THE OLD WORLD
Early man to the development of agriculture

ST. MARTIN'S SERIES IN PREHISTORY
Shirley Gorenstein and Robert Stigler, General Editors

PREHISPANIC AMERICA
THE OLD WORLD: EARLY MAN TO THE DEVELOPMENT OF AGRICULTURE

Forthcoming:

NORTH AMERICA
VARIETIES OF CULTURE IN THE OLD WORLD
A HISTORY OF AMERICAN ARCHAEOLOGY: METHOD AND THEORY

THE OLD WORLD
Early man to the development of agriculture

Robert Stigler
Ralph Holloway
Ralph Solecki
Dexter Perkins, Jr.
Patricia Daly

under the editorial supervision of
Robert Stigler

St. Martin's Press   New York

Library of Congress Catalog Card Number: 74-77528
Copyright © 1974 by St. Martin's Press, Inc.
All Rights Reserved.
Manufactured in the United States of America.
For information, write: St. Martin's Press, Inc.,
175 Fifth Avenue, New York, N.Y. 10010

AFFILIATED PUBLISHERS: Macmillan Limited, London—
also at Bombay, Calcutta, Madras, and Melbourne.

The editors dedicate this series to
William Duncan Strong
who provided a standard of excellence
toward which his students continue to strive

PREFACE

This volume is one of a series whose aims are to give a succinct introduction to the study of prehistory and to sum up the present state of knowledge concerning prehistoric cultural developments in the significant archaeological areas of the Old and New Worlds.

The study of prehistory has been going on in an organized way for more than one hundred years. The results have been presented in thousands of papers, monographs, and books. Indeed, by the beginning of this century the amount of published information had become so vast that archaeologists found it hard to be prehistorians of the world. Space and time were divided up, and researchers became specialists in certain geographical areas and sometimes in certain periods. In recent years it has become even more difficult for one archaeologist to write a global prehistory. The would-be generalist today is hard-put to keep abreast of a whole field which is subject to radical technical and theoretical advances as well as a continuing explosion of information. Furthermore, the archaeologist always has a tendency to favor the area or areas where he has worked and to slight others of which he has no first-hand knowledge.

To overcome these problems, we have arranged for each of the first four books in this series to be written by a team of several authors, all of them specialists in one or more regions or time periods. The author of each chapter had a free hand, subject to limitations of space, in presenting his view of the present state of archaeological knowledge in his area. In none of the volumes or chapters has there been any effort to impose a Procrustean uniformity, other than in the general length and depth of treatment given to coordinate subjects. The authors have subscribed, however, to an overall organizational plan which is meant to give the series coherence as well as balance. This plan is primarily geographical, though some volumes and chapters also have temporal and topical aspects. The final book of the series, written by one of the editors with an introduction by the other, will be a history of archaeological method and theory in America.

We are indebted to Barry Rossinoff, who conceived the format of the series and saw the books' preparation through tumultuous times. We are also grateful to Judy Hammond, who worked with intelligence as well as artistry in preparing the drawings, and to Brian Hesse, who was an innovative and indefatigable research assistant on the project.

SHIRLEY GORENSTEIN
ROBERT STIGLER

CONTENTS

INTRODUCTION by Robert Stigler   1

Chapter 1
FOSSIL MAN IN THE OLD WORLD by Ralph Holloway   9
Historical Outline, 11. Taxonomy, 15. The Fossils, 18. The Dynamics of Human Evolution, 35. Postscript, 42
Bibliographic Essay, 43

Chapter 2
THE OLD WORLD PALEOLITHIC by Ralph Solecki   45
The Lower Paleolithic, 53. The Middle Paleolithic, 57. The Upper Paleolithic, 63
Bibliographic Essay, 69

Chapter 3
THE BEGINNING OF FOOD PRODUCTION
IN THE NEAR EAST
by Dexter Perkins, Jr., and Patricia Daly   71
The Neolithic in the Near East, 72. Animal Domestication, 77. Plant Domestication, 83. The Archaeological Record, 87
Bibliographic Essay, 95

Chapter 4
THE LATER NEOLITHIC IN THE NEAR EAST
AND THE RISE OF CIVILIZATION by Robert Stigler   98
Jarmo, Jericho, and Çatal Hüyük, 100. Northern Mesopotamia, 108. Southern Mesopotamia, 111. Iran, 120. Anatolia, 121. Syro-Cilicia and the Levant, 122. The End of Prehistory, 124
Bibliographic Essay, 125

Chapter 5
EGYPT AND INDIA: PROBLEM AREAS by Robert Stigler   127
Egypt, 127. India, 143
Bibliographic Essay, 153

COMPLETE BIBLIOGRAPHY   155

INDEX   159

THE OLD WORLD
Early man to the development of agriculture

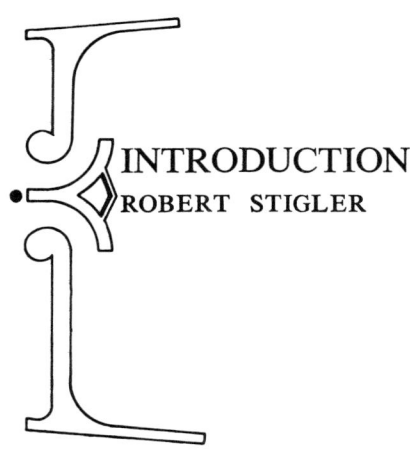

INTRODUCTION
ROBERT STIGLER

The Old and New Worlds each have a prehistory; that is to say, they both saw long periods of man's cultural development before the advent of written records which ushered in the historical era. But because of its much earlier beginnings, the prehistoric time span in the Old World is immensely longer than in the New; in addition, the geographical extent of the Old World is much greater. These facts in themselves make for a greater diversity in the subject matter and study of Old World prehistory. For example, involvement with *Homo sapiens*'s earlier stages of physical development and concern with the whole extent of Pleistocene chronology are necessary to the Old World archaeologist, while not at all to his New World counterpart.

Moreover, archaeology in the New World has had the advantage of its subject matter being all of a piece. Although such earlier forms of man as Neandertal, *Homo erectus,* and the australopithecines, along with their cultures, are lacking in the New World, the whole continuum of aboriginal culture that does exist, from "Early Man" to the Aztec and Inca, is by definition prehistoric, and one archaeological profession has always dealt with it. Plenty of argument and controversy takes place within that profession, but at the same time there has always been something of a unity of aim and understanding, and an emphasis on scientific or science-like procedures, in New World archaeology. Some Old World archaeologists even think that the American concern with archaeological theory is overdone. A recent sarcastic book review by an English archaeologist begins:

> From time to time, as the primitive Old World archaeologist squats on the shore of the primordial Atlantic, a passing current will wash up at his feet the ideograms of a distant civilization—the baneful signs of distant archaeologists. With curiosity and persistence the aboriginal may laboriously run his finger along familiar signs in unfamiliar and difficult constructions. . . . [Yet another] American book on archaeological theory. . . .

Nevertheless, New World archaeology has developed over the years a great number of useful conceptual frameworks and systematic aids to our understanding of prehistory that remain largely unused in the Old World. As a simple example, the geographical units which form the principal basis for the chapter-by-chapter organization of the volumes on the Old World in this series are not only larger but also more diffuse than those employed in New World archaeology. While they show a certain vague cultural coherence, they are hardly comparable to the much more precisely defined cultural and natural areas of the New World which have been so much a part of everyone's thinking in archaeology and ethnology for fifty years or more as to be taken for granted. Such delineations are only in their infancy in the Old World as a whole.

Unlike New World archaeology, Old World archaeology consists of two major branches: 1) prehistoric and 2) the archaeology of the literate periods, Bronze Age and after. *Prehistoric* archaeology in *Europe* grew up in the nineteenth century in close association with the natural sciences, such as biology and geology, while the other kind had a very raffish ancestry amid the temples and sculptures and lootable treasures of the eastern Mediterranean and Near East, catering to art museums and private collectors. When prehistoric archaeology in the Old World began to spread beyond Europe, especially to the Near East, it all too often came to be infected by the unsystematic and certainly unscientific atmosphere which characterized ongoing archaeological work there. One might say that in a general sense prehistoric archaeology in Europe (and the New World) had always been "problem-oriented" to a certain extent, but in the Near East much of what we know has been the result of random, accidental, or fortuitous choice in recovery. Consequently, shocking gaps of a kind unknown today in Europe and the New World still exist in the prehistoric record, despite a turn for the better in recent years. In Asia and Africa various historical factors have limited archaeological work until the last few decades.

Looked at from a worldwide viewpoint, there is an almost inescapable impression that if one could somehow quantify what we know or understand today, we would see that we have a much fuller picture, per square mile as it were, of New World prehistory than of Old. The very tired old archaeological cliché that "we have only scratched the surface" may no longer have any real validity in the New World, but it still deserves to be capitalized and underlined for the Old.

Be that as it may, a number of striking advances have been made in recent years in the study of Old World prehistory. The chapters that follow are an attempt to sum up the substance of what we know at present about the several aspects and major geographical areas of the subject.

One of the major milestones in man's quest to understand himself was the demonstration in the nineteenth century of the fact of human evolution, from earlier types up through the present-day form of man. Accumulating material evidence, fossil-hands-on-stone-tools as it were, showed that this process took place in conjunction with the earlier stages of cultural evolution. The first chapter of this volume is a review of the status of human biology today in its studies of the physical stages of man's emergence and development from prehominid primate stock. These successive forms of men were the creators of the succession of cultures which the Paleolithic archaeologist attempts to reconstruct, and as such are an integral part of prehistory. In "Fossil Man in the Old World" Ralph Holloway shows that the study of these fossils has become a highly technical and sophisticated science involving far more than just the measurement and comparison of bones, and that we seem to be on the threshold of a much fuller understanding of the ways in which man's earlier biological and mental attributes were intimately related to his social and cultural forms.

Like some archaeological finds, fossil man is a subject which readily lends itself to sensationalism. The discovery of a new skull or a new tooth is a welcome break in the otherwise somber news of our day-to-day affairs, and newspapers often give the impression that such discoveries have a more earth-shaking effect on physical anthropology than they actually do, or that the new tooth invalidates much of what has been said before on the subject of human evolution. In truth, the science is far beyond that condition. Legitimate controversies exist, as they do in any active science, and Holloway identifies them, but the questions that revolve around a new piece of evidence today are not whether it validates or invalidates the "theory of evolution" but, rather, where it fits in the evolutionary mosaic.

The next chapter, on the Paleolithic cultures of the Old World, deals with those two to three million years of man's culture history falling largely in the Pleistocene epoch. As a major branch of prehistory, Paleolithic studies always have been a relatively specialized field, and in recent years they have become even more so. A particular set of problems exists for the Paleolithic archaeologist: the need for an extensive knowledge of geology, since much of his material for study comes from radically different environmental settings and climatic conditions in the past; the fact that the physical preservation of such ancient materials is subject to severe limitations; the need for special analytic and interpretative techniques to deal with the very limited cultural repertories of the simple hunting and gathering Paleolithic societies. Both the subject matter and these common problems serve to delineate Paleolithic archaeology as a single field, so that, except for Holloway's chapter on Fossil Man, this is the only chapter in the Old World volumes in this series to give hemisphere-wide coverage.

We know that in the times before man became agricultural and settled down to more localized cultural patterns in the latest prehistoric period, the Neolithic, much broader traditions characterized the cultures of the Old World Paleolithic. A fundamental question in Paleolithic studies concerns the meaning of these broader traditions: What were their real limits? Put another way, what factors might make them appear broader to us than they actually were at the time?

Paleolithic archaeology was in the vanguard of prehistoric studies to emerge in the nineteenth century, but like all those studies it was centered in western Europe. Ralph Solecki's chapter on the Paleolithic, like all studies on the subject, shows that heritage and some of its problems. From late in the nineteenth century scholars have been concerned with the validity of employing the classifications and terminologies derived from western Europe in the interpretation of Paleolithic materials elsewhere in the Old World. As Solecki's chapter demonstrates, the problem is exacerbated by the few categories and forms of material to which the Paleolithic archaeologist is limited. Although the *numbers* of Paleolithic sites and the *quantity* of stone tools recovered from them present no problem, compare the *complexity* and *variety* of materials available here with those recovered from a Late Neolithic town site. Having to concentrate on very limited cultural evidence, Paleolithic studies today are one of the most active branches of archaeology in the development of innovative techniques of analysis and interpretation.

Around the end of the Pleistocene epoch many Late Paleolithic peoples began to alter their food-getting and other activities in distinctive ways. Heretofore, prehistorians have traditionally attributed this change to supposed climatic modifications which took place at the end of the Pleistocene, affecting animal and plant life in different parts of the world; but today the picture does not seem to be so simple. At any rate, like the Paleolithic, the cultural change involved here was first recognized by European archaeologists in the nineteenth century, principally through changes in the stone tool tradition, and the term "Mesolithic" was coined to refer to the period. Increasingly it came to be recognized as an intermediate period between the Paleolithic and the agricultural Neolithic in Europe.

Like "Paleolithic" and "Neolithic," the term "Mesolithic" was eventually extended to other parts of the Old World beyond Europe as prehistoric studies expanded. Some modern archaeologists, however, have come to abandon applying the terms—particularly

6 THE OLD WORLD

"Mesolithic" and "Neolithic"—outside Europe, as, for example, the periods in the Near East have been revealed to have been of a significantly different nature from their approximate European counterparts. Dexter Perkins, Jr., and Patricia Daly are among those authorities who choose not to employ the term "Mesolithic" for the transitional period between Paleolithic and Neolithic in the Near East, owing to the period's unique qualities there.

In their chapter "The Beginning of Food Production in the Near East" Perkins and Daly represent an important recent phenomenon in prehistoric studies—namely, the substantial use of a kind of archaeological evidence which until a few years ago was almost completely overlooked. In fact, they utilize this evidence to provide a new framework for understanding prehistoric cultural development. The practices in the Near East c. 9000–6000 B.C. relating to food-getting were ultimately of the greatest importance to most of the world, and for this reason it seems worthwhile, now that we are beginning to have real insight into the processes of plant and animal domestication in the ancient world, to view the prehistory of this period in the Near East from the standpoint of those basic economic processes. Perkins and Daly utilize the idea that a plant or animal whose form has been modified by several generations of domestication is as much an artifact as a stone hand-axe or a Neolithic pot. While it is true that for many decades archaeologists have dutifully saved a few animal bones from their sites (and then often gone on to misidentify them), it is only in recent years that specialists have entered this field and careful collections have begun to be made and analyzed by refined techniques. As a result, many old stereotypes are being overthrown, and a considerably more complex picture of the period is being uncovered.

Following the discussion of the early food-producing period in the Near East, the chapter "The Later Neolithic in the Near East and the Rise of Civilization" begins with a description of established village and town life in southwest Asia and goes on to a consideration of the factors which might account for the rapid development and increasing urbanization that progressively characterized the area. Much of the evidence of this Late Neolithic period is faulty, and much missing, for it is a phase of Near Eastern archaeology which has been pursued very haphazardly. With few exceptions in recent years, prehistoric archaeologists in the area have concentrated their energies on the earlier stages of development; the sixth, fifth, and fourth millennia B.C. are still understood largely through an antiquated body of studies with a heavy emphasis on pottery analysis and rather speculative interpretations of the social and cultural institutions of the time. A few authorities are at work on the problems of the period, but not enough.

The chapter attempts to depict the diversity that appears to have marked the Near East at this time in Mesopotamia, Anatolia, the Levant, and elsewhere and its implications for the approaching Bronze Age. These are the stages of cultural development in the Near East which have sometimes been compared with the high cultural developments of Mesoamerica and the Andean region of the New World, and it might be interesting for the reader to note the chapters on Mesoamerica and the Andes in the New World volumes of this series, observing similarities and differences in the ways various authorities have dealt with such concepts as "urbanism" and "civilization" in the two hemispheres.

The exact relationship of the Nile Valley to the rest of the ancient Near East constitutes a large problem. In one way or another, Egypt is usually considered to be a part of the cultural Near East, ancient and modern, but its prehistoric development represents enough of a special case to be discussed here separately from southwest Asia.

The author is aware of the seeming peculiarity of grouping Egypt and the Indian subcontinent together in the final chapter, "Egypt and India: Problem Areas," but there is a logic to it. Although the two areas had no direct cultural relation to each other in Neolithic or early Bronze Age times, both were dependent on the nuclear Near East in varying ways and to varying degrees at different stages in their development.

Despite a few recent advances in knowledge, the nature of the Neolithic in the Nile Valley remains today one of the most worrisome questions in Old World prehistory. There seems simply not to be enough of it, considering the cultural explosion that took place at the end of the period in late Predynastic and early Dynastic times. The final chapter begins with a description of the Neolithic in Egypt as we presently know it and goes on to consider its possible origins, presumably tied in some way to southwest Asia. There follows an appraisal of the state of affairs at the verge of the Dynastic era, again with what can only be called implications of southwestern Asian involvement.

On the Indian subcontinent matters are different. The area is one of those (like Africa) where a rather distinctive archaeological approach has grown up; neither the classifications nor the terminology employed by south Asian archaeologists is directly comparable to those used in other areas of the Old World. The chapter continues by outlining the later Stone Age cultures of India and Pakistan and moves on to a consideration of the Indus Valley civilization. This civilization raises special questions: its relation both to earlier and later cultures on the subcontinent, and, most importantly here, the degree to which it, too, should be considered a cultural outlier of the Near East. Technically speaking, the Indus civilization belongs to the Bronze Age and among the literate "B. A." civilizations, but partly because the Indus script has never been deciphered, and partly because it has simply become archaeological custom, the Indus remains and their discussion seem to have fallen more than a little into the hands of prehistorians.

1
FOSSIL MAN IN THE OLD WORLD
RALPH HOLLOWAY

The study of fossil man, or paleoanthropology, deals with the fossil remains of creatures evolving in both bodily and behavioral characteristics over some 3 to 5 million years. Thus its subject matter is the heritage and the property of all men, regardless of race, nationality, language, or customs. The fossil remains of man and near-man, combined with the archaeological evidence of stone tools, living sites, and animal and floral associations, are our unwritten biological and social history, the clues that are indispensable for teaching us what we are as a species and how we came to be this way.

The popular conception is that the study of fossil man is devoted to finding the "missing link" between ourselves and our ape-like ancestors who existed some 15 to 20 million years ago. Actually, every discovery is a "missing link." Not only do fossils teach us about the intermediate stages of our evolutionary passage; they also tell us about the biological variability of past populations and give us insights into the dynamics, the selection pressures of evolution, which led to our transformation. This goal of a more holistic understanding of ourselves does not rest alone on the mechanical analysis and description of fossilized bones and teeth or the stone tools of early man. Comparative psychology, primatology, the neurological sciences, indeed all of the biological and social sciences contribute to the unraveling of the empirical clues to our physical and cultural evolution, the remains of fossil man and his artifacts.

MAP 1.1   Distribution of early man sites in Africa.

This chapter will attempt to outline some of the major discoveries of the fossil record, describe their main characteristics, and present some speculations about the evolutionary dynamics which produced us. It is very likely that even as the chapter is being written, new discoveries are being made, and the fossil record of our evolution continues to grow.

· HISTORICAL OUTLINE

The idea that man is simply another member of the animal realm is an ancient one, but it was not until the appearance of Charles Darwin's classic works in the nineteenth century that the concept of man as a *natural evolutionary product* began to take hold. Although evolutionary theory has come a long way since the days of Darwin and his contemporary, Alfred Russel Wallace, the fundamental idea of gradual natural change, working over periods of millions of years and resulting from the differential reproduction of genetically advantaged variations in a particular ecosystem, has remained unchanged. It is still a basic tenet of all our present-day biological knowledge.

Darwin's insights and his voluminous documentation of *living* forms and their evolutionary adaptations did not enjoy the benefit of the large amount of fossil evidence relating to man (see Maps 1.1, 1.2, and 1.3) which has now accumulated. Actually, the first find which was accorded some possible status as an evolutionary precursor to modern man was made in 1856 in the Neander Valley in Germany. An earlier find, made in the caves of Gibraltar in 1848, was not recognized at the time as a possible ancestor, and was forgotten until more fossils were discovered between 1856 and 1889. It is in this period (albeit with considerable debate and even ridicule) that the real recognition came that the Neandertal peoples, their cultural artifacts, and peculiar associated animals such as giant cave bears, hyenas, mastodons, and rhinoceroses, were far older than modern man and represented a possible evolutionary stage in human development. The finds at Spy, Engis, and La Naulette (all in Belgium) and later at Le Moustier and La Chapelle-aux-Saints in France (1908) finally brought to an end the previous skepticism of the great German pathologist, Rudolph

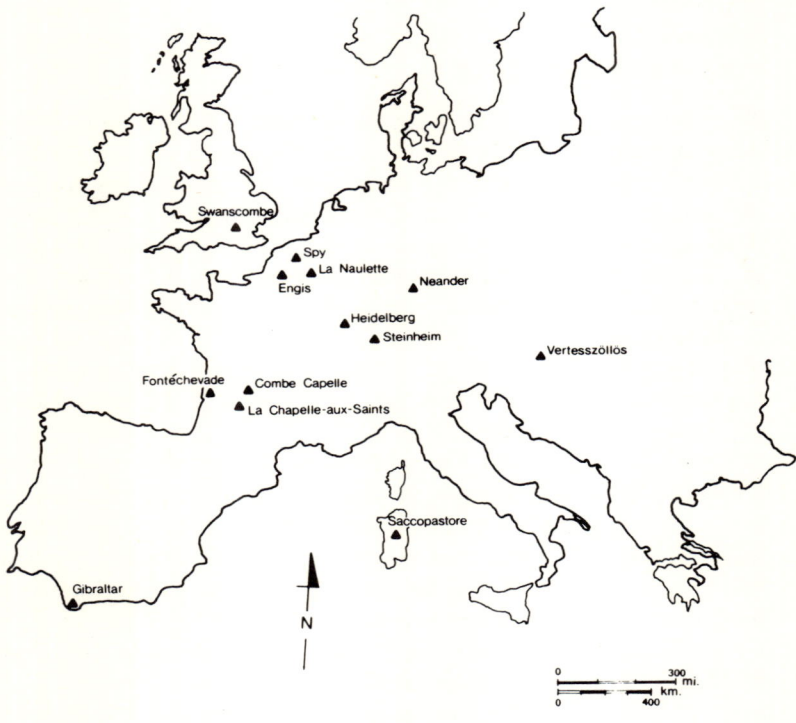

MAP 1.2   Distribution of early man sites in Europe.

MAP 1.3   Distribution of early man sites in Asia.

Virchow, and other eminent scientists, who had claimed that the remains discovered earlier were merely those of imbecile or idiot Hun horsemen or Russian Cossacks, Roman cretins, or other isolated pathological specimens from the not-so-distant past.

A second stage of fossil discoveries, from 1890 to 1921, produced even more primitive and older fossil hominids in Java and in Germany, represented by the *Pithecanthropus* finds of Eugene Dubois in 1891 and of Schoetensack, who uncovered a lower jaw in the Mauer sands near Heidelberg in 1907. In addition, more finds of Neandertals came to light, not only in western but also in eastern Europe (Yugoslavia and Russia) and in Northern Rhodesia (now Zambia). A most puzzling "find," the Piltdown skull and associated jaw discovered in England in 1912, left scientists with an impossible task for more than thirty-five years: to reconcile what appeared to be a modern man struggling to rid himself of a chimpanzee jaw. As we know now, Piltdown was a fraud.

Then, from 1922 to 1946, a large number of discoveries in Europe, Africa, and Asia produced more pithecanthropine types from Java and China (Choukoutien), Neandertals from Europe and especially the Near East, and still more primitive forms, the australopithecines from South Africa, discovered first by Raymond Dart and later by Robert Broom and John Robinson.

Meanwhile, associated discoveries of stone tools and of evidence for the habitual use of fire and a way of life based on cooperative hunting and gathering were also made, and gradually a picture emerged showing the progressive modernization and sophistication of both morphology and culture, spanning a period of from 500,000 to a million years ago up to the recent past. The quest originally was to understand the formal phylogenetic relationships between fossil types, and their progression, rather than the evolutionary dynamics that formed that progression.

From 1947 to 1965, the picture did not become simpler but more complex. Emphasis was increasingly placed on fitting the changes of morphology, as well as the possible social behavioral patterns that led to modern man, into evolutionary and genetic terms. Discoveries in southern China (Mapa), Iraq (Shanidar), and the Lebanon extended the range of Neandertal populations, whereas pithecanthropine finds were also made in North Africa, Java, China, and both East and South Africa. Acrimonious debates surrounding the australopithecines were partially submerged in the acceptance of these "missing links" as the earliest prehuman hominids through more discoveries of similar fossils at Olduvai Gorge in Tanzania.

Since 1965 the focus of attention has shifted almost exclusively to Africa, where at Olduvai Gorge in Tanzania, the valley of the Omo River in Ethiopia, and eastern Lake Rudolf in Kenya diverse dental and skull fragments of early australopithecines and even more modern-looking hominids have been discovered in clear association with stone tools dated absolutely by the potassium-argon method to around 3 million years ago. Most recently, a fragment of hominid mandible from Lothagam Hill, Kenya, has been dated to 5.5 million years, thus opening up the last part of the Pliocene to man's direct ancestors.

Recent years have also been a period in which data from primate studies, neuro-anatomy, comparative anatomy, and physiology have been used intensively to propose hypotheses about *how* we came to be. Furthermore, it is a period in which some even earlier candidates for inclusion in the family of man, the Hominidae, have been discovered, such as the *Ramapithecus* finds from eastern Africa dating to about 12–14 million years ago. *Ramapithecus* finds originally made in the early 1930's in the Siwalik Hills in northwestern India have also been recognized now as hominids.

· TAXONOMY

Today, biologists regard the species as the major unit of evolutionary importance. The concept of species which is most in use is based on criteria of reproductive isolation, a state closely related to the genetic level and thus to the concept of evolution as a change in gene frequencies through time. Indeed, species are regarded as the largest kind of evolving genetic system, within which members are able to reproduce with one another and produce fertile offspring. This genetic system is essentially *closed* to other populations (rather than *open,* as are subspecies or races), since interspecific fertile offspring are not possible.

Another concept of species is that of morphological species or morpho-species, populations separated on the basis of their differences in outward form. This concept is based on the surmise that populations having different morphological features are generally different taxonomic entities at the species, generic, or even higher levels, and that the degree of taxonomic separation depends on the kinds and amounts of morphological dissimilarity, which ultimately reflect different adaptations.

With living forms, one at least has the chance of testing whether or not populations are likely to be specifically distinct. With fossils, this is impossible, but the literature on fossil man is filled with controversy about whether specimens X and Y are the same or different species, genera, etc. This is particularly true of the older literature. Prior to the acceptance of the genetical species concept, the fossil hominid record was "classified" according to a strictly morphological concept of species, and because of a lack of understanding of the amount and nature of normal variations in populations, these classifications tended to subdivide species and genera to a point where almost any new discovery was given a new designation. This was particularly true in the case of the australopithecines and the Tertiary apes.

It is very important to realize that we do not have very good samples of any single fossil hominid group, at least in the statistical sense, and that considerable morphological variation is a usual feature of any population, for such variation is the grist for evolutionary change. In general, different morphologies reflect different adaptive patterns and thus suggest genetic or reproductive isolation, whether the forms compared existed at the same time or in some succession of time. There is, however, no way of telling from a comparison between modern man's jaws and the relatively similar jaws of Neandertals whether modern man and Neandertals should be considered as different or the same species. Nor is it possible to know, without a time machine, whether the large jaw of the gracile australopithecine is specifically, generically, or not at all distinct from the larger jaw of the robust australopithecine.

The jaws are different not only in size but in shape and in the proportions of the teeth. And as it happens, these differences are of such a nature that, when combined with the other skeletal evidence of the braincase, limbs, and pelvis, they suggest a different adaptational pattern and thus a good probability of at least specific difference.

These are vexed questions in the study of fossil man and are subject to interpretation. The classification used in this chapter is certainly open to debate and may indeed require change. But until more finds are made, and those already discovered fully described, the system set forth in Table 1.1 will at least provide a reasonable

TABLE 1.1   Taxonomic Breakdown of Fossil Hominids

Order Primates
  Suborder Prosimii (lemurs, tarsiers)
  Suborder Anthropoidea
    Infraorder Platyrrhines (New World monkeys)
    Infraorder Catarrhines (Old World monkeys)
      Superfamily Hominoidea (apes and man)
        Family Oreopithecidae (possible Pliocene swamp-dwelling ape)
        Family Pongidae
          Subfamily Parapithecinae (Oligocene apes)
          Subfamily Dryopithecinae (Miocene apes)
          Subfamily Pliopithecinae (Miocene fossil gibbon-like apes)
          Subfamily Hylobatinae (gibbon and siamang apes)
          Subfamily Ponginae (chimp, gorilla, orang, *Gigantopithecus*)
        Family Hominidae
          Genus *Ramapithecus*
            species, *punjabicus, wickeri* (?)
          Genus *Australopithecus*
            species, *africanus* (gracile)
            species, *robustus,* including *"boisei"*
          Genus *Homo*
            species, *habilis* (?)
            species, *erectus*
            species, *sapiens*
              subspecies, *neandertalensis*
              subspecies, *sapiens*

? indicates uncertainty—see text

beginning for further discussion. The taxonomic breakdown of the fossil hominids given here is, of course, only one possibility.

· THE FOSSILS

It is convenient to lump the fossils showing clear relationship to man into four groups, roughly successive in geological time, in modernness of bodily features, and in cultural associations. Any such scheme is somewhat arbitrary, of course, and it should be kept constantly in mind that the levels, stages, or whatever terms we apply are simply scientific conveniences for organizing our data and erecting hypotheses. The reality that existed in the past was that of groups of populations intermixing and evolving at different rates at different times in widely different environments and geographical locations. As evidence, we have no soft tissues, brains, muscles, or the like, only bones, teeth, and tools, and our total picture is a very fragmentary one indeed.

Earliest Prehominids or Hominids
It has been through the careful work of Elwyn Simons and David Pilbeam that discoveries made in the middle 1930's of teeth and jaw fragments from the Siwalik Hills of India may be seen as human precursors. These fragments, known as *Ramapithecus punjabicus* (see Figure 1.1) are dated at roughly 12–15 million years ago. No limb bones or skull fragments are known at present. One portion of an upper jaw contains two premolars, two molars, and the alveoli or sockets for the canine and lateral incisor teeth. The cusps and general morphological pattern of the molars and premolars are very human-like, a point made almost thirty-six years ago by G. E. Lewis, who described these finds. The socket for the canine is small, indicating that the root of the canine tooth and its crown must also have been small. There is a canine foss, and the nasal spine was close to the anterior incisor alveolar margin, a characteristic which is hominid. The shape of the dental row appears parabolic, and there is a good suggestion that the palate was arched. Both these traits are also hominid. There are also a few small pieces of mandible assigned to this genus which match very well with those in the upper jaw and which show a short

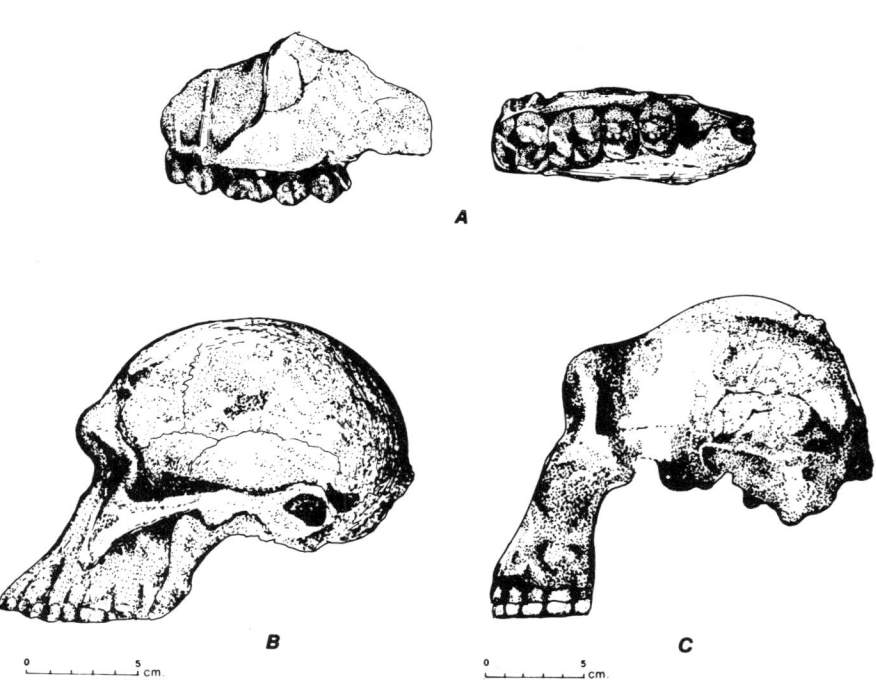

FIGURE 1.1 Early hominid fossils. (A) *Ramapithecus* jaw fragment. (B) Gracile australopithecine. (C) Robust australopithecine.

depth of the body of the mandible. Taken all together, these specimens seem clearly hominid. It has been speculated that the patterns they represent must have been associated with a short, relatively non-protruding face that was fairly vertical, and that therefore this creature was possibly bipedal, or beginning such an adaptation. Obviously, this is an extremely tenuous and unprovable speculation at present.

In Miocene deposits at Fort Ternan, Kenya, L. S. B. Leakey has discovered two fragments which he has named respectively *Kenyapithecus wickeri* and *Kenyapithecus africanus*. These date to the same period as *Ramapithecus,* and the former specimen, sp. *wickeri,* is practically identical to the Indian *Ramapithecus*. Thus Leakey's generic, if not specific, designations of this African find should be abandoned. The second specimen, sp. *africanus,* is not a *Ramapithecus* but a dryopithecine ape, according to Simon's study. No stone tools have been found in association with these materials. The reduced canine and absence of stone tools raise two important points: 1) if *Ramapithecus* is hominid, it is possible that our ancestors never had long, pointed canines which later became reduced, and 2) if they did have such teeth, the reduction took place long before stone tools were made, and therefore the development of tools cannot be responsible as a causal mechanism. Obviously, only more complete finds will answer critical questions about the evolutionary status and functional development of this fossil.

From this period of 12–15 million years ago, we have a complete hiatus until roughly 3–4 million years ago, when the evidence for at least two kinds of hominids becomes very clear.

Early Hominids: The Australopithecines

In 1924 a peculiar skull and natural endocast (brain cast) from the limeworks at Taungs in South Africa was brought to the attention of Raymond Dart. Dart immediately realized that the features of the teeth, face, and fossilized brain cast were more advanced than that of any known ape, even in the juvenile or young stage. He called the specimen *Australopithecus africanus* ("southern ape") and published his findings in *Nature* in 1925. A storm broke loose, the winds blown largely by the established anatomists in England. It was not until subsequent discoveries in South Africa were made at Sterkfontein in 1936 by Broom, at Swartkrans and Kromdraai by Broom and Robinson, and at Makapansgat by Dart that scientific opinion swayed in the 1950's to accept these creatures as definite hominids and precursors to man.

Two types (Figure 1.1) now seem to be established: 1) A form gracile in morphology, with large anterior teeth relative to the molars and premolars, and cranial capacities between 428 and 485 cc.; the skulls show many features which are advanced over the apes and which, in conjunction with pelvic and lower limb fragments, suggest almost full bi-pedalism. 2) A robust form, with more rugged skull, sometimes with a sagittal crest for additional attachment area for the large temporalis muscle needed to move the larger lower jaw; the premolars and molars are very large relative to the anterior teeth, and this form had a cranial capacity of about 530 cc. In both forms, the height of the braincase above the brow ridges is greater than in apes; the occipital condyles which help balance the head on the spine are placed more anteriorly than in apes, indicating an upright posture; the foramen magnum points downward, and the back portion of the skull where the neck muscles attach is also facing downward, rather than backwards. Based on these differing morphological patterns, Robinson has suggested that the two forms represent different ecological adaptations, and that the differences in dental patterns imply that the robust form was primarily herbivorous, while the gracile forms were at least partly carnivorous. Robinson also suggests that the bipedalism of the robust form was not as highly developed as in the gracile form. The gracile forms are known from Taungs, Sterkfontein, and Makapansgat, and are called *Australopithecus africanus,* while those from Swartkrans and Kromdraai are variously called *Paranthropus robustus* or *Australopithecus robustus.* It seems unlikely that the difference between these hominids is enough to warrant generic distinction, and the latter binomial is suggested as most appropriate for the robust form.

In total, there are some 1022 fragments of australopithecines from South Africa alone, including cranial parts, teeth (the majority), and postcranial bones. Unfortunately, all these finds occur in a very obdurate limestone breccia which so far has defied absolute dating. Combined faunal and geological evidence studied by C. K. Brain in Pretoria indicates that the gracile forms were earlier than the robust ones, although there was probably some overlap for an undetermined period. A number of primitive but undoubted stone tools have been found at Swartkrans, while Dart has claimed that the nature of the bone evidence from Sterkfontein and Makapansgat statistically demonstrates a preferential use by the gracile hominid of other materials which exhibit clear forms and which he has named the "osteodontokeratic culture." There is some controversy as to who made the stone tools known from Swartkrans, for as we shall see, there is evidence for a more advanced hominid living in the same period, both at Swartkrans and in Olduvai Gorge.

In 1959 Dr. Leakey and Mrs. Leakey made a spectacular discovery at Olduvai Gorge, Bed I, where they found an almost complete cranium (without the lower jaw) of a form very similar to the robust hominid types known from South Africa, in association with broken animal bones and stone tools. They gave it the name *Zinjanthropus boisei,* thus indicating not only that, as a species, it was reproductively isolated from its southern neighbors, but also that it was sufficiently distinct to be regarded as a separate genus. Comparisons with the South African material, however, make it clear that these specimens certainly belong to the same genus. P. V. Tobias, who has made an intensive study of "Zinj," prefers to call it *Australopithecus boisei*. Others regard it as a racial variant of *A. robustus*. More important, however, is the fact that the specimen could be accurately dated by the potassium-argon method to an age of 1.75 million years. Furthermore, the skull was found in direct association with stone tools and the remains of small mammals, birds, and reptiles, which were in a crushed condition. At the time, it appeared to offer conclusive proof that *Australopithecus* of the robust variety made and used stone tools and engaged in some hunting activity. Later finds of somewhat more advanced hominids have cast doubt on this assertion, as will be seen.

"Zinj," or Olduvai Hominid #5, shows some anatomical differences from the robust forms of South Africa in the teeth, mastoid region, and face, but it is impossible to claim that it must have separate taxonomic status, even at the species level, from those in South Africa. Farther south of Olduvai is Lake Natron, where in lacustrine deposits of comparable age there was discovered a complete lower jaw with beautifully preserved teeth, which fits the "Zinj" face very well and which is closely similar to some of the robust South African mandibles. The cranial capacity of "Zinj" is 530 cc., exactly the same as a new Swartkrans endocast found by Brain in 1966. My examination of this endocast indicates that not only is the size identical to the East African "Zinj" but that the two are also practically identical in shape. This argues strongly against species separation.

Since 1959 there has been an explosion of early hominid discoveries in East Africa, and a similar explosion of controversy over their taxonomic relationships. In addition to Olduvai Gorge, more recent discoveries have been made in the Omo River valley in southern Ethiopia and on the eastern shore of Lake Rudolf in northern Kenya.

OLDUVAI GORGE   Since 1960 a number of fragments have been discovered here, mainly in Beds I and II, representing as many as thirty individuals and suggesting a line or lines of hominid evolution separate from those of the robust australopithecines and possibly from those of the gracile ones also. Many of the finds are very fragmentary, and those of the limb bones, such as clavicles, foot, and hand bones, cannot really be assigned to any taxon because there are no comparable materials from South Africa or elsewhere. Although this is particularly so for those derived from Bed I, they have nevertheless been designated by their discoverer as *Homo habilis*. However, other materials, including teeth, mandibular fragments, and the partial skulls of two individuals—Hom. #7 and Hom. #24—have also been named *Homo habilis* to connote a creature more on the direct line to later forms of *Homo,* such as sp. *erectus* and sp. *sapiens*. The picture is a confusing one, because some of the features seem intermediate between gracile australopithecines and later Middle Pleistocene *Homo erectus* (see below). This is particularly true of many of the dental materials. The cranial fragments of Hom. #7, however, indicate a gracile, more advanced hominid, with an estimated cranial capacity of 652 cc. at a sub-adult age. This value, and the expected larger value if age is taken into consideration (687 cc.), is clearly beyond any of the other known australopithecines' capacities, the highest of which is 530 cc.

Hominid #9, near the top of Bed II, is unmistakably a robust form of *Homo erectus,* and some of the other dental and small cranial fragments found in Bed II which were previously referred to a *habilis* taxon are perhaps best considered as early forms of *Homo erectus,* possibly derived from the Bed I habiline fossils. It is also possible that some of the isolated teeth and indeterminate cranial fragments of Bed I localities, and those in lower Bed II, might be gracile australopithecines. Metric analysis alone is unlikely to settle these questions. The Hom. #7 specimens come from a slightly lower level than does Hom. #5, the famous "Zinj" skull. Stone tools are also known from these layers, and there thus exists the possibility that "Zinj" was not the maker of those found with his remains, and that he possibly was prey to some more advanced hominid, such as a habiline. Only additional finds will settle this perplexing problem.

LOWER OMO RIVER BASIN   An international research expedition involving Kenyan, American, and French explorers has uncovered evidence of fossil australopithecines dating back to between 3 and 4 million years ago, thus clearly showing that fossil hominids existed during the Upper Pliocene. As this article is being written, new finds are in the process of being excavated. Indeed, an age of 5.5 million years is suggested by a find at Lothagam Hill, Kenya.

Approximately twenty isolated teeth are known from Omo River localities dating between 2 and 3 million years ago, and these show clear affinities with the gracile form of *Australopithecus*. In addition, there are isolated teeth showing *robustus* affinities. The 1969 expedition led by Clark Howell discovered the posterior portion of a small cranium which is tentatively regarded as a gracile australopithecine, dated at about 2.6 million years. Two mandibular fragments are also known, one clearly referrable to the robust line; the other shows many robust features, but one of the first premolar teeth has some peculiarities in size not seen in other *robustus* teeth. The French contingent has also discovered some isolated teeth and a mandibular fragment without crowns of teeth. A *robustus* pattern is again suggested. Unfortunately, this find was named *Paraustralopithecus aethiopicus,* even though it is only a minor variant of the robust type. The Kenyan contingent, led by Richard Leakey, has uncovered the fragments of three crania which date to approximately 100,000 years and are surely *sapiens* both in form and endocranial capacity.

EASTERN LAKE RUDOLF This area, extremely remote and difficult to reach even on foot, is currently being explored under the direction of Richard Leakey. Thus far, two cranial portions have been discovered, associated with early Oldowan-type stone tools, from levels dating about 2.6 million years ago. One skull (E.R. 406), almost totally complete except for the teeth, is clearly a robust australopithecine. The second find is the right half and small basal part of a skull showing features which led its discoverer, Richard Leakey, to regard it as a possible *Homo habilis*. Having seen this second fragment, I would hesitate to call it habiline; it is most likely a female of the *robustus* type. The general region of the eastern shore of Lake Rudolf is expected to be one of the richest fossil hominid sites yet excavated.

Recently, Ron Clarke and F. C. Howell have determined that two fragments found earlier at the South African site of Swartkrans and originally attributed to a *robustus* type are possibly representative of a more advanced hominid, probably *Homo erectus,* although Tobias has suggested that this too might be a female *robustus* type.

Taken all together, these finds suggest a possible maximum of four kinds of hominids in the Upper Pliocene and Lower Pleistocene: 1) robust and 2) gracile australopithecines, 3) *Homo habilis,* and 4) *Homo erectus*. This is only one possible view, of course. Alternatively, one can argue that the habiline materials are really an East African variant of the gracile australopithecine form which later evolved into *Homo erectus*. The Hom. #7 from Bed I at Olduvai, however, makes this unlikely, since the cranial capacity is surely significantly greater than any of the gracile South African forms known.

In any event, two kinds of australopithecines seem to have existed from a time three million to about one million years ago, and it seems possible that the line of genus *Homo* may extend back to about two million years ago, regardless of what absolute dates may in the future be found for the South African fossils. Thus there is evidence for different kinds of hominids co-existing through perhaps two million years; one line, the robust one, most likely came to a dead end in terms of evolution. At present, we cannot know what kinds of social behavioral or even ecological relationships existed between these lines.

Middle Pleistocene Hominids: Homo erectus
As briefly mentioned above, fossil remains from both East and South Africa suggest the beginnings of the *Homo erectus* level of hominid evolution. This taxonomic group is represented by fossils from two localities in Europe (Germany and Hungary), from the Near East, South Africa, Java, and north and south China, and possibly from the Chad Republic and Israel. Thus it was a very widely spread group of hominids, showing features intermediate between the earlier australopithecines and the Neandertals of the third interglacial and fourth glacial periods of the Pleistocene. Most paleoanthropologists agree that this taxon is an intermediary link in human evolution, dating back from approximately 800,000 up to some 250–300,000 years ago. It is with the *Homo erectus* group (previously known as *Pithecanthropus erectus* in Java and *Sinanthropus pekinensis* in China) that we find clear evidence of the persistent hunting of large animals, stone tools fashioned to clear-cut standardized patterns (e.g., Chellean and Acheulean hand-axes, among other implements), the use of fire, fully human bipedalism, and brain sizes at the lower limits of modern man, i.e., 750–1100 cc. The teeth are clearly human, albeit larger than modern man's, and are set in jaws which while massive by our own standards show refinement over those of the preceding australopithecines. The brow ridges are usually very large. With the exception of some isolated thigh bones discovered in Java, no pelvic fragments are as yet reported. The femur is indistinguishable from that of modern man, and one example shows perhaps the earliest known example of pathology: an exostosis, or bony can-

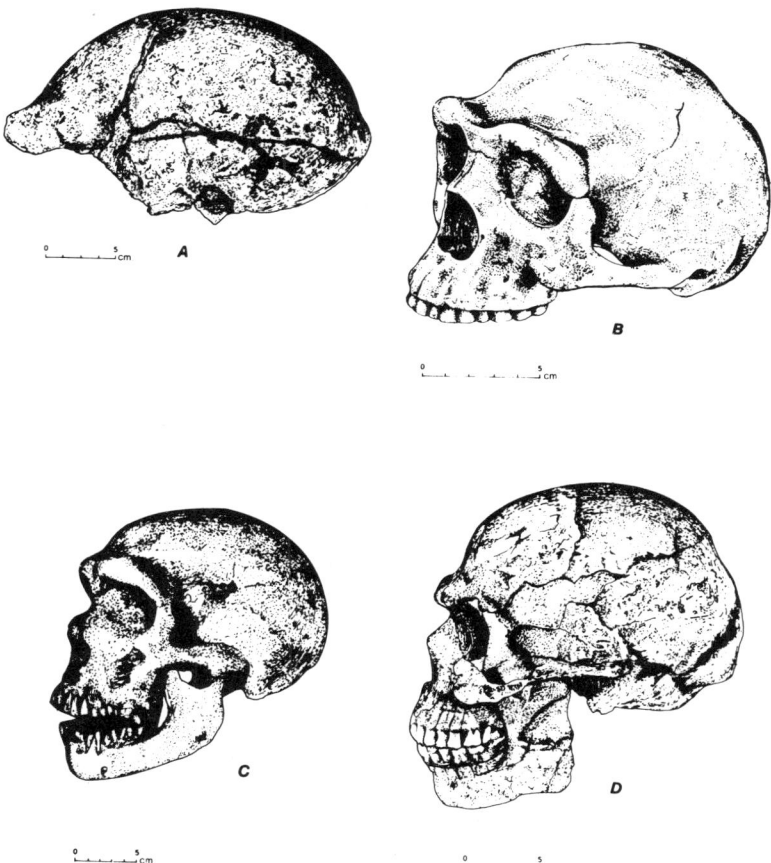

FIGURE 1.2   Early man skulls.   *(A) Homo erectus* from Java. *(B) Homo erectus* from Choukoutien.   *(C)* Neandertal from La Ferrassie.   *(D)* Early *Homo sapiens sapiens* from Skhūl.

cerous growth, on the main shaft, just beneath the point of articulation with the pelvis.

These specimens of *H. erectus* type were discovered in 1891 by the Dutch physician, Eugene Dubois, who specifically went to Java to discover the "missing link," a bold undertaking considering the academic climate at the time. His principal find consisted of a partial cranial vault (see Figure 1.2), found at Trinil, on the Solo River in the central part of Java. Additional finds have been made in Java since 1940 by G. H. R. von Koenigswald and from 1961–1966 by Sartono and Jacob. These have been variously dated between 595,000 and 435,000 years ago. (The Olduvai Hom. #9, from Bed II, a clear but quite robust *H. erectus,* has been dated at c. 750,000 years.)

In the late 1920's and 30's a number of caves were excavated in the region of Choukoutien in China, and a large sample of hominids very similar to those from Java was discovered, as well as evidence for the use of fire, together with stone tools made mainly from quartzitic rocks. These fossils, then known as *Sinanthropus pekinensis* (Figure 1.2), were the basis of a number of perceptive studies by the late Franz Weidenreich. Unfortunately, the fossils, the best population sample existing of fossil man, were mysteriously lost during the early part of World War II. Only casts and the excellent monographs of Weidenreich remain for further analysis. The fossils were somewhat more advanced than those known from Java, particularly in terms of cranial capacity, which averaged about 1050 cc. More recent discoveries (1964–1965) in the Shensi Province of China, known as "Lantian Man," are older than those at Choukoutien and, again, very similar to those in Java.

In North Africa, at Ternifine in Algeria and in three localities in Morocco, the late French palaeontologist, C. Arambourg, discovered partial fragments of teeth, jaws, and a parietal bone, associated with tools suggesting a Chellean pattern. It is on the basis of the tools, the faunal associations, and the morphology of the teeth and jaws that these finds are considered to be the same as the Javanese and Chinese *H. erectus* fossils. The designation given to them—*Atlanthropus mauritanicus*—should promptly be forgotten, as they are simply a North African variant of the basic *Homo erectus* pattern.

We now reckon two finds of *Homo erectus* material in Europe. The earliest, made in 1907 by Schoetensack in the Mauer sands near the city of Heidelberg, consists of a complete lower jaw with almost all the teeth intact. No stone tools were found with this fossil, and its dating is very difficult, being based on *relative* methods of faunal and geological comparison. The strata in which the find was made are attributed to the first interglacial period, with a date of roughly 500,000–600,000 years ago. The second find came in 1965, at the occupation site of Vertesszöllös in Hungary, and consists of a portion of the occipital bone and several teeth, with an associated stone tool industry of primitive choppers. The teeth and the faunal and cultural associations suggest a *Homo erectus* type, but estimates of the cranial capacity based on the occipital portion have been so large as to call for careful restudy, not to say skepticism.

In 1959 a few fragments of a skull and a tooth were found near Tell Ubeidiya, in Israel. Primitive stone tools and faunal remains of a Lower Pleistocene context were associated with the hominid bones. Unfortunately, these are not complete enough for any taxonomic assignment to be made.

In 1960 a broken frontal bone and some facial bones were found by Coppens in the Republic of Chad. There were no artifacts, but extinct elephant teeth suggest a date of late Lower or early Middle Pleistocene age. The name given the fossil, *Tchadanthropus uxoris,* must be dropped, as the fragments are really too incomplete to risk a binomial designation but not so unusual that they could not be fitted into either the *Australopithecus* or *Homo* genus.

Late Pleistocene Hominids:
The Neandertals and Homo sapiens sapiens

While the Middle Pleistocene hominids of the *Homo erectus* taxon present a fairly clear and relatively invariable pattern of morphological features, the Neandertals of the later part of the Pleistocene, from third interglacial times to about 35,000 years ago in the fourth glacial period, present an extremely complex picture that is currently full of controversy. It is impossible here to do more than introduce these finds and underline some of the major aspects of the group which are in question.

First of all, there is quite good agreement that these fossils should be included within the taxon of *Homo sapiens,* since they show only racial distinction from modern man. Like *Homo erectus,* they are widespread throughout western and eastern Europe and East and South Africa, in Israel, Lebanon, and Iraq in the Near East, and possibly in Java (as *Homo soloensis*), and China ("Mapa Man").

Two patterns of morphological features have been suggested to have existed, leading to a division into the so-called Classic and Progressive Neandertals. The "Classic" Neandertals are believed to have been a specialized development which occurred in northwestern Europe, becoming extinct after modern *Homo sapiens* came into the area, with the retreat of the last glacial period. The "Progressive" Neandertals are believed to have evolved from the *Homo erectus* groups and were 1) earlier in time than "Classics" in eastern Europe and parts of the Near East and 2) more modern in appearance, lending themselves more readily to some ancestral group from which modern *Homo sapiens* could have evolved.

The "Classic" features (Figure 1.2) which suggest some distinctiveness from modern *Homo sapiens* are large, uninterrupted brow ridges, a bun-shaped occipital bone, a long prognathous face with no canine fossa (maxillary indentation), and cranial capacities that are similar to our own and sometimes larger, i.e., up to 1650 cc. The "Progressive" Neandertals are very similar but have less accentuation of these features and thus a more modern appearance.

At the caves of Skhūl and Tabūn, at Mount Carmel in present-day Israel, there were discovered in the early 1930's the remains of possibly two groups of "Progressive" Neandertals, dated c. 30,000 to 40,000 years ago and separated by perhaps 10,000 years. The earlier population came from the Tabūn cave, the later from the cave of Skhūl, and it is the latter group (Figure 1.2) that shows features intermediate between Neandertal and modern man. The question has long been raised whether the latter population represents a hybrid group whose ancestors were both Neandertals and some as-yet-unfound group of modern *Homo sapiens* from the east, or whether they were a group in the process of evolving into modern man.

Further to the east are the remains from Shanidar Cave, in Iraq, dated around 45,000 years ago, which seem to be "Classic" Neandertals.

When all the finds are considered, it is apparent that the Neandertals were a widely spread and highly variable group. It is inescapable that some of their populations, most likely the earlier ones of eastern Europe and the Near East, were ancestral to modern man, and that some of these populations probably did evolve characteristics found in the true "Classic" types of northwestern Europe and eventually became either extinct through isolation or were absorbed by later, more modern populations. The contention of Loring Brace that we evolved from "Classic" types, and that any other view is a Catastrophist hang-on from the days of Cuvier, is not an unpopular one, but I think the more conservative view given above, which does not necessarily entail Catastrophist views, is a workable position until further finds are made.

In Java, between 1931 and 1933, some eleven calvaria were found, all of them without faces, making proper comparison with other Neandertals impossible. They occurred in a stratigraphic and faunal zone which suggested an Upper Pleistocene context. The cranial capacities are smaller than the European Neandertals, averaging around 1150–1200 cc., and the morphological patterns have suggested to several paleoanthropologists that these "Solo" calvaria show true resemblance to earlier *Homo erectus* finds from Java and China.

Another find which expands considerably the possible range of Neandertals was made in 1958, in Kwantung Province, China. Its date is unknown, but the partial facial and skull fragments certainly suggest a Neandertal pattern. It is known as Mapa Man.

At the cave of Broken Hill, Zambia (the former Northern Rhodesia), a skull was found in 1921, along with a broken portion of another upper jaw, and arm, leg, and pelvic fragments. Associated with the bones were cultural artifacts of a type known as Proto-Stillbay. The brain size of this hominid was about 1300 cc. Although he has an enormous brow ridge, large teeth, and dental arch, he is clearly not a simple "Classic" Neandertal but a somewhat different pattern, a variant on that theme. The fossil is known as Rhodesian Man.

Much further to the south, some eighty miles north of Cape Town, South Africa, yet another fossil was discovered, blown out from the sandy plains west of Hopefield along the coast of Saldanha Bay. This find shows only the upper part of a calvarium, but is almost identical to that of Rhodesian Man. It is roughly of the same age, i.e., some 30,000–40,000 years ago, and associated with late hand-axes, which suggests that Saldanha Man was just slightly earlier than Rhodesian Man. The question is: Are these African remains too specialized, with their primitive features such as brow ridges, and yet too late in time to be possible ancestors of modern man, or are they to be interpreted as racial variations which became isolated and did not continue to evolve further? The latter seems most probable.

Whatever the controversial nature of the Neandertals in terms of their taxonomic position and their relationship to modern man, they are clearly advanced hominids, making sophisticated stone tools, hunting large and dangerous animals, and having apparent religious convictions, as judged by some of their ritual burials. It has been suggested more than once that clean-shaven, dressed in a grey suit, and hanging from a subway strap, a Neandertal could not be distinguished from any other New York troglodyte. I think he might be noticed by a few, but that is all. As to what ever happened to the Neandertals of western Europe, we do not really know. It has long been held that their stone tool industry, the Mousterian, was discontinuous with later levels of Upper Paleolithic blade industries, such as the Aurignacian, Solutrean, and Magdalenian, and that this hiatus was as extreme as the purported disjunction between Neandertal and modern *Homo sapiens* types as represented by the fossils of Combe Capelle and Cro-Magnon. The picture appears far more complex today, and there seem to be suggestions of a gradation, at least in some localities, from Mousterian-Levalloisian to true blade industries; but transitional morphological patterns between "Classic" Neandertals and modern man have not been discerned as yet in western Europe.

Some Problematic Fossils: Steinheim, Swanscombe, Fontéchevade
There are two fossil finds dating from between the second interglacial and the fourth glacial which suggest an appearance more modern than the typical *Homo erectus* pattern of the time, discussed earlier, and which could have led to both "Progressive" and "Classic" Neandertals in later hominid evolution. These are Steinheim in Germany and Swanscombe in England. Steinheim consists of a skull found north of Stuttgart in 1933. Judged as a female because of a gracile appearance, "she" shows a number of traits that could place her as ancestral to both Neandertals and modern *sapiens*. Steinheim has an elevated forehead, a rounded contour in the back part of the skull, and a cranial capacity of about 1150 cc. The brow ridges are heavy, and it is easy to derive a Neandertal face from hers, although the teeth suggest that the lower jaw would not have been as large as those of later Neandertals.

At Swanscombe, in gravel sediments of late second interglacial age, an occipital bone and the left parietal bone were discovered in 1936; then, almost twenty years later in 1955, the right parietal of the same individual was found! The layer from which the finds came also produced hand-axes of the Acheulian III stage. No Swanscombe facial fragments have yet been found. The occipital and parietals suggest a well-rounded skull with a modern appearance and a cranial capacity of possibly 1300 cc. The vault is low, however, with very thick bones, and there is a Neandertal feature in the region of junction of the lambdoid, parietals, and temporal bones. In other words, most of the features of this Swanscombe skull are more modern than the "Classic" type of western Europe and thus could be of the same population as the Steinheim skull. But without the frontal bone and face we cannot be certain. In any event, these two finds show that the modern contours of the skull were already evolved during the second interglacial, perhaps as much as 400,000 years ago.

Lastly, there are the two cryptic fragments from Fontéchevade, in central France, discovered in 1947. These occur in a cave level containing a Tayacian stone tool industry and faunal remains of a date before the end of the third interglacial. One fragment is a small piece of the frontal bone, the second a larger piece of the top part of the skull. The second fragment suggests a skull indistinguishable from that of modern man, with a possible endocranial capacity of 1450 cc., even though it is a thick skull. The forehead region is missing, but a small portion of the frontal sinus is still intact, and its position makes it most unlikely that this skull had the forehead region of any "Classic" Neandertal. The first fragment is also thick but shows unmistakably that the brow ridges of this hominid were like those of modern *Homo sapiens*. Of course, it is possible to argue that these fragments were only the gracile extreme of a population which also included "Classic" Neandertals. It is also possible to claim the opposite, that here was a population almost completely modern in appearance, *prior* to "Classic" Neandertal and thus extending the hominid record of *Homo sapiens* (*recens*) at least to third interglacial times.

In my opinion, it is very unparsimonious to declare Fontéchevade to be the extreme of a yet undiscovered population, and I would therefore, on the basis of these finds and the others at Steinheim, Swanscombe, Tabūn, and Skhūl, as well as of the eastern European Neandertals, including Saccopastore, opt for the appearance of modern man either before or at least contemporaneously with the "Classic" Neandertals. How these two varieties of *Homo sapiens* existed, or rather co-existed, is another matter. Certainly, it need not have been violently. Thus, again, I do not believe that our present evidence necessarily proves that the "Classic" Neandertals represent an intermediate stage of hominid evolution between *Homo erectus* and modern *Homo sapiens*.

Finally, there are the broken skulls of Kanjera, Kenya, on the eastern shore of Lake Victoria, found in 1932 by the elder Leakey. These skulls were eroded out of deposits which unfortunately were not marked by the discoverer, and thus their validity with respect to age is in question. Nevertheless, careful dating work, using fluorine analysis by K. Oakley, has shown that the skull fragments are in the same fossilized state as mammal bones of the Middle Pleistocene, with associated hand-axes. The best guess provides an age of not less than seventy thousand years. Now, while the bones are quite thick, they show perfectly modern features of the brow, occipital, and other regions; one even has a depression in the cheek, the canine fossa, which is also modern in appearance. These, therefore, are certainly not "Classic" Neandertals, and they come earlier in time than either the Rhodesian Man or Saldanha finds.

Even more recently, the remains of three crania have been found from deposits in the Omo River basin in Ethiopia. These give an absolute date of roughly 120,000 years ago and seem quite modern in appearance, with fully modern-sized endocranial capacities. They were discovered in 1967 by the Kenya group and are judged by their describer, M. Day, to be *Homo sapiens* types, showing a curious mixture of both modern and more primitive *erectus*-like features, with a range of variation not unlike that of present-day *sapiens*.

In Sarawak, on the northern shore of Borneo, an important discovery was made in 1958 by T. Harrison, who found an almost complete skull of an adolescent male, along with chopping tools, and was able to get a charcoal sample which provided a radiocarbon age of 40,000 years. This skull is clearly that of a modern *Homo sapiens*, quite unlike the finds from Solo in Java. In fact, it is even less primitive looking than the skulls of modern Australian aborigines, although without a larger sample such a statement should be regarded tentatively. All of this, if confirmed, makes it further clear that modern forms of *Homo sapiens* existed both before and along with the Neandertal peoples called "Classic."

This is hardly the extent of the true fossil record. What has been related thus far comprises only the fossil highlights, so to speak. There are many other fragments, particularly of Neandertals and Late Pleistocene *Homo sapiens*, which have not been covered here.

· THE DYNAMICS OF HUMAN EVOLUTION

The foregoing has presented the major empirical evidence of human evolution, the fossilized bony remains of past man. Our description has not dealt at all with the questions of how and why these transformations took place during the last 12–14 million years. Certainly many factors have played an important part in transforming a *Ramapithecus* or even an *Australopithecus* hominid into what we are today, and one can only provide speculation as to how these changes came about. This must be done, of course, within the boundaries of modern genetics and evolutionary theory, comparative and functional anatomy, primatology, and the presumed significance of the cultural associations (living sites and other faunal remains) as well as the fossil record itself.

The factors involved in the dynamics of human evolution, as listed in Table 1.2, are not meant to be all-inclusive, or even independent of one another; they are merely suggestive. As such, they represent logical developments from what we know of comparative anatomy and behavior. In attempting to explain the dynamics of human evolution, the challenge is to put these factors into a synthesized whole that is at once parsimonious, defensible within the frameworks of genetic and evolutionary theory, and based on known morphological-behavioral-ecological relationships. Some scientists like to place the items in a particular time sequence, indicating that this happened first, then this, next that, and so on; but there is no way of looking at the endocranial casts of early hominids, for example, or the cubic centimeters of cranial capacity, and deciding whether or not such-and-such a hominid possessed language. There is likewise no way of looking at these materials and saying exactly what kind of social structure the hominid had, or whether he was peaceful or aggressive.

We *can* be certain that bipedalism and social behavior were key elements in man's evolution. The pelvic remains of the gracile australopithecines indicate that this hominid was capable of upright bipedalism, even though it had a cranial capacity below the average of the gorilla and not very different from the chimpanzee. The endocasts themselves, however, show modern configurations, clearly proving that even by this time the brain had become reorganized in the human direction. What seems to have followed thereafter was principally a process of selection for *larger* brains and body sizes. This also meant selection for a prolonged duration of growth, and for a longer post-natal dependency of the infant upon the mother. These features suggest in turn that behavioral adjustments in the nature of cooperative social behavior were also selected for quite early in the course of hominid evolution. This eventually entailed a separation of roles between male and female, with the male doing the hunting for animal proteins while the female very likely gathered the vegetable complements and supplements to the diet.

TABLE 1.2 A Partial List of the Interrelated Variables in the Dynamics of Hominid Evolution *

+	1.	Bipedal locomotion—upright posture, striding gait.
+	2.	Increasing use of hands to carry, manipulate objects.
+	3.	Dentition related to differing food habits: possible reduction in shape and length of canines, molarization of premolars.
+	4.	Increase in both relative and absolute brain size; reorganization and refinement of various brain regions, particularly cerebral cortex.
(+)	5.	Prolonged gestation and postnatal dependence of offspring.
(+)	6.	Retardation of growth rates with prolongation of duration.
+	7.	Increase in body size.
+	8.	Decrease in sexual dimorphism associated with gross size.
(−)	9.	Increase in sexual dimorphism associated with secondary sexual characteristics—fat deposition, permanent enlarged breasts, hair distribution; more permanent sexual receptivity of the female.
+	10.	Increased dependence on scavenging and/or hunting for protein-rich food.
(−)	11.	Sexual division of labor, domestication of the male; females complement males' hunting by gathering vegetable foods.
(−)	12.	Increased capacity for social density, and possibly greater disease resistance through increased protein consumption; drop in intra-group aggression, or increase in threshold of aggression. Increased sociality.
(+)(−)	13.	Psychosocial evolution—language through symbols, cognitive capacity and management of complexity of both social and material environments.
+	14.	Increasing use of wood, bone, horn, stone tools, fire—cultural adaptation.
+	15.	Gracilization of face and teeth, loss of body hair, sapientization.

* This list is not regarded as complete, nor is it organized according to any necessary time sequence.
+ indicates empirical support directly possible from fossil and archaeological record.
(+) indicates support possible with larger samples and specimens.
(−) indicates inference.

Likewise, necessary differentiations in physiognomy between male and female are suggested, not so much in skeletal and dental traits but rather in those features that interest us the most—sexual attractants such as permanent breasts, facial and bodily hair patterns, etc.—and that are associated with the permanent sexual receptivity of the female and a concomitant domestication of the male. These changes may have included psychological variables as well, and they must have involved a different focus of interactions between the endocrine glands and their target tissues. On another level changes in the social nurturing and teaching of *cultural* routines to the young would have become necessary.

It is my contention that when one has proof that stone tools were made to a definite standardized pattern, there is also a very good possibility that language existed. Once social changes in the direction of greater cooperation and role-segregation between the sexes came about, natural selection could operate on other changes which resulted in longer growth durations and postnatal dependency time, an increase in body size, an increase both in absolute brain size and in brain size relative to the body, and increased dependency on a hunting and gathering existence mediated through symbolically based social relationships and thus providing a cultural way of life. Once hunting, stone-tool making, and increased brain size become constant features of the pattern, it is possible to see them as interdependent variables operating as positive feedback factors for each other.

The next question that should be asked is, What set this process of interdependent reinforcement going? We need to visualize some "initial kick" which, once in motion, sets off a positive feedback cycle that selects positively for both cultural and brain complexity—this complexity mediated through prolonging growth duration and dependence and also through emphasis on cultural learning and strong social ties within groups. I would suggest three phases or stages of this process, as follows:

STAGE 1 From the end of *Ramapithecus* and early australopithecine phase, with major emphasis on social behavioral adaptations, involving bipedalism and endocrine and neural reorganization (but not necessarily neural enlargement).

STAGE 2 Late australopithecine-habiline phase, with major emphasis on consolidation and refinements of innovations or "initial kick" of Stage 1.

STAGE 3 Late habiline-early *erectus* to Neandertal-*sapiens* phase, with emphasis on elaboration of cultural skills in positive feedback relationships with brain enlargement.

Obviously, any attempt to go beyond the vague outlines of the empirical information of the fossil bone fragments can be little else than speculation: a sort of "just-so" story. Still, it is worthwhile to make an attempt, so that one can gain some idea of what might interrelate with what and suggest some coherent synthesis of the scattered facts. My own theory goes as follows:

Sometime back in the mid-to-late Miocene, the then-current apes, the dryopithecines, underwent an adaptive radiation, leading to increasing specialization within ecological niches and producing such types as those ancestral to the gorilla, chimpanzee, and orangutan, more adapted to arboreal conditions at a time when forests were retreating during desiccation. Another line, however, took on the challenge of the increasing retreat of forested zones and began a development based on adaptation to a *savanna* existence, perhaps utilizing seeds and grasses; this line was represented by *Ramapithecus* at the end of the Miocene.

With the beginning of the Pliocene or a few million years later, this group underwent another small adaptive radiation, resulting after about five million years in two ecologically distinct but overlapping (sympatric) groups: 1) a large-bodied, robust, mainly herbivorous type, *Australopithecus robustus,* and 2) a more gracile, more omnivorous type, *Australopithecus africanus,* which gradually increased its reliance on scavenging carnivore kills and hunting small animals. Both groups evolved increased degrees of cooperative, social intra-group behavior, which was effective in withstanding any significant carnivore predation, and which was based on the larger, better organized brains that had resulted from increased growth-time and juvenile dependency. Neither canine teeth, claws, nor stone weapons would have been necessary to these creatures.

Then, about three to four million years ago, these two groups made significant adaptive "choices": the robust group continued a mainly herbivorous adaptation, while the gracile group came to rely more heavily on animal flesh as a source of essential protein. The results were numerous and far-reaching. The robust group relied on larger body sizes, speed, and threat display, thus focusing selection pressures on bigger teeth for vegetable diets and increased sexual dimorphism in body size. The gracile forms "opted," in a sense, for increasing behavioral plasticity and effectiveness in securing protein-rich sources found in animal flesh. This resulted in increasingly effective bipedal locomotion for hunting, scavenging, and particularly carrying and for traveling between water holes and home bases. Increased prolongation of gestation and postnatal dependence times were necessary concomitants of selection for better brains, a resultant of increased mitotic division of nerve cells (hyperplasia) and increased size (hypertrophy) of nerve cells, with more branching and connections. These prolongations in mitotic division and neuron growth, resulting in larger brains both relatively and absolutely, could not have occurred without reliance upon, and availability of, rich protein sources. (The medical literature is rich in sources showing the awful effects of protein malnourishment on the normal growth of the brain.)

An increased prolongation of dependence and growth meant an attending change in relations between the sexes, and between males of the groups. It probably meant increased degrees of affective ties among all group members: between males for cooperation in hunting; between females for caring for and feeding the young, which are dependent longer; and between males and females in food sharing and division of labor. The main adaptation was thus a better brain and cooperative social behavior to nourish it and "program" (teach) it for a hunting adaptation, with prolonged growth and dependence a necessary step in the evolution of bigger and better brains and more effective learning abilities. Sexual division of labor undoubtedly became highly adaptive as females supplemented the protein-rich meat diets with further small game and necessary vegetable foods (particularly for vitamins) while taking care of the young.

These interconnected sets of adaptations probably continued to develop until roughly a million years ago, with little enmity between the two groups—which is another way of saying that there was probably not much economic competition for ecological resources between them. Then, as the gracile group increased its prolongation of growth under positive selection pressures, both brain *and body size* increased to some point where the environment could no longer support both hominid lines. From here, it would have been a short time until the decline of the robust group, while the selection pressures for increased brain, body size, and effective hunting led to the evolution of the gracile group into *Homo erectus*. Perhaps at this point they even preyed upon the remnants of the robust line.

The combination of increased body and brain size probably reached a plateau near the middle of the Pleistocene with late *Homo erectus* types (such as at Choukoutien), when further selection and ecological requirements came to favor increased behavioral efficiency through better and bigger brains, without any further significant increase in body size. Along with increasing dependence on hunting, which had characterized the gracile australopithecines, there would have been growing pressures for better stone-tool making, communication, and social control. Language by symbol systems, associated with all three of these processes, must have depended on a specific neural organization and socialization process for its success. Language creates environmental differentiation or complexity and control over that environment. Thus the dynamics outlined here should be seen not only as interrelated but as processes which also further changed selection pressures through time. It is suggested that these operated in a positive feedback way, involving increasing perfection of brain, intelligent behavior, bipedalism, hunting, sociality, cognitive capacity, language, and toolmaking. The morphological correlations are increased size of body and brain; changes in the pattern of sexual dimorphism; perfection of bipedalism. The behavioral correlations are increased sophistication in perceiving and manipulating environments through language and intelligence, and increased cooperation, sociality, and complementation of sexual division of labor. The physiological correlates of these are, of course, numerous but surely must have included endocrine-target tissue changes leading to reduced intragroup aggression, increased sexual-signaling features (i.e., permanent breasts, permanent receptivity of females, etc.), prolonged gestation, dependence, and growth.

This is just one possible explanation, extremely brief, of the interacting dynamics of human evolution. While much of the account rests on a number of assumptions that might be disproved, the task facing the paleoanthropologist is not only to construct hypotheses which explain the evolutionary sequence of the fossils and the dynamics involved, but also to do it in such a way that the hypotheses are testable and thus go beyond a mere description of the morphological changes shown in the fossils. It is a very challenging process.

• POSTSCRIPT

As I indicated earlier, knowledge of our evolutionary development is a year-to-year matter. Since the time when this book was submitted for publication, new discoveries in Africa have been reported, some of which not only expand our sample of hominid specimens but also introduce a new dimension into our considerations. Just such a find is the new E.R. (East Rudolf) 1470 cranium discovered by Richard Leakey's team during the latter part of the 1972 season. Although the lower jaw is missing, this is an almost complete cranium of a hominid found at East Rudolf at a level below the KBS tuff, which has been dated as $2.6 \pm .21$ million years old. Since the cranium was found almost 30 meters lower, its own age is reckoned at about 2.9 million years! In addition, it is clearly not australopithecine in form, but rather is from an early species of *Homo,* with a cranial capacity of at least 775 cc.! The date is a good 1.0 million years earlier than that of the bottom of Bed I at Olduvai Gorge. Until the specimen is fully studied and the results published, it would be premature to speculate about its relationship to other hominid fossils. However, we probably must now consider at least three different early hominid types, or species, in the Lower Pleistocene in Africa. To complicate matters more, there were still more discoveries in 1973 which have yet to be fully reported.

The reader will thus appreciate that the scheme this chapter presents may be significantly altered by these new discoveries. Such is the nature of the game!

• BIBLIOGRAPHIC ESSAY

Of the books and articles relating to fossil man, probably the best available are W. E. LeGros Clark's *Fossil Evidence for Human Evolution,* published by the University of Chicago Press in 1964, as well as the classic by M. Boule and H. V. Vallois, *Fossil Men,* published by Dryden Press in 1957. An excellent article is F. Clark Howell's "Recent advances in human evolutionary studies," published in 1964 in the *Quarterly Review of Biology,* Vol. 42, pages 471–504. This article is also available in S. L. Washburn and Phyllis Dolhinow's reader, *Perspectives on Human Evolution 2,* published in 1972 by Holt, Rinehart and Winston, pages 51–128. An excellent recent discussion including the newest fossils can be found in W. W. Howells' *Evolution of the Genus Homo,* published by Addison-Wesley in 1973. For more technical information about the discoveries made by R. E. Leakey's team at East Rudolf, the reader should consult recent numbers of *Nature* and the *American Journal of Physical Anthropology.*

As a first step in a search for further information concerning the evolutionary dynamics of early man, the volumes *The Neanderthals* (1973) and *The Missing Link* (1972) in the Time-Life Books series, as well as the book entitled *Early Man* (1965) in the Life Nature Library, should be consulted. Other works which would prove valuable to the student are F. E. Poirier's *Fossil Man: An Evolutionary Journey,* published in 1973 by C. V. Mosby; David Pilbeam's *The Ascent of Man* in the Macmillan Series in Physical Anthropology, 1972; M. F. A. Montagu's edited work, *Culture: Man's Adaptive Dimension,* published by Oxford University Press in 1968 (see particularly chapters 2, 3, 4, 6, and 7); and the first chapter of W. Etkin's edited volume, *Social Behavior and Organization Among Vertebrates,* published by the University of Chicago Press in 1964.

If further information is desired concerning the evolution of the brain, the reader is directed to some of the author's articles on the subject: "Cranial capacity, neural reorganization and hominid evolution: a search for more suitable parameters," in *American Anthropologist,* Vol. 68 (1966), pages 103–121; "The evolution of the human brain: some notes toward a synthesis between neural structure and the evolution of complex behavior," in *General Systems,* Vol. 12 (1967), pages 3–19; "The human brain in evolutionary perspective," in the second edition of Morton Fried's edited work, *Readings in Anthropology,* Vol. I, pages 215–223, published by Crown in 1968; "The evolution of the primate brain: some aspects of quantitative relationships," in *Brain Research,* Vol. 7 (1968), pages 121–172; "Some questions on parameters of neural evolution in primates," in the *Annals of the New York Academy of Sciences,* Vol. 167 (1969), pages 332–342; "Neural parameters, hunting and the evolution of the human brain," in *Advances in Primatology,* Vol. 1, pages 299–309, edited by C. R. Norback and W. Montagna and published by Appleton-Century-Crofts in 1970; and "Australopithecine endocasts, brain evolution in the Hominoidea and a model of hominid evolution," in *The Functional and Evolutionary Biology of Primates,* pages 185–204, edited by R. Tuttle and published by Aldine in 1972.

2
THE OLD WORLD PALEOLITHIC
RALPH SOLECKI

Traditionally, Paleolithic archaeology has consisted principally of the study of stone tools made by man before the time when he began to manufacture pottery and use polished and ground stone implements. Since the latter period, the Neolithic, and all of subsequent history take up less than one half of one percent of man's known life on earth, the Paleolithic can be seen to have been immensely long.

Of course, Paleolithic archaeology includes more than the mere classification of stone tool types. Differences inherent in the modes of manufacture of the tools are sought. These tool-making techniques, in turn, are bound up inextricably with the economic techniques by which tool-makers gained a livelihood. Again, at a higher level of abstraction economic techniques are tied in with the social organization and other activities of the tool-makers, hints of which can be seen fleetingly in the remains archaeologists find.

Although Stone Age archaeology had been foreshadowed earlier, it was not until the middle of the nineteenth century that the first real strides were made. By the beginning of the present century the young social science was well established in western Europe, and Paleolithic archaeology, particularly in contrast with Neolithic and classical, had become closely identified with the geology and paleontology of the Pleistocene period.

Following the scheme adopted by the early prehistorians, the Paleolithic period has been divided into three parts: Lower, Middle, and Upper. This western European scheme is basically a chronological one, but it also involves the geological, faunal, and floral histories of the natural areas concerned. The Paleolithic stages were originally identified by the occurrence in them of various special tool types, which became the hallmarks or "index fossils" of the particular periods. Indeed, geologists seized upon these markers for the identification of geological strata in the sometimes mistaken opinion that they were infallible guides. Prehistorians trained in the tradition of geologists treated the study of prehistory as a kind of adjunct to geology, emphasizing stratigraphical relationships, artifact types (like index fossils), and chronology to the detriment of other aspects of the study. What many prehistorians overlooked is the fact that early man, like modern *Homo sapiens,* was a thinking animal and could not be made to fit into a single mold. Prehistorians found this out increasingly when they tried to apply the neat and familiar western European systems of Paleolithic archaeology to other parts of the Old World, namely sub-Saharan Africa and Asia east of India, although at first the systems seemed to fit well enough.

As man is today, man in the past was heavily dependent upon the characteristics of his natural surroundings: soils and the attendant flora and fauna of his times, commonly called his environment. Today we designate the special studies of the two-way relations between man and his environment by the term "cultural ecology." The prehistorian relies on the geologist for the identification of strata and the study of the soils of ancient environments; on the palynologist (pollen analyst) for the identification of the floral evidence found in the soils; and on the paleontologist for the identification of the faunal remains—splintered and broken animal bones—recovered from the archaeological deposits. Since most perishable remains have usually disappeared, the cultural evidence itself is quite meager when compared, for example, to that which the classical archaeologist obtains as his reward. Consequently, the prehistorian of the Paleolithic has especially turned to the natural sciences for aids to his own study of the artifacts, which consist mainly of flints, although bone implements and objects also form a valuable part of his collections where the conditions of preservation are favorable.

Largely as a result of researches which were by-products of the Second World War, prehistorians have been given the tools with which to date both their oldest (back to about three million years ago) and their relatively younger but still prehistoric archaeological remains. These methods, mainly dependent upon forms of radioactivity, use different materials for dating. The most precise of the methods utilizes the carbon-14 isotope, which occurs commonly in materials found in archaeological contexts. These include charcoal or burned wood from hearths (and even unburned wood where preserved), burned bone, and unburned shells, the reliability of the dating decreasing in that order. There are presently about fifty laboratories in the world dating materials by the radiocarbon method. Because of technical difficulties and various uncertainties of the results, practically all these laboratories limit dating to about forty thousand years ago, only two or three producing dates to fifty or sixty thousand years. These dates cover all of the Upper Paleolithic, Mesolithic, and subsequent periods but only the very end of the Middle Paleolithic. They show that modern man, or *Homo sapiens sapiens,* whose origins are generally ascribed to the Upper Paleolithic, dates back no more than 35,000 to 40,000 years at most, or a mere one percent of the life of the Hominidae, who are ultimately traceable to around 3 to 4 million years ago in eastern Africa, and even much earlier in some classifications of the group.

All forms of tool-making and -using men, from the earliest varieties, are to be found within the confines of the geological Pleistocene and Holocene periods of the Quaternary. Various ages have been suggested for the Pleistocene since it was first distinguished in the nineteenth century, and its various subdivisions have consequently been alternately expanded and contracted. Most generally, an age of one million years has been attributed to it, but hardly two decades ago a conservative date of 300,000 years was put forth. This last made more than one physical anthropologist unhappy, because it did not allow sufficient time for man's evolution. The situation was corrected with the invention of K/A (potassium/argon) dating, which first gave us ages of 1.9 million years for early Pleistocene finds in Olduvai Gorge in Tanzania and more recently 3 to 4 million years for material from the Omo Valley in

Ethiopia. The potassium-argon method depends on the radioactive processes found in certain kinds of basaltic rock such as lava flows and other stones of molten origin.

The Pleistocene is recognized as a period of great worldwide fluctuations of temperature, from very cold to very warm. With the cooler temperatures came the coincident increase of glaciations in the higher altitudes (mountain glaciation) and in the northern latitudes (continental glaciation). The growth of glaciers is intimately bound up with the water in the major water-bearing body on earth, the sea. Thus when the glaciers grow, the sea level falls (or regresses), and when the glaciers melt, it rises (transgresses). Four major periods of glaciation are recognized for the Pleistocene in Europe, with three intervening periods of warmth, the interglacials. The glaciations, Günz, Mindel, Riss, and Würm, were named after localities in the Alpine area where the first studies were made. These glacial periods have been more finely subdivided into stadial periods. Correspondingly, the interglacials suffered minor periods of coolness. The last glacial, the Würm, ended about eleven thousand years ago with a sudden upsurge of worldwide warmth.

These glacials and interglacials were closely related to the spread of man over the earth, permitting him at some times to extend into continental areas released from the grip of the glaciers and at other times to cross dry-shod (or -footed) into new areas and land masses normally barred by shallow-water straits. Thus, England was a part of continental Europe as late as about eight thousands years ago. As climate fluctuated, glaciers waxed and waned, and the sea level receded and rose, the flora and fauna of the world were affected. This, in turn, had repercussions upon man, who at first had few means to protect himself against a cold, harsh climate, though the giant herbivores prospered under such conditions. It was perhaps for this reason that the ancestors of modern man flourished originally in the warmer areas of Africa and the more southerly parts of Asia. When they learned how to cope with the weather and to adapt their equipment to their environment, they moved from their homeland to regions where the possibilities of the hunt were richer.

A phenomenon intimately tied up with Pleistocene chronology

is the periodic reversal of the earth's magnetic poles (dated by the K/A process). One of these reversals, the "Olduvai event," marks the time of the hominid occupation at Olduvai Gorge. Another occurred at about the time of the appearance of the pithecanthropines in Java around 700,000 years ago. Although just what the broader effects of these reversals might have been is at present very controversial, the coincidences with major stages of human evolution are suggestive, since there seem to have been increases of cosmic radiation at the times of pole reversal; and these increases are also believed to have had climatic consequences.

Within each of the three major periods of the Old Stone Age, the Lower, Middle, and Upper, we have the assignment of diagnostic tool types. Thus, for the *Lower Paleolithic* (see Figure 2.1) there are the pebble tools and choppers (the African Oldowan) and the hand-axes (the western European Abbevillian and Acheulian). The makers of the African Oldowan were the australopithecines; of the hand-axes, the pithecanthropines. Flake tools were characteristic of the *Middle Paleolithic* (Figure 2.2), the Levalloiso-Mousterian types being made by Neandertals, although uncertainty surrounds those of the Tayacian and Clactonian. Finally, blade tools are one of the distinguishing features of the *Upper Paleolithic* (Figure 2.3), represented in western Europe by the Aurignacian, Perigordian, Solutrean, and Magdalenian cultures, and made by *Homo sapiens.*

The evolution of tool-making can now be traced from the pebble-tool stage through the various grades of hand-axes. The use of flake tools, which were present from the earliest period of tool manufacture, became paramount only later in the prehistory of man. This represented an economic use of the raw stone material, permitting the production of many tools from the same poundage of flint that it had earlier taken to make a single hand-axe. Better technological grasp of flint-working, a kind of revolution associated with the coming of modern man, is reflected in the still more economical production of the blade tools from prismatic-shaped cores or nuclei of stone. Tool types became much more varied in Upper Paleolithic times, and indeed for a single specific function several designs of tools were purposefully made. Bone tools became very much in evidence in the same period, fabricated

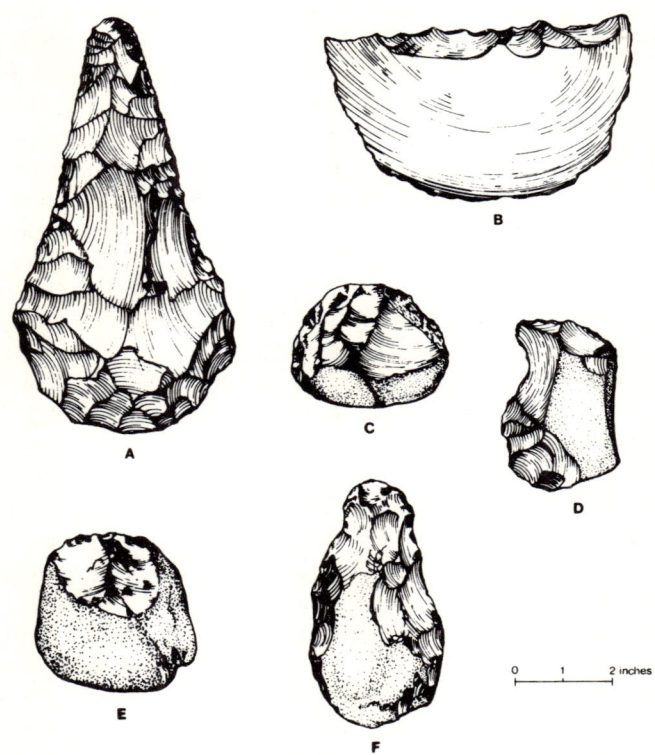

FIGURE 2.1 Lower Paleolithic tools. *(A)* Micoquian biface. *(B)* Choukoutien chopping tool. *(C)* Oldowan pebble tool. *(D)* Clactonian flake. *(E)* Oldowan pebble tool. *(F)* Abbevillian hand-axe.

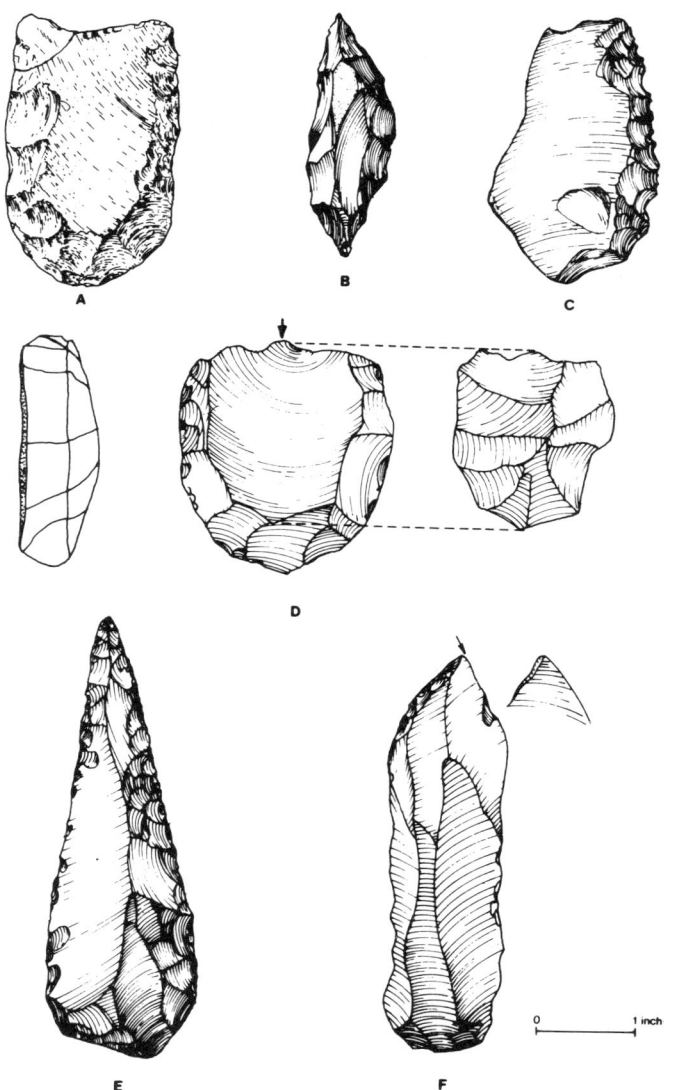

FIGURE 2.2 Middle Paleolithic tools. *(A)* Fauresmith cleaver. *(B)* Tayacian point. *(C)* "Denticulate." *(D)* Steps in the Levallois technique. *(E)* Mousterian point. *(F)* Burin.

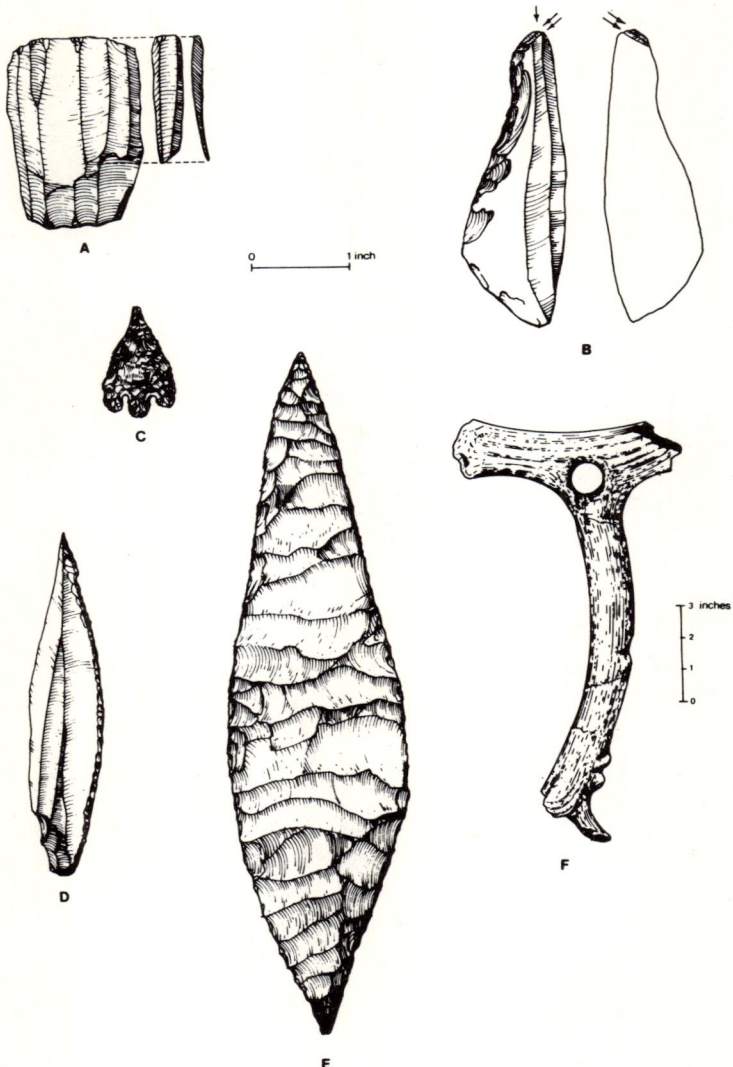

FIGURE 2.3 Upper Paleolithic and Mesolithic tools. *(A)* Mesolithic blade core and blade. *(B)* Burin. *(C)* Parpallo point. *(D)* Gravettian point. *(E)* Solutrean spear point. *(F)* Shaft straightener.

mainly for the function of tipping hunting lances, although other uses for cut bones seem also to have been developed. In the immediately post-Paleolithic period, the Mesolithic, technology developed to a degree which indicates that the *most* economical use of flint had finally been found, in the production of "microliths."

Seen on a graph, man's technology progressed ever so slowly and gradually from his dim origins about 3 million years ago to c. 700,000 B.P., when the development of the hand-axe cultures had their beginning. The rise of technology was slightly steeper up to the time of the origins of the flake cultures, roughly 150,000 years ago and culminating about 40,000 B.P. At that point, stone technology spurted sharply with the development of the great Upper Paleolithic technological advances of blade production; and finally the ascendance was even more marked with the coming of the Mesolithic period. In the later stages we also see the development of artwork and the diversification of tool types and materials. (See Figure 2.4.)

· THE LOWER PALEOLITHIC

The area famous for the earliest tool-making and tool-using hominids is in eastern Africa, notably in the Olduvai Gorge area of Tanzania, the Lake Rudolf area of Kenya, and the Omo Valley of southern Ethiopia. All of these places have one thing in common: they lie within the African Rift system, a zone of geologically disturbed strata which is also represented in the submerged valley of the Red Sea and the northern extension of that same valley into the Dead Sea and Jordan River areas of Palestine.

Discoveries in the basal Olduvai Gorge deposits indicate the certain coexistence of extremely crude, chipped-stone pebble tools, little more than battered and fractured cobbles about the size of a golf ball, together with the bones of australopithecines, members of the Hominidae who stood erect to approximately four feet in height and had small cranial capacities of about 600 cc. These creatures seem to have cooperated in the hunt, and with pebble tools they were able to cut the flesh of the large beasts which had successfully been downed. The method of tool manufacture consisted of little more than putting the pebble on an anvil (another stone) and smashing it with a heavy cobble.

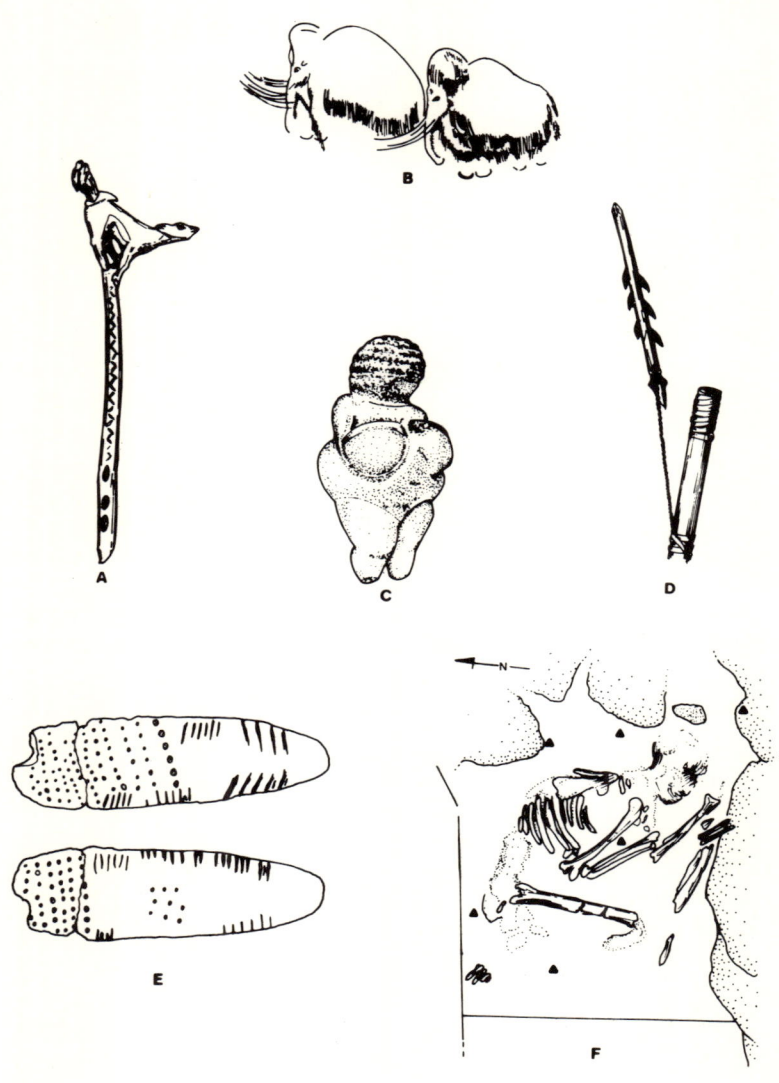

FIGURE 2.4 *(A)* Magdalenian spear thrower. *(B)* Upper Paleolithic cave drawing of mammoths. *(C)* "Venus" figurine. *(D)* Magdalenian harpoon. *(E)* "Calendar" bone. *(F)* Neandertal burial in Shanidar Cave showing location of flower pollen samples.

The earliest bone- and stone-bearing layers at Olduvai rest upon basalt lava which came from nearby volcanoes. These rocks, as well as those of volcanic origin associated with the primary bed, are datable by the K/A process, and indeed, as mentioned earlier, have yielded dates of about 1.9 million years ago. Still earlier dates have been found for rather similar tools and associated australopithecine bones in the Omo Valley and the Lake Rudolf areas, with ages in excess of three million years. These fossil remains have been assigned to the geological sub-period called the Villafranchian, at the base of the Pleistocene. Evidence of the very primitive industry associated with the Australopithecinae, the making of pebble tools, has also been found at Vallonet in southern France, remote from the original find spot in Africa and separated from it by a sea. The faunal material from this site is assigned the date of Upper Villafranchian, making it more or less contemporary with the basal hominid-containing deposits of Olduvai.

Slightly more advanced stone tools called "choppers" (the cutting edge flaked from one side) and "chopping tools" (the cutting edge flaked from two sides) have been found in other places in Africa, notably in Chad, Ain-Hanech in Algeria, Casablanca in Morocco, and the alluvial deposits of the Vaal River in South Africa. Choppers were usually made of thin flat pebbles, whereas the chopping tool was flaked on a thicker pebble.

Stepping across to Asia, these crude-edged stone "chopping" implements occur in the Jordan Valley at Ubeidiya in Israel, and in India. The chopping tool persisted for a long time in the Far East, notably in China, where at the famous cave of Choukoutien it had been taken over by later hominid types, the *Pithecanthropus erectus* species of man which was originally discovered in Java.

It is believed that the chopper or its variant, the chopping tool, evolved by degrees to the bifacially flaked hand-axe. This tool, also made with percussion blows from a stone hammer, has been identified in higher levels of the classic geological sequence at Olduvai Gorge. Associated with the first crude hand-axes are spheroids of flaked stone ranging from about the size of a tangerine to the size of a large orange. These balls have sometimes been identified as bolas, although this use is conjectural. In Europe the earliest hand-axe cultures have been called Abbevillian (formerly Chellean) in France, after the type-station where very crude examples were found well over a hundred years ago.

The hand-axe cultures, associated with the pithecanthropines, ranged over Africa, southern Asia, and that part of Europe which was not covered by heavy glaciation, i.e., non-Arctic Europe. As noted earlier, the pithecanthropines of eastern Asia appear mainly to have continued to use the more rudimentary choppers, instead of the hand-axes, although the latter do occur sporadically in the area. The date of the emergence of *Pithecanthropus* and the hand-axe cultures is roughly 700,000 to 750,000 years ago. As a predominant tool technique it lasted to about 125,000 years ago. With the hand-axes have been found occasional burins and flakes which presumably served as supplemental tools.

It is not known exactly what hand-axes were used for, since they often do not appear to show any wear. However, the association of these large implements with elephant bones at butchering sites such as Torralba in Spain suggests that they were used to flay the hides of the larger beasts, as well as to cut through the limb joints. Hand-axe sites of one kind or another are fairly numerous compared to those of the earlier chopper-chopping tools, some 180 having been tallied in the Near East alone, but *dwelling* sites with hand-axes present are a rarity.

Despite a very slow rate of change, the hand-axe makers were not entirely stagnant culturally, since they did improve their techniques of manufacture. In the later stages, called the Acheulian after St. Acheul in France, the place of the original finds, a wood, horn, or bone baton was favored over the stone pebble as a percussion or striking instrument for flaking the axe. The softer material produced a straighter, more even cutting edge and was capable of more precision than the stone hammer. The Acheulian hand-axe users seem to have been hunters of the larger animals (where they were available), attacking them in small bands at favored strategic spots where the beasts were at a disadvantage. The Acheulian peoples lived in tents with an oval-shaped ground plan or other shelters of a temporary nature. For some unknown reason they appear sometimes to have shunned caves, which were ready-made homes needing only a little modification. The reason may be logical enough—the larger beasts such as the elephants were not adapted to mountainous cave country or, alternatively, the caves were not in close proximity to the normal haunts of the quarry.

The Near East seems to have been the funnel through which the hand-axe cultures spread out from Africa, where it is presumed that the tool type first developed. On the trail are found the sites of Ubeidiya in Israel, Joub Janine in Lebanon, and Latamne in Syria.

· THE MIDDLE PALEOLITHIC

The production of hand-axes dwindled and fell into disuse over its area of dominance as the smaller and handier flakes which mark the opening of the Middle Paleolithic in western Europe came into fashion. Actually, there were areas in northern and eastern Europe where hand-axes never had come *into* vogue in any strength. On the other hand, there were "islands" where the bifacial tool-making tradition lingered, as exemplified by the Fauresmith and Sangoan cultures in Africa south of the Sahara. The latter traditions appear to have been adapted to open- and forest-type environments respectively. From them stemmed a number and variety of tool technologies parallel in time to the Upper Paleolithic and Mesolithic in the northern hemisphere of the Old World.

One of the African innovations, the Levallois technique, heralding the Middle Paleolithic age proper, appears to have been developed in southwest Africa and to have spread rapidly over the continent to Asia and Europe. This technique became part of the Mousterian tradition, well known as associated with the new species of man, *Homo sapiens neandertalensis*.

The Middle Paleolithic is characterized by the predominance of flake tools—that is, tools made on flakes which had been struck from flint cores especially prepared for the production. The Middle Paleolithic horizon is restricted to the area of continental Europe, North Africa, and eastward in Asia to India. There are also reports of artifacts made in the flake tradition from sporadic points as far east as eastern Siberia.

While we generally associate the Middle Paleolithic in prehistory with the Mousterian flake tradition, two other minor traditions are recognized—the Clactonian and Tayacian, found in western Europe. The Tayacian has also been identified in the Near East. The Clactonian is an industry of flake tools, generally of large size, struck off by stone-hammer percussion from the parent core. It is localized in northern France and England and probably dates to the Mindel-Riss interglacial, possibly 400,000 years ago. It was first discovered at Clacton-on-Sea in England and later found in the Seine Valley of France. No human remains have as yet been discovered with it.

The Tayacian industry is more widespread, ranging from sites in the Near East (Levant) to southwestern France, where it was first recognized in the heart of the classic area for prehistoric studies near Les Eyzies in the Dordogne Valley. It has been called a "phantom" industry, probably a variety of the Levalloiso-Mousterian. In any case, it definitely occurs at the base of the Levalloiso-Mousterian sequence at a number of sites, and appears to date to the Riss-Würm interglacial (c. 100,000 years ago), although some investigators would place it in the preceding Mindel-Riss interglacial, at least in the Near East, where some five localities have been found bearing materials of this type. The sites are Mugharet-et-Tabūn and Qafsa in Israel, Yabroud in Syria, and Bahsas and Ras Beirut in Lebanon. The Tayacian is marked by a particular type of point which is steeply retouched on the sides by the stone-hammer percussion technique. The flakes were evidently struck off from large cores without elaborate preparation of the raw material. No human skeletal remains have been found associated with this industry.

The Levalloiso-Mousterian, originally divided up as two elements, one chronologically succeeding the other, was first recognized in France, where the names originated. Levallois is a station on the Metro subway system of Paris, and Le Moustier is a little village in the Dordogne area of southwestern France. Both are near sites identified with a special method of fashioning or preparing the parent core of flint from which the flakes to be utilized were struck off. First, the cortex of a nodule of flint was removed down to a shape resembling a tortoise, hence the term "tortoise-core," and then the Levallois flake was struck from the flat underside of this prepared core. The expert flint-knapper thus produced a flake already pointed, razor-sharp, and ready for use. The method of production can be duplicated today by trained flint-knappers, using a handy-sized pebble to strike with. Another kind of core, the discoidal, is similarly tortoise-shaped, but instead of producing a single flake, the prehistoric flint-knapper struck off flakes from the perimeter toward the center, achieving a kind of circular "mousetrap" effect, as opposed to the Levallois core technique, which produced what may be likened to a rattrap shape. Before the flake was struck off, the place of intended impact on the core perimeter was very often "burred" with a brusque succession of blows faceting the core edge. This gives the edge a prepared striking-platform, enabling the artisan to achieve better control and assuring the detachment of a more perfect flake.

The production of flakes from cores is less wasteful of raw material than the production of hand-axes, which are themselves cores. By using the Levallois tortoise-core technique, the prehistoric artisan could detach from the same kilogram of flint which produces one Acheulian hand-axe at least a dozen usable flakes and points, whose total cutting edges equaled at least ten times the length of the usable edge on the hand-axe. By the discoidal core technique, the amount of cutting edge possible is even greater, giving the flint-knapper as much as twice again the amount of usable flakes and points gained from the tortoise-core technique.

It appears that the single difference between the so-called Mousterian point, the hallmark of the Mousterian industry, and the Levallois point is the heavy side-retouch on the Mousterian and the slight side-retouch or absence of side-retouch on the Levallois. This has led one investigator to the hypothesis that the reason for the difference was the availability of raw material. For instance, in northern France and Belgium, where good sources of fine flint abound, one finds the "rich man's Levalloisian"; in southwestern France, where flint is in shorter supply and of poorer quality, the raw material was conserved, and the tools saw much more use and resharpening—hence the "poor man's Levalloisian," or Mousterian.

The Levalloiso-Mousterian has been subdivided into four major industries, called traditions, on the basis of the percentages of artifact types included, such as hand-axes, scrapers, points, and denticulates. These industries are considered to be traditions because of their long persistence in time. Following the above scheme we have the recognition of 1) the Mousterian of Acheulian tradition, with a heavy relative percentage of Acheulian hand-axes present; 2) the Mousterian of Quina tradition, typified by a special kind of scraper with a curvate or "rocking-chair" bottom; 3) the Mousterian of Denticulate tradition, marked by a relatively large percentage of toothed tools; and 4) the typical Mousterian tradition, dominated by a large proportion of Mousterian-type points.

We still have gaps in our knowledge of the area, but there is enough evidence to indicate that the four major types of the Levalloiso-Mousterian are also to be found in the Near East, especially in the Levant, with some suggestions in North Africa as well. In the Zagros Mountains, which appear to be an especially homogeneous ecological area, only one tradition, the typical Mousterian, seems to have flourished. One of the major sites in the Zagros area is the cave of Shanidar in Iraqi Kurdistan. In the Levant area, at the paramount cave and shelter sites of Mount Carmel, Yabroud, the Kheritoun Valley, Adlun, Masloukh, and Nahr Ibrahim and other sites in Lebanon and Israel, there have been enough representatives of the four traditions for us to be sure that southwestern France holds no monopoly in this regard.

The movement of peoples is favored here as a hypothesis to account for the similarity of these tools, since transferral of ideas without the mechanism of peoples would surely involve a language use more precise than we believe these peoples had. Concerning the actual carriers of the Levalloiso-Mousterian culture, the type of fossil was originally named "Neanderthal," after the little valley of Neander near Düsseldorf in western Germany. The Neandertals appear to have been ecologically the first broadly adaptable people on earth. They were distributed through many different environmental situations, from the seaside, through steppe and forest, to high mountains. Some places, like northeastern Europe and northern Siberia, must have been too cold or forbidding for Neandertal man, although Mousterian flints have been reported in southern Siberia and northern China, in places well to the north of the present frost line. Neandertals were thoroughly familiar with the use of fire, and undoubtedly used skin coverings for the body.

From the number of sites, western and southern Europe and the Near East would seem to have been especially favored by them, but this appearance may be largely circumstantial, since these are the areas that have been most intensively explored by prehistorians. And while it cannot be denied that the same areas presented excellent cave fronts and rock shelters, ready-made homes which were favored by some early men, we must not lose sight of the fact that deposits in such shelter and cave sites had a better chance of survival and preservation than those in the open. Undoubtedly there were many open sites in northeastern Europe (Germany, Poland, Russia) which were wiped away by the last glaciation. Many regions farther east in the U.S.S.R. were simply unsuited for habitation during the Middle Paleolithic period.

It is very difficult to count the exact number of Neandertal skeletons, or parts of individuals, which have been found in the world, or of the sites involved; however, there are at least 44 sites with 86 Neandertals in Europe, 12 sites and 45 individuals in the Near East, and 12 sites and 24 individuals elsewhere (not including Africa south of the Sahara). The approximate total of sites thus is 68, and the number of Neandertal skeletons or individuals represented is about 155. Recent reports indicate that current excavations at Jebel Qafsa in Israel have produced at least a dozen skeletons.

My own finds at Shanidar Cave in Iraq are interesting not only because some nine individuals are represented but because of the associated information. One of the individuals, Shanidar I, found in a horizon dated 46,000 B.P., was a male about forty years old who could hardly have fended for himself in the outside world because of old injuries and a deformity from birth. Another individual, also adult, had suffered a stab wound in his ribs and was recovering on his bed when, as in the case of Shanidar I, a rock-fall brought death. The most remarkable find (Figure 2.4) is a grave interment in which some eight species of flowers were laid. From the flowers, which were identified by the pollens found in the grave, it has been determined that the individual, Shanidar IV, had been buried some time between the end of May and the beginning of July. Nearly all the flowers have medicinal properties, but this may be only coincidence, since there is no other evidence that the Neandertals of Shanidar knew the virtues of plants for medicine. This is the first time floral evidence has been found with any kind of prehistoric skeletal remains. It gives us a further appreciation of the human aspect of the Neandertals, and removes them further from the bestial kind of characterization handed down to us from the time of the original find in the nineteenth century.

Contemporary with the types of flake cultures represented in southwestern Asia and much of Europe was a related kind in northeastern and central Europe and North Africa. In these parts of Europe the variety of the Mousterian is replaced by a procedure of bifacial tool preparation known as the Szeleta and Osmaniwicza cultures. In North Africa there are also areas of local and individual industries which developed seemingly without antecedent, and disappeared similarly without trace, such as the Tabelablat industry in Tunisia. Recent investigations in the Nile Valley have shown a rich and varied industry of flake cultures whose importance is just now being realized.

South of the Sahara, and east of India, the flake cultures are again unlike the familiar Mousterian. Instead, in Africa we have pockets of localized flake cultures developing in the wake of the hand-axes, which persisted here long into the period (some fifty thousand years ago at Kalambo Falls in Tanzania) when hand-axes dwindled in importance in the Near East and Europe. These African hand-axe cultures were replaced by the Sangoan and Fauresmith about thirty or forty thousand years ago, marking a strange parallel with the situation in central and eastern Europe.

In India, which is recognized as the division between the so-called hand-axe traditions of the west and the chopper traditions of the east (one writer calls it the "Movius line" after its original describer), both the successors of the chopper tools called the Soan, and the Mousterian occur. The several types of Mousterian have not been discovered yet in this area, nor have complete industries been recognized. One of the problems is that we do not have clearly stratified finds, neither open sites nor cave sites here giving us the required controls. East of India, the industries seem to be either a continuation of the chopper variety of simple tools, or rudimentarily developed beyond it, though still very much related.

· THE UPPER PALEOLITHIC

The Upper Paleolithic appears as a tangible entity first in the Near East about 37,000 years ago, so far as we can presently pinpoint it. Rather strong arguments have been advanced for the original transition of the Middle Paleolithic to the Upper Paleolithic in France, but so far the edge on priority appears to rest in the Near East, both on skeletal and cultural evidence. If we believe the evidence of the radiocarbon-dated sites, the Upper Paleolithic spread thence westward, where it reached an efflorescence in southwestern and western Europe, richer by far in terms of preserved traces than anywhere else in the world. The spread of this new horizon is typified by the "blade culture" industries, so called because the stone implements were not made exclusively on simpler flakes, but on elongated flakes or blades struck by a special material-saving coring technique. The carriers of these blade-tool industries were all *Homo sapiens sapiens.*

The most economical view of the replacement and complete submergence of the Middle Paleolithic cultures in western Europe and their Neandertal bearers is that the Upper Paleolithic peoples overwhelmed and usurped their territory. If a catastrophic disease wiped out the Neandertals, it must have been brought in with the conquerors, because there is no indication of a prolonged interruption in the occupation of the same sites by the Neandertals and their immediate, more modern successors. Just as effective as a new epidemic disease would have been the relatively high technological advantage possessed by the modern men over the culturally poorer Neandertals, and it could certainly have been a factor in their displacement.

The new techniques of flint-knapping gave the Upper Paleolithic successors the capability to extract roughly thirty times as much cutting edge from the same kilogram of flint as the Neandertal predecessor was able to get. Moreover, Upper Paleolithic man had a knowledge of advanced wood-working, and probably of basketry, which the Neandertals seemingly did not possess. This is evidenced by the kind of stone scrapers and varieties of special burins which the new modern men had, plus the bone awls which could have served as perforators of hides or for the manipulation of grasses and twigs in the manufacture of baskets. These latter would have been extremely useful in providing storage for collected natural foods, such as nuts, as a supplement to hunted game. In effect, modern man had this great advantage over the Neandertals: he did not have to hunt tirelessly day in and out—he was able at last to relax and devote time released from the hunt to other pursuits. This was manifest in art, which seems to be absent from the home of the Upper Paleolithic in the Near East but which flourished in southwestern and western Europe.

Beside the newer technical craft of flint-knapping, which had its foreshadowing as far back as the Lower Paleolithic in the form of an occasional burin and some prismatic cores and was seen throughout the Middle Paleolithic in similar occasional manifestations, we find a method of indirect percussion with a rod and hammer, and later the use of the pressure technique of finely finishing the work with deliberate pressing-off of flakes. Crutch-like tools, special anvils, instruments of horn, and other devices were used to produce the beautifully contrived blades of the Solutrean, for instance. Rotary motion in the form of drilling operations was introduced, reminding us that lathes and drill presses, among the major tools of the modern age, had their origins far back in antiquity.

The culture of the Neandertals is certainly not to be compared with the Upper Paleolithic cultures, as is evident from a mere scanning of the chipped stone tools laid side by side in two collections. Concerning man himself, there are skeletal differences between the Middle and Upper Paleolithic populations, most obviously in the skull, even though the cranial capacities are about the same. It has been suggested that the cultural superiority of the Upper Paleolithic *Homo sapiens sapiens* peoples over Neandertals was due to the possession of a more highly articulate language, or more precise language usage. In other words, the moderns were able to transmit instructions about things that mattered, as in the preparation of highly involved kits which included tools to make tools, and to communicate ideas about religion, art, and nontangible things, which the Neandertals never possessed, and all the lore of nature, which was so important to men's livelihood.

One of the most important things in their existence, the predictability of the seasons, seems to have been known to these new moderns. Evidence that the Upper Paleolithic men inscribed a lunar count on batons of bone and on stone has been found from the shores of the Atlantic to eastern Europe. (Probably because perishable materials were used, similar evidence is lacking for the period in the Near East, not appearing until about twelve thousand years ago at Shanidar Cave.) In Western Europe not only were lunar counts kept, but seasonal correlations were made with the occurrence of such natural events as the return of the salmon on their upstream journeys, the mating of the deer, the leafing of trees, and the blooming of certain flowers. These mnemonic devices would have given Upper Paleolithic man a certain *control* over nature. One can imagine that with the powerful array of knowledge, speech, technology, and predictive information about nature, this modern man was able to adapt himself to territories which were forbidden to the Neandertals; and this he did.

In southwestern France in Upper Paleolithic times we have the appearance of two cultures, the Aurignacian and the Perigordian, which run almost side by side in the same region. With the exception of the manifestations of art and the highly developed horn and bone work of the Aurignacians, the chipped stone assemblages in the Near East provide a parallel to these western European ones, even to the specialized treatments of the burin. This could not be mere coincidence because of the highly involved preparations involved. (The same kinds of analogies seem to be lacking in northern Europe; at least, all the parallels to western Europe have not been found there.) There appears to be a general resemblance between the Perigordian and the backed-blade culture horizons in the Levant, but the distinctions are not yet finely drawn because studies in the Near East have not advanced far enough. It can be said, however, that the Aurignacian is quite widespread there, through Turkey and the Zagros Mountains as far as Afghanistan.

India seems to have its own special blade-and-burin culture, which may have been a kind of peripheral adjustment of the Aurignacian tradition.

In southwestern Europe we have the replacement of the Aurignacian and Perigordian about nineteen thousand years ago, during the height of the Würm III period, by the Solutrean tradition. The Solutreans were expert in stampeding whole herds of horses and cattle, which they drove over cliffs and slaughtered in great numbers, reminding one of the bison drives of the American Indians. The Solutreans manufactured very beautifully made bifacial blades, earlier using the percussion method, and then evolved to shouldered points, using controlled pressure. They occupied the same caves that Aurignacians, Perigordians, and the Neandertals before them had lived in. Through radiocarbon dating, it has been learned that the Solutrean culture lasted two thousand years or more, about sixteen thousand years ago.

The next cultural tradition, the Magdalenian (named after another type-site in the Dordogne area, La Madeleine), also came into existence and flourished during the height and the waning of the Würm III glacial. The Magdalenians were an extremely artistic people, as evidenced by their home art (portable art works) and their cave art; they were also very adept technically. Living in an environment seemingly as cold as that experienced by the Eskimos today, like the Eskimos they adapted themselves by means of a very advanced technological tool kit. They disappeared as a cultural tradition about twelve thousand years ago. Neither the Solutrean nor the Magdalenian cultures was ever manifest in the Near East, undoubtedly because they were largely oriented to Arctic or sub-Arctic climates, conditions that did not quite hold in the Near East during the times.

Beyond western Europe proper there seems to have been a continuation of the blade-and-burin cultures of the Perigordian and Aurignacian type, practically to the close of the Würm III glacial. In western Russia and the valley systems of Czechoslovakia plains-adapted dwellers had a backed-blade culture emphasizing bone work to a high degree. These people hunted the giant herbivores, the greatest meat providers of them all, the elephant-like mammoths, which they pursued to the brink of the Asian continent, the

Pacific Ocean. They carved figures and idols in the ivory of the animals they killed, and made figurines of stone and sometimes of clay. Like their cousins in western Europe, they possessed knowledge of the lunar count and of the cycles of nature, which gave them the edge over their quarry. The famous sites of Willendorf in Austria, Dolní-Vestonice in Czechoslovakia, and Kostienki in the Ukraine, all dating from about twenty thousand years ago, contain great communal houses near rivers.

As the climate ameliorated, the glaciers receded in the Alps, and the continental glacier covering Scandinavia diminished, the flora and fauna followed by the hunters encroached northward. In northern Germany and Poland there arose the tradition of the deer-slayers, called the Hamburgian people in Germany and the Swiderians in Poland. They were the precursors to the Mesolithic populations in northern Europe. These people and their predecessors in France, the Magdalenians, were also communal, much like the mammoth-hunters of central and eastern Europe, living in long houses with two or three hearths and undoubtedly having a tight-knit social organization which made certain kinds of family and societal adjustments necessary.

In the Near East, toward the end of the last glacial, there also appear cultural changes, but not with the same kind of severe wrench as in northern Europe. The time about twelve thousand years ago is marked by the Kebaran, a terminal Paleolithic or Mesolithic culture which introduced smaller and neater flint blades detached from small polyhedral flint cores or nuclei. These flints were fashioned into what are called backed bladelets, inserted into wooden hafts and forming composite implements. Again, in terms of the economical use of a kilo of flint, it has been estimated that the Mesolithic peoples were able to produce about thirty to forty feet of cutting edge, truly a long way from the six inches or so achieved from the same weight by the Acheulian hand-axe maker. Admittedly, the purposes of the tools were not the same, but it is to be supposed that the Mesolithic people could easily have contrived a hand-axe if they wished, as their successors again did in the Neolithic age.

North Africa appears to have gone its own way during the height of the last glaciation and down to the end of the period, which was locally felt as a moist climate. None of the splendid cultural traditions such as the Solutrean and Magdalenian were experienced. Indeed, viewed subjectively, the existence of these North African peoples in late prehistoric times must have been rather meager: they fed almost exclusively on snails. The Oranian culture seems to have something in it in common with the twelve-thousand-year-old Kebaran of the Levant. Dating before the Oranian in North Africa is the so-called Dabban tradition, localized in the north Libyan area. To the south of the Sahara are found a number of cultural traditions, evidently descendent from the Fauresmith and Sangoan, which date to about thirty thousand years ago. There are intensive ecological adaptations evidenced in the forest belt of the Congo on the one hand and in the savannah and highlands on the other, but they have none of the singularity and rich diversity of their European contemporaries.

Eastward toward India there was the same shift toward smaller and neater stone implements, manufactured from small prepared nuclear or pyramidal cores. Farther east, in southeast Asia and eastern Asia, the tradition was content to continue to manufacture the same kind of flake tools as before, although of smaller size. Australia was entered, presumably by boat, about thirty thousand years ago, by a people who laid the foundation for the occupation of that part of the southern hemisphere. Dated sites (Lake Mungo) ranging from 25,000 to 30,000 years old have yielded relatively crude scrapers and some human bones.

Contrasting with the other larger islands to the south, including Indonesia and the Philippines where abundant evidences of Paleolithic culture have been discovered, very little is known at present concerning the Paleolithic of Japan. The Nyu industry appears to be related typologically to the Anyathian of Burma, the Patjitanian of Java, and the Choukoutienian of China. There are choppers and hand-axe implements in the assemblage. Japan's Paleolithic culture seems to be extremely retarded, and it is thought that this is attributable to isolation. Later, stone blade-points reminiscent of the European Solutrean appear, in marked contrast to the earlier and cruder assemblages. This stage was followed by a microlithic technique having counterparts in Alaska.

Across Bering Strait, where evidence indicates there was a land bridge during and at the end of the last glaciation, came a people at the latest by fourteen thousand years ago—possibly twenty thousand years ago and possibly much earlier—carrying with them a hunting tradition. Massive choppers and cleavers made by the percussion technique and resembling Siberian counterparts have been found in the Arctic of North America. Burins and long, well-made bifacial points shaped by the pressure technique similarly occur in ancient contexts. The newcomers appear to have entered the New World by way of the valley of the Mackenzie River, taking advantage of an ice-free corridor which led them to the heart of the North American continental plains area and the big game that flourished in a world empty of man until that time.

· BIBLIOGRAPHIC ESSAY

Although the books on prehistory since George Grant MacCurdy's basic work, *Human Origins, A Manual of Prehistory,* published by D. Appleton in 1924, are fairly numerous, one can still dip into these two volumes for useful basic information and descriptions. Among the later general works on prehistory is M. C. Burkitt's *The Old Stone Age,* published by Cambridge University Press in 1949; this revision of an earlier work (1921) is a forerunner of the "compact study of palaeolithic times," the type of publication that has appeared to replace the older, heavier texts on prehistory.

F. E. Zeuner's *Dating the Past, An Introduction to Geochronology,* published by Methuen in 1959, was, and still is, an invaluable aid to understanding the background of prehistory. Before the popularization of ecology and environmental studies, J. G. D. Clark's book, *Excavations at Star Carr,* published by Cambridge University Press in 1954, served nearly a generation of students with tremendous impact. Kenneth Oakley's *Frameworks for Dating Fossil Man,* published by Weidenfeld and Nicolson in 1964, is a useful little volume which has found a niche in its field. A giant without peer, revised and brought up to date, is Richard Foster Flint's *Glacial and Quaternary Geology,* published by Wiley in 1971. This study is basic to an understanding of Stone Age prehistory concerning the habitat of early man. Among the "compact study" type of works on prehistory, François Bordes' *The Old Stone Age,* published by McGraw-Hill in 1968, is perhaps too concisely written for the beginning student, and since text references are not given, the student who wishes to do further research on a line of investigation finds he must pick and choose from the works cited in the bibliography.

In Jacques Bordaz's *Tools of the Old and New Stone Age,* published by The Natural History Press in 1970, the student will find a lengthy bibliography with a useful key. Finally, although it duplicates Bordaz's work in many regards, the author still likes Kenneth Oakley's *Man the Toolmaker,* a Phoenix Book published by the University of Chicago Press in 1957.

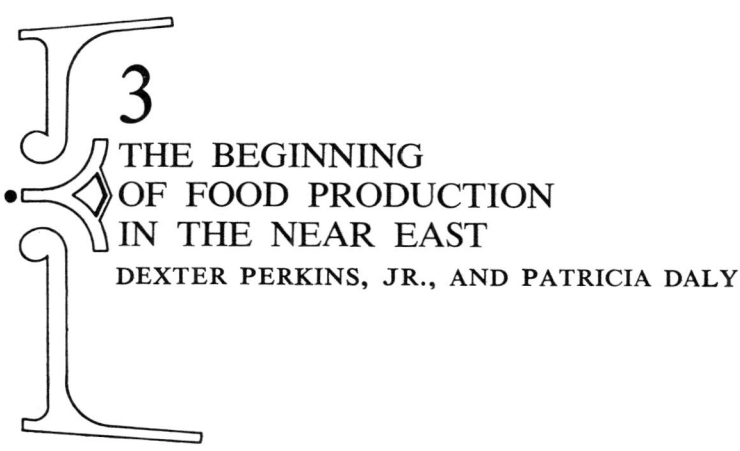

3
THE BEGINNING OF FOOD PRODUCTION IN THE NEAR EAST
DEXTER PERKINS, JR., AND PATRICIA DALY

Near East and *Middle East* are terms variously used to include the countries of southwest Asia, Egypt, and the Balkans. For our purposes, however, we will define the Near East as the area comprising the modern states of Turkey, Iran, Iraq, Syria, Lebanon, Jordan, and Israel. The territory along the eastern coast of the Mediterranean Sea is often called the Levant, and the part of the area which now includes Israel and the western portion of Jordan is frequently referred to as Palestine. These are convenient geographical terms, and we will use them.

The Near East can be roughly divided into three major vegetational zones:

1) The Mediterranean zone, extending in a narrow band along the eastern shore of the Mediterranean Sea and the southern and western coasts of Turkey. The vegetation consists largely of evergreen trees, plants, and shrubs, and in contrast to the third zone, the various plant species are not adapted to resist cold temperatures.

2) The desert and desert steppe zone, comprised of the deserts of Syria, Jordan, and Iraq and the steppe on their periphery, including Mesopotamia, the area around the lower reaches of the Tigris-Euphrates river system. Rainfall is low and the plant cover is sparse.

3) A highland zone, partly between and partly surrounding these two zones, including the Lebanon Mountains of the Levant, the mountains of eastern Turkey, and the Zagros mountain chain,

which extends the length of the western border of Iran and into the northern portion of Iraq. In most of these areas 8000-foot heights are common, with a number of peaks rising well over 2000 feet higher. To the west of this arc of mountains is the Anatolian plateau, with an average altitude of 4500 feet. In much of this zone the characteristic vegetation is a temperate forest, consisting, of oak, fir, pistachio, and juniper, which apparently spread throughout the highland areas of the Near East at the close of the Pleistocene. Also present are many edible fruits, nuts, and wild cereals, as well as large numbers of sheep, goats, cattle, and pigs. In view of its plant and animal occupants, it seems likely that it was in this zone that food production first began.

Within these broad zones, there is a great deal of local variation, with many ecotypes occurring within relatively small areas. This is in part due to rainfall patterns, and in part to vertical elevation. Rainfall is not sufficient to support large perennials in most areas, so much of the plant cover consists of quick-growing annuals, which can complete their growth cycle before the winter moisture is gone. The harvest period is extremely short, although early collectors could have extended it in a sense by following the ripening of successive stands at higher and higher elevations, as do many of the animals. Thus there would be a tendency for both animals and people to move from lowland to highland in the spring and summer, and return to the lowlands for the winter. Although there were areas (such as around Suberde and Mureybat) where such migration was not necessary, the seasonality of many resources over much of the Near East must have had its effect on the movements of animals and people, especially upon the utilization of what Kent Flannery calls a "broad spectrum" of food sources, and upon the degree and kind of contact between groups, which may have come together seasonally to exploit a particular ripening.

· THE NEOLITHIC IN THE NEAR EAST

The Neolithic period was originally defined in terms of the artifacts recovered—pottery, and polished rather than chipped stone tools —at the same time that it implied an economic base of agriculture. This definition, based on northern European cultural remains,

The Beginning of Food Production 73

could never have been very useful for the Near East, where the appearance of domestic plants and animals preceded the earliest pottery and polished stone and, more importantly, where the first food-producing cultures evolved. Although a similar adaptation occurred at a later date in the New World, it is the Near Eastern innovation which is in the direct line of development of Western civilization. While perhaps too much emphasis has been placed on the "Fertile Crescent" and the "Cradle of Civilization," the fact remains that the Near East *is* where it all began, and we are all its inheritors.

We propose to start our discussion with a definition of the Near Eastern Neolithic based on the economic status of communities known from the archaeological record. Those which show evidence for food production are considered Neolithic in functional terms. If Man the Toolmaker is by definition one who makes tools to a set and regular pattern, one who has learned to manipulate inanimate material, perhaps it would be useful to think of Neolithic Man as Man the Food Producer, one who to some degree controls animate nature, i.e., plants and animals.

Archaeological evidence shows that domestic animals were present in the Near East, specifically at Zawi Chemi Shanidar in Iraq, about eleven thousand years ago. Since it is unlikely that we have discovered here the *one* site which is the earliest case of animal husbandry, we must assume that the keeping of animals may have begun earlier, and perhaps in some other area. It is possible that domestication and effective food production began in the Near East as much as twelve thousand years ago, but we have no direct evidence. Although hunting and gathering continued to be of varying importance until quite recent times, by about 9000 B.C. some people had begun to replace the old way of life with at least a partial reliance on domestic food sources. We begin to find settled villages as well as the kill-sites and seasonal camps of hunters. Local population densities increased, and we find evidence for a fairly complex pattern of socio-economic relationships among various communities. By 7500 B.C. there was an extensive, though probably informal, trade in obsidian, and to a lesser extent in copper, extending from central Turkey to southern Jordan, and from eastern Turkey to the Zagros Mountains. By 6000 B.C. there were at least two settlements that have been called cities, although by many definitions of urbanism they might not strictly qualify. The face of the land had been changed by man and his artifactual plants and animals to such a degree that today we find it hard to believe that hunting and gathering could ever have been a feasible way of life in the area. Man the Hunter had become Man the Pastoralist, the Farmer, the Villager, and the Townsman.

These changes took place in such a relatively short time and were of such fundamental importance that the question immediately arises: Why did they occur? Why did a life-style that had been successful for tens of thousands of years give way to one so different? Modern hunting peoples, though living for the most part in marginal areas, are frequently better nourished and always more leisured than their agrarian neighbors. Barring massive interference from other cultures or from the environment, hunters seem to remain in comfortable equilibrium with their environment. Agrarian peoples not only must work a good deal harder for their sustenance but are also much more precariously balanced in relation to their environment, since they have substantially altered the natural ecology of their surroundings. Because we are no longer obliged to regard any step "up" the scale of cultural evolution as the natural order of inevitable Progress, it is necessary for us to at least speculate about possible causes for the change, which is in many ways so extraordinary. There are no sure answers at the moment, and it is unlikely that there will ever be anything better than varying degrees of probability.

Climatic change at the end of the glacial period has long been invoked as the crucial factor in causing the change from hunting and gathering to food production. The retreat of the glaciers was assumed to have shifted the rain belts, causing increasing desiccation all over the Near East, and crowding men, plants, and animals into a few dwindling oases, where close association led to domestication. This theory has numerous flaws. First and most basic is that it is becoming more and more doubtful that any of the agreed-upon climatic crises, such as the retreat of the last glaciers (c. 11,000 B.C.) or the latest altithermal (c. 4000 B.C.), bear a useful relationship to the evidence for early food production in the area. The modern aridity of the Near East is almost certainly more the result of the presence of domestic animals and the use of the natural plant cover for fuel than of any major climatic shift. Domestic goats in particular have probably caused more loss of ground cover and consequent erosion than any climatic factor acting on the area in the last ten thousand years.

The second flaw is the idea that upland animals, such as sheep and goats, would descend to riverine bottomlands to become trapped as unwilling co-inhabitants with hunters, or that upland plants, such as wild wheat, would do the same. This notion is totally at odds with everything that is known about these plant and animal species, and about human behavior as well. Numerous attempts to raise wild sheep and goats in zoos have shown that these animals will simply not survive without the most sophisticated care in conditions of terrain, air pressure, and humidity to which they are not accustomed; nor would they seek them out, being much more likely to remain in *higher* altitudes with their higher rainfall. The same is true of the wild cereals: only with great care (and a careful selection of better-adapted mutants) can they be made to survive at all outside their natural habitats, which in no case are riverine oases. In a way, human behavior furnishes an even stronger argument against the idea. In the unlikely event that men and animals became close neighbors in a closed environment, the most probable result would be that the men would hunt the animals to extinction rather than domesticate them.

Another theory has been that the end of the glacial period caused either the extinction or the retreat of the bigger game animals from the area, necessitating a switch to smaller and more amenable animals. It is difficult to find much evidence for this in the faunal record. An essentially modern fauna is present in the food remains as early as the Middle Paleolithic in the Near East, as shown by Shanidar Cave and Mount Carmel. With the exception of the woolly rhinoceros, all the animals hunted by man persisted until historical times. The principal food animals remain the same for fifty thousand years: sheep, goats, cattle, pigs, red deer, roe deer, fallow deer, gazelle, and the various equids. Elephants, lions, leopards, and bears are equally durable in the record, although obviously never an important dietary source. Sheep and goats were important prey for millennia before they were brought under cultural control, but there is nothing in the record to relate their change in status to any major climatic event. Neither paleontological nor palynological data show any significant climatic change for many thousands of years on either side of the period which apparently saw the first attempts at food production.

If we reject climate, in any of its possible effects, as a fundamental cause of the switch to food production, we are left to find another explanation. It is our opinion that population increase is a most likely cause for a marked change in economic strategies: overcrowding makes it imperative to find new resources, and to find new methods of exploiting existing resources. Of course, postulating population pressure as a cause only pushes the question back one level to: What caused population increase? Modern hunters seem to maintain themselves at or below the effective carrying capacity of their environments, as do most predators. Their natural increase is limited by various biological factors, such as the lessened fertility of the well-nourished and the starvation of the undernourished, and by cultural factors, such as senilicide or infanticide. Although ethnographic parallels are always risky, there is evidence that modern hunting people are better nourished with less effort than their farming neighbors, and there is also reason to believe that with more game and fewer people, Upper Paleolithic hunters would have been even better off. Given the almost automatic biological controls on population and an abundance of animal and plant foods, what factor could have led to the population increase which would have necessitated altered economic strategies?

In the ecosystem, human hunters are predators. Predators are necessarily much rarer than their prey, and man, as a slow breeder, was surely among the rarest of predators. Even with the advantage afforded by tools and weapons, it was surely a long time before he offered any serious competition to other predators or pressed to any great degree upon the carrying capacity of the environment. But there are two important differences between human and animal predators. First, man's role as a predator differs in its zoo-geographic effect from that of carnivores. Wolves preying on herds of wild sheep or deer commonly take the newborn, the very old, or the diseased, thus in effect culling the herd of its weakest members.

The result is that the herd's breeding capacity is in no way diminished, and the predation may even be beneficial. Human hunters act in a quite different and more destructive way, since all evidence seems to show that they take a high percentage of healthy adults and seldom the kinds of animals taken by carnivores. This behavior has an immediately injurious effect on flocks of herbivores and, if carried out over a long period, would undoubtedly deplete the supply of hunted animals. This in turn would have its effect on man's animal competition: when the game diminished, the carnivores would be hard pressed to find food, while omnivorous man could turn to other food sources—wild cereals, fruits, seeds, and nuts. Simply by his differing role as a predator, man could not only reduce his primary economic competition; he could also learn, perhaps, to move into ecological niches which might not support specialized hunters but *would* support people who had begun to utilize a broader spectrum of resources. As with any animal which expands the economic possibilities of its role in the ecosystem, human population increase then is not only possible but inevitable. The hunters remain, as in fact they do virtually until our time, but other adaptations become increasingly important. And these adaptations are not, for the time being, food producing.

· ANIMAL DOMESTICATION

Before we discuss the beginnings of animal domestication, we must define what we mean by a "domestic" animal (see Figure 3.1). The appearance and behavior of modern domestic animals are quite different from those of their wild ancestors. Changes have taken place in their skeletons as well, and are known as far back as 6500 B.C. Thus we may define a domestic species osteologically as one that is so different in its hard anatomy from its wild ancestor that a zoologist would consider it a new species. However, in the earliest stages of domestication such changes may not have taken place or may have been so slight as to be undetectable (although recent work suggests that there were changes in the micro-structure of some bones). For the archaeologist, then,

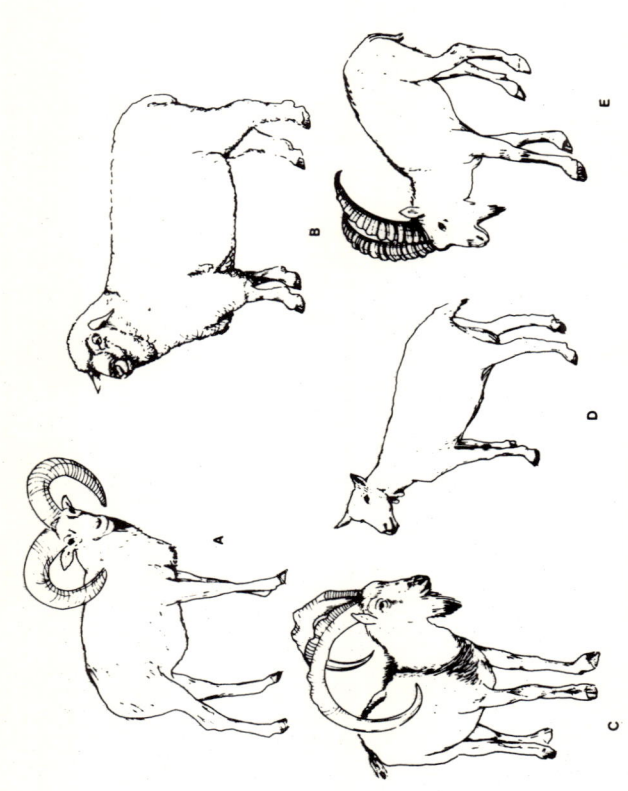

FIGURE 3.1 *(A)* Wild urial sheep.   *(B)* Domesticated wool sheep. *(C)* Wild bezoar goat.   *(D)* Domesticated goat.   *(E)* Wild Nubian ibex.   *(F)* Wild pig.   *(G)* Domesticated pig.   *(H)* Wild aurochs bull.   *(I)* Domesticated cow.

the zoological differentiation between wild and domestic forms may not be useful, and we must define a domestic animal in another way.

A domestic animal, by our criteria, is one that breeds in captivity and is of significant economic importance. Archaeological evidence for cultural control may be artifactual (harnesses for draft animals, for example, or plastic and graphic art showing animals in domestic situations) or from analysis of the bones themselves showing the age-grade composition of the population to be different from that of a wild group. As a hunter/predator, man apparently did not make any purposeful selection of particular age groups in the animals he hunted. As mentioned earlier, hunters, unlike animal predators, take all age groups including a high percentage of adults. But the evidence indicates that the earliest stock-raisers in the Near East selected more immature animals than adults to be killed, thus maintaining an adult breeding population.

It is commonly assumed that the first domesticated animal was the dog. If so, this is not reflected in the archaeological record from the Near East. In fact, sheep and possibly goats were domesticated earlier. There is no indication that the dog was ever important in the Neolithic economy, either as a food animal or as a shepherd dog. Far more important was the domestication of sheep, goats, cattle, and pigs—in short, the development of diversified stock-raising, which, with the cultivation of a variety of domesticated grains, was the prelude to the growth of urbanism (see Map 3.1).

Before this stage was reached, however, there was a long period during which stock-raising was of a simpler kind, based on no more than one domestic animal. Unfortunately there are few data from this period, roughly spanning two thousand years from 9000 to 7000 B.C. Five sites have been excavated and dated: Zawi Chemi Shanidar (9000 B.C.) in northern Iraq, Çayönü (7000 B.C.) in southeastern Turkey, Ganj Dareh (7500 B.C.) and Ali Kosh (7000 B.C.) in western Iran, and Mureybat (8000 B.C.) in northern Syria. Domestic animals have been found at every site except Mureybat: sheep at Zawi Chemi Shanidar and Çayönü and goats at Ganj Dareh and Ali Kosh. Apparently sheep were first domesticated at the northwestern end of the Zagros Mountains;

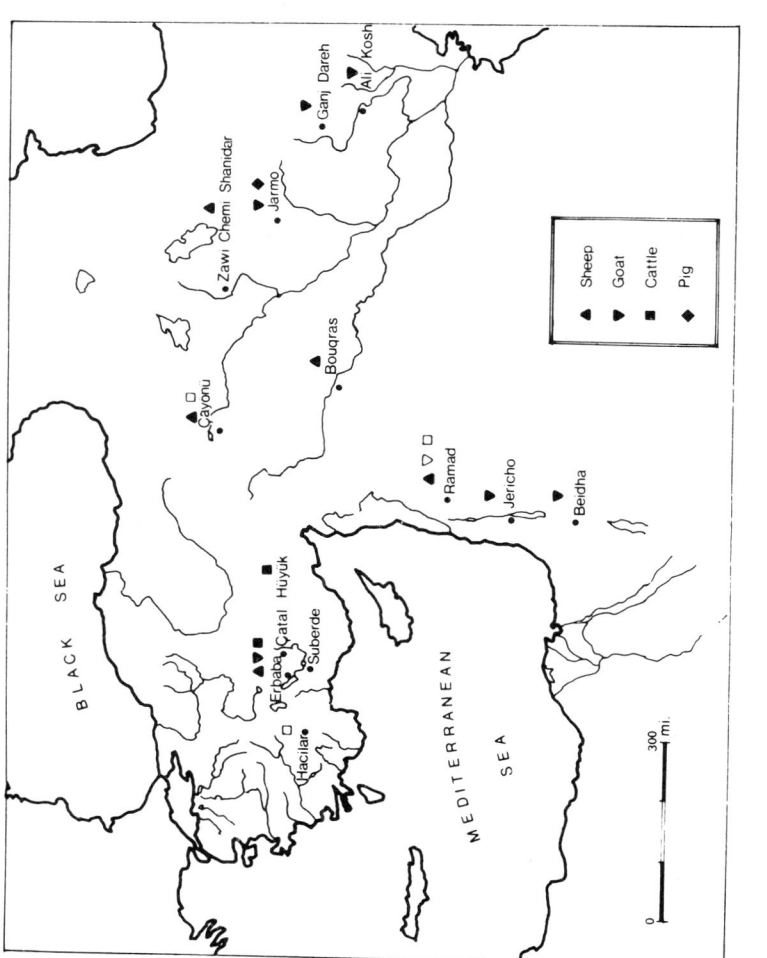

MAP 3.1 Distribution of domestic animals, 9000 to 6000 B.C. Hollow symbols indicate that domestication is reported but not confirmed.

goats were first domesticated at the southeastern end of that mountain chain.

The seventh millennium saw the domestication of cattle and pigs and the spread of animal husbandry throughout the Near East. Domestic cattle, perhaps introduced from Europe, are found at Çatal Hüyük in Anatolia in 6400 B.C. No other domesticates are present, paralleling the situation at the sites where the earliest domestic sheep and goats appear.

The domestication of the pig was a special case. Domestic pigs are not recorded until the end of the seventh millennium, and unlike the other domesticates, at the time of their first appearance they are never the sole domesticate. At no time were pigs an important economic factor in the Near East, perhaps because, unlike the other domesticates, pigs do not normally eat rough fodder but actually compete with man for food.

By 6000 B.C. there are indications that animal husbandry had become more diversified and had spread throughout the Near East, in conjunction with, and perhaps partially the result of, the development of a variety of domesticated grains. However, it is difficult to discern any logical pattern in the development of animal husbandry. Certainly the domestication of one animal did not lead immediately to the domestication of others in a particular area, although all the potential domesticates were widespread throughout the Near East. The archaeological record suggests that, with the exception of the pig, each animal was domesticated in a different region: cattle on the Anatolian plateau, sheep in the uplands of the Turkey/Iraq border, and goats in the Zagros Mountains in Iran. Why this should be so remains a mystery. A possible explanation is that a single domesticate was sufficient if the animal was kept solely for meat, but each of the three primary domesticates has its own valuable secondary products—wool from sheep, milk from goats, and milk and hides from cattle. As these products became known throughout the Near East, their desirability may have been the incentive for acquiring a variety of domestic animals.

One may ask: Other than the dog, why were the four animals, and only these four animals, successfully domesticated? Some authors have suggested that they were peculiarly "pre-adapted" for domestication. However, the Egyptians of the Old Kingdom kept a variety of domestic animals other than the four major domesticates, all of them equally "pre-adapted." None was ever important economically, and all were eventually given up. Therein lies the key. Quite simply, domestic sheep, goats, cattle, and pigs were economically more productive than the others.

· PLANT DOMESTICATION

It has been established that the development of agriculture in the Near East was based on the cultivation of three domesticated grains: einkorn wheat (*Triticum monococcum*), emmer wheat (*Triticum dicoccum*), and two-row barley (*Hordeum vulgare* ssp. *distichum*). Archaeologists have assumed that the domestication of these cereals (see Map 3.2) occurred roughly contemporaneously with the domestication of the important food animals, but this does not appear to be the case. The earliest cultivated grains occur no earlier than c. 7000 B.C., two thousand years after the appearance of the earliest domestic animal. Furthermore, they seem to have made a surprisingly small contribution to the diet until a thousand years later.

Unlike the earliest domestic animals, the earliest domestic grains, particularly domestic wheats, are readily distinguished from their wild ancestors, so we are not faced with the problem of definition on other than morphological grounds (see Figure 3.2). And domesticated cereals are different from their wild ancestors in another important respect. The spike (the seed-bearing portion of the plant) is brittle in the wild forms, facilitating the scattering of the seed. In domestic grains the spike is much less fragile, and the seeds are not dispersed when the grain is reaped. The selective reaping of the tough-spiked grain would not favor its increase in the next crop, since the brittle-spiked grain would be left in the field. What is required is the deliberate sowing of the seeds of the tough-spiked grain. Domesticated grains, therefore, are entirely dependent on man for their survival.

Einkorn Wheat
Recently it has been established that wild einkorn (*Triticum boeoticum*) is the sole ancestor of domestic einkorn (*T. monococcum*). The distribution of the wild plant is extensive, ranging from the

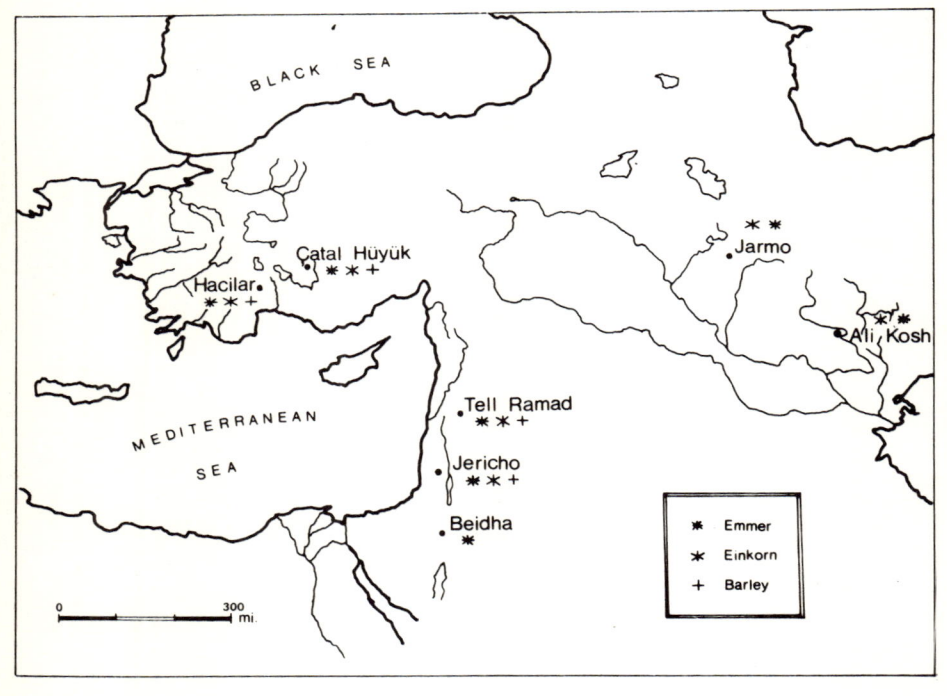

MAP 3.2   Distribution of domestic grains, 9000 to 6000 B.C.

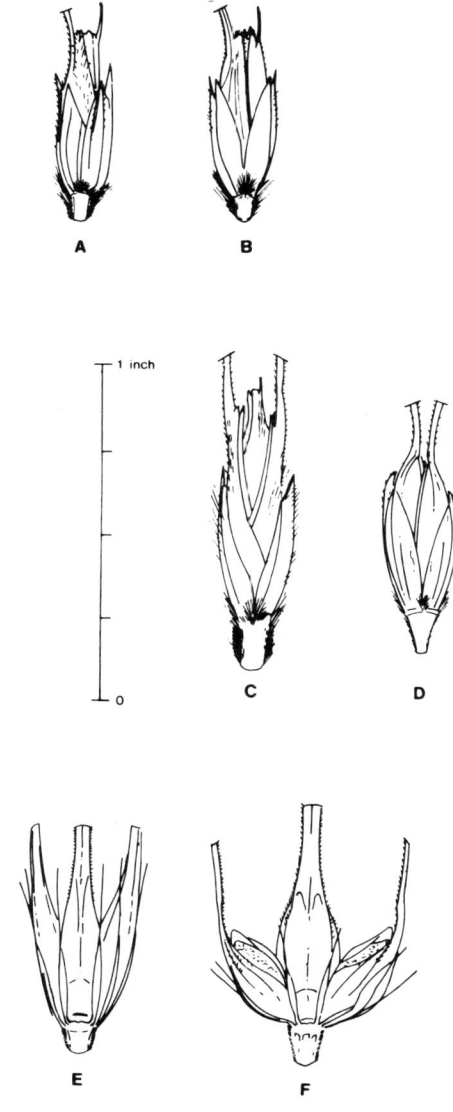

FIGURE 3.2 *(A)* Wild, and *(B)* domesticated einkorn wheat. *(C)* Wild, and *(D)* domesticated emmer wheat. *(E)* Wild, and *(F)* domesticated barley.

Peloponnesus in Greece to Afghanistan. Its distributional center —that is, the areas in which it occurs in massive stands—lies in the mountains of southeastern Turkey and the Zagros Mountains of Iraq and Iran. The first finds of domestic einkorn are in the eastern part of this area, at Ali Kosh (7000 B.C.) and Jarmo (6750 B.C.). Wild and domestic einkorn are very similar genetically and are distinguished by their method of seed dispersal, which is reflected in the structure of the spike.

Emmer Wheat
Domestic emmer (*Triticum dicoccum*) is derived from wild emmer (*T. dicoccoides*). Wild and domestic emmer are morphologically similar, and hybrids between them are fully interfertile. Like domestic einkorn wheat, domestic emmer is distinguished from its wild progenitor by the presence of a sturdier spike. The distributional center of wild emmer has been thought to be much smaller than that of wild einkorn, covering a small area in south Syria and Palestine, where it still occurs in dense stands. However, new finds suggest that the distribution of wild emmer paralleled that of wild einkorn. The earliest domesticated emmer is found at sites outside the presumed distributional center: at Ali Kosh (7000 B.C.) and Jarmo (6750 B.C.) in the Zagros Mountains and at Beidha (6800 B.C.) in southern Jordan.

Barley
Unlike the two cultivated wheats, domesticated barley occurs in a variety of forms. All are descended from a single wild barley species (*Hordeum spontaneum*). Like einkorn wheat, it is found from Anatolia to Afghanistan. Its distributional center is roughly the same as einkorn, except that it extends to the uplands of the Levant as far south as southern Jordan. The earliest finds of domestic barley are at the extreme ends of the distributional center: at Ali Kosh (7000 B.C.) and Beidha (6800 B.C.).

Throughout their distributional centers all three of the wild ancestors of the domestic grains occur in natural stands almost as dense as in cultivated wheat fields. A botanist has demonstrated that experienced plant collectors, harvesting during the three-week period when wild wheat ripens, could gather more grain than a family could possibly consume in a year. This being so, what would be the stimulus to develop domesticated grains? It has been suggested that cultivation began as an attempt to produce artificially, around the margins of the distributional center, stands of cereals as dense as those in the primary habitat. We believe, however, that there is an alternative. It is quite possible that the domestication occurred within the primary cereal centers. Domestic animals apparently were present before the earliest domestic plants, and today, under heavy grazing pressure, wild cereals tend to die out. Their place is taken by less palatable herbs, and only when the grazing pressure is relaxed do the wild grasses re-establish their dominance. The development of domestic grains could have been forced upon the owners of the early domestic animals.

The beginnings of agriculture differ from the beginnings of stock-raising in two important respects: 1) Multiple domestication occurs very early, as, for example, at Ali Kosh. Mixed field cultivation apparently resulted in the simultaneous domestication of all three of the important grains, more or less inadvertently. 2) The domesticated plants, in the earliest stages of their development, were relatively unimportant in the economy.

· THE ARCHAEOLOGICAL RECORD

We feel that, in the period from c. 9000 to 6000 B.C., the available evidence indicates a sequence of adaptations along the following lines.

Some groups of hunters may have either reduced the local game supply or themselves over-bred in their "optimum" hunting area, forcing moves to less favored areas and increased dependence on a greater variety of plant and animal resources. This in turn apparently led to two forms of specialized sedentarism without actual food production: those groups that utilized abundant stands of wild cereals (such as the various Natufian sites), and those groups that seem to have found reliable sources of game, as at Suberde, described below. Whether the original basis of a settled village was game or wild grain, the next step seems to be the domestication of *one* animal for meat and its gradual establishment as an important dietary source. Zawi Chemi Shanidar represents this stage. However, the presence of an important domestic animal probably changes the local ecology to such a degree that dependence on wild grains is no longer practical, and cultivation of the wild cereals, either for human or for animal consumption, follows single animal domestication, as at Ali Kosh. Then further animals are domesticated, for products other than meat, and a pattern of food production not unlike the modern one in the Near East is essentially established.

In the short survey of sites which follows (also see Chart 3.1), we have chosen to describe sites representative of the various stages we have postulated. In view of the fact that by 7500 B.C. at the latest there was an extensive trade in obsidian and other useful imperishables throughout the Near East, it seems only reasonable to suppose that none of these sites was effectively autonomous or isolated, although the degree and kind of relationship between sites of differing economic patterns is not well understood at present.

The Natufian: Sedentary Collectors of Wild Grain
A series of sites in the Levant are designated Natufian, after the type-find in the Wadi en-Natuf in Israel. Because of the predominance of microliths in the stone industry (as well as the time of its appearance) the Natufian has sometimes been referred to as Mesolithic. The best-known sites are in the Mount Carmel area and the Jordan Valley; especially in the latter does there seem to have been particular cultural elaboration, as in burial practices. Dating of the sites involves problems, but some of them seem clearly to go back to the ninth millennium, 8000 B.C., and perhaps a thousand years earlier than that.

The Natufian is characterized generally by permanent villages, relatively large populations, numbers of mortars and grinding stones used apparently for grinding grains and seeds, and many toothed sickle-blades of flint, resembling those of later farming peoples and often showing a use-polish along the cutting edges. No domestic plants or animals have been identified at any of the sites, although the bones of many hunted animals are present and it has been further shown that wild emmer wheat formerly was **at home in the area, particularly in the Jordan Valley.**

	DATE	DOMESTIC ANIMALS PRESENT	DOMESTIC PLANTS PRESENT
NORTHERN ZAGROS			
Zawi Chemi Shanidar	c. 9000 B.C.	sheep	none
Çayönü	c. 7000 B.C.	sheep, ?cattle	---
SOUTHERN ZAGROS			
Ganj Dareh	c. 7500 B.C.	goat	---
Ali Kosh (Bus Mordeh phase)	c. 7000 B.C.	goat	Emmer, Barley
Ali Kosh (Ali Kosh phase)	c. 6750 B.C.	goat	Emmer, Barley
Jarmo (preceramic)	c. 6750 B.C.	goat	Einkorn, Emmer, Barley
Jarmo (ceramic)	c. 6300 B.C.	goat, pig	Einkorn, Emmer, Barley
SYRIA-PALESTINE			
Mureybat	c. 8000 B.C.	none	none
Beidha	c. 6800 B.C.	goat	Emmer
Bouqras	c. 6500 B.C.	sheep	---
Jericho	c. 6500 B.C.	goat	Einkorn, Emmer, Barley
Ramad	c. 6200 B.C.	sheep, ?goat, ?cattle	Einkorn, Emmer, Barley
ANATOLIA			
Aceramic Hacilar	c. 7000 B.C.	?cattle	Einkorn, Emmer, Barley
Suberde	c. 6600 B.C.	none	none
Çatal Hüyük	c. 6400 B.C.	cattle	Einkorn, Emmer, Barley
Erbaba	c. 6000 B.C.	sheep, goat, cattle	---

CHART 3.1 The earliest appearances of domesticated plants and animals in the Near East.

It has been said many times that agricultural surpluses make sedentism possible. The Natufian type of community suggests that good stands of wild wheat and/or other wild grains made it *necessary:* it has been demonstrated in stands of wild wheat that while the grain is ripe in an optimum area, a ton or more of clean grain can be harvested by very few people. The problem would then become one of what to do with it. Add to this the harvest of other wild cereals, legumes, and seasonal fruits, and the seasonal wandering and the following of migratory animals becomes not only unnecessary but impractical. Storage, preservation, and protection of wild crops would be the problem, but they do not constitute food production.

Suberde, the Hunters' Village
This site is located in the northeastern foothills of the western Taurus range in Turkey, on the edge of the Anatolian plateau. It was occupied for about six hundred years, beginning around 6600 B.C. Despite its relatively late date and the fact that it almost certainly had contacts with far more sophisticated sites such as Çatal Hüyük, Suberde is functionally a sedentary village of hunters, dependent entirely upon the taking of wild game. The site was occupied year-round, not seasonally, and there is evidence that the presence of the village had a marked effect on the local game populations.

The prehistoric levels at Suberde show poorly preserved remains of mud-brick walls, fragments of plastered floors, and burned remnants of wattle-and-daub, either from roofs or upper walls. There are grinding stones and large clay storage bins but no pottery. Polished stone celts are found in the later part of the deposit. A few lightly (and perhaps accidentally) baked figurines of animals and humans are present. The chipped stone material is more than 90 percent obsidian, from sources near Çatal Hüyük; it is remarkable for the small size of its tools and for the amount of use made of the waste flakes, implying that the obsidian was both scarce and expensive. Many flint blades show sickle sheen, the result of cutting cereal stems or reeds. A number of marine invertebrate shells suggests that Suberde had contacts with the Mediterranean coast.

All of the animals eaten at Suberde were wild, and the pattern of their skeletal remains suggests that they were killed at some distance from the site. The area around Suberde is classic sheep terrain, and throughout the occupation sheep constitute the major portion of the remains, both numerically and in terms of meat. However, the later levels show a decline in the proportion of sheep to the larger game, wild cattle and red deer. This suggests that human predation on the sheep either reduced the flocks or drove them away, necessitating a shift to the larger game. There is no evidence that the people of Suberde domesticated any animal but the dog at any time, and it is not inconceivable that the site was abandoned because the area would no longer support a hunting economy.

Zawi Chemi Shanidar: Earliest Evidence of Food Production
On superficial comparison, Zawi Chemi (near Shanidar Cave) in northern Iraq might seem to be an example of a type of exploitation similar to that of Suberde and the Natufians. It also, at first glance, resembles nearby sites in the western Zagros of similar age (c. 10,000–9000 B.C.). The stone tool industry has a large percentage of relatively small artifacts, including microliths, and there are a great many grinding stones, mullers, and querns, presumably for the processing of various seeds, grains, and nuts. There are indications of permanent year-round occupation and several building periods. House foundations consist of circles of stones which probably supported less substantial upper walls. There are no cultivated plants, and there is much evidence for the hunting of wild game.

However, Zawi Chemi Shanidar differs from other Near Eastern sites of this period in one very important respect: analysis of the animal bones reveals that the *sheep* among them were domesticated, and were an important part of the diet. Whatever the stratagem of overall control employed, the bones demonstrate that a high percentage of the sheep remains were of immature animals, suggesting a selective slaughtering not characteristic of hunters. Moreover, the bones also show a certain pattern of cellular change (from the bones of wild animals) which we are coming to associate with the domestic state.

Shanidar Cave and the open site of Zawi Chemi Shanidar constitute an archaeological continuum. The lower levels of these sites show that wild sheep were not common in the immediate surrounding area, wild goat and red deer being much more so, yet in the upper levels sheep having the attributes of domestication come rather rapidly to constitute (numerically) 80 percent of all food animal remains. It therefore seems to us unlikely that the *initial* control and domestication of sheep occurred in the immediate vicinity but rather in some other locality, perhaps not too distant and even earlier.

In any event, Zawi Chemi Shanidar is the earliest example known today, by at least a thousand years, of human control of food production in the Near East, and since the botanical evidence clearly establishes that there were no cultivated plants present, it strongly suggests that the domestication of animals preceded that of plants.

Tepe Ali Kosh: Increasing Dependence on Cultivated Grains
Tepe Ali Kosh is situated on the Deh Luran plain in southwestern Iran. In the earliest period of occupation (the Bus Mordeh phase, c. 7000–6750 B.C.) houses were made of slabs cut from a natural red clay deposit and used as unfired "bricks." Floors were of stamped mud or clay. The subsistence pattern was characterized by high dependence on the collecting of seeds from plants native to the Deh Luran plain. Emmer wheat and hulled two-row barley were cultivated but comprised only a third of the total weight of vegetal food. The Bus Mordeh people herded domestic goats, but the hunting of wild ungulates supplied the bulk of the meat supply.

In the second period of occupation (the Ali Kosh phase, c. 6750–6000 B.C.) the architecture was more elaborate. The walls were held together by mud mortar and frequently finished with a coat of smooth plaster. Most important, there was a great change in the economic base. Emmer wheat and hulled two-row barley now provided more than 90 percent of the total weight of plant food, although the seeds of native wild plants continued to be collected. Goats were still the only domestic animals present, and the hunting of large ungulates, such as the wild ox, actually increased. Trade, which had not been important during the Bus Mordeh phase, was now much more extensive. Obsidian from the Lake Van region in Turkey comprised a significant percentage of

The Beginning of Food Production 93

the chipped stone, and there is evidence of contacts with the Iranian plateau and the Persian Gulf. Perhaps these contacts led to the next stage in food production, when more than one animal was domesticated.

Erbaba: Multiple Domestication of Animals

This site, located near the shore of Lake Beyşehir in Turkey and dated to about 6000 B.C., is the earliest known example of the domestication of more than two animals, presumably for secondary products rather than meat. While the botanical specimens have not yet been reported upon, the presence of a complex of domestic plants in the region at this period, at the sites of Çatal Hüyük and Hacilar, suggests strongly that such a complex was also present at Erbaba. More unusual is the presence here of domestic sheep, goats, and cattle and the complete absence of hunted animals, such as red deer or pig. The dog, which was present six hundred years earlier at Suberde, was absent at Erbaba, suggesting that hunting dogs were of no use and that shepherd dogs had not yet been developed.

The houses were constructed of cobbles which were not found in the immediate vicinity and which are a unique building material in this region. The chipped stone industry is about half Anatolian obsidian, but the amount of debitage indicates some possibility that the obsidian arrived at Erbaba in the form of blanks rather than raw chunks, and that both flint and obsidian were utilized in quite specialized fashion. Grinding stones were common and pottery was present, but the only figurines were human, not animal. The impression is that the people of Erbaba had completely abandoned hunting and collecting and depended entirely on their flocks and fields. Just how each species of animal was used is not yet clear, but sheep were probably the important meat source, while goats and cattle were kept for other products. The importance of this stage in the developmental pattern of the Near East is that it is the earliest example of the self-sufficient food producing economy common even today in the region.

Çatal Hüyük and Jericho: Towns and Trade

Throughout the period we are considering, there were settlements of widely varying economic pattern whose relationship is not clear.

Probably many of them represent "part-cultures" in that they were not fully self-sufficient but somehow dependent on other groups in a variety of ways. In the case of these two sites we are clearly dealing with quite a different level of cultural elaboration. In both cases the period of occupation was very long, the artifacts were remarkably sophisticated, and the evidence for extensive and substantial trade is demonstrable. These sites represent not so much early urbanism as a stage in the economic development of the Near East which inevitably led to cities and city-states.

Çatal Hüyük is situated on the Konya plain in Turkey. The deposit apparently covers about thirty-two acres, of which one acre has been excavated. It was occupied from about 6500 B.C. to about 5600 B.C. Many of the rooms excavated appear to have served as shrines or temples, which may indicate that the site was specialized, like New World ceremonial centers, or that the various functions of the town were segregated into neighborhoods or quarters. In either case, the unique character of Çatal Hüyük is clear: it was larger, more crowded, more specialized, and richer than any other site in the Anatolian plateau in this time period. All contemporary sites in Anatolia had obsidian from a source near Çatal Hüyük; only Çatal Hüyük itself had obsidian from farther east in Armenia. Mediterranean shells and other materials not available locally attest to the extent and amount of long-distance trade.

The people of Çatal Hüyük had a wide variety of domestic plants, and from the earliest levels domestic cattle were present. Although many of the famous murals in the ceremonial chambers depict hunting scenes, there are virtually no remains of hunted animals in the deposit, and it is probable that such hunting as there was had been reduced to sport or ritual, of no economic importance. A principal basis of the economy seems to have been a mixture of control of some scarce commodities, such as obsidian, and whatever profit may have accrued from a great number of impressive shrines, which are unique for the area and the time. The gradual decline and final destruction of Çatal Hüyük may have resulted from growing competition from other incipient market centers, as full food production became widespread.

The site of Jericho, in Palestine, shows an even longer occupation, although there are some gaps in the sequence. There is evidence that an early, Natufian-like occupation was replaced sometime in the early eighth millennium or earlier by a series of round houses, and soon after that the spectacular first fortifications of Jericho were begun. There was no pottery and no evidence for domestic plants or animals at this period, although somewhat later goats were domesticated. Without apparent food production it is unclear how the people of Jericho could have accumulated the surplus wealth and energy to make such massive defenses either possible or necessary. Trade seems to be the answer. Salt, bitumen, and sulfur from the Dead Sea may have been traded for Anatolian obsidian and nephrite, Sinai turquoise, and Red Sea shells. That there was a sufficient supportive hinterland for such a trade center is attested by the fact that Jericho was persistently rebuilt and reoccupied after a series of destructions, both by the original occupants and by immigrants from the north. In such a situation, wild cereals and hunted animals may have provided adequate sustenance, since the people of Jericho could have traded over a wide area to acquire what might be locally lacking. Eventually domestic plants and animals may have been brought into the area by invading peoples or obtained as part of the trading operation.

Each of these two sites represents a regional climax for the period, but the contrast between them implies a marked difference in the economic bases of the towns, as well as in their individual details. While it is difficult to extrapolate to thirty-two acres of deposit from the one acre excavated, the number and richness of the shrines at Çatal Hüyük, persisting through a long period, suggest that Çatal Hüyük functioned as a regional ceremonial center for religious activity, as well as a clearing house for traded materials. Jericho, on the other hand, impresses chiefly as a fortress designed to protect a rich market town. Perhaps at Çatal Hüyük exotic materials came to the town because it was a religious center, while at Jericho trade goods created the market town. Both sites indicate that towns are a logical response to a broadly supportive countryside and not an independent cultural innovation.

· BIBLIOGRAPHIC ESSAY

Among the most thoughtful of the articles concerned with the general dynamics of the shift to food production are Kent Flannery's article, "The ecology of early food production in Mesopotamia," *Science,* Vol.

147 (1965), pages 1247–1256; L. R. Binford's article, "Post-Pleistocene adaptations," in *New Perspectives in Archaeology,* edited by S. R. Binford and L. R. Binford and published by Aldine in 1968; and Philip E. L. Smith and T. Cuyler Young's article, "The evolution of early agriculture and culture in greater Mesopotamia: a trial model," in *Population Growth: Anthropological Implications,* edited by Brian Spooner and published by the M.I.T. Press in 1973. Besides these papers the reader is directed to two comprehensive compilations of essays: P. J. Ucko and G. W. Dimbleby's *The Domestication and Exploitation of Plants and Animals,* published by Aldine in 1969, and E. S. Higgs' *Papers in Economic Prehistory,* published by Cambridge University Press in 1972.

For discussion of other aspects of early Neolithic development, the interested reader is directed to Frank Hole's article, "Evidence of social organization from Western Iran, 8000–4000 B.C.," in *New Perspectives in Archaeology,* mentioned above, and to Gary A. Wright's volume, *Obsidian Analyses and Prehistoric Near Eastern Trade: 7500 to 3500 B.C.,* Museum of Anthropology, University of Michigan Anthropological Papers, No. 37, 1969. Finally, for the student who has gained a grasp of some of the details of cultural development in the ancient Near East, Jane Jacobs' little book, *The Economy of Cities,* published by Random House in 1969, will prove very thought provoking.

If more detailed information about the development of domestic plants is desired, the new book by Jane Renfrew, *Palaeoethnobotany,* published by the Columbia University Press in 1973, is suggested. Probably the best place for someone interested in the domestication of animals to start is F. E. Zeuner's classic, *A History of Domesticated Animals,* published by Hutchinson in 1963. Also to be recommended for its extensive bibliography and monumental wealth of detail is H. Epstein's *The Domestication of Animals in Africa* (two volumes), published in 1972 by Africana Press. The most recent volume on the problem is János Matolsci's edited work, *Domestikationsforschung und Geschichte der Haustiere,* published by Akadémiai Kiadó in Budapest in 1973.

For those interested in specific examples of detailed research on Near Eastern collections, the authors' article, "A hunters' village in Turkey," *Scientific American,* Vol. 210 (1968), No. 5, as well as Dexter Perkins' articles in *Science,* "Prehistoric fauna from Shanidar,

Iraq," Vol. 144 (1964), pages 1565 and 1566, and "Fauna of Çatal Hüyük: evidence for early cattle domestication in Anatolia," Vol. 164 (1969), pages 177–179, can be recommended. For other neighboring areas, see Robert J. Braidwood and Bruce Howe's book, *Prehistoric Investigations in Iraqi Kurdistan,* Studies in Ancient Oriental Civilization, No. 31, University of Chicago Press, 1960, and Frank Hole, K. V. Flannery, and James A. Neely's *Prehistory and Human Ecology of the Deh Luran Plain,* Memoirs of the Museum of Anthropology, No. 1, University of Michigan, 1969.

Finally, for general overviews of Near Eastern cultural development that give more attention to the particulars of tool assemblage than has been possible in this chapter, James Mellaart's *Earliest Civilizations of the Near East,* published by McGraw-Hill in 1966, and Sonia Cole's *The Neolithic Revolution,* 5th edition, Publication No. 541, Trustees of the British Museum (Natural History), 1970, can be recommended.

4
THE LATER NEOLITHIC IN THE NEAR EAST AND THE RISE OF CIVILIZATION
ROBERT STIGLER

As recently as the 1940's the emergence of Neolithic culture in the Near East (see Map 4.1) was thought to have taken place within the "Fertile Crescent," the arc of rich, mostly alluvial soils stretching up from the valleys of the Tigris and Euphrates across northern Syria, down the Levant, and extending into the Nile Valley. The two extremes of this arc, Mesopotamia and Egypt, were guessed to be the places where agriculture had been first invented. Beginning in 1948, the work of Robert Braidwood and his students represented a giant step away from this preconception and forever reoriented prehistoric research throughout the Near East.

The preconception had been based on the fact that at the *end* of the Neolithic era there had appeared literate Bronze Age civilizations in Egypt and Mesopotamia; hence it had seemed logical to conclude that the predecessors of those civilizations had evolved *in situ*. Where else but in the fertile valleys themselves? Braidwood questioned this logic, and began excavations at Jarmo in northeastern Iraq, not far as the crow flies from the Tigris Valley but in a distinctly different environmental setting. His interpretation of the meaning of Jarmo has changed over the last twenty years, and his original hypothesis concerning the ecology of the early stages of food production has been broadened; but certain principles that he put forth have been fully borne out.

As prehistorians developed better insights into the processes of incipient animal and plant domestication, the view that these might have taken place in the large river-valley systems such as the

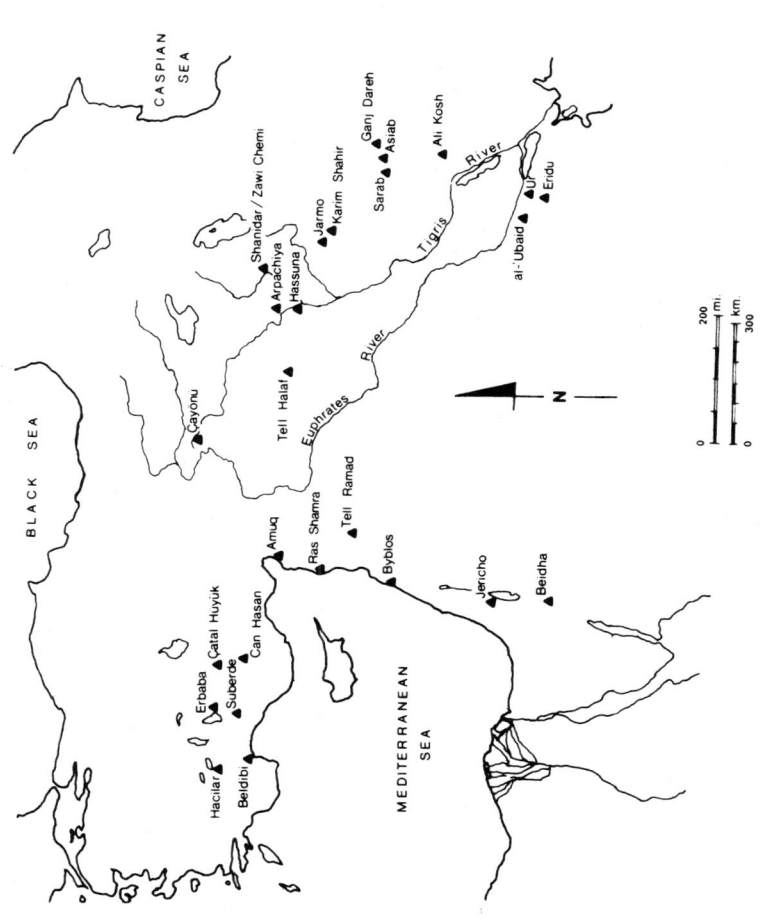

MAP 4.1 Important Neolithic sites in the Near East.

Tigris-Euphrates and the Nile seemed more and more insupportable on at least two counts: 1) it came to be realized that the earliest farmers with the simplest of tools could not be expected to have coped with the problems of cultivation on the valley floors, which, though fertile, required a rather more sophisticated technology than had as yet been developed; and 2) despite the old "oasis theory," there was no evidence that the *wild* forms of the later domesticated plants and animals were at home in the alluvial valleys in late Pleistocene or post-Pleistocene times.

Braidwood formulated the concept of the "nuclear area," where a series of wild plants and animals suitable for domestication existed at the time of man's initial steps toward food production. In southwest Asia such a nuclear area can be drawn with varying borders (owing to some remaining uncertainties about the natural ranges of flora and fauna), but essentially 1) it constitutes the intermediate uplands regions from about one thousand to five thousand feet above sea level which are adjacent to but outside the Fertile Crescent proper; 2) it contains from one locality to another several members of the sheep-goat-cattle-pig-wheat-barley complex which was eventually domesticated; and 3) it is marked in most localities by rainfall which is low in quantity but sufficient for simple dry-farming techniques. Today it is fairly clear that in the Near East the early stages of food production did indeed take place in such mostly upland country, and only afterward did Neolithic settlement begin to fill the alluvial valleys and lowland plains. Before discussing these later developments, it seems worthwhile to begin with a few words about three archaeological sites which precede the wider spread of food-producing communities and which in one way or another must eventually be fitted into our picture of the Neolithic in the Near East.

· JARMO, JERICHO, AND ÇATAL HÜYÜK

These three sites were all occupied during either the eighth or the seventh millennium B.C., i.e., sometime after the period which has given us evidence of the *earliest* steps toward food production but before a uniform Neolithic economy became common in the Near East. The sites are widely separated and radically different in form and size (see Figure 4.1), and although in the broadest sense they

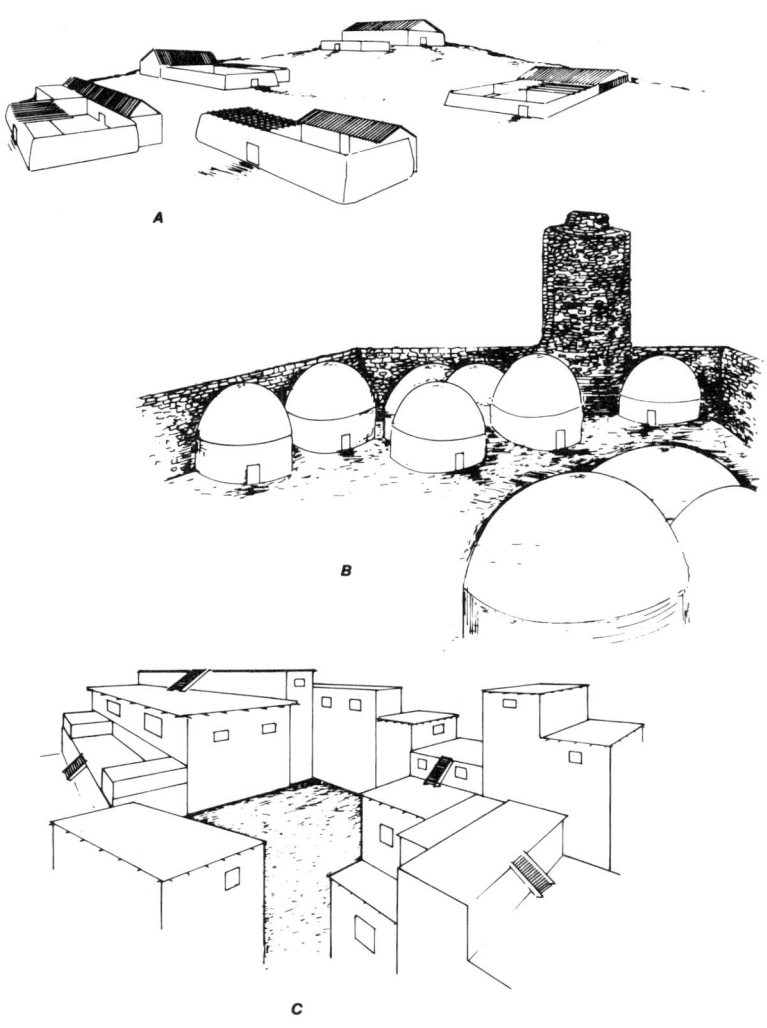

FIGURE 4.1 Artist's reconstruction of the appearance of three early Neolithic settlements. *(A)* Jarmo. *(B)* PPNA Jericho. *(C)* Çatal Hüyük.

lie within the nuclear area just defined, their specific environmental settings are also strikingly different. Just what they tell us, singly and together, about the seventh millennium is still very unclear, but their individuality, at the same time that they were more or less contemporary, is extremely intriguing.

Jarmo is on the hilly western flanks of the Zagros Mountains in northeastern Iraq, in the same region and setting as the earlier Shanidar Cave, Karim Shahir, and Zawi Chemi Shanidar. Occupied c. 6750–6500 B.C., it was a small village of simple sedentary farmers, who had domesticated goats, sheep, and pigs, barley, and einkorn and emmer wheat but who also hunted wild game in the area and ate a species of land snails. The site covers no more than four acres atop a bluff overlooking a small stream and apparently never contained more than about twenty houses at any one time, with an estimated population of 150 people. The houses often had crude stone foundations supporting puddled-mud walls, with brush-and-mud roofs. "Art" consisted of small clay figurines of animals and humans (especially pregnant women), undoubtedly of ritual significance. Pottery was manufactured only in the latter part of the occupation.

In an area where we now know there was earlier incipient animal domestication (Zawi Chemi Shanidar) and a series of smaller settlements which can be taken as those of the hunting-and-gathering forebears of Jarmo, this small village would seem to be a perfect example of the first full-time farming and herding communities, representing the transition from the earlier hunters, gatherers, and occasional sheepherders of the hilly flanks of northeastern Iraq to the village and town dwellers of the alluvial valleys. As such, it presents a readily understandable and satisfying picture, but that this was the *principal* type of transition in the Near East is now in question.

Just what early Neolithic Jericho represents is more puzzling. It is located, not in uplands, but the total reverse—about seven hundred feet below sea level near the deepest part of the Jordan river valley. It is one of the most unusual environments and geological features on earth, but despite this, it can in a certain sense be considered a part of the Near Eastern nuclear area: the small, below-sea-level valley is immediately enclosed by extremely dry uplands, and at least some wild cereals and goats were present.

A large natural spring at the site has occasioned settlement at least since Mesolithic times, as well as attracting animals and water birds. The "Pre-pottery Neolithic" levels of Jericho overlie a Natufian stratum and are older than Jarmo by several centuries, going well back into the eighth millennium B.C. The town (no village this) covers some ten acres and had an estimated population of two to three thousand. Well-built houses of regularly shaped mud bricks are tightly grouped, and at a certain point before 7000 B.C. the whole settlement was surrounded by a massive stone wall of fortification, incorporating at least one large watch tower. This wall was later rebuilt, still within the "pre-pottery" period. The necessity for such defenses in Neolithic times is wholly at odds with our conception of the period: one scholar has said that it could only be an early case of urban paranoia! In any event, there is nothing to indicate against whom the walls were built.

The Pre-pottery Neolithic was of long duration at Jericho. It was followed after a lapse by a "Pottery Neolithic," probably around 6000 B.C. There is no *direct* evidence of the domestication of plants or animals here until after the pre-pottery period, and this has led to several avenues of speculation. On the one hand, it is difficult at present to envision a community of this size subsisting by hunting and gathering and/or by trade, and many archaeologists have simply assumed the presence of agriculture back to the beginnings of the ten-acre Pre-pottery Neolithic "A" (PPNA) town. On the other hand, it is becoming evident that in favored areas elsewhere in the Near East permanent communities, though smaller, did exist without food production; and it must be added that the Jordan Valley is a unique and lush environment, with waterfowl and rich vegetation (including wild emmer wheat), and it certainly must also have attracted wild game from the surrounding desert and dry hills.

A still more surprising seventh millennium site is that of Çatal Hüyük, about three thousand feet above sea level in the Konya plain of the south-central portion of the Anatolian plateau. Although fertile the Konya region is dry, having only sixteen inches of annual rainfall, but the site of Çatal Hüyük is located on the small Çarşamba River, which probably provided more water in the seventh millennium than it does today.

We have a mixture of over-abundant data on some aspects of

the site and inadequate evidence of others. The deeper portions of the *tell,* or mound, site were not excavated, so that the antecedents of the climactic period are unknown. The Konya plain was an especially rich part of the southwest Asian nuclear area, one that abounded in wild but domesticable animals and cereal grasses, and it is only to be expected that the earliest steps toward domestication will eventually prove to have taken place here, too, but Çatal Hüyük represents a later stage. The excavated levels and accompanying radiocarbon dates of the site form a complex picture, but speaking summarily they seem to extend from around 6500 to c. 5750 B.C. The unique cultural features are said to go back at least to the 6500 date, but they cluster around 6000 B.C. Even if they were confined to the latter date, they would still be remarkable.

Çatal Hüyük was a town covering some thirty-two acres, three times the area of Jericho, eight times that of Jarmo. Apparently something of a fire-trap, it repeatedly burned and was repeatedly rebuilt, always to the same basic plan: a maze of houses and rooms enclosed by an unbroken peripheral circle of chambers having entrances only through the roofs, presenting a blank facade to the outside world. The excavator James Mellaart sees this as a defensive arrangement.

In the excavated part of the site an unusually high percentage of the rooms appear to have been ceremonial in nature, containing a variety of frescoes, wall-reliefs, free-standing sculpture in clay, and figurines, depicting animals, human females, scenes of the hunt, and other topics. The richness of this art is unique for the Old World Neolithic anywhere. Pottery at Çatal Hüyük, on the other hand, consists of undistinguished plainware and seems even to be absent in some levels. Cattle were domesticated, as were no fewer than fourteen different food plants, including einkorn, emmer, and hexaploid bread wheat, peas, lentils, and other species; but hunting continued to provide a major portion of the diet.

Our knowledge of Anatolian prehistory is too recent to allow definitive statements, but Çatal Hüyük would appear to be by far the dominant site in the area for its time. Whatever its antecedents, it must be thought of as a special case, and special explanations must be adduced to account for it. One which has been put forth is the suggestion that trade in obsidian made the town wealthy, and that, in turn, it became a ceremonial or pilgrimage center for a wide area. Two recently active volcanoes at the east end of the Konya plain provided abundant quantities of obsidian, and trace-element studies show that this material of specifically Konya provenience is present in archaeological sites in Cyprus, Syria, the Levant, and elsewhere in the Near East. It was clearly an important item of trade in the seventh and sixth millennia. In the vicinity of Çatal Hüyük there is known to have existed contemporaneously at least one village of hunters, Suberde, and the suggestion has been made that these hunters traded wild game to the town in return for religious services (obsidian being rare at Suberde).

The existence in the Near East of three such diverse communities as Jarmo, Jericho, and Çatal Hüyük raises more questions than can be answered at this point. Jarmo is the only one with a fully satisfactory sequential context: obvious predecessors in the same area and, as we shall see, successors nearby. PPNA Jericho, despite the Natufian level at the bottom of the mound, still appears rather suddenly and inexplicably, and on an unknown economic base. Trade has also, not very convincingly, been postulated here, not only to account for the size of the town but also to explain the possible absence of agriculture and husbandry. Jericho is close by the Dead Sea with its resources of salt, bitumen, sulfur, and potash, while imported turquoise, lapis lazuli, and the like have been found in the site; but preservation conditions are not good at Jericho, and the nature of its food supply—wild, domesticated, or traded in—is simply unknown.

Çatal Hüyük is more readily believable as a trading and ceremonial center and at the same time provides evidence of a flourishing agricultural system. It nevertheless does seem to represent a peculiar success for such early times, again without obvious forerunners or descendants known at present.

These, of course, are only three settlements dating before 6000 B.C. which raise certain kinds of questions. A number of other sites are known from the same period—Suberde, Ali Kosh, Erbaba, Beidha, and Çayönü, to name a few which were referred to in the preceding chapter. Taken all together, their differences are most striking. At present the eighth and seventh millennia show the most variegated scene of any of the prehistoric periods in the Near East, marked by the widest diversity in the forms of its communities and societies. However this archaeologist's jigsaw puzzle is finally put together, it is bound to yield further surprises. The sixth, fifth, and fourth millennia might almost seem transparently clear and "normal" by comparison.

Those, however, are rash words if not deceptive, in view of the fact that the Later Neolithic period is an archaeologically neglected one in the Near East, and a great deal remains to be learned about it. Since World War II most prehistoric archaeologists have concentrated their efforts on the early stages of food production and the earlier Paleolithic era, while historical archaeologists have seldom had a direct interest in later prehistory. It is rather symbolic of the "no-man's-land" character of the period that the time span from around 5600 B.C. until 3500–3000 B.C. is commonly called Chalcolithic by historical archaeologists, while prehistorians usually avoid that term and employ "Late" or "Later Neolithic," if they consider the age at all.

Far too much of what we know about the Near East from c. 6000 B.C. to c. 3200 B.C. is based overwhelmingly on pottery styles (Figure 4.2). Very little can be said specifically or in detail about other evolving technologies, changing settlement patterns, or emerging new forms of economic organization. Even cultural sequences are still confused, although a welter of sites is known from all over the Near East. This must have been an era of very widespread establishment of village and town life throughout the area, based now on fairly uniform systems of agriculture and herding, revolving around the whole complex of domesticated sheep-goats-cattle, wheat, barley, and various other food plants. Hunting would have continued as a subsistence activity, of relatively less importance than in early Neolithic times.

The Near East is a large area of great environmental diversity, but despite local adaptations in the Late Neolithic, on the whole there do not appear to have been the blatant eccentricities of the seventh and eighth millennia. The Neolithic occupation of the Tigris-Euphrates valleys began around 6000 B.C., and parallel developments in Anatolia, the Levant, and Iran took place around

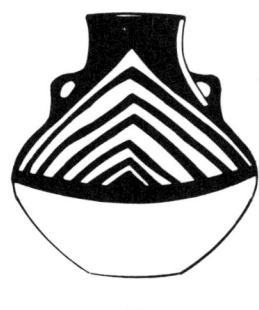

FIGURE 4.2 Pottery of the Later Neolithic. *(A)* Hassuna. *(B)* Halaf. *(C)* Samarra. *(D)* Sialk. *(E)* Hacilar.

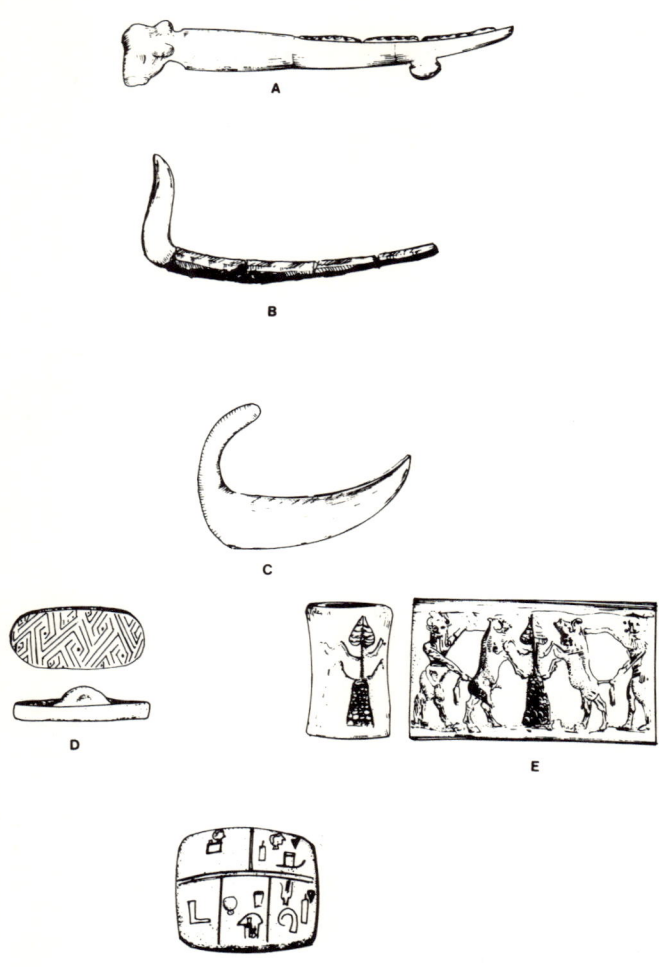

FIGURE 4.3 Near East artifacts, from c. 9000 to c. 3000 B.C. *(A)* Natufian sickle, for reaping wild grain. *(B)* Later Neolithic sickle of common pattern, with flint blades set in wooden haft. *(C)* Baked clay sickle from southern Mesopotamia. *(D)* Clay stamp seal of the Late Neolithic period in Mesopotamia. *(E)* Cylinder seal (left), with rolled-out impression. *(F)* Limestone tablet showing the first, pictographic stage in the development of cuneiform writing, c. 3500 B.C.

the same time—a period of the "settling-in" of agricultural peasant communities. (See Figure 4.3.)

· NORTHERN MESOPOTAMIA

Hassuna
The first Neolithic culture in Mesopotamia proper is commonly considered to be the Hassunan, named after the site of Tell Hassuna on the west side of the middle Tigris River twenty miles south of modern Mosul. While the country is rolling and merges imperceptibly with the uplands, it is "valley" as opposed to the hilly flanks where nearby Jarmo is located. Other sites of the Hassuna culture are restricted to similar terrain in a rather limited region of northern Iraq. In content and style the early Hassunan materials are easily seen as a continuation of Jarmo, as though an expansion of Jarmo culture down the flanks and to the west had taken place. Both the simple pottery and the stone tools show this. Although house construction improves during the course of Hassunan development, it remains simple, with the settlements no more than villages of farmers cultivating the now standard repertory of Near Eastern domesticates.

Hassunan pottery falls into three categories: 1) an earlier plainware with relations to Jarmo; 2) a simple decorated ware with relatively crudely painted geometric motifs; and 3) "Samarran" ware of considerably greater refinement and artistry, utilizing both geometric designs and stylized figures of animals, birds, insects, fish, and humans.

The ways in which Samarran ware has been interpreted show very well the problems faced by prehistorians interested in this period. At one time the pottery itself was elevated to the status of a "culture" because of its difference from other known styles, especially Hassunan proper. Then it was demoted to being a "ware" when it was realized that it frequently occurred in the upper levels of otherwise Hassunan sites. Second thoughts on this subject have led one present-day archaeologist to return to a "Hassuna-and-Samarra cultures" terminology. Furthermore, a number of authorities who deal with the material engage in a favorite sport of Old World archaeologists (sometimes jokingly referred to as the "Old Testament effect"), namely, attributing the appearance of any cultural innovation to an immigration of peoples from the outside: Samarran ware has in the past often been taken to indicate such a movement of new peoples into the area.

Samarran pottery does present problems because its associations are somewhat mixed. It has never been altogether pinned down as merely a component of Hassunan culture; it is sometimes found with "later" Halafian ware. At present the most economical solution would seem to be to regard it not as a separate culture but basically as a pottery style which at least overlaps with some later Hassunan materials, though it is found in other contexts as well, and leave the matter there until further excavation clarifies the problem.

Two old radiocarbon determinations from Hassunan sites give dates of 5100 and 5600 B.C. Another indirect carbon-14 date places some Hassunan material at 5800 B.C. *Guess*-dates for a beginning of the period around 6000 B.C. and a termination c. 5200–5000 B.C. seem reasonable.

Halaf

The next phase of Late Neolithic culture in Mesopotamia is usually considered to be that represented by the discovery almost sixty years ago of a distinctive pottery style at Tell Halaf on the Syrian-Turkish border, midway between the Tigris and Euphrates. Later work showed that, like the Hassunan culture, the Halafian was centered in northern Iraq, but it was distributed considerably more widely (or at least its pottery was).

Halafian settlements were still only of "village" size, but construction techniques improved, and cobbled streets were laid between houses. Although packed mud walls continued to be employed, at least at some sites the first mud bricks in Mesopotamia appear. Also for the first time in Mesopotamia structures or chambers different from dwelling or other utilitarian units appear in some Halafian sites. These are vaulted circular rooms, "beehive" in shape, ranging from about fifteen to thirty feet in diameter, and built of packed mud. Rectangular antechambers are sometimes attached. These structures have, unhappily, been called *"tholoi,"* after the much later, larger, stone-built *tholos*-tombs of Mycenae in Greece—a farfetched terminology indeed. At one site at least, the chambers appear to have been lived in, but elsewhere their use seems to have been a special one. They were not tombs, mostly being found empty, although burials with grave offerings are sometimes grouped around them. The buildings perhaps represent the first steps toward the ceremonial temple architecture later to loom so large in Mesopotamian civilization.

Halafian pottery was the finest ever produced, before or since, in prehistoric Mesopotamia. It was still hand-made but with thin walls of a very fine clay. Decoration consisted of the carefully and skillfully applied painting of geometric motifs and occasional figures of animals, birds, and flowers. Flat stamp seals of steatite or other stone, used to impress marks of ownership on lumps of clay attached to goods, make their first appearance in the Halafian.

Halafian sites and/or pottery show a distribution into northern Syria even to the Mediterranean, into southeastern Turkey, and somewhat farther down the Tigris and Euphrates than Hassunan materials. The dating of the complex again is troublesome. There is a radiocarbon date of 5288 B.C. from Tell Arpachiya near Mosul, but other indications go back to the early (high) 5000's. Braidwood stresses the likelihood of this earlier age for the Halafian, which would then considerably overlap Hassuna, and, by utilizing some ambiguities in the dating, suggests that Çatal Hüyük is only a western variant outpost of the culture. Mellaart on the other hand regards northern Mesopotamia in the sixth millennium, Hassuna and Halaf alike, as the *beneficiary* of an Anatolian stimulus.

More to fill in the yawning gaps in the sequence than on the basis of any direct evidence, various authorities extend the end of the Halafian culture well down into the fifth millennium, as late as 4300 B.C., before it is replaced by another recognizable entity.

In broadest outline the 1500 years or so from c. 6000 to c. 4500 B.C. saw the settlement of the middle reaches of the Tigris and Euphrates valleys in northern Iraq, or Mesopotamia, by farming peoples who had probably moved in from one or more regions of the "nuclear area" to the east, north, and west. Farming techniques were secure but not elaborate, allowing for only a moderate

THE OLD WORLD

expansion in size, quality, and numbers of settlements during the period. Some development is noticeable: native copper was occasionally worked, though not for the first time in the Near East; aesthetically and technologically, pottery improved greatly; and one notable advance was that of plow agriculture, as distinct from the use of a digging stick wielded by the farmer. But on the whole the period was one of relatively stable peasant-village life, not markedly different here from what was happening very widely in the Near East in the sixth and early fifth millennia.

· SOUTHERN MESOPOTAMIA

Below present-day Baghdad, on a roughly east-west line drawn a little to the north, the character of the Tigris-Euphrates system changes to broad, extremely flat, alluvial valleys, desert-like in appearance once one is away from the margins of the rivers, though the soil is exceptionally fertile if water is applied. The lower reaches of the system are marshy. Owing to the flatness of the land and the periodic flooding of the rivers, the region has been said to "hover between desert and swamp." Rainfall is almost nonexistent.

In the lowest levels of several sites which flourished here in later times, there have been found types of pottery, "Eridu" and "Haji Mohammed" wares, both owing something to the Halafian and Samarran pottery of the north and indicating an occupation of this country at least from around 5000 to 4300 B.C. For that matter it is most likely that small numbers of gatherers and fishers had earlier exploited the riverine marshes.

At Eridu, slightly west of the present-day course of the Euphrates, a series of small square rooms fitted with altars has been found in the very early levels associated with early "Eridu" ware. They represent the simplest beginnings in the south of the long, much elaborated tradition of temple architecture in Mesopotamia referred to earlier. (See Figure 4.4.)

There is a great need for more study of these earlier levels of the Neolithic in southern Mesopotamia, for we can really say very little about the origins of settlement there. The only reasonably well-known prehistoric period begins around 4300 B.C.

FIGURE 4.4 Architectural development in Mesopotamia. *(A)* Halafian *"tholos."* *(B)* Ubaidian temple at Eridu. *(C)* The Warka-Jemdet Nasr White Temple at Uruk. *(D)* The *Ziggurat* of Ur.

Ubaid

The Ubaid culture is named after the small type-site of al-'Ubaid, which with nearby Ur and Eridu forms a triangle just west of the lower course of the Euphrates. Ubaidian remains are known from both northern and southern Mesopotamia, but the south saw a much more florescent aspect of the culture than the north. As usual, based on pottery analogies, the origins of Ubaid have often been attributed to a new people coming into the area (from southwestern Iran), but until more is known about the local and other Mesopotamian antecedents of the culture, this seems a fairly gratuitous speculation. The pottery style is widespread in several directions, while most of the major communities are definitely located in southern Mesopotamia.

The Ubaid period lasted from at least as early as 4300 B.C. to perhaps as late as 3500 B.C. In its homeland it can be seen as a town *and* village society, i.e., larger settlements surrounded by satellite communities, a pattern which evolved into the city-states of later times. Ubaidian towns were dominated by their temples, and this temple architecture underwent a rapid development from the simple pre-Ubaidian structures at Eridu to fairly "monumental" examples showing the characteristic Mesopotamian pilaster-facades and having elements probably foreshadowing the *ziggurat*.

It has been said that the larger Ubaidian settlements were probably market towns as well as religious centers, both for the local satellite communities and for wider trade. Southern Mesopotamia had few natural resources other than fertile soil (and local artisans) at this time, and there is evidence of the import of raw materials. But in the light of what we know about later historical Mesopotamia, it is possible that much or all of this Ubaidian "trade" was in the hands of the temple administrators, consisted largely of offerings, tribute, or levies, and did not involve actual markets for its distribution.

The earlier carefully produced and beautifully decorated pottery of Mesopotamia (Halafian and Samarran) gave way in Ubaid times to technologically competent but mass-produced wares decorated in an often careless manner. Some pottery was manufactured on the *tournette,* a forerunner of the fast-spinning potter's wheel. Stamp seals, engraved only with simple geometric figures in the

The Later Neolithic in the Near East

earlier Halafian period, now depict animals and humans together in scenes. Stone work of any kind is rare in the stone-poor country of southern Mesopotamia, but these stamp seals are common at Tepe Gawra and other northern Mesopotamian sites in Ubaidian times.

A number of other technological innovations have been determined in the Ubaid assemblages: the *casting* of copper, especially in northern Mesopotamia; the use of fired bricks in construction; and simple sailboats for river transport, to name a few.

While agriculture in southern Mesopotamia must have been extremely productive, it seems likely that a different order of wealth, whether based on mercantile trade or the temples' command of tribute and organization of commerce, was growing at this time. Of course, only agricultural surpluses could have made this possible in the first place, feeding artisans, mass-producers of pottery, construction workers, temple authorities, and other town dwellers. Whether as a result of population expansion, trade, or some other force, the vitality of Ubaidian culture was such that its influence was widespread, at the same time that much of the ground-plan of the later historic periods in Mesopotamia was being laid down here.

Warka

Our focus is now entirely on the south, for the provincial quality of northern Mesopotamia in Ubaidian times is even heightened in this period, and although we have almost no details concerning immediately post-Ubaidian times in the south, it is only reasonable to assume a continuing intensification in the pace of development here.

It would serve little purpose to detail the arguments-in-a-vacuum, the terminological variations, and chronological uncertainties of this period in southern Mesopotamia beyond a few words. Warka is the modern Arabic name of the site of ancient Uruk or Erech, east of the modern course of the Euphrates, around 50 miles northwest of Ur-Eridu-Ubaid, and about 150 miles southeast of Baghdad. Most historical archaeologists continue to speak of the "Uruk" period, but the designation "Warka" is preferred by prehistorians, reflecting a more recent interpretation of the last prehistoric stages.

Dating of the Warka or Uruk period is purely interpretive. Some historians allow it only the two hundred years from 3300 to 3100 B.C., but there are also reasons to date it back to the earlier fourth millennium. If we use the terminology Ubaid→Warka→Proto-Literate rather than the alternative Ubaid→Uruk→Proto-Literate, it should be understood that "Warka" includes only the first half of "Uruk," the latter half falling into the "Proto-Literate" period of the former scheme.

This leaves us with almost nothing to say at present concerning Warka, since its existence has been detected only through a new pottery style present in the lower levels of two or three sites. This pottery retains a few features of the Ubaidian, but since the most typical forms do not show the painted designs of long-standing tradition in Mesopotamia, an "Uruk invasion" has been invoked. Otherwise, the most we can say about the Warka period is that it is transitional, in time at least, from the Ubaid to the Proto-Literate, and that it is probable that the first cylinder seals in Mesopotamia began to be developed here.

The Proto-Literate

As we get this close to Sumerian civilization, chronology becomes firmer. The Proto-Literate period can be reasonably bracketed by the dates 3200–3100 B.C. to 2800 B.C. In the other terminology the Proto-Literate consists of Uruk IV and "Jemdet Nasr" materials.

Virtually the whole constellation of traits comprising the most widely accepted definition of "civilization" is now demonstrably present in southern Mesopotamia—the potter's wheel, the vehicular wheel (on wagons and what seem to be chariot-like carts), bronze metallurgy, and writing, as well as urbanism and other forms of social elaboration.

At Warka-Erech, early in the Proto-Literate period, the huge temple of the goddess E-Anna was constructed, measuring 100 by almost 250 feet and having an associated *ziggurat* and subsidiary buildings. In form it and other temples of the period show a direct development from Ubaidian models. In this temple were found the earliest clay tablets with pictographic forms of writing, which quickly evolved into the standard cuneiform of later Mesopotamia.

Estimates of population as high as fifty to eighty thousand have been made for later Proto-Literate cities, but these are notoriously shaky figures; certainly they represent upper limits, if indeed any settlements reached this size.

We are told that the earliest Proto-Literate writing is in the Sumerian language and that the whole Proto-Literate period is culturally "Sumerian," a prelude to the emergence very close to 2800 B.C. of the historically known and named kings and dynasties of the city-states of ancient Sumer. At the same time, the origins, linguistic and otherwise, of the Sumerians is a most complicated and debated question. It cannot be pursued here, but, needless to say, alternative explanations involving invasions-migrations and *in situ* development have been put forth. If the prehistorian can plead incompetence to judge these matters and at the same time take a prehistoric bird's-eye view of Mesopotamian cultural development ranging from c. 6000 to 2800 B.C., then we can say that the panorama, for all of the gaps in our knowledge, is one of a steadily evolving series of Neolithic cultures, increasingly able to exploit the fertility of the river valleys, ultimately intensifying in the richer south (Chart 4.1). Technological innovations are steadily added, perhaps by some diffusion into the area but much more likely by local invention: all the circumstances were propitious.

Irrigation

Artificial distribution of water to arid land occurred frequently in ancient times in several parts of the Old and New Worlds, while the control of excess water, as in the Nile floods, was also a periodic necessity. It seems a safe assumption, however, that the various techniques of water manipulation required a degree of technological sophistication beyond the attainments of the earliest farmers, who must have relied rather on rainfall and/or natural ground moisture. But in order for more land to be brought under cultivation farther from the immediate banks of the Tigris and Euphrates, the Nile, the small rivers on the desert coast of Peru, etc., systems of irrigation ditches and canals would have been necessary.

For many years a school of archaeological-historical thought, led notably by the historian Karl Wittfogel, has held that irrigation technology was a crucial factor in the political, economic, and so-

LEVANT	MESOPOTAMIA	ANATOLIA
3000 B.C.	2800 B.C.	3000 B.C.
↑ SLOW GROWTH OF COASTAL TOWNS	PROTO-LITERATE *CITIES*	↑ SLOW CHALCOLITHIC DEVELOPMENT
	3100 B.C.	
	WARKA	
	3500 B.C.	
	HALAF	
	5200 B.C. SAMARRA	
"POTTERY NEOLITHIC"	HASSUNA	HACILAR
6000 B.C.		6000 B.C.
	DIVERSITY BEFORE 6000 B.C.	
PPNB		ÇATAL HÜYÜK
PPNA	JARMO	HACILAR
JERICHO and BEIDHA		SUBERDE
NATUFIAN	KARIM SHAHIR and ZAWI CHEMI SHANIDAR	BELDIBI
9000 B.C.		9000 B.C.

CHART 4.1   Outline of Neolithic development in the Near East.

The Later Neolithic in the Near East 119

cial development of a number of ancient societies. The arguments of this school are elaborate and far-reaching, but one of them, in simplified form, goes as follows:

In order to be effective, irrigation systems necessitate first the cooperation of individuals, and then cooperation between communities, to construct and maintain the ditches and canals. Moreover, the mobilization of these cooperating elements, combined with rights, claims, and disputes over the water itself, requires some authority to bring them about and preside over them. Thus the irrigation complex is seen as a whole distinct feature of certain Neolithic and Bronze Age cultures which is lacking in other areas where agriculture does not have the water problem. The "irrigation hypothesis" holds that this accounts not only for the more rapid development of the irrigating Neolithic societies but also for a particular emerging pattern of political, economic, and social organization which reaches a climax with the attainment of Bronze Age civilization.

While it is doubtless true that there is a notable association of large-scale irrigation and water manipulation with the more advanced cultures of the ancient world in the Nile, the Tigris-Euphrates, the Indus, and the Hwangho (Yellow) river valleys, as well as in Peru and the Valley of Mexico, in most of these cases the Neolithic origins of the irrigation tradition are virtually unknown. In terrain which has been occupied and cultivated for centuries and millennia, to trace ancient ditch systems in the open countryside is difficult enough; to identify them with specific cultural periods is almost impossible, especially in the case of the earlier, simpler instances. In Mesopotamia at a certain point the presence of fairly elaborate irrigation networks becomes presumptive, as in Ubaid times, even if they were not physically observable by then. But by Ubaid times the character of Mesopotamian civilization was just about set, or at least already adumbrated, and for the earlier periods in the Tigris-Euphrates valleys, we are left with only the hypothesis, undemonstrated and perhaps undemonstrable.

A rather more generalized interpretation of the rapidity of cultural development from 6000 to 3000 B.C. in Mesopotamia, as compared with other areas of the Near East, could be phrased in terms of 1) the immediate adjacency of the heart of the "nuclear area," which in a sense had provided a pre-adaptation of the earliest valley settlers in northern Mesopotamia, and 2) the extraordinary fertility of the alluvial valley system itself, as rich as any in the world.

· IRAN

Within the last decade the eastern slopes of the Zagros range in western Iran have been shown to be a fully participating region of the nuclear area of the Near East, evidenced by the sites of Ali Kosh, Ganj Dareh, Tepe Asiab, Sarab, Guran, and others of the eighth and seventh millennia B.C. If 6000 B.C. may be taken in a very general sense as a significant time-line throughout the Near East, after which the variety of the seventh millennium sites gave way to a more standardized pattern of Neolithic culture, Iran seems to participate in the phenomenon. Although the archaeological evidence today is very spotty, a number of archaeologists are engaged in the excavation of Neolithic sites of both pre- and post-6000 B.C. Excellent painted pottery has long been known to have been a marked feature of the later Neolithic cultures of Iran, often called Chalcolithic—Susa, Sialk, Giyan, Cheshmeh Ali, and many others. The wares are distinctive in detail, and to describe them in the over-simplified terms employed in this essay would make them sound more like Mesopotamian pottery than in fact they are.

The existence of this Iranian painted pottery tradition has long been a convenience to the type of Mesopotamian archaeologist who seeks "outside influences" each time a new style emerges in his own pottery. If anything, the direction of influence is more likely to have been the reverse. It is interesting to note, however, that the earliest known pottery anywhere in the Near East has very recently been turned up at Ganj Dareh on the eastern slopes of the Zagros in Iran, dating to before 7000 B.C. The excavator, Philip Smith, points out that the simple pottery was originally fired very lightly, and probably would not have recognizably survived had not an accidental conflagration in the level where it was found hardened it by means of a higher-temperature baking. Perhaps there is something to the independence of the Iranian pottery tradition, but Smith rather questions whether the numerous "aceramic" or "pre-pottery" Neolithic levels elsewhere in the Near East and eastern Mediterranean area might not also have contained such perishable pottery.

Iran is partly open to Mesopotamia, in the south, and partially isolated from it by the Zagros. While a certain degree of independence can be seen at all times in the Neolithic and Bronze Ages, it is equally likely that in the Later Neolithic Age and the Bronze Age events in the dominant Tigris-Euphrates valleys had a relatively one-way effect on Iran.

· ANATOLIA

As recently as fifteen years ago statements were made to the effect that there had been no Neolithic on the Anatolian plateau (though a later "Chalcolithic" had long been recognized). But by virtue of sites such as Suberde, Erbaba, Çatal Hüyük, Aceramic Hacilar, and Can Hasan, the area today is one of great interest to the Neolithic prehistorian.

What we know of the later Neolithic on the Anatolian plateau can perhaps be briefly formulated best in terms of the site of Hacilar, about 130 miles west of Çatal Hüyük. Hacilar is a small mound excavated in the late 1950's by Mellaart, before his work at Çatal Hüyük. A Neolithic level without pottery at the base of the site is estimated (reckoning from Çatal Hüyük) to date to c. 7000 B.C. There follows a long hiatus in occupation, lasting until c. 5750 B.C., a gap which is neatly filled by the evidence from Çatal Hüyük itself. Mellaart labels the period from 5750 to 5600 B.C. at Hacilar as Late Neolithic, which leads without break into an "Early Chalcolithic" phase ending at 5000 B.C. with the abandonment of the site. Pottery contemporary with this Early Chalcolithic at Hacilar also comes from later levels at Can Hasan, fifty miles east of Çatal Hüyük, and other sites, including Çatal Hüyük *West,* a post-Neolithic mound just across the Çarşamba River from Early Neolithic Çatal Hüyük.

The Late Neolithic pottery at Hacilar shows general resemblances to the undecorated wares of Çatal Hüyük, with the exception that a small amount of painting occurs. But then in the Early Chalcolithic phase at Hacilar, Çatal Hüyük West, and Can Hasan,

122 THE OLD WORLD

painting is elaborated into beautifully decorated wares whose designs revolve principally around bold geometric patterns.

By employing a considerably later chronology for the Halafian culture than the one recently favored by others, and by stressing an "Anatolianness" in the Halafian tradition (in pottery decoration, copper metallurgy, a religious bull-cult, etc.), Mellaart manages to suggest a strong Hacilar-Çatal Hüyük West influence in the establishment of that tradition. On the other hand, earlier dates for the Halafian would make this clearly impossible and lead to the opposite conclusion.

Whatever its uniqueness and innovative development in Early Neolithic times up until about 6000 B.C., it looks today as though Anatolia was in later times more the recipient than the creator of major new features of culture. Its Late Neolithic, or Chalcolithic, cultures, located as they were in a different environmental setting, had some individuality, but when bronze technology, for example, made its way into the area, it was unaccompanied by writing, and when urbanism finally appeared, it was from different sources altogether.

· SYRO-CILICIA AND THE LEVANT

"Syro-Cilicia" refers to the regions adjacent to the northeast corner of the Mediterranean, where Syria meets Turkey. It includes the plains around Antioch and Aleppo, and the nearby coastal plain of the Turkish province of Cilicia. The term *Levant* is here extended to include not only the coastal strip and towns of Syria, Lebanon, and Israel but inland to the desert as well. There is some justification for considering all these areas together as one.

Northern Syria is relatively low-lying country, constituting a break between the Turkish Taurus and the Lebanese ranges to the south. It is the only part of this whole area to have relatively direct access to the Tigris-Euphrates and Mesopotamia.

Natufian occupations, though centered in Palestine, are known sporadically from the southern Levant northward and extending well west on the southern coast of Turkey to Beldibi Cave beyond Antalya. After the Natufian the next major phase of development recognized is that of a "pre-pottery Neolithic" at a number of sites—Beidha, Jericho, Ras Shamra (Ugarit) on the Syrian coast, Tell Ramad near Damascus, and others. By its size and its various anomalies Jericho stands out among these. Dating is various at the different sites but comes down close to 6000 B.C. in some cases.

Pottery appears in a number of sites within a couple of hundred years on either side of the 6000 B.C. time-line—e.g., at Mersin in Cilicia, the Amuq sequence in northern Syria, Ras Shamra, Byblos on the Lebanese coast, and Jericho.

These cultural levels are said to represent a break with the earlier pre-pottery horizon in ways other than just the addition of pottery, but much more excavation across the transition is necessary before this ceases to be a highly speculative matter. Although it has been claimed that the new pottery has origins on the Anatolian plateau, this is not easily demonstrable. What impresses one about both the pre-pottery and pottery-bearing early Neolithic periods in Syro-Cilicia and the Levant is an interplay, complex and changing but definite, between sites, involving burial practices, house forms, stone implements, and specific pottery types, all of which give something of an internal unity to the area. Pottery in the early levels of the coastal sites decorated with impressions made by the edge of a *cardium* shell is an example of this.

These post-6000 B.C. cultures are presumably contemporaneous with Hassuna, but influence from Mesopotamia proper is not noticeable. Halafian influence is another matter, since the Halaf culture itself extended farther to the west, abutting the area under consideration. This influence, however, appears only later in the local pottery records, as at Ras Shamra, Mersin, and Amuq in the late sixth millennium.

A time of troubles and impoverishment, causes unknown, appears to have smitten much of this area in the fifth millennium. Some sites are considered to have become only semi-sedentary, occupied by nomads (who have been suggested as creating the troubles), and it has been proposed that the Halafian culture itself suffered its end this way. In any event, with the recovery strong Ubaidian influence, at least in pottery, appears throughout the area. From this time on, the growing Mesopotamian civilization strongly affected the whole Near East; as in Anatolia, elements came piecemeal to Syro-Cilicia and the Levant—e.g., bronze before writing. But urbanization (and writing) along the Mediterranean coast took indigenous forms, and we can see the eventual emergence here of increasingly mercantile-maritime oriented cities in contrast to the political-religious centers of Mesopotamia.

· THE END OF PREHISTORY

"Civilization" is a generic concept about which most Old World archaeologists intuitively agree, but when it comes to objective criteria and specific cases, there are occasional problems. One point should be held in mind: the archaeologist's use of the term does not constitute a value-judgment. Who today would define cultural development and a growth in complexity as betterment or Progress? We are free then to formulate the definition as rigorously as we wish, and stick to it, with the understanding that we are labeling only a measurable degree of cultural complexity, nothing more.

With few exceptions the term *civilization* as applied to ancient societies in the Old World has been limited to those showing the presence of at least a majority of the following traits: the plow, wheeled carts, and traction animals, the sailing boat, the smelting of copper ores (implying bronze metallurgy), monumental architecture, a solar calendar (as opposed to simple lunar ones), writing, some kind of mathematics, standardized measurements, irrigation, specialized craftsmen, cities, and food surpluses to sustain the non-farmers in the population. This list was put forth by V. G. Childe some years ago, obviously with Mesopotamian civilization in mind (there was no wheel other than the potter's, and a lack of cities, in early Egypt), and it still stands up well as a checklist of features. If a majority of these are present in the archaeological-historical evidence, we know that a major cultural threshold had been crossed.

Furthermore, we know historically that these features tend to cluster in all the known Old World instances; that is to say, after centuries of slower piecemeal innovation by Neolithic societies, certain of them in favored environmental locations reached a stage in their development where technological advances then took place on a broad front in a short span of time, leading rapidly to the new level of cultural complexity.

This list refers almost exclusively to technological and material traits, and it appeals to many prehistorians because it consists of the kind of evidence that can most readily be ascertained archaeologically. But of course we know both logically and historically that there were socio-cultural correlates as well: new patterns of political and religious authority, class stratification, division of labor along different lines, newly appearing economic institutions, mechanisms for apportioning wealth. These institutional changes might take differing forms from one early civilization to another —e.g., in the political realm the competing city-states in Sumer contrast with the early unification of authority in Upper and Lower Egypt, a theocratic orientation in Mesopotamia and Egypt seems different from the "secular" appearance of Indus civilization, and so on.

One can evaluate these differences in different ways, and depending on the purpose, one's methods, or inclination, either minimize them or stress the individuality; but it is not difficult to determine that the early civilizations in the Old World, led by the one in Mesopotamia, represented *quantitatively* a new degree of broad-based technological complexity which had emerged in conjunction with the exploitation of certain favored environments. In the Old World these environments seem all to have been large river valleys with arid or semi-arid climates.

· BIBLIOGRAPHIC ESSAY

In recent years a number of general books have appeared that cover in more detail the cultural processes and developments it was possible only to outline here. These include James Mellaart's *Earliest Civilizations of the Near East,* published by McGraw-Hill in 1966, and W. Hallo and W. Simpson's *The Ancient Near East,* published by Harcourt Brace Jovanovich in 1971, as well as *Early Man: Prehistory and the Civilizations of the Near East* by C. G. Starr, published by Oxford University Press in 1973. A good reader covering many aspects of the development of the Near East is C. C. Lamberg-Karlovsky's edited paperback, *Old World Archaeology: Foundations of Civilization,* published by W. H. Freeman in 1972.

Two symposia that would enrich the student's understanding of the enormous changes undergone by ancient Near Eastern peoples are C. H. Kraeling and R. M. Adams' *City Invincible,* published by the University of Chicago Press in 1960, and *Man, Settlement and Urbanism,* edited by Peter J. Ucko, Ruth Tringham, and G. W. Dimbleby and published by Duckworth in 1972.

Two very important books dealing specifically with Mesopotamia are those by Robert M. Adams, *Land Behind Baghdad: A History of Settlement on the Diyala Plains,* and *The Uruk Countryside: The Natural Setting of Urban Societies* (written with Hans Nissen), published by the University of Chicago Press in 1965 and 1972, respectively. Another book by Adams, *The Evolution of Urban Society,* published by Aldine in 1966, is also well worth reading.

For readers interested in grappling with material from other specific areas in the Near East, James Mellaart's two books, *Çatal Hüyük: A Neolithic Town in Anatolia,* published by Thames and Hudson in 1967, and *Excavations at Hacilar,* published by Aldine in 1970, are suggested for Anatolia, as well as Seton Lloyd's *Early Highland Peoples of Anatolia,* published by McGraw-Hill in 1968. Kathleen Kenyon's *Archaeology in the Holy Land,* 3rd edition, published by Praeger in 1970, is a good source on the Levant.

For more detailed information on the whole Near East, the reader is directed to the relevant chapters of the *Cambridge Ancient History,* Volume I, Part I, *Prolegomena and Prehistory,* edited by I. E. S. Edwards, C. J. Gadd, and N. G. L. Hammond and published by Cambridge University Press in 1970.

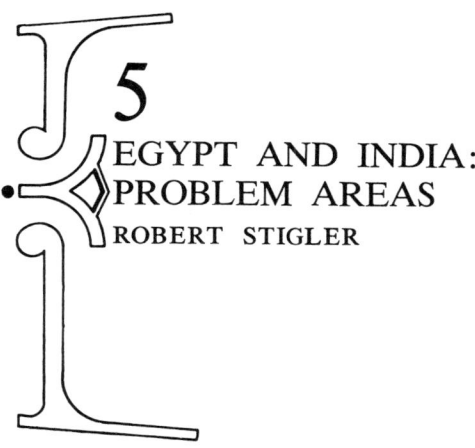

5
EGYPT AND INDIA: PROBLEM AREAS
ROBERT STIGLER

· EGYPT

Seen from the deck of a steamer or photographed by an orbiting satellite, the Nile is like no other river on earth. It snakes its way through a narrow green valley, usually bordered by hills or cliffs and always by stark desert, for more than 1600 miles without a tributary. (See Map 5.1.) Upstream, there are almost 2500 miles more of it, penetrating into the central African lake country and the Ethiopian highlands. The last 800 or so miles, the lower Nile, run through present-day Egypt.

Because the Nile flows northward and all life in its vicinity is totally river-oriented, a somewhat confusing terminology has existed since ancient times. *Down* the river is northward, "above Wadi Halfa" means *south* of the town, and Lower Egypt is north of Upper Egypt.

Between Khartoum, the capital of the Republic of the Sudan, and the town of Aswan about 150 miles north of the modern Sudanese-Egyptian border, a distance of more than 1200 miles on the river, there is a series of six widely spaced cataracts created by exposed low granitic bars running transversely across the river bed. At these cataracts the river is wide, shallow, and turbulent, usually preventing the passage of boats. In between them are long placid reaches. The cataracts still affect river traffic, local economies, and cultural patterns today. Ancient and modern Nubia, until it was flooded out of existence in the 1960's, was the land and peoples between the First and Third Cataracts. Although

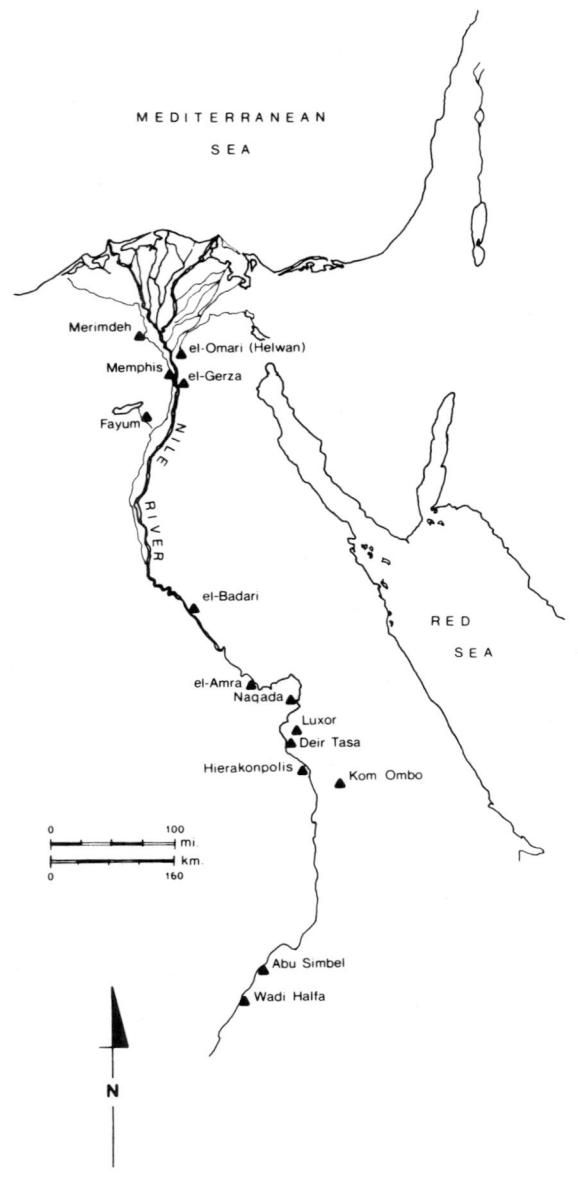

MAP 5.1   Some major archaeological sites in Egypt.

Egypt and India: Problem Areas 129

periodically in ancient Dynastic Egypt the construction of fortresses, monuments such as Abu Simbel, and other relatively minor instances of cultural penetration across the cataract barrier into Nubia and even farther upstream took place, ancient Egypt as a "culture area" consisted essentially of the Nile Valley from the First Cataract at Aswan north to the Mediterranean, an unimpeded reach of the river. "Upper Egypt" was and is the five-hundred-mile stretch from Aswan to the head of the Delta, where present-day Cairo is located, and "Lower Egypt" is the Delta itself, the last northerly 150 miles of territory between Cairo and the sea.

Nile archaeology is beset with problems. Although the present aridity of the North African deserts is a modern phenomenon, at least since Mesolithic times some degree of dryness in the area has forced settlement close to the main stream itself or to related ancient waterways. The annual Nile flood and the deposition of silts have undoubtedly played havoc with many early simple archaeological sites, either washing them away or burying them too deep to recover. Intensive human habitation and cultivation for thousands of years must account for the destruction of additional prehistoric remains.

Finally, to a greater degree than anywhere else in the Near East, there has been a simple neglect by archaeologists of the surviving *prehistoric* remains here. Altogether we have a very inadequate picture of the Neolithic in the Nile Valley, a situation which may or may not be correctable in the future. (See Chart 5.1.)

Mesolithic Indications

At present the most that can be said about the Mesolithic period in most of Egypt is that there is one known occurrence of a Natufian-like industry at the site of Helwan (el-Omari) on the right bank of the Nile just south of Cairo. This is the southernmost known occurrence of specifically Natufian types of microliths, but the distance from other sites of that culture is actually not very great—about 230 miles in a direct line to Beidha in southern Jordan. Natufian sites can be very simple and unprepossessing, and it is certainly possible that others on the lower Nile have been destroyed or overlooked, although before too many assumptions

	FOURTH DYNASTY	Great Pyramid of Cheops
	2680 B.C.	
	THIRD DYNASTY	First or Step Pyramid of Zoser
Unification of Lower and Upper Egypt	**SECOND DYNASTY**	
	FIRST DYNASTY	Mastabas
	3200 B.C.	
Mesopotamian Elements Appear	**GERZEAN**	Well-Made Trench Tombs
	3600 B.C.	
First Settlement on Valley Floor	**AMRATIAN**	Wattle-and-Daub Houses and Simple Pit or Trench Burials
	3800 B.C.	
Settlements on Hills Overlooking Valley	**TASIAN-BADARIAN**	
	4000 B.C.	
Introduction of Agriculture	**FAYUM A**	Crude Shelters at Merimdeh
	4400 B.C.	
	HELWAN MESOLITHIC	

CHART 5.1   Outline of Neolithic development in Egypt.

Egypt and India: Problem Areas 131

are made on this score it should be pointed out that the riverine flora and fauna in Egypt were considerably different from those of Palestine and the coast to the north, and any Mesolithic adaptation here can be expected to have taken at least somewhat different forms from the typical Natufian. Helwan was excavated many years ago, and all we know of the Natufian-like occupation is the presence of similar microlith types. The site is totally undated and floats freely in the charts of different archaeologists (there being a lot of empty time around it); but in southwest Asia the Natufian seems to have been a very brief period, however significant, and is dated to the late tenth and early ninth millennia B.C.. Whatever the date for Helwan may be, there follows a total blank in the archaeological record in the lower Nile Valley until the middle of the *fifth* millennium B.C.

But recent work in Upper Egypt and Nubia, growing out of the archaeological salvage program that was undertaken in the early 1960's behind the new Aswan Dam construction, has shown us the presence of several extraordinarily early microlithic stone industries both above and below the town of Aswan itself. These industries have been termed Final Stone Age in the Africa-based terminology employed, but they might well qualify for the designation Mesolithic used in other parts of the world. If so, they are the oldest known Mesolithic cultures.

At least one of these industries, the Halfan, goes back to c. 17,000 B.C. and is found as far north as Kom Ombo in Egypt and to some distance south of the now-drowned town of Wadi Halfa in the Sudan. Another of the industries, the Qadan, centered in Nubia, is dated back to 12,500 B.C. and is associated with other extremely interesting features. First, a number of the microliths themselves have a sheen or "polish" along one edge, which presumably comes from their repeated use in cutting cereal grasses, the same as the sickle blades of the Palestinian Natufian. Furthermore, the Qadan assemblage includes large flat grinding stones accompanied by smaller hand-held mullers, also a feature of the Natufian. This is not to imply that the two are related, for the dates on the Qadan are at least two to three thousand years older than the Natufian, a remarkably ancient adaptation of this kind.

It is often suggested that the Natufians in the Jordan Valley and vicinity were reaping wild emmer wheat now known to have grown wild there, but so far there is no evidence that any of the southwest Asian grasses (wheats or barley) were indigenous to the Nile Valley. Other seed-bearing grasses, however, may well have been. In addition to grinding wild seeds, grains, or other vegetal food, the Qadan peoples fished the river and hunted wild cattle, gazelle, hartebeest, hippopotamus, and hyena.

These early microlithic industries of Nubia, here considered Mesolithic, lasted quite late in southern Egypt and the northern Sudan, even into the fourth millennium B.C. They do not provide any evidence, however, at least as yet, of having given rise to food-production itself, as the southwestern Asian Mesolithic cultures did. Hence they may be regarded as a kind of false dawn of the Mesolithic era.

The Egyptian Neolithic
The Egyptian Neolithic (see Figure 5.1) has traditionally been divided into five periods—the Fayum, Tasian, Badarian, Amratian, and Gerzean—of which the second and third can be combined into one.

THE FAYUM   The first evidence of early agricultural peoples in the Nile Valley was discovered in the 1920's by the English archaeologist Gertrude Caton-Thompson in the Fayum Depression some twenty miles west of the Nile, about forty miles south of Cairo. The Fayum is an ancient lake bed, itself the relic of an ancient course of the river. In the Neolithic period the lake was larger than in modern times, and close to a former shoreline located higher up on the slopes of the depression Caton-Thompson found the remains of settlements of Neolithic farmers. That they hunted and fished in an environment still lusher than that of today is shown by fish-hooks, a harpoon, projectile points, and wild animal remains, but they also kept domesticated sheep, goats, cattle, and pigs and grew domestic emmer wheat and barley, which they stored in basketry-lined pits. Traces of linen cloth were found, and simple pottery, adequately made but without obvious affilia-

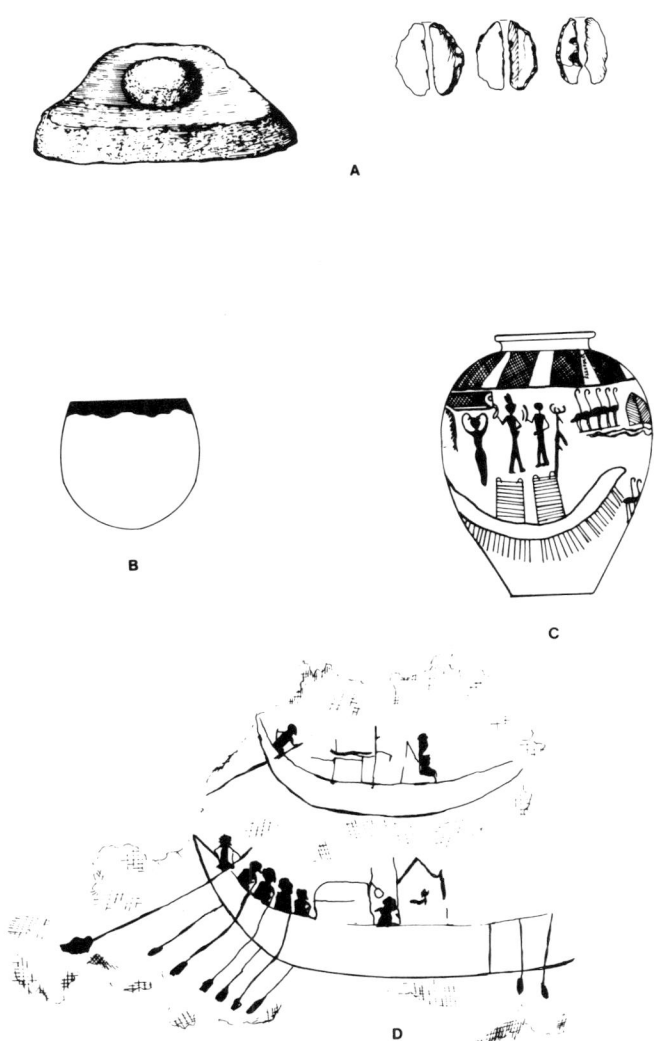

FIGURE 5.1 Mesolithic and Neolithic artifacts of the Nile Valley. *(A)* Stone grinder, and microlithic sickle blades with edges polished by use, from the Qadan culture of Nubia. *(B)* Badarian "black-top" ware. *(C)* Gerzean jar—note rowed boat with "cabins" and "totemic" standard. *(D)* Gerzean textile fragment with painted figures of boats.

tions to other (Near Eastern) styles of the times. House remains were nonexistent, leading to the conclusion that in the benevolent climate nothing more than tents or other flimsy shelters were necessary. The most specific links of this "Fayum A" culture to the rest of the world are the domestic animals and plants. None of the wild forebears of the domestic sheep, goats, pigs, and wheat present were indigenous to Egypt or any other parts of Africa and hence must have derived from southwest Asia. The stone tools, however, are considered to be more in the lithic traditions of the Saharan and North African regions than those of southwest Asia.

Radiocarbon determinations push the age of the Fayum Neolithic back to c. 4400 B.C. at the earliest. Not many miles away in Palestine, four thousand years of town life had already passed by this time. This is what is meant by the inexplicable lateness and simplicity of the Egyptian Neolithic.

A site obviously related to this Fayum A culture, and perhaps more typical of the period, was subsequently found not far away in the earlier levels of an occupational mound at Merimdeh, on slightly raised ground immediately at the edge of the Nile Delta itself, near Cairo. Essentially the same repertory of animals, plants, tools, and other artifacts characterized this assemblage, the difference being that it was a larger settlement, with a feeling of somewhat greater "richness" relatively speaking, and it contained in the related levels structures which show a development from earlier very simple arrangements of poles supporting woven reed screens to the later more substantial houses with walls of packed mud, though still nothing to arouse the envy of a Mesopotamian of the time.

Both these sites can be considered to pertain to Lower Egypt. For the next stages of Neolithic development we must look southward to Upper Egypt, realizing that this most likely reflects the poverty of our knowledge rather than a geographical shift of any historical or cultural significance. We have to piece together the Egyptian Neolithic as best we can.

TASIAN-BADARIAN Most of what we know about the next period comes from grave excavations going back to the days of

Sir Flinders Petrie. At several sites in Upper Egypt, especially at el-Badari near Assiut and at Deir Tasa, there have been found cemeteries containing evidence of one or two distinct cultural groups. At Badari there are two kinds of graves in the same cemetery. Elsewhere there seems to be a partial segregation of the materials. Nowhere is there evidence of archaeological stratification to indicate that the "Tasian" precedes the "Badarian," and there are only a few faintly perceived settlement remains which show the whole group together stratigraphically to underlie the succeeding Amratian period. It therefore seems best at present to speak only of a Tasian-Badarian period.

Several pieces of evidence point to these peoples' living on spurs of higher ground which project into the valley, farming the valley floor with emmer and barley, and keeping cattle, sheep and/or goats, but evidently no pigs. Hunting was still an important subsistence activity. Badarian graves are richer than Tasian ones, containing ivory combs, hammered (i.e., not smelted) native-copper beads, small stone palettes for cosmetics, and other offerings. Not only were humans interred wrapped in textiles, but on occasion domestic animals were given the same treatment. The burial pits, somewhat elongated, are described as trench graves. Badarian pottery contains two very distinctive wares, 1) the so-called "black-top," produced by keeping oxygen away from the insides and rims of the vessels during the process of firing; and 2) "ripple" ware, whose surfaces before firing were first delicately striated with a comb-like device and then highly burnished with a polishing stone, producing a most attractive tactile and visual texture.

Tasian burials contain different pottery, decorated with white paint-filled incisions, and show no evidence of copper, but otherwise there is insufficient evidence all around to establish what might have been merely coexisting burial practices as two separate and successive cultures.

Presumptive dates on this Tasian-Badarian complex would fall in the early fourth millennium, perhaps c. 4000–3800 B.C. It seems still to be a remarkably simple culture, but interesting for certain features such as animal burial and trench graves, which foreshadow later Egyptian developments. (See Figure 5.2.)

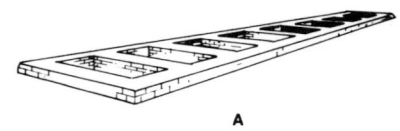

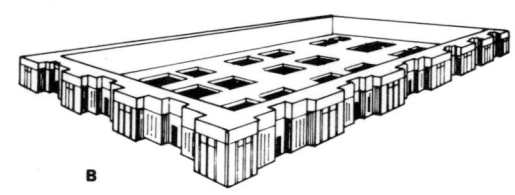

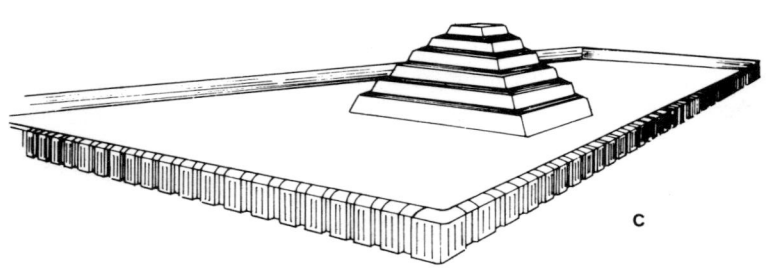

FIGURE 5.2   The development of Egyptian tomb architecture.   *(A)* Late Predynastic compartmented trench tomb.   *(B)* Early Dynastic *mastaba*.   *(C)* The first pyramid, the Step Pyramid of Zoser.

Egypt and India: Problem Areas 137

The two remaining prehistoric periods in Egypt have been given various names:
    Amratian = Naqada I = Early Predynastic
    Gerzean = Naqada II = Late Predynastic.

AMRATIAN The Amratian culture, named after the village of el-Amra, is also well represented at the larger site of Naqada, both on the west bank not far north of Luxor. These apparently were the first people to live on the valley floor itself, but the Naqada settlement was still a simple one, scarcely three hundred feet in diameter and consisting of simple wattle-and-daub or reed-and-mud structures. Known settlements and cemeteries of the Amratian period are more numerous than those of the Tasian-Badarian, perhaps indicating an expansion of population, but from all the evidence a simple peasant-village economy still prevailed, based on barley-wheat and cattle-sheep-goats. The common practice of scratching various animal figures on pottery has been called "totemic" and thought perhaps to foreshadow the use of similar emblems in Dynastic times to mark local political or territorial divisions.

Exceptionally well-made flint implements are present, developed from a tradition traceable back to Fayum A and earlier Saharan times. In pottery black-top ware continued, and new styles were invented, but on the whole the quality of pottery declined as finer alabaster and other stone vessels were increasingly produced. Native copper cold-hammered into trinkets, pins, etc., continued as the only form of "metallurgy," occurring in such small quantities that even Egyptologists mostly refrain from employing the term Chalcolithic. Burial practices generally followed the Badarian pattern, though a few of the trench graves were now walled with mud plaster. Drawings of boats indicate that sailless rowed vessels constructed of papyrus reeds were used on the river at least by this time.

By projecting back from the fairly secure later historical chronology, the Amratian period can be dated approximately from 3800 to 3600 B.C.

Up until the end of the Amratian there are no specific elements in the Egyptian Neolithic which indicate connections with the rest of the Near East in southwest Asia, other than the domesticated plants and animals of provenience there. These, of course, are highly important exceptions, but otherwise, both in form and content and in size and quality, the Fayum A, Badarian, and Amratian remains are distinctive. If they show any affiliations, these are of a rather generalized African nature. This latter situation continues into Dynastic times, when, for example, pharaonic rule has been compared in form with the historical kingdoms of the Upper Nile and West Africa, known from later times but perhaps of earlier origin, and contrasted on the other hand with political institutions in Mesopotamia and elsewhere in southwest Asia. But in the Late Predynastic Gerzean period there is some concrete evidence, as well as evidence of a more abstract nature, showing contacts and influences from Asia. (See Figure 5.3.)

GERZEAN The Gerzean takes its name from el-Gerza, technically in Upper Egypt but actually quite far north, on the left bank of the Nile at the latitude of the Fayum Depression, about forty-five miles south of Cairo. Gerzean remains, however, extend to the south, where they are well represented, for example, at Naqada, overlying Amratian ones; farther south, as in the Aswan area, the Gerzean style never did replace the Amratian. In the north, far beyond any known Amratian occurrences, the Gerzean is distributed right up to the Delta area, which was itself at the time occupied by a somewhat different cultural entity.

In several respects the Gerzean can be seen as an outgrowth of Amratian culture. Black-top ware and stone vessels continued in the same tradition, as did trench graves—which were now regularly plastered, and in some cases fitted with compartments, built-in benches or ledges, and other features. Gerzean houses were more substantially but still quite simply built, of mud, straw, and reeds. Hunting by this time became a minimal subsistence activity.

But a number of rather more striking technological developments and advances, or importations, characterize the period. Larger rowed papyrus boats with cabins evolved from simpler Amratian types, and a different type, with a sail, also appears in drawings. Egyptian faience (the misnomer is derived in a tortuous

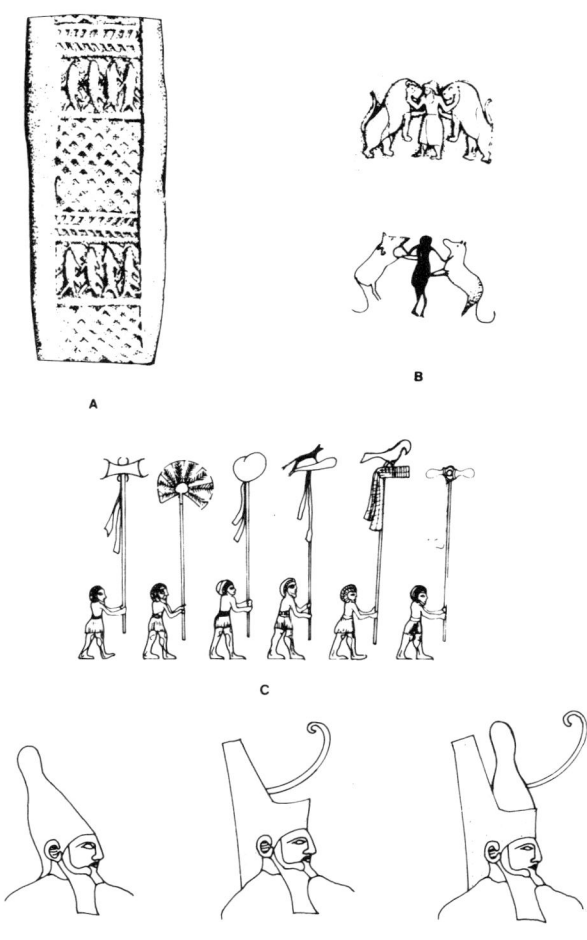

FIGURE 5.3 The Late Predynastic and Early Dynastic periods in Egypt. *(A)* Rolled-out impression of Mesopotamian Warka-like cylinder seal found in Gerzean cemetery. *(B)* Late Predynastic bone carving and textile painting, both showing a typical Mesopotamian motif of a man dominating two lions. *(C)* Artist's reconstruction of standard bearers; the standards possibly represent totem-derived emblems of the nomes. *(D)* The crowns of Upper and Lower Egypt, and their combination after unification.

way from glazed earthenware made since medieval times in Faenza in Italy; the French termed it "faience" and then applied the same name to a quite different substance from ancient Egypt) was undoubtedly a local Gerzean invention, later to be made much use of in scarabs, *ushabti* figures, and the like.

The finely flaked flint work of earlier Badarian and Amratian times continued, but *cast* copper knives, daggers, and axes were made as well. Lead and silver from southwest Asia and lapis lazuli from Afghanistan turn up in locally made objects. Most tellingly, an Egyptian copy of a Mesopotamian cylinder seal of Warka type (c. 3500 B.C.) was found in a Gerzean grave at Naqada. In short, while the period saw a definite expansion of local technology and the probable emergence of a variety of town-dwelling artisans and craftsmen, trade and contacts with the much more advanced cultures of southwest Asia, including Mesopotamia and beyond, were taking place, seemingly for the first time.

Also probably for the first time the valley floor was completely tilled. It is hopeless to expect to find archaeological evidence of irrigation or flood control dating to Gerzean or earlier times, but the Nile more than any other river requires prediction and manipulation, and it is almost a certainty that by now some form of hydraulic control was well under way.

The later Dynastic written sources indicate that by Late Predynastic times two parallel lineages of "kings" ruled Upper and Lower Egypt respectively, and that these kings had contrasting totems and wore different regalia, notably crowns of different color and shape. There is no contemporary (Gerzean) archaeological evidence to bear this out, at least as an overriding political characteristic of the times, and it seems more likely that a series of chieftainships from Aswan to the Delta constituted the effective political organization of the Gerzean period. A chieftainship would probably have consisted of a small town center and adjacent villages, with a distinctive totem-derived emblem, and the chief might either have been also a priest or have had priests with him in the administration of the territory. There is no reason not to identify these chieftainships with the "nomes" of the time of unification, c. 3200 B.C., and later; but unfortunately all of these socio-cultural and institutional aspects of the period can only be

Egypt and India: Problem Areas   141

reconstructed by speculation until more is known about the archaeology of the Gerzean. The dates for the period are from c. 3600 to c. 3200 B.C.

Entry into the Historical Period

As we understand it today, the pattern of the entry of Egypt into the civilized, literate, historical period is wholly at variance with that of Mesopotamia. Ancient Egyptian historians credit one man with setting the process in motion by unifying Upper and Lower Egypt. While many modern Egyptologists think the unification more likely to have been a slightly longer process, over two or three generations, it is apparent that from shortly after 3200 B.C. the iconography, the accounts of the times, and all the other evidence indicate the presence of a succession of strong, effective, and individual rulers over all of Upper and Lower Egypt.

The mythologized later accounts of the period do not allow us even to be sure of the name of the first Pharaoh (a later title), whether he was "Menes," "Narmer," or another person designated by the "Rosette-Scorpion" hieroglyph; and the political activities of this First, Second, and Third Dynasty "Archaic" period from around 3200 to 2680 B.C. are equally hazy, although the unification itself seems to have comprised the incorporation of the twenty-two nomes of Upper Egypt and the twenty of the Delta under the now-double crown.

What is clearer is that the Archaic period witnessed an explosion of technological advance, with evidence that Mesopotamian influences played an even larger part in the developments. The hieroglyphic system of writing is first found just at the end of Predynastic times, engraved on portable slate tablets. It appears fully developed from the beginning, containing pictographic, ideographic, and phonetic elements together, unlike the early stages of cuneiform in Mesopotamia, which underwent a rapid evolution from pictographs to an ideograph-*cum*-phonetic system, as most other forms of writing are known to have done. Most linguists and some Egyptologists agree that this instantaneous birth of a mature system can only have been the result of an awareness of cuneiform, made likely by the presence of other Mesopotamian elements.

THE OLD WORLD

Gerzean trench graves came above-ground in Dynasties I and II, taking the form of large and elaborately compartmented *mastabas,* built of the first mold-made sun-dried bricks in Egypt, all earlier mud architecture being of *pisé* or *"tuf."* The elaborate pilaster-facades of these structures, however, are often considered to be an echo of Mesopotamian temple architecture, showing the same general type of feature. By the Third Dynasty in the twenty-eighth or twenty-seventh century B.C., the huge Step Pyramid of Zoser was constructed of stone by Imhotep, who invented pyramid architecture by piling six *mastabas* atop one another. The architectural progress from puddled-mud huts, within about five hundred years, was enormous.

Wheeled vehicles appear only from the sixteenth century B.C. in Egypt, the lateness undoubtedly being due to the convenience of the river for travel and transport, plus constant occasions to shuttle back and forth across it. But this item and a lack of large urban centers are the only two traits at variance with V. G. Childe's checklist of the features he took as the criteria of "civilization."

Students of modern cities have not yet managed to standardize a city-town-village terminology with objective definitions, and prehistorians are even worse off. One respectable archaeologist has called Pre-pottery Neolithic Jericho a "city" and a "civilization." At the other extreme it has been called a large village. Another authority has answered that it is none of these and that it is not a town either: it is an *agro-town.*

Egyptologists speak of "capital cities" in the Dynastic period, at the same time pointing to the lack of urbanization. The capitals, Memphis, Hierakonpolis, etc., were perhaps no more than politico-religious or ceremonial centers without sizable secular populations. The question is controversial. There is no physical evidence indicating anything like Ur, Eridu, or Lagash, or Mohenjodaro on the Indus, or Anyang, Tenochtitlan, or Cuzco, but some archaeologists assert that the cities are surely there, under the Nile silts. On the other hand, the geography of the Nile is so peculiar, so *linear,* and transportation, while slow, is so easy, that it does seem entirely conceivable that these factors militated against the growth of large clusters of population, even when the existing institutions would have brought them about in a different setting.

Egypt and India: Problem Areas 143

What seems to have been a basically African, or non-Asian, form of society arose in the lower Nile Valley from at least 4500 B.C., reaching its first climax toward the end of the fourth millennium. At both ends of this continuum there is evidence of southwest Asian contributions. Especially around 3000 B.C. it is possible that these contributions accelerated the pace of development, although the specific material instances are no more than artistic motifs and themes, ceremonial objects, and traded raw materials. An Egyptian *awareness* and knowledge of Mesopotamia was probably much more important than the material objects themselves; but in any event the elements present in the Nile Valley at that time, whatever their origins, were, in a unique environment, molded into a unique civilization.

· INDIA

As shown at all points in its cultural history, the Indian subcontinent is something of a world in itself. Some periods show stronger links with outside areas and cultures, others weaker ones, but at all times a distinctive stamp appears, or is quickly given, to cultural development in the area. One would expect no less, the distinctiveness being logically a result, at least to a large degree, of the relative geographic isolation of the subcontinent. This isolation derives from the desert, the jungle, and above all the huge mountain chains that separate India-Pakistan from Iran to the west, central Asia and Tibet to the north, and Burma and southeast Asia to the east.

Although the subcontinent itself is immensely varied in its topography, climate is something of a unifying factor. The prevailing heat and the rain systems, induced by the mountain barriers against cold winds from the north and by the surrounding warm waters of the Indian Ocean, have surely played a role in bringing about a series of local cultural adaptations differing from those of the rest of the continental mass and subject only to occasional injections of outside influence. In a general way the process is analogous to that of prehistoric cultural development in Africa.

As in the case of Africa, for more than a decade archaeological work on the Indian subcontinent has come to reflect its distinctiveness by the adoption of an archaeological terminology different from the prevailing one used elsewhere in the Old World. For the stages of cultural development prior to the appearance of the agricultural Neolithic, the terms Early, Middle, and Late Stone Ages have come increasingly to be employed in recent years. While these terms may be partly a result of archaeological fashion, they also indicate some substantive differences from the outside world in those periods. Consequently no one-to-one correlation is possible, but in general the "Early Stone Age" in India-Pakistan can be taken as the stage parallel to the Lower and Middle Paleolithic elsewhere, the "Middle Stone Age" to the Middle and Upper Paleolithic, and the "Late Stone Age" to the Mesolithic. While more exact equivalents are either very complex or impossible, they are of no moment to us now, since this chapter is primarily concerned only with the Neolithic and subsequent periods. However, some general comments on this "Stone Age" background to the Neolithic are first necessary here.

Background to the Neolithic
The Late Stone Age or Mesolithic cultures of India-Pakistan are extremely widespread and populous and seem to represent a hunting-fishing-gathering exploitation of a rich natural environment. Many of the stone tools and weapons employed consisted of microliths set in composite implements, similar to worldwide Mesolithic practice.

In southwest Asia and Europe the local Mesolithic cultures indisputably developed out of the terminal Pleistocene Upper Paleolithic, and a number of Indian and Pakistani archaeologists likewise view the microlithic Late Stone Age assemblages of the subcontinent as arising locally from the cultures of the Middle Stone Age. But the Middle Stone Age in India-Pakistan is as yet very poorly known; while perhaps parallel in time or as a stage, it seems very unlike the Upper Paleolithic elsewhere, and furthermore the nature of the transition to Late Stone Age times is very unclear. Consequently, other archaeologists prefer to regard the microlithic Late Stone Age of the subcontinent as having been derived mainly from outside the area, specifically from the Mesolithic of southwest Asia.

In any event, while the dating of the period in India-Pakistan is still tentative, it appears at present to go back no farther than the fifth millennium B.C., i.e., later than its counterparts to the west.

The larger question, however, is the relation of the India-Pakistan Late Stone Age or Mesolithic to the rise of food-production on the subcontinent. A number of years ago Robert Braidwood suggested the possibility that the area at this time may have been part of a larger *oikumene,* including southwest Asia, throughout which intensive food collectors were experimenting or drifting into new relationships with potentially domesticable *local* animal and plant species. The details of this process are just now coming to light in southwest Asia, but it is much too early to attempt to prove the same thing for India-Pakistan, since the links between the Mesolithic and the Neolithic are still missing from the archaeological record here, not to mention the detailed faunal and floral records necessary.

Because for many years the best-known Neolithic materials on the subcontinent have come from the northwest and have shown certain affiliations with southwest Asia, an aura of interpretation has grown up around the whole of India-Pakistan derived from that northwestern subsection. But many basic questions concerning the origins or advent of early agriculture in different parts of the whole subcontinent remain not only to be answered but even to be asked. While present discussion of the Neolithic must be based largely on a one-sided body of information, such factors as the recent surprising discovery in south*east* Asia of remarkably early agriculture, as well as the large amount of work yet to be done throughout India, suggest that the picture we have today may eventually be greatly modified. The recent recognition of a major independent agricultural tradition in sub-Saharan Africa might well provide a cautionary example to the Indo-Pakistani archaeologist.

The Neolithic
South of the giant mountain ranges the Indian subcontinent is conventionally sub-divided geographically into 1) the Indo-Gangetic plains created by the two great rivers of Pakistan and India,

and 2) the geologically ancient low plateau of "Peninsular" India farther to the south. Because of limitations of space, the only portion of this vast area which can be discussed systematically here is the Indus Valley and immediately adjacent regions. The least that can be said is that the basic elements of what is commonly meant by Neolithic culture appear to us today to have been present first in this northwestern periphery of the subcontinent, and they seem to have been the result of diffusion from southwest Asia. Map 5.2 shows the major sites.

BALUCHISTAN The earliest dated farming communities known to be of direct relevance to the subcontinent proper are located in Baluchistan, the rough mountain-and-hill-country of western Pakistan, which extends over into both Iran and Afghanistan. Topographically this hill country of Baluchistan is intermediate between the Iranian plateau and the broad expanse of Sind, the flat alluvial valley of the lower Indus River. Baluchistan itself is ecologically varied: on the whole it is arid, with much barren land, but a number of small valleys are well-watered. *Extensive* tracts of watered or irrigable farm land do not appear.

Within the last three to four decades a growing number of Neolithic sites and "cultures" have been uncovered in northern and central Baluchistan, ranging from c. 3500 B.C. onward. Many of the sites have not been dated directly, and taken as a whole the body of data indicates that these locally early Neolithic cultures represent a variety of micro-adaptations to the ecologically diverse region, so that it is difficult to arrange them simply in a chronological or developmental sequence; but some can be singled out as representative.

The site of Kile Gul Mohammad in the Quetta Valley of northeastern Baluchistan is a cornerstone of the Baluchistan Neolithic, providing the earliest carbon-14 dates for the period in all of India-Pakistan as well as containing some of the simplest materials in its first phase. This earliest phase (KGM I) at the site lacks pottery but contains evidence that a Neolithic people living in a small settlement of simple *pisé* houses reaped grain and kept goats, sheep, and cattle. The *end* of this phase is dated to c. 3500 B.C., and the excavator estimates that the beginning may go back to 4000.

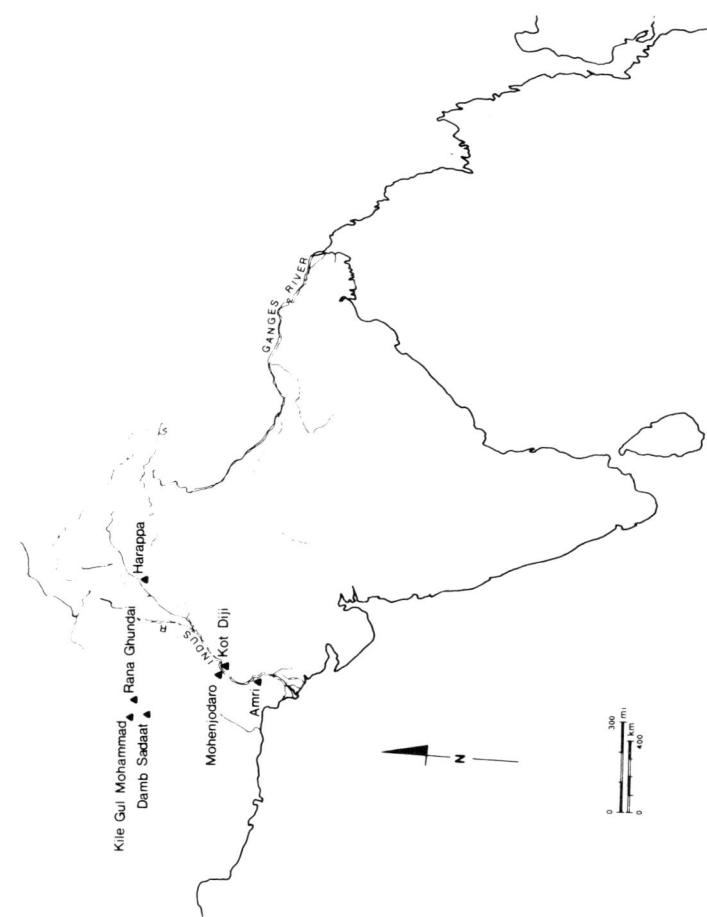

MAP 5.2 Sites in Baluchistan and the Indus Valley.

In Phase II a crude, basket-marked pottery as well as mud bricks are added. Phase III sees the introduction of wheel-made pottery with painted designs which have analogies westward via Afghanistan to the Iranian plateau and ultimately to Mesopotamia. The story does not rest alone on Kile Gul Mohammad, of course; other later fourth millennium and third millennium sites abound in central and northern Baluchistan: Damb Sadaat, Rana Ghundai, those of the Zhob, and others. In the phase following Kile Gul Mohammad III, pottery with extremely fine decoration appears.

From the beginning to the end of this Neolithic sequence in central and northern Baluchistan, there is a steady growth in the size and quality of settlements and in the refinements of artifact production down to perhaps 2500 B.C. But though some of the later sites are moderately impressive in their extent—up to fifteen acres—it is principally in pottery that the successive elaboration shows best at present. While the stylistic connections of this pottery tradition rest on intricate site-to-site comparisons, they overwhelmingly point to the Iranian plateau as their place of origin.

Although this series, as it grows, compares favorably with the Neolithic sequence in the Nile Valley discussed earlier in this chapter, one gets the feeling that in its continuing presumed dependence on outside stimuli, and in its continuing *relative* simplicity, it does not prepare us for the emergence sometime after 2500 B.C. of the Bronze Age civilization of the Indus Valley nearby. Walter Fairservis, whose familiarity with the problems of this area and these times is second to none, has put forth a cogent line of reasoning concerning this problem. He sees first the settlement of northern and central Baluchistan by simple food producers, perhaps at first more pastoral than agricultural, followed by the increasing development of a locally adapted and well-established agricultural system. Rainfall patterns and the nature of the country facilitated this process. At a certain point in the sequence some of these peoples moved into southern Baluchistan, which has direct access to the Indus Valley.

Southern Baluchistan is more arid than the center or the north. Small rivers flow and torrential rains occur, but the water is less available naturally to vegetation here than it is under the different geographic and regime conditions farther north. Here in the south

Egypt and India: Problem Areas 149

the local manifestations of the Nal and ultimately the Kulli cultures seem to represent late Neolithic (c. 2500 B.C.) derivatives from Kile Gul Mohammad-like sources, with the addition of an agricultural system employing dams on smaller rivers and terrace-like arrangements on the run-off slopes for purposes of impounding or retaining water. Of no great scope, these devices nevertheless became part of an agricultural technology which was a preparation for coping with the greater hydraulic problems of the Indus Valley itself, once the great alluvial plain began to be settled and farmed.

Fairservis believes that a number of other features in the assemblages of these later cultures show a growing independence of invention and less reliance on southwest Asian motifs and styles.

Two partial analogies may be drawn here. First, this eminently reasonable reconstruction resembles the situation in Mesopotamia with the descent from the hilly flanks into the Tigris-Euphrates valleys. In Baluchistan the Neolithic cultures developed much further than those of northeastern Iraq (Jarmo) before the descent began, but a comparison of the fertility of the two upland areas would probably explain that difference. The other analogy is with the Nile Valley. There is nothing in Pakistan like the elaborate Ubaid and Warka cultures of Mesopotamia in "late Neolithic" times. If such comparisons are valid at all, the Baluchistan sequence (and what is known of the pre-Indus sites in the valley itself) appear more on the order and scale of the Neolithic in the Nile Valley, and again we are left with a presently rather inexplicable cultural explosion, around 2300 B.C., unsupported by what would appear to be an adequate previous development.

This is not, of course, to suggest that some romantic archaeological mystery exists or that some unheralded burst of creative genius wrought civilization out of nothing. Rather, the problematical aspects of the emergence of civilization in both the Nile and Indus valleys derive from the current state of archaeological knowledge. The first features of an ancient culture that we learn about are the material remains—artifacts, architecture, etc. At a subsequent level of greater sophistication we can place these in an environmental context and ecological relationship. Less open to our inspection at present are such intangible aspects of ancient cultures as the social, economic, and political systems which in-

150   THE OLD WORLD

formed them. Archaeology everywhere is only beginning to devise means to understand these cultural features.

Under the circumstances it seems only reasonable to suppose that, despite the contrast in the *material* remains across the Neolithic-Bronze Age time-line, in both the Indus and Nile valleys in late Neolithic times social, economic, and political innovations with a material or ecological basis were taking place that account for the momentous changes to come. Archaeology has not yet perceived these innovations satisfactorily, but one of its major tasks is to do so.

THE INDUS VALLEY   By 2300 B.C. a full-fledged, literate, Bronze Age civilization arose in the Indus Valley. Authorities are split in designating this civilization the Indus or the Harappan, but the term Harappan Civilization appears to be gaining in preference. In geographical extent this was the largest of the four "primal" civilizations of the Old World—Egypt, Mesopotamia, the Indus, and China—stretching some thousand miles along the great alluvial river valley.

The Indus, one of the world's most enormous rivers, is fed principally by the snows of the giant mountain ranges to the north but significantly by rainfall as well. Its volume is twice that of the Nile, and like the Nile it carries a heavy burden of silt, which it deposits in an alluvial plain extending from the Punjab to the sea. Unlike the Nile Valley, the Indus Valley is not closely confined but rather is bordered by the foothills of Baluchistan at varying distances to the west and by arid desert to the east. The floodplain of the river is consequently immense, and flooding is a major factor in any extensive agricultural cultivation of the valley. Hydraulic works and devices are a necessary concomitant to such cultivation.

At least two pre-Harappan occupations of the valley, which in one way or another can be seen as a prelude to the civilization to come, may be singled out for notice.

The first is the site of Amri, on a low gravel terrace just above the cultivated alluvium, at the base of foothills which at this latitude extend eastward close to the river. The site itself is subject to flooding today. The settlement was that of a small village

Egypt and India: Problem Areas 151

which developed through several phases. The earliest contains wheel-made pottery with painted decoration showing clear relations to the later Neolithic wares of central and northern Baluchistan. Of equal significance is the fact that the Neolithic levels of the site are overlain by an occupation of the Harappan period. From the earliest times onward the inhabitants kept cattle, sheep, goats, and donkeys, but the hunting of wild game was also important to the diet. Although direct evidence of plant foods is absent, presumably the inhabitants of Amri cultivated wheat and barley as is documented for the later Harappans. Amri represents the earliest (late though it is) Neolithic occupation of the Indus Valley proper and shows both its derivation from the Baluchistan hill country and the stratigraphic succession to Harappa.

Kot Diji, upstream and on the left bank of the Indus in Upper Sind, is another small site of the late Neolithic period; in fact its pottery shows it to be simply a variant of that of Amri. Here too the site eventually saw a Harappa-period occupation, but even more important is the evidence of Kot Diji-type materials at the base of the great site of Harappa itself, in the Punjab. If this Amri-Kot Diji occupation of the alluvial valley can be taken as having entered from the southwest, the presence of a Kot Diji settlement as far to the north as Harappa bespeaks a significant spread of Neolithic peoples into the valley in pre-Harappan times. But at present little more can be said about this phenomenon.

Harappan Civilization
Although it sometimes has been treated as a "prehistoric" culture, because the Indus script has never been deciphered, in form the Harappan culture belongs together with those of Pharaonic Egypt and the city-states of Sumer, the Bronze Age civilizations whose description is outside the province of this book. (See Figure 5.4.) But a few observations may be made to conclude this chapter.

As in the case of Egypt, the preceding Neolithic sequence has been viewed as too brief and unwontedly simple, at least in the material manifestations, to account satisfactorily at present for the complex cultural developments that followed virtually immediately. Furthermore, some kind of dependence on southwest Asia is assumed, not only for the Neolithic cultures but into early

FIGURE 5.4 Artifacts of Baluchistan and the Indus Valley. *(A)* Nal ware from Baluchistan. *(B)* Clay model of ox-drawn cart, Harappan culture. *(C)* Harappan jar. *(D)* and *(E)* Stone seals of the Harappan culture, showing characters of the Indus script.

Egypt and India: Problem Areas 153

Bronze Age times as well. In the case of the Egyptian Neolithic this debt to southwest Asia seems primarily to rest in the plants and animals which formed the core of domestication in the Nile Valley, while a handful of trade objects and some vague stylistic resemblances at the outset of Dynastic times have been credited with symbolizing a process of stimulus diffusion which triggered the explosion of civilization.

In Pakistan, in the absence of good evidence concerning domesticates in the Neolithic, pottery relations to southwest Asia have been stressed. Again, trade objects with Mesopotamia at the beginning of Harappan times, a few stylistic parallels, and a domesticated fauna and flora which might or might not be indigenous have also been pointed to as continuing evidence of influences from farther west.

Both these interpretations may well turn out to be the story, and there is no intention in this chapter to attempt to create a controversy where no grounds for one exist at present; but it can be pointed out that both the Nile Valley and the Indus Valley are backed by vast territories, Africa and the Indian subcontinent, whose relations to the valleys themselves are as yet far from clear. The full picture will not be known until these contexts are provided.

· BIBLIOGRAPHIC ESSAY

The great majority of books on ancient Egypt deal more with the Dynastic periods than with the prehistoric, but W. C. Hayes' *Most Ancient Egypt,* published by the University of Chicago Press in 1965, can be profitably read, as can W. Hallo and W. Simpson's *The Ancient Near East,* published by Harcourt Brace Jovanovich in 1971 (the first half of this work deals with Mesopotamia).

Two volumes by Cyril Aldred, *The Egyptians,* published by Praeger in 1961, and *Egypt to the End of the Old Kingdom,* published by Mc-Graw-Hill in 1966, also give good standard coverage. Walter Emery's *Archaic Egypt,* published by Penguin in 1961, concentrates on the vital Late Predynastic and Early Dynastic phases of Nile culture. One of the very few strictly anthropological treatments of prehistoric Egypt is Bruce Trigger's short but very rewarding book, *Beyond History: The Methods of Prehistory,* published by Holt, Rinehart and Winston in 1968.

The massive and often quite technical two-volume set, *The Prehistory of Nubia,* edited by Fred Wendorf and published by Southern Methodist University Press in 1968, does not deal directly with Egypt proper, but parts of the work have considerable relevance to the area.

For the archaeology of the Indian subcontinent the reader is directed to the recent and outstanding book by Walter A. Fairservis, *The Roots of Ancient India,* published by Macmillan in 1971. Another excellent work is Sir Mortimer Wheeler's *The Indus Civilization,* 3rd edition, published by Cambridge University Press in 1968. A view of Pakistani-Indian archaeology from a different standpoint is provided by S. C. Malik in *Indian Civilization: The Formative Period,* published by the Indian Institute of Advanced Study in 1968; Malik is critical of many of the more standard interpretations. Finally, a worthwhile collection of articles covering India and Pakistan, as well as outlying areas such as Nepal, Afghanistan, and Sri Lanka, appears in *South Asian Archaeology,* edited by Norman Hammond and published by Noyes Press in 1973.

COMPLETE BIBLIOGRAPHY

Adams, R. M., 1965, *Land Behind Baghdad: A History of Settlement on the Diyala Plains,* University of Chicago Press, Chicago.

———, 1966, *The Evolution of Urban Society,* Aldine, Chicago.

Adams, R. M., and H. J. Nissen, 1972, *The Uruk Countryside: The Natural Setting of Urban Societies,* University of Chicago Press, Chicago.

Aldred, C., 1961, *The Egyptians,* Praeger, New York.

———, 1966, *Egypt to the End of the Old Kingdom,* McGraw-Hill, New York.

Binford, L. R., 1968, "Post-Pleistocene Adaptations," *New Perspectives in Archaeology,* S. R. Binford and L. R. Binford, editors, Aldine, Chicago.

Bordaz, J., 1970, *Tools of the Old and New Stone Age,* Natural History Press, Garden City, N. Y.

Bordes, F., 1968, *The Old Stone Age,* McGraw-Hill, New York.

Boule, M., and H. V. Vallois, 1957, *Fossil Men,* Dryden Press, New York.

Braidwood, R. J., and B. Howe, 1960, *Prehistoric Investigations in Iraqi Kurdistan,* Studies in Ancient Oriental Civilization, No. 31, University of Chicago Press, Chicago.

Burkitt, M. C., 1949, *The Old Stone Age,* Cambridge University Press, Cambridge, Eng.

Clark, J. G. D., 1954, *Excavations at Star Carr,* Cambridge University Press, Cambridge, Eng.

Clark, W. E. LeGros, 1964, *Fossil Evidence for Human Evolution,* University of Chicago Press, Chicago.

Cole, S., 1970, *The Neolithic Revolution,* 5th edition, Trustees of the British Museum (Natural History), Publication No. 541, London.

Edwards, I. E. S., C. J. Gadd, and N. G. L. Hammond, editors, 1970, *Cambridge Ancient History,* Volume I, Part I, *Prolegomena and Prehistory,* Cambridge University Press, Cambridge, Eng.
Emery, W., 1961, *Archaic Egypt,* Penguin Books, Baltimore.
Epstein, H., 1972, *The Domestication of Animals in Africa,* Volumes 1 and 2, Africana Press, New York.
Etkin, W., editor, 1964, *Social Behavior and Organization Among Vertebrates,* University of Chicago Press, Chicago.
Fairservis, W. A., 1971, *The Roots of Ancient India,* Macmillan, New York.
Flannery, K., 1965, "The Ecology of Early Food Production in Mesopotamia," *Science,* Vol. 147, pp. 1247–1256.
Flint, R. F., 1971, *Glacial and Quaternary Geology,* John Wiley and Sons, New York.
Hallo, W., and W. Simpson, 1971, *The Ancient Near East,* Harcourt Brace Jovanovich, New York.
Hammond, N., editor, 1973, *South Asian Archaeology,* Noyes Press, Park Ridge, N. J.
Hayes, W. C., 1965, *Most Ancient Egypt,* University of Chicago Press, Chicago.
Higgs, E. S., editor, 1972, *Papers in Economic Prehistory,* Cambridge University Press, New York.
Hole, F., 1968, "Evidence of Social Organization from Western Iran, 8000–4000 B.C.," *New Perspectives in Archaeology,* S. R. Binford and L. R. Binford, editors, Aldine, Chicago.
Hole, F., K. V. Flannery, and J. A. Neely, 1969, *Prehistory and Human Ecology of the Deh Luran Plain,* Memoirs of the Museum of Anthropology, University of Michigan, No. 1, Ann Arbor.
Holloway, Ralph, 1966, "Cranial Capacity, Neural Reorganization and Hominid Evolution: A Search for More Suitable Parameters," *American Anthropologist,* Vol. 68, pp. 103–121.
———, 1967, "The Evolution of the Human Brain: Some Notes Toward a Synthesis Between Neural Structure and the Evolution of Complex Behavior," *General Systems,* Vol. 12, pp. 3–19.
———, 1968, "The Evolution of the Primate Brain: Some Aspects of Quantitative Relationships," *Brain Research,* Vol. 7, pp. 121–172.
———, 1968, "The Human Brain in Evolutionary Perspective," *Readings in Anthropology,* M. Fried, editor, 2nd edition, Vol. I, pp. 215–223, Crown, New York.
———, 1969, "Some Questions on Parameters of Neural Evolution in Primates," *Annals of the New York Academy of Sciences,* Vol. 167, pp. 332–342.

―――, 1970, "Neural Parameters, Hunting and the Evolution of the Human Brain," *Advances in Primatology*, C. R. Norback and W. Montagna, editors, Vol. 1, pp. 299–309, Appleton-Century-Crofts, New York.

―――, 1972, "Australopithecine Endocasts, Brain Evolution in the Hominoidea and a Model of Hominid Evolution," *The Functional and Evolutionary Biology of Primates*, R. Tuttle, editor, pp. 185–204, Aldine, Chicago.

Howell, F. Clark, 1964, "Recent Advances in Human Evolutionary Studies," *Quarterly Review of Biology*, Vol. 42, pp. 471–504.

―――, editor, 1965, *Early Man*, Life Nature Library, Time-Life, Amsterdam.

Howells, W. W., 1973, *Evolution of the Genus Homo*, Addison-Wesley, Reading, Mass.

Jacobs, J., 1969, *The Economy of Cities*, Random House, New York.

Kenyon, K., 1970, *Archaeology in the Holy Land*, 3rd edition, Praeger, New York.

Kraeling, C. H., and R. M. Adams, editors, 1960, *City Invincible*, University of Chicago Press, Chicago.

Lamberg-Karlovsky, C. C., editor, 1972, *Old World Archaeology: Foundations of Civilization*, W. H. Freeman, San Francisco.

Lloyd, S., 1968, *Early Highland Peoples of Anatolia*, McGraw-Hill, New York.

MacCurdy, G. G., 1924, *Human Origins, A Manual of Prehistory*, Volumes 1 and 2, D. Appleton, New York.

Malik, S. C., 1968, *Indian Civilization: The Formative Period*, Indian Institute of Advanced Study, International Publications Service, New York.

Matolsci, J., editor, 1973, *Domestikationsforschung und Geschichte der Haustiere*, Akadémiai Kiadó, Budapest.

Mellaart, J., 1966, *Earliest Civilizations of the Near East*, McGraw-Hill, New York.

―――, 1967, *Çatal Hüyük: A Neolithic Town in Anatolia*, Thames and Hudson, London.

―――, 1970, *Excavations at Hacilar*, Volumes 1 and 2, Aldine, Chicago.

Montagu, M. F. A., editor, 1968, *Culture: Man's Adaptive Dimension*, Oxford University Press, London.

Oakley, K., 1957, *Man the Toolmaker*, Phoenix Books, University of Chicago Press, Chicago.

―――, 1964, *Frameworks for Dating Fossil Man*, Weidenfeld and Nicolson, London. Revised edition, 1968, Aldine, Chicago.

Perkins, D., 1964, "Prehistoric Fauna from Shanidar, Iraq," *Science,* Vol. 144, pp. 1565–1566.

———, 1969, "Fauna of Çatal Hüyük: Evidence for Early Cattle Domestication in Anatolia," *Science,* Vol. 164, pp. 177–179.

Perkins, D., and P. Daly, 1968, "A Hunters' Village in Turkey," *Scientific American,* Vol. 210, No. 5, pp. 96–106.

Pilbeam, D., 1972, *The Ascent of Man,* Macmillan Series in Physical Anthropology, Macmillan, New York.

Poirier, F. E., 1973, *Fossil Man: An Evolutionary Journey,* C. V. Mosby, St. Louis.

Renfrew, J., 1973, *Palaeoethnobotany,* Columbia University Press, New York.

Smith, P. E. L., and T. C. Young, 1973, "The Evolution of Early Agriculture and Culture in Greater Mesopotamia: A Trial Model," *Population Growth: Anthropological Implications,* B. Spooner, editor, M.I.T. Press, Cambridge, Mass.

Starr, C. G., 1973, *Early Man: Prehistory and the Civilizations of the Near East,* Oxford University Press, London.

Time-Life Books Editors, 1972, *The Missing Link,* The Emergence of Man Series, Time-Life, New York.

———, 1973, *The Neanderthals,* The Emergence of Man Series, Time-Life, New York.

Trigger, B., 1968, *Beyond History: The Methods of Prehistory,* Holt, Rinehart and Winston, New York.

Ucko, P. J., and G. W. Dimbleby, editors, 1969, *The Domestication and Exploitation of Plants and Animals,* Aldine, Chicago.

Ucko, P. J., R. Tringham, and G. W. Dimbleby, editors, 1972, *Man, Settlement and Urbanism,* Duckworth, London.

Washburn, S. L., and P. Dolhinow, editors, 1972, *Perspectives on Human Evolution 2,* Holt, Rinehart and Winston, New York.

Wendorf, F., editor, 1968, *The Prehistory of Nubia,* Southern Methodist University Press, Dallas.

Wheeler, M., 1968, *The Indus Civilization,* 3rd edition, Cambridge University Press, Cambridge, Eng.

Wright, G. A., 1969, *Obsidian Analyses and Prehistoric Near Eastern Trade: 7500 to 3500 B.C.,* Museum of Anthropology, University of Michigan Anthropological Papers, No. 37, Ann Arbor.

Zeuner, F. E., 1959, *Dating the Past, An Introduction to Geochronology,* Methuen, London.

———, 1963, *A History of Domesticated Animals,* Hutchinson, London.

INDEX

Abbevillian culture, 55–56
Abbevillian tool types, 49, *50*
Abu Simbel, 128, 129
Acheulian culture, 33, 56
Acheulian tool types, 49
agriculture, and effect on ecology, 74–75; and population increase, 76; *see also* domestication of plants
Ain-Hanech site, 10, 55
Ali Kosh site, 80, 81, 84, 86, 87, 88, 89, 92–93, 99, 120
al-'Ubaid site, 99, 114
Amratian culture, 130, 137–138
Amri site, 147, 150–151
Amuq site, 99, 123
Anatolia, 118, 121–122
animal burial, 135
Arambourg, C., 28
art, *54,* 64, 65, 66, 67, 80, 102, 104
Atlanthropus mauritanicus, 29
Aurignacian culture, 49, 65
Aurignacian tool industry, 32
australopithecines, 14, 16–17, *19,* 20–26, 36, 38–39, 41, 42, 49, 55
Australopithecus, 24, 29, 35
Australopithecus africanus, 19, 20–21, 39

Australopithecus boisei, see Zinjanthropus boisei
Australopithecus robustus, 19, 21, 39
awls, 64

Badarian, *see* Tasian-Badarian period
Baluchistan, 146–150, 152
barley, 84, *85,* 86, 89, 92
baskets, 64
Beidha site, 81, 84, 86, 89, 99, 105, 118, 123
Beldibi Cave site, 99, 118, 122
bipedalism, 21, 36, 38, 40
bladelets, backed, 67
blade tools, 49, *52,* 63–68
boats, papyrus, 137, 138
Bouqras site, 81, 89
Brace, Loring, 31
Braidwood, Robert, 98, 100, 111, 145
Brain, C. K., 22
Broken Hill Cave site, 10, 31
Broom, Robert, 14, 21
burins, *51, 52,* 64, 65, 69
Byblos site, 99, 123

"calendar" bone, *54*

calendrical knowledge, 65, 67, 124
Can Hasan site, 99, 121
Çatal Hüyük site, 81, 82, 84, 89, 94, 95, 99, *101*, 103–105, 118, 121, 122
Caton-Thompson, Gertrude, 132
cattle, *79*, 81, 82, 83, 89, 93, 104
Çayönü site, 80, 81, 89, 99, 105
Chad, Republic of, sites in, 29
Chalcolithic, 106, 118; see also Neolithic period, Later
Chellean culture, see Abbevillian culture
Childe, V. G., 124, 142
"choppers," 55, 56
"chopping tools," *50, 55*, 63
Choukoutien site, 13, 14, 28, 55; skull from, *27;* tool from, *50*
civilization, concept of, 124–125
Clactonian culture, 49, 58; tool from, *50*
Clarke, Ron, 25
"Classic" Neandertals, 30, 31, 32, 33, 34
climatic changes, 48–49
Combe Capelle site, 12, 32
Coppens, Y., 29
cosmic radiation, 49
cranial capacity, 36
Cro-Magnon man, 32
Cuvier, Baron Georges, 31

Damb Sadaat site, 147, 148
Dart, Raymond, 14, 20, 21, 22
Darwin, Charles, 11
dating techniques, 46–49
Day, M., 35
Deir Tasa site, 128, 135
"denticulate" tools, *51*, 60
diet, effect on hominid development, 40
dogs, 80, 83, 91, 93
Dolní-Vestonice site, 67
domestication of animals, 73, 75–76, 77–83, 87–88, 89; effect on Near East, 74–75
domestication of plants, 83–87, 88, 89
drilling, 64
dryopithecines, 39
Dubois, Eugene, 14, 28

E-Anna, goddess, 116
Egypt, 127–143; Neolithic period in, 7–8, 132–141; unification of, 139, 141
einkorn wheat, 83–86, 89; illustrated, *85*
el-Amra site, 128, 137
el-Badari site, 128, 135
el-Gerza site, 128, 138
emmer wheat, 83–86, 88, 89; illustrated, *85*
Engis site, 11, 12
Erbaba site, 81, 89, 93, 99, 105, 121
Erech, see Warka period
Eridu site, 99, 112, *113,* 114, 115
"Eridu" ware, 112
evolution, human, 35–42

"faience," 138–140
Fairservis, Walter, 148, 149
Fauresmith culture, *51, 57,* 68
Fayum period, 130, 132–134
Fayum site, 128, 132–134
feedback factors, 38
"Fertile Crescent," 98, 100
flake tools, *50, 57*–63
Flannery, Kent, 72
flint-knapping, 64
Fontéchevade site, 12, 33–34
foramen magnum, 21
Ft. Ternan site, 10, 20

Ganj Dareh site, 80, 81, 89, 99, 120
Gerzean period, 130, *133,* 138–140
Gibraltar caves, 11, 12

glaciation, 48, 61, 66, 67–68, 69; and climate changes, 74–75
goats, 75–76, 78, 81, 82, 83, 89, 92, 93
grave interment, 61–62
graves, trench, 130, 135, 136
Gravettian point, 52

Hacilar site, 81, 84, 89, 93, 99, 118, 121–122; pottery from, 107
"Haji Mohammed" ware, 112
Halafian culture, 107, 110–112, 113, 118, 123, 131
Hamburgians, 67
hand-axe, 50, 55–57, 59, 62
Harappan civilization, 147, 150–153; illustrated, 152
Harrison, T., 35
Hassunan culture, 107, 109–110, 118
Heidelberg site, 12, 14, 29
Helwan site, 128, 129, 130, 131
Hierakonpolis, 128, 142
hieroglyphic writing, 141
hominid evolution, interrelated variables in, 37
hominids, 18–42; taxonomic breakdown of, 17
Homo erectus, 17, 24, 25, 26–29, 34, 39, 41, 42; illustrated, 27
Homo habilis, 17, 23, 25, 39
Homo sapiens, 17, 29, 30, 34, 35, 39, 49
Homo sapiens neandertalensis, 17, 57; *see also* Neandertals
Homo sapiens sapiens, 17, 27, 47, 63–65
Homo soloensis, 30
Hopefield site, 10, 32
housing, 56, 61, 67, 90, 92, 95, 102, 103, 110–111, 130, 134, 137, 138, 142
Howell, F. C., 25
human evolution, 35–42
hyperplasia of nerve cells, 40
hypertrophy of nerve cells, 40

ibex, 78
Imhotep, 142
"index fossils," 46
India, 143–153
Indus Valley civilization, 8, 150–151, 152
Iran, 120–121
irrigation, 117–119

Jacob, T., 28
Jarmo site, 81, 84, 86, 89, 98, 99, 100–102, 105, 118; illustrated, 101
Jemdet Nasr tradition, 113, 116
Jericho site, 81, 84, 89, 94–95, 99, 101, 102–103, 105, 118, 123
Joub Janine site, 57

K/A dating, *see* potassium/argon dating
Kalambo Falls site, 62
Kanjera site, 10, 34
Karim Shahir site, 99, 102, 118
Kebaran culture, 67, 68
Kenyapithecus africanus, 20
Kenyapithecus wickeri, 20
Kile Gul Mohammad site, 146–148
Kom Ombo site, 128, 131
Kostienki site, 67
Kot Diji site, 147, 151
Kromdraai site, 10, 21
Kulli culture, 149
Kurotoro site, 10
Kwantung Province, sites in, 31

labor, sexual division of, 40
La Chapelle-aux-Saints site, 11, 12
Lake Mungo site, 68
Lake Natron site, 10, 23
Lake Rudolf, 10, 15, 23, 25, 42, 53, 55
La Naulette site, 11, 12

language development, 41, 60, 64–65
"Lantian Man," 28
Latamne site, 57
Leakey, Dr. L. S. B., 20, 22, 34
Leakey, Mrs. L. S. B., 22
Leakey, Richard, 25, 42
Le Moustier, finds at, 11
Levalloiso-Mousterian tradition, 49, *51*, 57–60, 62; distinction between Levallois and Mousterian, 59
Levant, the, 71, 118, 122–124
Lewis, G. E., 18
Lothagam Hill site, 10, 15, 24
lunar calendar, 124
lunar count, 65, 67
Luxor site, 128, 137

Magdalenian culture, 49, 66, 67
Magdalenian tool industry, 32, *54*
magnetic poles, reversal of, 49
Makapansgat site, 10, 21
Mapa Man, 30, 31
Mapa site, 13, 14, 30, 31
mastabas, 130, *136*, 142
Mellaart, James, 104, 111, 121, 122
Memphis, 128, 142
Merimdeh site, 128, 130, 134
Mersin site, 123
"Mesolithic," limits of term, 5–6
Mesopotamia, northern, 109–112; southern, 112–120
Mohenjodaro site, 142, 147
Morocco, sites in, 28
Mt. Carmel sites, 13, 30
Mousterian tool industry, 32, *51*, 58–63
"Movius line," 62
Mureybat site, 80, 89

Nal culture, 149, *152*
Naqada site, 128, 137, 138
Natufian culture, 87–90, 103, 105, *108*, 118, 122, 131–132

Nature, 20
Neandertals, 11, 14, 16, 26, *27*, 29–35, 39, 49, *54*, 60–62, 63, 64, 65
Neander Valley site, 11, 12
Near East, described, 71–72; desiccation of, 74–75
"Neolithic," limits of term, 5–6
Neolithic period, 72–95
Neolithic period, Later, 98–125
nerve cells, development of, 40
neural reorganization, 38
nomes, 139, 140
Nubia, 127–128, 131, 133
nuclear areas, 100, 111, 119–120
Nyu industry, 68

Oakley, K., 34
occipital condyles, 21
Oldowan tool types, 49, *50*
"Olduvai event," 49
Olduvai Gorge site, 10, 15, 22, 23–24, 42, 47, 49, 53–55
Omo River site, 10, 15, 23–25, 35, 47–48, 53, 55
Oranian culture, 68
Osmaniwicza culture, 62
"osteodontokeratic culture," 22

"Paleolithic," limits of term, 5–6
Paleolithic period, 45–53; Lower, 53–57; Middle, 57–63; Upper, 63–69
Palestine, 71
Paranthropus robustus, 21; see also *Australopithecus robustus*
Paraustralopithecus aethiopicus, 25
Parpallo point, *52*
pathology, bone, 26
Perigordian culture, 49, 65
Petrie, Sir Flinders, 135
pictographs, *108*, 116
pigs, *79*, 81, 82, 83, 89
Pilbeam, David, 18
Piltdown fraud, 14

Index 163

pithecanthropines, 49, 56
Pithecanthropus erectus, 14, 26, 55; *see also Homo erectus*
potassium/argon (K/A) dating, 47, 48
pottery, 102, 103, 106, *107*, 109, 111, 112, 118, 120-121, 123, *133*, 135, 137, 148
pressure technique in flaking, 64
"Progressive" Neandertals, 30
protein, effect on brain of, 40
Proto-Literate period, 116-117, 118
Proto-Stillbay artifacts, 31
pyramids, 130, *136*, 142

Qadan industries, 131-132, *133*

radiocarbon dating, 47
Ramad, *see* Tell Ramad site
Ramapithecus, 15, 18-20, 35, 38, 39
Ramapithecus punjabicus, 18-20; illustrated, *19*
Rana Ghundai site, 147, 148
Ras Shamra site, 99, 123
Rhodesian Man, 32, 35
Rift system of Africa, 53
Robinson, John, 14, 21

Saccopastore site, 12
sagittal crest, 21
Saldanha Man, 32, 35
Samarran ware, *107*, 109-110, 118
Sangiran site, 13
Sangoan culture, 57, 68
Sarab site, 99, 120
Sarawak site, 13, 35
Sartono, S., 28
Schoetensack, O., 14, 29
seals, cylinder, *108*, 116, *139;* Harappan, *152;* stamp, *108*, 111, 114-115
seasons, predictability of, 65, 67
sedentarism, 87, 90

sexual differentiation, 38
Shanidar Cave site, 13, 14, 31, 60, 61, 65, 91-92, 99
sheep, 75-76, *78*, 80, 81, 82, 83, 89, 91-92, 93
Shensi Province site, 13, 28
Sialk pottery, *107*
Sidi Abderrahman site, 10
Simons, Elwyn, 18
Sinanthropus pekinensis, 26, 28; *see also* Choukoutien site, *Homo erectus*
Siwalik Hills site, 13, 15, 18
Skhūl cave site, 30; skull from, *27*
Smith, Philip, 120
Soan tradition, 62
social behavior, 36
solar calendar, 124
Solutrean culture, 49, 64, 66
Solutrean tool industry, 32, *52*
Spy site, 11, 12
Steinheim site, 12, 33
Sterkfontein site, 10, 21, 22
strata identification, 46
Suberde site, 81, 89, 90-91, 99, 105, 118, 121
Sumerian culture, 117
Swanscombe site, 12, 33
Swartkrans site, 10, 21, 22, 23
Swiderians, 67
Syro-Cilicia, 122-124
Szeleta culture, 62

Tabelablat industry, 62
Tabūn cave site, 30
Tasian-Badarian period, 130, *133*, 134-135
Taungs site, 10, 20, 21
taxonomy of hominids, 15-18
Tayacian tool industry, 33, 49, *51*, 58
Tchadanthropus uxoris, 29
Tell Arpachiya site, 99, 111
Tell Halaf site, 99, 110
Tell Hassuna site, 99, 109

Tell Ramad site, 81, 84, 89, 99, 123
Tell Ubeidiya site, 12, 29, 57
Tepe Ali Kosh site, *see* Ali Kosh site
Tepe Asiab site, 99, 120
Tepe Gawra site, 115
Ternifine site, 10, 28
tholoi, 110, *113*
Tobias, P. V., 22
tombs, *see* graves, *mastabas,* pyramids
tool-making, 38; evolution of, 49–69
tool types, diagnostic, 49, *50–52*
Torralba site, 56
tournette, 114
towns, 93–95, 118
trade, 93–95
Trinil site, 13; cranial vault from, 27, 28

Ubaid culture, *113,* 114–115, 116, 119, 123
Ubeidiya site, 13, 29, 55, 57

Ur site, 99, *113,* 114, 115
Uruk, *see* Warka period

vehicles, wheeled, 142
Vertesszöllös site, 12, 29
Virchow, Rudolph, 11–12
volcanoes, 105
von Koenigswald, G. H. R., 28

Wadi Halfa site, 128, 131
Wallace, Alfred Russel, 11
Warka period, *113,* 115–116, 118
Weidenreich, Franz, 28
wheat, 83–86, 88, 89; illustrated, *85*
Willendorf site, 67
Wittfogel, Karl, 117–119
writing, 116, 117, 141, 151, *152;* pictographic, *108,* 116

Zawi Chemi Shanidar site, 73, 80, 81, 88, 89, 91–92, 99, 118
Zhob sites, 148
ziggurat, 113, 114, 116
Zinjanthropus boisei, 22–24

Other Books of Interest from University Press of America

MASS PARTICIPATORY ECONOMY: A DEMOCRATIC ALTERNATIVE FOR KOREA
 Kim Dae Jung

KOREAN STUDIES IN AMERICA: OPTIONS FOR THE FUTURE
 Edited by Ronald Morse

TESTING DEMOCRATIC THEORIES IN SOUTH KOREA
 Sung M. Pae

FINANCE AND HOUSING QUALITY IN TWO DEVELOPING COUNTRIES: KOREA AND THE PHILIPPINES
 Raymond J. Struyk and Margery Austin Turner

REFLECTIONS ON A CENTURY OF UNITED STATES-KOREAN RELATIONS
 Edited by Ronald Morse

ASIAN ISSUES 1985
 Eduardo Lachica, Evelyn Colbert, Lloyd I. Rudolph, and Linda Y.C. Lim

BLIND PARTNERS: AMERICAN AND JAPANESE RESPONSES TO AN UNKNOWN FUTURE
 Edited by Ronald A. Morse and Shigenobu Yoshiba

LETTERS OF A JAVANESE PRINCESS BY RADEN ADJENG KARTINI
 Edited by and with an introduction by Hildred Geertz

THE UNITED STATES ACQUIRES THE PHILIPPINES: CONSENSUS VS. REALITY: VOLUME XV, THE CREDIBILITY OF INSTITUTIONS, POLICIES AND LEADERSHIP SERIES
 Louis J. Halle

VIETNAM AS HISTORY: TEN YEARS AFTER THE PARIS PEACE ACCORDS
 Edited by Peter Braestrup

THE GERMAN PRISONERS-OF-WAR IN JAPAN, 1914-1920
 Charles Burdick and Ursula Moessner

0-8191-605

Two Koreas— One Future?

A Report Prepared for the American Friends Service Committee

Edited by
John Sullivan and Roberta Foss

**University Press
of America**

**American Friends
Service Committee**

Copyright © 1987 by

University Press of America,® Inc.

4720 Boston Way
Lanham, MD 20706

3 Henrietta Street
London WC2E 8LU England

All rights reserved

Printed in the United States of America

British Cataloging in Publication Information Available

Co-published by arrangement with the
American Friends Service Committee

Library of Congress Cataloging in Publication Data

Two Koreas—one future?

"Co-published by arrangement with the American
Friends Service Committee"—Verso t.p.
  Bibliography: p.
  1. Korean reunification question (1945-   )
2. Korea—History—Partition, 1945.   3. Korea (South)—
Politics and government.   4. Korea (North)—Politics
and government.   I. Sullivan, John, 1917-   .
II. Foss, Roberta.   III. American Friends Service
Committee.
DS917.25.T85   1987   951.9'04   86-30762
ISBN 0-8191-6049-0 (alk. paper)
ISBN 0-8191-6050-4 (pbk. : alk. paper)

All University Press of America books are produced on acid-free
paper which exceeds the minimum standards set by the National
Historical Publication and Records Commission.

Acknowledgments

Thanks for this publication are due to the participants in the three AFSC conferences on Korean unification, held in 1981, 1982 and 1983, at which many of the issues discussed in this book were explored. In particular, we appreciate the support from the many people in the Korean-American community who urged us to prepare this work and provided the inspiration for doing so. The Board of Directors of the American Friends Service Committee aided us with helpful perspectives on the opening and concluding chapters. Our colleagues at the American Friends Service Committee provided encouragement that enabled us to be patient and to persevere over the many months of preparation and editing. Our thanks also to Stephen Thiermann who contributed early drafts of the final chapter, and to Sally Harrison and to Haeng Woo Lee, each of whom helped in the many tasks of editing and shepherding the book through to completion.

John A. Sullivan　　　　　　　　　　　　　　　　Roberta Foss
Vashon, Washington　　　　　　　　　　　　　　Philadelphia

October 1986

Table of Contents

Chapter	page
1. Introduction	1
2. The Division of Korea *Bruce Cumings*	5
3. The Economies of North and South Korea *Jon Halliday*	19
4. The Military Situation on the Korean Peninsula *Stephen Goose*	55
5. The Politics of Korea *Gregory Henderson*	95
6. The Major Powers and the Korean Triangle *Ilpyong J. Kim*	119
7. Korea Today, Korea Tomorrow—A Korean Perspective *Kyungmo Chung*	135
8. AFSC Perspectives on Korea	159

Chapter 1

Introduction

On June 25, 1950, a bitter war between North and South began in Korea. On July 27, 1953, a cease-fire was finally arranged at Panmunjom. The hostilities, which were put in a state of suspension, had confirmed militarily what had already been established politically in 1945: a Korea divided.

Now there was a cease-fire line and a demilitarized zone (DMZ) between the two republics. The cease-fire remained a nervous one, marked by suspicions, clashes, and occasional casualties. No peace agreement has ever been achieved. After the signing of the armistice, extraordinary reconstruction and separate development began on both sides, in which the two republics became integrated into rival economies, one of Western capitalism and the other of Eastern socialism. In many other ways the republics grew apart as their political and social systems followed starkly differing models.

Some warning voices were raised against hardening the line of separation, even during the war. In 1952 a U.S. political advisor to Syngman Rhee, Robert T. Oliver, argued for a neutral Korea, saying:

> It is increasingly evident that in Asia's long history, Korea has been a crucial area. Its primary role has been that of a buffer state. Never strong militarily and never ambitious for expansion, Korea has not in itself been a threat to anyone. Its significance lies now (as it has in the past) in the fact that it occupies the strategic heartland of north Asia, surrounded by China, Japan and Siberian Russia. So long as Korea is truly independent, these powers are kept apart and the peace of Asia is safe. As soon as Korea is dominated by one of them, the other two are endangered. This truism is impossible to avoid. It is the basis for Korean claims that (like Switzerland in

Europe) it is to the fundamental advantage of the great powers to insure two things: (1) that Korea be protected against aggression; and (2) that this be accomplished without reducing it to a pawn or satellite of any one or any group of outside nations. If this contention seems self-contradictory, the answer is that it once was done for Belgium and still is being done for Switzerland; it must be done for Korea if the consequences of general war are to be avoided.[1]

This thoughtful warning was not heeded, but the argument made in 1952 is telling today. Korea still remains the "strategic heartland" of Northeast Asia where the interests of four great powers converge, three geographically—China, Japan, and the Soviet Union, and one by virtue of its strategic reach and troop presence—the United States. The sixth and seventh largest armies in the world face each other at the 38th parallel on the Korean peninsula and their allies arm them and back them up. Further, on the southern side of the line, there are 40,000 U.S. troops and 150 or more U.S. nuclear weapons.

Incidents have occurred sporadically across the DMZ. Prudent people must fear that one of these incidents may get out of hand and begin an escalation which, in the worst case, could lead to nuclear confrontation. A major outbreak of hostilities would involve not only the U.S. troops on the scene, but could also draw in other U.S. troops stationed in Japan, Okinawa, the Philippines, Hawaii, and the western U.S. mainland.

It is now a crossroads time in Korea. The forty-year history of mistrust motivates each side to maintain a state of hostility toward the other. But there is also evidence of efforts at accommodation and reconciliation. The mid-1980s are witnessing a new round of contacts between Red Cross and government officials from North and South, with a series of meetings and family visits across the DMZ. The pace of history has quickened.

At such a time, it seems important to the American Friends Service Committee to review the situation with the aid of scholars and Korea specialists, seeking a direction to suggest for decisions about the future of Korea. Koreans have encouraged the AFSC to undertake such a task. In the late 1970s increasing numbers of Koreans in the United States became interested in discussing their thoughts and hopes about Korea and the prospects for reconciliation, which might lead eventually to reunification. At the same time a few of them began to visit the North, many meeting family members from whom they had been separated for thirty years. Some of these Koreans asked AFSC to sponsor off-the-record conferences where people interested in discussing Korea could do so freely in an atmosphere of trust. Such conferences were held in 1981, 1982, and 1983, with markedly increased frankness of exchange in successive meetings.

Conference participants urged AFSC to prepare a document on Korea which would focus on reunification, provide information about the North and the South from a variety of viewpoints, and include an AFSC perspective. This book is the response to that request.

Publication of this book is the latest event in a chain of AFSC-Quaker-Korean contacts that began in 1917, when Gilbert Bowles, who was in Japan representing the Religious Society of Friends (Quakers), went to Korea to investigate allegations of atrocities by Japanese during the occupation they had imposed in the wake of the Russo-Japanese War of 1904-1905. On his return to Tokyo from this and later visits, Bowles submitted reports of brutal treatment of Koreans. His reports and other pressures led in time to removal of the Japanese governor general who headed the occupation of Korea. Later Bowles commented, "It was perhaps the most important mission of my life."

Immediately after the Korean War, the AFSC, together with its sister British agency, the then Friends Service Council, engaged in post-war reconstruction in Kunsan, South Korea. Attempts to begin work in North Korea were not successful. AFSC went on to sponsor international work camps in the 1960s in South Korea, Okinawa, and Japan, all involving Korean youth, has made frequent visits to South Korea, and has sent two delegations to North Korea, in 1980 and 1984. Following the AFSC work in post-war South Korea, a group of Koreans formed the first Friends Meeting for Worship in Seoul. Its best known member is Teacher Ham Sok Hon, historian, philosopher, and champion of human rights and social justice who has sometimes been called "the Gandhi of Korea." He is quoted here in the final chapter, in which an AFSC perspective on the future of Korea is presented.

In fashioning this book, AFSC sought out several Korean specialists and scholars to lend their considerable knowledge to the examination of Korean affairs. A brief biographical sketch of each author appears at the end of the chapter that he contributed. Chung Kyungmo and Bruce Cumings, in quite different styles, have provided information on the recent history of Korea, especially since the end of World War II. Recently declassified documents have provided Cumings with a wealth of new information about the period between the end of World War II and the Korean War. Chung lived through and participated in many of the events he describes. Ilpyong Kim undertakes in his chapter to portray the geopolitical context in which Korea relates to the superpowers. Three specialists—Jon Halliday, Stephen Goose, and Gregory Henderson—provide comparative insights into the two republics and their economies, military establishments, and politics. Finally, the AFSC offers its perspective and some recommendations for action.

In recent years there has been some increase in literature about Korean reunification and a growing body of printed materials available in the United States about North Korea. In offering this publication, AFSC believes it provides readers with some information which is not readily available in other forms, however. First, it attempts to present facts and comparisons where possible about North and South Korea, an exercise made somewhat difficult by the relative scarcity of reliable information and statistics about the North. Second, in the chapter by Kyungmo Chung there is a revelation of the depth of feeling that Koreans have about their country, their cultural roots and the role of Japan. Third, to the best of AFSC's knowledge, this is the first book of its kind offered by a concerned U.S. religiously-based organization. AFSC brings to this work a belief in the fundamental right of self-determination of the Korean people—indeed of all people.

The pages that follow do not present a unified opinion or viewpoint, but rather a variety of vantage points, approaches and individual opinions. The book does not purport to present all views. The individual authors do not necessarily represent the views of the AFSC. Rather the book presents substantial information and comparison, and a sample of the opinions of those who are committed to reunification. The AFSC's attitudes are presented in the final chapter.

1. Choy, B.Y., *A History of the Korean Reunification Movement: Its Issues and Prospects,* (Bradley University: Research Committee on Korean Unification Institute of International Studies, 1984), p. 239.

Chapter 2

The Division of Korea

Bruce Cumings

In the life of every nation there is a moment in the movement of time, the significance of which is appreciated only in retrospect—the British defeat of Napoleon at Waterloo, the Southern shot fired on Fort Sumter, the halting of the Nazi legions at the gates of Moscow in 1941. The significant moment for Korea in the last four decades was the national division—not the Korean War, not the rise to economic power of the South, not the socialist revolution in the North. What remains to be explained is why that moment of division remains so profoundly misunderstood; its history is as little known as its authorship, its causes are misconstrued time and again. Even the year when division occurred is misplaced. A forty-year parenthesis of division is taken to be the norm for a nation that was unified for more than a millenium. And today, daily acts contributing to this division continue to occur under the same authorship.

In any standard, conventional history of the 1940s, the story of the division runs as follows. The responsibility for division rests on the Soviet Union, which came into Korea in the last minutes of World War II, set up a puppet regime under Kim Il Sung, their hand-picked leader, and then organized the Democratic People's Republic of Korea as a satellite state, the effective year of division being 1948. The United States more or less oozed into its Korean commitments in a half-hearted, ill-prepared manner. Having no policy toward Korea, the United States did not know whom to support and therefore improvised policy, always in reaction to Soviet initiatives.

After a three-year period of U.S. military government—always treated in standard texts in the most cursory fashion, as if it were unimportant—and after heroic attempts to get the Soviets to cooperate in unifying Korea, the United States transferred the Korean problem to the United Nations, which in turn sponsored and observed elections. These elections brought forth the Republic of Korea, led by a patriot named Syngman Rhee who was a tough curmudgeon for the United States to deal with. U.S. observers blanched at his authoritarian tendencies, but he was a patriot with nationalist credentials superior to those of Kim Il Sung. Thus Korea was divided; Koreans blame the division on the great powers while the great powers blame each other.

We might call this the Peer Gynt argument: The United States, the well-intentioned bumbler, doing ill when it tries so hard to do well, never quite sure how it all happened.[1]

Four decades after the fact, this account remains the standard interpretation, even though it does not seem to explain present-day Korea. For example, if one observes the situation at that salient of division where two sides still meet, Panmunjom, no Soviets are visible. Hard-faced North Korean soldiers, arms folded and eyes staring coldly, confront U.S. soldiers, chosen for their height and presumably for their capacities to match cold stares with cold stares. South Korean officers and soldiers are in a palpably secondary role on this piece of ground that is, in effect, a U.S. military base. It is held by the "Manchu Battalion," whose namesake helped to suppress the Boxer Rebellion and lift the siege of the legations in China in 1900. The name is a symbol, in other words, of Western imperialism in Asia. As if to make this point, the battalion displays gaudy posters showing a Hercules-like Caucasian warrior bringing an ax down upon the head of a cringing "Oriental."

This symbolism seems to be an errant counterpoint to the roseate image of a United States bereft of responsibility for the division of Korea. Is the symbolism therefore misleading? What about the substance of the U.S. role? South Korea is the only country in the world where the United States operationally controls the presumably sovereign armed forces of another state. In only one of the past forty years, June 1949 to June 1950, has the United States not commanded the Korean Army. So, the substance is the story. It is unlikely that there is another country in the world where the United States bears more responsibility for the existing state of affairs. The Korea problem, which is in most ways a problem of national division, is also a U.S. problem.

We were more than present at the creation, as Dean Acheson put it. The United States was an initiator, planner, and author of the division of Korea; if it does not bear the whole responsibility, it bears the major responsibility. That this is still so poorly understood only begins to get at the excavation that has to be done. If the division is ever to be ended, its origins have to be grasped, and these origins cannot be grasped without plowing under and below the mountains of rhetoric and special pleading that have obscured the conditions of Korea's partition.

When Did The Division Occur?

The answer is 1945, not 1948. The division of Korea occurred in the last five months of 1945. The first act occurred during a night-long session of the State-War-Navy Coordinating Committee in Washington, D.C., August 10-11, 1945. Assistant Secretary of War John J. McCloy, a figure of maximal importance in postwar U.S. diplomacy, later to be designated by *New Yorker* political correspondent Richard Rovere as the "chairman" of the eastern establishment, asked two young colonels, Dean Rusk and Charles Bonesteel, to withdraw to an adjoining room and find a place to draw a line across Korea; they were given thirty minutes. Rusk, of course, went on to become a key figure in U.S. Asian diplomacy in the 1950s and later secretary of state during the Kennedy and Johnson administrations. Bonesteel later commanded U.S. forces in Korea.

Rusk later said that he chose the thirty-eighth parallel because it included the capital city, Seoul, in the U.S. zone. He acknowledged that this line was "further north than could be realistically reached …in the event of Soviet disagreement," since U.S. armed forces would be unable to land in Korea for three weeks.[2] The Soviets, in other words, acquiesced to the proposed partition when their troops, already engaging the Japanese in Korea, could have marched on to Pusan. Rusk understood this to be a test of Soviet intentions and was "somewhat surprised" when the Soviets agreed.

This decision was made in the harried days just before the war ended and has been attributed both to that confusion and to a simple U.S. desire to find a line to demarcate Soviet and U.S. responsibilities in accepting the Japanese surrender. But any number of decisions critical to the postwar period were taken at the same time. Furthermore, as Gabriel Kolko has shown, the developing power relationship in East Asia was contingent on who received the surrender, and where, on the principle that "military victory would define local politics."[3] The Korean partition mimicked a similar American decision in China, designed to get the Japanese to surrender to nationalist rather than communist troops.

The decision on the thirty-eighth parallel, although made in thirty minutes, was based on years of planning, as were other decisions at the time. Within a year of Pearl Harbor, planners in the State Department had begun to worry about Soviet involvement in or control of Korea, viewing this as a threat to Pacific security. They thus began the decisive reversal of the traditional U.S. policy toward Korea, one of non-involvement and acquiescence in or support for Japanese designs on the peninsula. They never wavered from this new position.

Fears of Soviet penetration of Korea were the basic reason for the dispatch of troops to occupy Korea in September 1945. Even when U.S. troops were temporarily withdrawn from Korea, in 1949-1950, the State Department continued to define the security of Korea as important to Pacific and U.S. security. At this time Korea was given low priority in the military-strategic field by the

War Department, partially because of the cost involved, but it had high political-strategic priority in the State Department. The decision to intervene in the Korean War was primarily a State Department decision, hammered out and pushed through by the Secretary of State, Dean Acheson, over substantial military objections. There is, thus, a stunning consistency in the basic political assumptions behind U.S. policy toward Korea from 1943 to 1950.[4]

President Franklin D. Roosevelt rarely consulted the State Department, and probably did not know about this planning. His pet idea was to place Korea under a paternal great-power trusteeship, guiding and tutoring the Koreans toward an independence that, in his mind, would not come for several decades after the end of the war. He wanted to involve the Soviets in this trusteeship, while assuring that, with British and Chinese participation, the United States could always outvote the Soviets. FDR nurtured this plan from early 1943 until his death in April 1945. It had the virtue of anticipating a unified, not a divided, Korea and of assuming that the Soviets would have interests in Korea that would have to be acknowledged. It had the flaw of utterly overlooking strong desires in Korea for immediate independence after the Japanese demise. With Roosevelt's death, Korea policy devolved to bureaucrats who misunderstood and distrusted the presidential vision; it was they who wrote the basic plans for a military occupation of Korea.

If the United States had occupied southern Korea merely to disarm the Japanese, its soldiers could have left within a few weeks. By September 8, 1945, when U.S. forces finally landed, the Japanese were in no mood to fight and had already begun a rapid liquidation of the colonial presence. But even while U.S. occupation forces were still on Okinawa, they received messages from Japanese commanders worried about a very different enemy—the Korean people themselves. From August 15 onward, Koreans had organized peacekeeping forces, local self-governing committees, labor unions to run Japanese factories and, on September 6, a Korean People's Republic headquartered in Seoul. Although this explosion of political participation was led by people of various ideological complexions, excluding only rank collaborators with the Japanese, the Japanese had little trouble convincing U.S. commanders that communists were behind the movement. It was this development that transformed the basic purpose of the U.S. occupation. The occupation would not simply disarm the Japanese; it would not simply block the southward flow of Soviet power. It would also seek to root out this movement.

Formerly classified documentation makes clear that counterrevolutionary goals became the overriding concern of the occupation, giving a distinctly reactionary cast to U.S. policy and drawing the United States into commitments that it maintains to this day.[5] It was this desire to hold the South against both the Soviets and indigenous revolutionaries that transformed a temporary partition into a solidified division, and it did so by the end of 1945.

In September and October, the U.S.-sponsored conservative, anticommunist political parties, led mostly by wealthy landowners and reconstituted Korean elements of the colonial police force, began the creation of a southern army, brought back anti-communist politicians like Syngman Rhee from the United States and Kim Ku from China, and began serious planning for a separate southern government. The initiative for these actions came mostly from U.S. military and State Department representatives on the scene in Seoul, bringing the cold war to Korea months or years before it began elsewhere. Until early 1946 official U.S. policy continued to envision a trusteeship for Korea, even though little was done to bring such a policy to fruition. At critical points, however, the local decisions were supported by such central figures in U.S. foreign policy as McCloy, Averell Harriman, and George Kennan. These decisions developed into the sinews of a southern regime that finally became the Republic of Korea in 1948.[6]

The Soviets had interests in Korea and were not likely to leave without securing them. But early postwar history does not suggest that these interests were nearly as important to them as U.S. interests in the South were to the United States. The Soviets stopped their march south at the thirty-eighth parallel three weeks before U.S. forces arrived. In December 1945 during the Moscow Foreign Ministers' Conference they compromised on a U.S. plan for trusteeship. They worked through a coalition of nationalists and communists until early 1946 and did not try to set up national police and military forces or a separate central administration for the North. All such initiatives in the South came from the United States.

The Soviet occupation reacted to the U.S. decisions by helping to set up an Interim Central People's Committee in the North in February 1946, the time from which most scholars date Kim Il Sung's ascendancy. They did not set up a military government but retreated to the background to give the impression that administration was solely in Korean hands. After six months of supporting a coalition leadership, the Soviets sponsored Kim's assumption of power in February 1946. It is by no means clear that he was their first choice, however, or that they thought they had found a docile puppet. Kim's rise to power meant that a host of hardened guerrillas now ruled North Korea. Indeed this same core group continues to hold maximum power today, even though many of the original group have died. Therefore, this Korean leadership was quite different from the pliable groups the Soviets installed in many East European countries. From 1946 to 1949 the Kim group allied first with groups of Koreans associated with the Chinese communists in Yenan, then with pro-Soviet groups, and finally merged again with pro-Chinese factions in 1949 in a consolidated leadership. The Soviet sponsorship of Kim is ill-understood and no doubt was a mixed blessing for them.

Kim Il Sung is widely thought to be an imposter who stole the name of a famous Korean resistance fighter. This myth, fostered originally by South Korean intelligence circles, persists today in spite of much recent scholarship that clearly shows Kim to have been among the leading anti-Japanese fighters in Manchuria and gives details on his background during the period 1931-1945. Kim's relationship with the Soviets is somewhat less clear, but it appears to have involved little more than Soviet training of Kim and his guerrillas for forays into Korea from just across the Soviet border in the period 1942-1945. Kim had joined the Chinese Communist Party in the 1930s and had a much more important relationship with Chinese guerrilla leaders than he had with the Soviets.[7]

There is no question that the Soviets sought to control and dominate North Korea in the 1947-49 period, but they did so primarily through loyal Koreans from the USSR or the Comintern, not through Kim and his allies. A decisive reversal of Soviet influence occurred early in 1949 when, after the withdrawal of Soviet troops from North Korea (the last ones left in December 1948), tens of thousands of Koreans who had fought in the Chinese civil war returned to Korea. These troops were highly Sinicized and battle-hardened, and Kim Il Sung and his supporters used these returned "volunteers" to fashion a measure of autonomy from the Soviets.[8]

Both the Soviets and the Kim group must share responsibility for the division of Korea. The Soviets acquiesced in the U.S. decision on the thirty-eighth parallel and were never willing to negotiate for Korean unification if their hold in the North would be threatened. Kim Il Sung and his allies busily went about setting up separate administrative, party and military structures at the center in Pyongyang. But in much of the country the Soviets were invisible and the northern regime based itself in the people's committee structure that had emerged on a nationwide basis, thus giving the North a tremendous political advantage over the South. Their form of government, the people's committees, was widespread in the South as well, whereas conservative political organizations often existed only in Seoul, not in the countryside where the mass of the population lived, and certainly not in North Korea.

So, the record is clear that Korea was, in effect, divided by early 1946. Most of the initiatives for division came from the U.S. occupation and its conservative Korean allies, who faced a strong left in both North and South. But the Soviets and their northern allies responded to these initiatives with divisive ploys of their own. In retrospect, responsibility for the division of Korea is shared by the Soviet Union and the United States and by leading Korean groups in both North and South. As U.S. citizens, we should both acknowledge this responsibility, as we have yet to do, and recognize that amongst the parties to the division, the United States comes first. Most of the important initiatives that would have lasting impact came from the South in the last months of 1945, bringing Syngman Rhee to effective power.[9]

Attempts to Resolve the Division

Although the United States bears the major share of responsibility for the national division, and although the same basic assumptions were influencing U.S. positions, U.S. policy was not uniform throughout the period 1945-1950. Different officials and bureaucracies sought through diplomacy and negotiation to unify Korea. Three efforts toward this end are particularly important: (1) the trusteeship agreement and the Joint Commission meetings in 1946; (2) attempts to forge a left-right coalition, also in 1946; and (3) the U.S. role in turning the Korean problem over to the United Nations in 1947.

At the end of December 1945 foreign ministers of the United States and the USSR agreed in Moscow to sponsor jointly the creation of a unified provisional government of Korea and, if necessary, to place Korea temporarily under a four-power trusteeship. Within a month, this agreement was effectively undone.

Although the trusteeship imbroglio is complex and still misunderstood, it is a fascinating example of how day-to-day politics undermines solemn diplomatic agreements. First, those U.S. policy makers who supported a trusteeship were from a small group of internationalists, mostly in the State Department, people increasingly in jeopardy for being "soft on communism." John Carter Vincent was perhaps the most prominent example. He became a prime antagonist of occupation policy in Korea. Second, the occupation did not support trusteeship, because any involvement of the Soviets or the left in administering Korea threatened the economic and political positions of Koreans whom the United States supported.

When the Moscow agreements were announced, they were interpreted in the South as calling for an immediate trusteeship over Korea, a plan said to have been authored by the Soviets. The occupation command connived in these gross distortions. In fact, the United States had pushed trusteeship first and foremost in Moscow and had made no arrangements for a provisional government staffed by Koreans. It was the Soviets who pushed for a provisional government and wanted to play down trusteeship arrangements. Although Washington planners thought they had achieved an agreement with the Soviets at the highest level on how to unify Korea, within a month the agreement had more or less collapsed, mainly because of the actions in South Korea of the U.S. command and its Korean allies, such as Syngman Rhee.[10] Desultory proceedings to try to establish a provisional government went on for several months in Soviet-U.S. Joint Commission meetings, but the die had been cast and the Joint Commission failed by the summer of 1946.

A handful of liberals in the occupation and the State Department tried to retrieve the situation in the South by sponsoring meetings between left and right in July 1946, aimed at establishing a coalition leadership which would isolate extremes of the right (Syngman Rhee) and the left (Kim Il Sung and the southern communist leader

Pak Hon Yong). This was perhaps the first postwar attempt at creating a "Third Force," presaging similar efforts in China and Vietnam. The primary U.S. official behind the coalition effort, Leonard Bertsch, sought to give southern Korea the political center it so desperately needed to stabilize its politics. But the center could not hold because it had no base in the population, such as a stable middle class. The effort dissolved in the fall of 1946 when massive rebellions broke out in the southeast and southwest.

The U.S. decision to move the Korea question to the United Nations ostensibly came only after the Soviets refused to bend their positions at the Joint Commission's second set of meetings in 1947. Of all the U.S. actions in Korea, the move to the United Nations remains both the key element justifying the U.S. role (now the whole United Nations was behind it) and that part of U.S. policy least understood, most subject to mystification. Newly declassified documents now make clear that this decision was taken well before the collapse of the second Joint Commission, and in the context of an abrupt change of course in U.S. global policy.[11]

In March 1947 President Harry S. Truman enunciated his containment policy, known as the "Truman Doctrine," pledging U.S. aid to nations threatened by communism. Although a de facto containment policy had existed for some time in many parts of the world, including Korea, the public trumpeting of the new policy made clear that Truman had decisively moved away from Roosevelt's internationalist policy of accommodation with the Soviets. The civil war in Greece and the defense of Turkey were the ostensible objects of this policy. Most scholars still assert that the Truman Doctrine represented an application of containment only in western and southern Europe, and that containment came to East Asia only with the Korean War in 1950.

Declassified documentation has now made clear, however, that State Department officials had hoped to include South Korea along with Greece and Turkey as key, threatened nations worthy of U.S. economic and military aid. Planners drew up a program costing what for that time was a whopping $600 million for Korea. At about the same time Dean Acheson, by then a key official in the Truman administration often functioning as acting secretary of state, told Congressional representatives in secret testimony that the United States had drawn the line in Korea.[12]

In 1947 the U.S. defense budget was exceedingly small by current standards, about $12 billion, and various bureaucracies fought over small pieces of the pie. The War Department had responsibility for the occupation of Korea and had suffered much criticism from State Department people who thought something they called "the military mind" was in the saddle in Seoul. Given severe limitations on funds and a thankless and difficult occupation, the War Department resisted the new program for Korea. After several weeks of wrangling, it became apparent that Korea would have to be dropped, leaving Greece and Turkey in the containment program.

The State Department still thought, however, that containment should be applied to South Korea. Failing a commitment from the War Department or from Congress, State planners sought a compromise by getting the fledgling United Nations to provide some sort of collective defense of South Korea. This was the basic reason for the U.S. decision to seek UN backing for the southern regime.[13] From 1947 on, we may say that important officials like Acheson in the State Department placed high value on what might be called the political-strategic value of Korea. The U.S. role in South Korea was a test case of its credibility—of the U.S. capacity to be a good anticommunist manager—in direct confrontation with the Soviets. The War Department, strapped for funds and with all sorts of new commitments around the world, placed Korea low in terms of military-strategic priorities; this peninsula was the wrong place to take a stand in time of general war. Right up to the Korean War in 1950 these different estimates of Korea's value persisted and were the main reason for seeking United Nations help in securing South Korea from communism.

The moving of the Korean question to the United Nations was the final act in the division of Korea. Given the overwhelming U.S. dominance of the United Nations at that time, making it easy to line up various friends and allies behind U.S. policy, Soviet and North Korean opposition to a UN role in Korea was a foregone conclusion. When the United States secured a UN commission to observe elections in Korea in 1948 and requested its entry into the North, the North refused, saying that the United Nations had no competence regarding the Korean question and that the commission itself included members from countries like Nationalist China, the Philippines, Canada and Costa Rica, all of which could be counted on to line up with U.S. policy. The UN commission therefore observed an election in the South alone, resulting in the formation of the Republic of Korea in August 1948, led by Syngman Rhee. The United States rode herd on all the members of this commission, bringing tremendous pressure to bear on the home governments to assure a successful outcome. The finding that this election had been conducted in a "free and fair" atmosphere then became the primary source of legitimacy for the southern regime, which in fact differed very little from the de facto government that had emerged in the South by the end of 1945.

The Resistance to a Separate Southern Government

A separate southern regime appealed mostly to those elite or wealthy Koreans who feared any kind of coalition with the left or participation by the Soviets in Korean affairs. From October 1945 onward, a separatist southern solution was the preferred strategy of the Korean right wing. Syngman Rhee publicly voiced this demand as early as May 1946. But the vast majority of Koreans wanted immediate reunification; thus there developed a broad and deep resistance to the threatened partition of Korea.

All through the first year after liberation, Koreans in the southern countryside sought to build, sustain, or rebuild people's committee structures like those that had emerged in the North. Although conditions varied from province to province, generally speaking the occupation was hostile to these local self-governing organs. The Korean right wanted them rooted out at all costs. A year of provincial repression ended in the autumn of 1946 with a massive uprising in the four southernmost provinces, those that contained a majority of the southern population.[14] The primary demand of the rebels, as acknowledged by head of the U.S. Military Government General Hodge himself, was the restoration of the people's committees.

In spite of severe repression that left hundreds dead and thousands in jail, resistance continued in the summer and fall of 1947, mainly in the form of countless local village struggles between left and right. With the decision to hold a separate election for the South in early 1948, the resistance grew and became particularly pronounced in those regions where the left was strongest, primarily the Southwest and Cheju Island. Cheju, off the southern coast, had been ruled until 1948 by a people's committee under very loose supervision by U.S. officers. In March 1948 Cheju islanders launched an armed struggle against the separate elections, a struggle which evolved into a guerrilla war that lasted about two years.

The authorities in Seoul responded by bringing in mainland police, most of whom had served the Japanese, and large numbers of men from the so-called Northwest Youth, a terrorist organization made up of dispossessed Koreans from the north. These elements launched a reign of terror on the island that included huge population relocations, burning of countless villages, and systematic torture and murder of captured guerrillas. Some estimates suggest that as much as one-third of the population of the island may have perished in these counterinsurgency campaigns.[15] By early 1950 the resistance was destroyed and Cheju was pacified.

In the fall of 1948, guerrilla warfare had spread from Cheju to the mainland. The detonator of this resistance was a mutiny by soldiers in the southwestern port city of Yosu, who refused orders to embark for Cheju Island to fight against the guerrillas. Although this revolt was suppressed within a week, large numbers of rebels escaped to nearby mountains and inaugurated a guerrilla campaign that lasted until the outbreak of the Korean War, and was not finally extinguished until the U.S.-sponsored "Operation Ratkiller" wiped southern Korea clean of remnant guerrillas in 1954.

Space does not permit a thorough treatment of this guerrilla movement, except to remark that (1) the vast majority of guerrillas were native southerners, indeed coming from the southernmost parts of the peninsula, well away from North Korea; (2) U.S. officers, mainly those from the Korean Military Advisory Group, participated directly in the suppression of the guerrillas; (3) Specific geographic characteristics of Korea limited the extent and success of the movement. Resupply of guerrillas from the North (as in Vietnam) was almost impossible and the South could be effectively sealed. In addition, harsh winters denuded the mountains of foliage, making it very difficult for guerrillas to survive from the autumn to the next spring; and (4) the effective defeat of the southern guerrillas was obvious by the spring of 1950, and probably caused the North Koreans to move from unconventional to conventional warfare in seeking to unify Korea.[16]

Conclusions

This essay has argued that the prime responsibility for the division of Korea rests on the shoulders of the United States. The Soviets and the leaders of North and South Korea share that responsibility, but in a hierarchy of causation, U.S. actions come first. The United States never saw unification to be in its interests, with one exception—after the Inchon landing in September 1950 when a temporary advance on the battlefield opened the way to a unification imposed on U.S. terms. Then officials in Washington discovered a touching regard for the aspirations of the vast majority of Korea's citizens to see their homeland reunified. Otherwise, U.S. policy was much like that later in Vietnam—a success, a "win," was defined as a permanently separated southern state, allied to the United States. The fundamental reason for seeking a separate southern state, in both Korea and Vietnam, was that the forces of the left had completely organized the North and also constituted a potentially strong alternative regime in the South, whereas the forces we supported had a lame grip on their part of the country and next to none on the opposing side.

Does this question of historical responsibility matter? Four decades have passed since Korea was divided; what difference does it make that major authorship rests with the United States? This would be a legitimate question, if an historically myopic one, if the United States had washed its hands of its Korea commitments. Yet today of all the major powers, the United States is the one that persists in an anachronistic, confrontational policy in Korea, as if nothing had changed since 1945 or since the end of the Korean War. The Soviets withdrew their troops in 1948 and did little to help North Korea during the Korean War. Since the early 1960s their relationship with the DPRK has been either cool or at times tempestuous. It was China that pulled Kim Il Sung's chestnuts out of the fire during the Korean War, and it is China that has been Pyongyang's key strategic ally for the past three decades. Yet China has become a strong friend of the United States and has been pushing for far- reaching diplomatic changes on the Korean peninsula for several years. It clearly wants relations with the South and has an ever-growing indirect trade with Seoul. It is the United States, with its forty one thousand ground troops and its one hundred fifty nuclear weapons, that remains committed to a belligerent, uncompromising posture in Korea, refusing to open diplomatic talks or relations with the other side as the fifth decade of North Korea's existence begins.

So, some reflection by U.S. citizens on the U.S. role in Korea has not simply an academic or historical value, but a direct relation to ongoing events on the peninsula today. A tense confrontation that could erupt in war at any time still is the defining characteristic of the Korean situation, as it has been since the late 1940s. Although three of the four major reasons for the division still exist (U.S. commitment to the South, the instability of the southern political system, and the ambition of Kim Il Sung and his supporters), there have been radical changes in the environment surrounding Korea. Korea is a cold war island in a post-cold war sea. Growing economic exchange is eroding old, seemingly impermeable political barriers throughout East Asia. Witness Hong Kong, Taiwan, or the indirect trade, amounting to almost $1 billion in 1984, between China and South Korea. The time is at hand for the U.S. government, and its citizens, to reflect on its historical and contemporary responsibility for the continuing tension on the Korean peninsula and to move toward entirely new policies that would seek reduction of tension, relations with the North, and the eventual reconciliation and reunion of the two Korean states.

Reconciliation and reunification does not have to mean the dominance of one side over the other. Perhaps through their talks North and South Korea can agree on some sort of structural arrangement which would put emphasis on those things which both sides favor and which would be mutually beneficial, such as trade, and which would not focus primarily on the issues of disagreement.

Notes

1. Edgar E. A. Johnson, *American Imperialism in the Image of Peer Gynt* (Minneapolis: University of Minnesota Press, 1971). Johnson was part of the economic aid mission in Korea in the late 1940s.

2. *Foreign Relations of the U.S.*, 1945, v. 6, Dean Rusk, memo for the record, July 12, 1950.

3. Gabriel Kolko, *The Politics of War: The World and U.S. Foreign Policy 1943-45* (New York: Random House, 1968), p. 140.

4. I have argued this point at length in my "Introduction," in Cumings, ed., *Child of Conflict: The Korean-American Relationship, 1943-53* (Seattle: University of Washington Press, 1983).

5. Bruce Cumings, *The Origins of the Korean War: Liberation and the Emergence of Separate Regimes* (Princeton: Princeton University Press, 1981), pp. 135-262.

6. McCloy visited Korea in November 1945 and sided with the occupation in its disputes with the State Department; Harriman made a hasty trip to Seoul in early 1946, and gave strong backing to Hodge; Kennan wrote memos in this period that tended to see Korean politics through the lenses of Soviet policies in Eastern Europe—a very different situation. See Cumings, ibid., pp. 183-85, 230.

7. Some of the best information on Kim's activities, from an unimpeachable source, is to be found in a manuscript based on American interviews with two former Japanese officers in the Kwantung Army, assigned to chase down Kim Il Sung and other guerrillas, in National Archives, *Manuscripts of the Office of the Chief of Military History*, Box 601, "Military Studies on Manchuria," chapter nine, "Bandits and Inhabitants."

8. Perhaps as many as 150,000 Koreans fought in the Chinese civil war, and they began returning to northern Korea when most of the fighting for north and northeast China was finished, that is, in 1949 and early 1950. See Bruce Cumings, *The Origins of the Korean War,* volume two, chapter seven, "North Korea's China Connection."

9. Cumings, *Origins,* v. 1, pp. 135-209.

10. The occupation commander, General Hodge, sought to make it look as if the Soviets were the authors of the trusteeship idea, when in fact the United States had been behind this plan since 1943. See Cumings, ibid., pp. 215-226.

11. Cumings, *Origins of the Korean War*, volume two, chapter three; the decision to take the Korean case to the United Nations happened at the same time as the enunciation of the Truman doctrine, in March 1947.

12. Cumings, "Introduction," *Child of Conflict*, op. cit.

13. Ibid.

14. Cumings, *Origins*, v. 1, pp. 351-379.

15. John Merrill, "Internal Warfare in Korea," in Cumings, ed., *Child of Conflict*.

16. Cumings, "Introduction," *Child of Conflict*.

Bruce Cumings is associate professor of International Studies at the University of Washington and director of a research project on the Korean War. He has a doctorate from Columbia University in Political Science and East Asian Studies. Cumings has recently completed the second volume in his *Origins of the Korean War*. A frequent writer for *The Nation, Pacific News Service* and *The Seattle Weekly*, he has published numerous other articles.

Chapter 3

The Economies of North and South Korea

Jon Halliday

At the time of the Japanese surrender in August 1945, which marked the start of the de facto division of Korea, the northern and southern parts of the country were left with very different economic endowments. The North had most of the heavy industry and mines. The South had most of the good agricultural land and the light industry (cf. Table I).[1]

Table I

Distribution of Resources at Partition, 1945

Sector	North Korea %	South Korea %
Heavy Industry	65	35
Light Industry	31	69
Agriculture	37	63
Commerce	18	82

Japanese colonial rule had lasted an entire generation, since 1910. During this period, contrary to widespread belief, Japan had considerably promoted economic growth in Korea, although this growth was heavily lopsided and geared toward the advantage of Japan, not

Korea. As Bruce Cumings has pointed out, "If there has been a miracle in East Asia, it has not occurred just since 1960; it would be profoundly ahistorical to think that it did."[2] Growth in Korea over the period 1911 to 1938 seems to have been higher than in Japan itself.

The nature of this growth is significant. Korea was in essence integrated into a much larger, Japan-centered unit, along with Taiwan and (later) northeast China. The core of Japanese colonial policy was maximum development with maximum extraction. This was true of both industrial and agricultural policy, both of which were geared toward export. The figures on rice dramatically show the relationship between increased production, increased exports, and declining consumption by the Koreans themselves. (cf. Table II).[3]

Table II

Production and Consumption of Korean Rice

Year	Total Output	Export to Japan (in million koku)	Total Consumption within Korea	Annual Percapita Consumption (in koku)	
				Korea	Japan
1912	11.6	0.5	11.1	0.78	1.07
1915	14.1	2.3	11.8	0.74	1.10
1918	13.7	2.2	11.6	0.68	1.14
1924	15.2	4.6	10.8	0.60	1.12
1930	13.7	5.4	8.6	0.45	1.08
1931	19.2	8.4	10.5	0.52	1.30
1932	15.9	7.6	8.4	0.41	1.01
1933	16.3	8.7	8.5	0.41	1.10

To sustain both industrialization and the transport of agricultural produce, Japan set up an extensive communications network, particularly railroads. Once again, this was geared not to the domestic needs of Korea, but "externally" to those of the Japanese empire, with the linkages going from mines to the coast. The railroads also linked northern Korea closely to northeast China and to southern Korea and Japan. Strong north-south communication lines, especially the railroad, contributed to the economic unity of the peninsula.

Japanese policies had considerable longer-term effects as a result of the enormous population displacement which they caused. The standard literature acknowledges the extensive Japanese takeover of Korean farmland, but it tends to understate the degree to which colonial rule over Korea and the annexation of Korea and its population as a subordinate part of the Japanese empire dislocated and ravaged Korean society. Perhaps as much as one-third of the entire population of the country was displaced under Japanese pressure. More than four million Koreans were taken to work (in the worst jobs) in Japan and at least two million in Manchuria (not all at the same time). There was also considerable migration within Korea itself, mainly from southern rural areas to new industry in the north. This dislocation was a major factor in post-1945 events, especially on the land-holding situation in the south.[4]

Two other general points are worth mentioning. The first is that the promotion of industrialization was not accompanied by a commensurate promotion of Korean cadres and skilled personnel. Japanese virtually monopolized skilled jobs in industry. In 1945 the country was thus left without the personnel able to run (or rehabilitate) much of the machinery surviving. On the other hand, the Japanese virtual monopolization of assets and top jobs meant that, with the chief exception of the Korean landlords and a small Korean entrepreneurial and middle class, there was relative equality in the standard of living of the Korean population—the equality of the dispossessed.

The Legacy of the North

As Table I shows, the North inherited most of the country's heavy industry and a proportion of the light industry only slightly less than its proportion of the population. However, it is most uncertain what the real value of this legacy was. First of all, as George McCune states, "Industry in Korea was such an integral part of the economy of Greater Japan that most of the industrial plant existing in Korea at the end of the war was incapable of independent existence."[5] Second, although damage from the fighting between the Soviet Red Army and the Japanese Army seems to have been relatively slight, damage from Japanese sabotage was heavy: nineteen hydroelectric plants were put out of operation, sixty-four mines were totally flooded, 178 partially flooded, six enterprises (including the Pyongyang Aircraft Factory) completely destroyed and forty-seven enterprises partially destroyed. In addition, wartime overuse had reduced much factory equipment to an appalling condition. In 1945, according to Chung, "North Korean industry was in a state of chaos and disrepair."[6] Many Western sources emphasize the North's advantage in inheriting a large proportion of the country's heavy industry. North Korean sources tend to stress the degree of Japanese sabotage. The North was fortunate in its mining resources but the industrial legacy was dubious. In many cases it probably took almost as much work to get factories going again as it would have done to build them from scratch.

Post-Liberation Reforms in the North

North Korea was occupied by the Soviet Union from August 1945 until September 1948 (formally, troops were withdrawn by the end of December 1948). There is controversy on two key factors: how to characterize the Soviet occupation and the degree of autonomy of the new Korean administration in the north. Very briefly, it would seem that after a poor start, the Soviet occupation made an energetic attempt to get the economy going again, and that after the first few months, while providing the essential guarantee of force, it allowed the local Korean regime considerable autonomy.

The first priority was to immobilize the Japanese and confiscate all Japanese-held assets. The Soviet Red Army played a major role in this and certainly provided the context within which rapid confiscation was made possible throughout the North. However, it would also seem that large numbers of Japanese were kept on, many in skilled jobs (detailed figures on this neglected aspect are lacking).

The Soviets were liberating and occupying a "Third World" country for the first time (with the partial exception of Mongolia) and to some extent they wanted to present North Korea as a showcase for socialist-type development in the Third World. North Korea also lent itself well (atypically well, it should be said) to Stalinist "industry-first" development.

However, under this Soviet umbrella, the evidence is that the new Korean regime exercised considerable autonomy.[7] Between March and August 1946 the new administration (the North Korean Interim People's Committee: NKIPC) enacted a series of radical reforms covering every field of policy: Agrarian Reform (March 5), Labor Law (June 24), Law on Equality of the Sexes (July 30) and Law on the Nationalization of Industry, Transport, Communications, Banks, etc. (August 10). Although these reforms fall manifestly within the general area of Moscow-approved socialism of the epoch, there is plenty of evidence to show that they also had specifically Korean characteristics, and were not just carbon copies of Soviet reforms. The Law on Equality of the Sexes, for example, took close account of the specific situation of women, and of patriarchy, in Korea. Yet it also broke very sharply with traditional Korean practices; for a traditionally Confucian society, it was an extremely advanced reform, which brought about fast changes in the position of women.

The 1946 Land Reform, too, was probably more successful than is generally recognized in the West. It was a basic "land-to-the-tiller" type of reform, establishing small holdings, not collectivization. It had two striking features. First, it was by far the fastest—and therefore probably the most peaceful—land reform in any socialist country ever, taking (officially) only three weeks to implement. Second, it allowed large landlords to own the same size farms as anyone else, provided that they moved to another district (most in fact fled to the South). However, it must also be said that there is not enough evidence to make a definitive evaluation of the 1946 land reform. It is notoriously hard to raise agricultural output immediately after any major upheaval, even by liberating the elan of the population, and the base years taken for comparison are statistically unsatisfactory.

Some idea of the gains made in the years between 1945 and the Korean War can be gleaned from Table III.

Table III[8]

North Korea: Indices of Key Economic Variables, 1946-1953
(1946 = 100)

	1946	1949	1953
National Income	100	209	145
Gross value of industrial production	100	337	216
Production of the means of production	100	375	158
Production of consumer goods	100	288	285
Gross value of agricultural production	100	151	115

One big unknown in this early period is the real extent of Soviet aid. Soviet and Korean accounts do not tally on this. The Koreans, much later, accused the Soviets of unequal exchange.[9] The Soviets have published figures to indicate that they gave extensive aid. Of course, both statements may be true—and probably are: that is, that the Soviets did indeed play a major rule in rehabilitating industry and agriculture in the North, as well as providing aid, but also took sizable deliveries of raw materials, including gold, at rates which were disadvantageous to the DPRK.

What is not in dispute is that by 1950 the North was recovering well from Japanese colonialism and there had been a big influx of Koreans from Japan.[10] The North was in much better shape than the South, particularly in regard to food supply.

The Legacy of the South

As Table I shows, the South inherited most of the country's agricultural land, most of its light industry[11] and most of the service sector, not least because it inherited the nation's capital, Seoul, a factor of considerable political importance. Although most of the mineral resources lay in the North, the South had sizable tungsten, coal and graphite deposits. At the moment of Japan's surrender on August 15, 1945, the South had a higher proportion of assets in working order than did the North. This was so because the fighting between the Soviet Red Army and the Japanese army took place only in the northern part of the peninsula and especially because the Japanese did not carry out as much sabotage in the South as in the North.

The economic policies pursued in the South differed markedly from those followed in the North in the years 1945-1950.[12] Redistribution of confiscated Japanese assets proceeded much more slowly. The U.S. occupation regime and the Korean regime headed by Syngman Rhee moved much more slowly and much less decisively to tackle the land-holding and food supply situations. In the initial period, rice production fell sharply, due partly to the absence of fertilizer, which had come from the North, but also because rice was hoarded and failed to reach the urban areas. Only imports of U.S. wheat prevented mass hunger and famine. The tenancy situation and land hunger were aggravated by the return of large numbers of Koreans from Japan, northeast China and northern Korea. The land situation contributed to widespread uprisings in the South in the fall of 1946, memorably described by the journalist Mark Gayn, who was an eye witness.[13]

In 1948 the U.S. military occupation made a first move toward alleviating the crisis by selling some 278,000 hectares of confiscated Japanese-owned lands to some 587,974 families. After prolonged wrangling and watering-down, a land reform bill was finally passed, just before the Korean War broke out. In theory, this mandated the distribution of the lands of big landlords to some nine hundred thousand households.[14]

The liberation of Korea from the Japanese empire, along with the division of the country, produced the same sorts of problems in industry in the South as in the North: an unbalanced and unintegrated manufacturing sector, but in this instance light industry rather than heavy. By 1946 manufacturing plants had been reduced to less than half the pre-1945 figure. According to Hatada, production in 1948 was only twenty percent of the 1940 figure.[15]

Estimates differ widely on the success of the newly independent regime of the Republic of Korea under Syngman Rhee after 1948. In many ways this regime was a retread of the Yi system, basically stagnation-oriented.[16] Others suggest that the period 1948-1950 "was a period of substantial progress,"[17] with coal production rising (from a very low base) by forty percent, electrical power by thirty percent, and industrial production as a whole by fifty percent.

Such gains as there were were made possible almost wholly by foreign (i.e., U.S.) aid. According to Hatada, this amounted to $550 million by the end of 1949,[18] a sizable sum for the time. Most sources concur in stating that this aid was largely dissipated in supplying consumer goods. In January 1950 the U.S. House of Representatives voted against a bill for further aid to the Republic of Korea (ROK). It was only when then Secretary of State Acheson argued that the ROK would collapse in two or three months without U.S. aid that a bill was passed in March 1950 granting Seoul $100 million.

One reason the country was in dire straits was that by FY 1949 approximately sixty percent of the budget was being spent on military and security affairs. This both hampered the chances of economic development and greatly contributed to inflation, which was in the runaway category prior to the outbreak of full-scale war in June 1950. The economic situation was so serious that the National Assembly was deadlocked on the FY 1950 budget in April (1950) and the situation was only unblocked by an explicit threat by Acheson to cut off all economic aid, which would, in effect, have meant letting the ROK collapse.

The Impact of the Korean War

It is hard to overstate the devastating impact of the Korean War. Both human and material destruction were on an appalling scale. Although the whole of the peninsula and all its inhabitants suffered great hardship and high casualties, the North suffered considerably more than the South.

- The South

Between June 25 and the end of September 1950, ninety percent of the South (maximum from late July to mid-September) was occupied by the North. The joint North Korean/Chinese forces also occupied a sizable part of the South for several months again in early 1951. Seoul was reoccupied between January 4 and March 14, 1951.

As W.D. Reeve points out, "The damage inflicted by the war...is difficult to assess in concrete terms."[19] UN estimates in September 1951 suggest that physical damage in the South in the first year may have amounted to nearly $2 billion, which would be greater than the value of the South's GNP in the year prior to the start of the war. In Seoul over eighty percent of industry, public utilities and transport, three-quarters of the offices, and more than half of the dwellings were in ruins. There was also heavy loss of livestock and much damage to irrigation works. Agricultural output dropped twenty-seven percent between 1949 and 1952; GNP fell sixteen percent. Inflation was acute: five hundred percent in 1951, one hundred percent in 1952. The war also had a profound impact on Korean society, to some extent leveling social distinctions, as well as causing considerable population dislocation.

But there were other effects which are less often emphasized. By far the most important is the paradoxical one that the North Koreans, by carrying out a radical land reform in the South in the summer of 1950 (a fact which is omitted from many standard texts), helped unblock the logjam in rural landholding and, in a sense, contributed to making it possible for the Rhee regime to survive by enacting a more timid land reform on the back of the communist reform.[20] A second major effect, rather hard to quantify, was the impact of the presence of a vast U.S. army and air force, equipped with the latest technology. The spin-offs from this were certainly enormous, not just in giving their start to most of the *chaebol* (big conglomerates), but in spreading technological know-how and money through the economy.[21] This experience and the personal contacts that went with it, among other things, led directly to the ability of Korean companies to bid successfully for big contracts during the Vietnam War and later to major construction projects in the Middle East. In addition, the large-scale militarization of ROK society, including a proportionately large army, military training in schools and a heavy military budget, can be attributed in part to the war of 1950-53.

There is no agreed figure for the human losses. Well over one million Koreans died in the South during the war (total population in 1950: just over twenty million). Of these, probably about eighty-five percent were civilians.[22] Among the economic costs resulting from this human devastation must be included that of maintaining large numbers of orphans and disabled people.[23]

- The North

Like the South, the North had ninety percent of its territory (and population) occupied for up to three months, between early October and the end of December 1950. But whereas the South suffered heavy destruction for less than one year (up to the spring of 1951), the North was very heavily bombed from both air and sea for the entire period of the war—three years.

The Democratic People's Republic of Korea (DPRK) was more devastated than any country had been during World War II, and more than North Vietnam during the Vietnam War. Total material damage has been estimated at 420 billion *won*.[24] Much of the destruction was caused by the intensive bombing, but many towns and villages were burned down by U.S.—and British— troops during the retreat from the Yalu in November-December 1950.

By the end of the war virtually every town and village was completely destroyed. Less than one-third of the way through the war the head of the U.S. Bomber Command in the Far East, General O'Donnell, told the MacArthur hearings, "Everything is destroyed. There is nothing standing worthy of the name. Just before the Chinese came in [four or five months into the war, J.H.] we were grounded. There were no more targets in Korea."[25] By the end of the first year of the war, the U.S. Air Force had dropped 7.8 million gallons of napalm on the North, as well as ninety seven thousand tons of bombs. North Korea claims that the United States dropped more than fifteen million napalm bombs on the DPRK in the first two years of the war, and that the capital, Pyongyang, received one thousand bombs (including delayed action bombs) per square kilometer. The capital had been a city of four hundred thousand people. When the war ended it is reported to have had only two buildings intact. Photographs taken in 1953 show it looking much like Hiroshima after the atomic bomb. A British navy officer P.O.W. returning home through Pyongyang in late summer 1953 wrote starkly, "The city has ceased to exist."[26]

Every major industrial enterprise was destroyed. In 1953 power production was only twenty-six percent of what it had been in 1949, fuel eleven percent, chemicals twenty-two percent and metallurgy ten percent. In addition to power plants, the United States bombed a number of major dams in May 1953, causing extensive loss of life, flooding, and threat to the rice crops.[27] Long before the end of the war, much of the population of the North was living in caves or in holes in the ground. Much industry had been moved into underground installations. Farming was done mainly at night.

The DPRK will not give overall figures for population losses during the war. A Soviet source states that the population fell by 11.76 percent between 1949 and 1953 (males from 4,782,000 to 3,982,000;

females from 4,840,000 to 4,509,000).[28] A generally accepted estimate is that about one-third of the deaths were military casualties, the rest civilian. The DPRK's population loss was proportionately higher than that of the USSR in World War II, resulting in a comparable sex imbalance. Among the costs that are impossible to quantify are the high expense of looking after many orphans, disabled, and limbless people, and many thousands, perhaps hundreds of thousands, of people scarred physically and mentally by napalm.

Like the South, the North became a highly militarized society, with very large armed forces and a heavy defense budget. Again as in the South, there were undoubtedly technological spin-offs from using and repairing military equipment, although, on the whole, this technology was not as advanced as that used by the United States. The DPRK also acquired considerable experience at earth-moving and underground construction, which has enabled it, at high cost, to locate many strategic installations deep below ground to this day.

The utter devastation also had tremendous impact on the land system. Almost all property lines were destroyed during the war, and agriculture perforce moved onto a de facto collective basis. Immediately after the war ended, the North instituted collectivization (called "cooperativization"); this was completed by 1958. As Bruce Cumings has pointed out, these cooperatives, which "correspond[ed] to the old natural villages rather than huge state farms," have produced "one of the more successful socialist agricultural systems."[29]

The DPRK recovered amazingly fast from the war. Undoubtedly, its own extraordinarily high level of mobilization was a major factor behind this recovery. But foreign aid was also crucial. Apart from financial aid, particularly from the USSR and China, and food and clothing, mention must be made of the exceptional input provided by hundreds of thousands of Chinese troops. They helped with farming, irrigation and repair work during the war and very large numbers stayed in Korea up to 1958, working on reconstruction projects. This huge extra labor force was probably the single most important external factor allowing the North to rebuild to prewar levels within a few years.[30])

• Socialism in the North

In view of the North's very poor reputation in the West and frequent predictions of economic failure, it is perhaps worth noting that many experienced observers have rated its achievements quite highly. Harrison Salisbury, a highly astute observer of communist countries, who visited the North in 1972, wrote of "a tremendous technical and industrial achievement" and "on a per capita basis...the most intensively industrialized country in Asia, with the exception of Japan." The French agronomist René Dumont claimed in the late 1960s, "In agriculture and probably industry, too, North Korea leads the socialist bloc." And Joan Robinson wrote, after a visit in 1964, "All the economic miracles of the postwar world are put in the shade by these achievements."[31] Admittedly, these comments refer to the period of the mid-1960s and early 1970s. Although the observations are dated, it is important to note that they refer to a period when the DPRK economy was being written off by Seoul and some Western sources as a failure on the brink of disaster in very much the same terms as are currently deployed by its critics. Moreover, the fact that the economy had had some two decades of high growth means that one can state that it had been soundly established, which does not preclude later slowdown, or even decline. The extent of the transformation of the society can be seen from Table IV.

Table IV[32]

Share of Industry and Agriculture in National Income (Percent)

	1946	*1965 1970*	*1983*
Industry	16.8	64.265	66
Agriculture	63.5	18.320	10

This has, naturally, been accompanied by a big shift in the proportions of the population in rural and urban areas. It is reckoned that the urban population rose from 17.7 percent of the total in 1953 to between sixty and seventy percent by the early 1980s.

North Korea claims to have built "an excellent independent national economy which is well-rounded, equipped, up-to-date, fed with our own raw materials, operated by our own cadres and techniques."[33] It claims that growth has been sustained at a high rate and has been balanced between agriculture, light industry and heavy industry. That is, growth has been achieved without squeezing the rural sector excessively and without sacrificing the consumer, as happened in other communist countries. It claims balanced growth among the different areas of the hilly and mountainous country.

The basic strategy of *juche* (roughly "self reliance") calls for the economy to rely, when it can, on domestic resources in all sectors, for sixty to seventy percent of supplies. Where key raw materials are not available, the policy is to substitute domestic resources, e.g., limestone for making textiles, coal for producing fertilizers. Substitution is a key component of juche. Contrary to some suggestions, Pyongyang, while endorsing autarchy (self reliance) explicitly rejects autarky (self sufficiency) and strongly favors international economic cooperation, especially South-South cooperation.[34] According to Kim Il Sung in 1979, the juche strategy meant that the DPRK "is immune from the effects of worldwide economic upheavals, and it is crisis-free."[35]

Agriculture has been the big problem area in almost all socialist societies. The DPRK claims to be self-sufficient in food overall, with unhusked grain production having reached ten million tons by 1984. Unfortunately, the DPRK will not release comprehensive statistics on its food trade. Working back from statistics of its trading partners, it appears that it probably does export more food, mainly rice, in both quantity and value than it imports, mainly wheat. The *Asia 1984 Yearbook* listed North Korea as the only country in the Asia-Pacific area other than New Zealand whose percentage of imported food consumption was nil.[36] Perhaps the best single reason for giving credence to the basic DPRK claims is that the figures for rice yields (7.6 tons per hectare) and total cereal production (then "approaching ten million tons annually") were accepted by a highly qualified independent observer, the chief editor of the Food and Agricultural Organization magazine *Ceres*, based on a first-hand inspection tour in May 1983.[37] Furthermore, this overall self-sufficiency seems to be at a fairly high level. The World Bank's *World Development Report 1984* gives the daily calorie supply per capita as three thousand or 129 percent of requirement, a higher figure than that for Australia, Japan or Sweden.[38]

The North's achievement in agriculture is impressive, especially given its harsh climate and shortage of good land. Land available for agriculture is to be expanded through massive projects scheduled for completion in 1990. The plan is to reclaim three hundred thousand hectares of land from the sea and to extend the area of cultivable land by an additional two hundred thousand hectares, through terracing and other methods. Among the technical factors contributing to the North's success in agriculture are very high use of fertilizer (more than one and a half tons per hectare by 1978), an extensive irrigation system, and high mechanization (e.g., tractors and rice transplanters).[39]

It is more difficult to evaluate the impact of the two land reforms in 1946 and in the post-Korean War collectivization.[40] As everywhere else, agriculture had to produce the "surplus" for other sectors. The agricultural tax, which started at twenty-five percent, was gradually phased out until it was abolished in 1966. The official claim that even during this initial period the rural population was not squeezed excessively is difficult to evaluate. In fact, the tax was on planned, not actual output, and only best-quality grain was accepted in payment. When the tax was abolished in 1966 the growth rate declined.[41] The regime claims that since 1966 the urban areas subsidize the rural ones. This is impossible to confirm, since information on prices and subsidies is far from comprehensive. There is a large subsidy for rice, but there is no hard information on subsidies for fertilizers and other inputs.

The centerpiece of DPRK strategy has been its drive for industrialization. North Korea is probably still, as when Harrison Salisbury visited it, the second most highly industrialized country in Asia, after Japan. The regime claims very high growth rates: 23.5 percent average increase in gross industrial output between 1954 and 1970, and an annual average increase of fifteen percent in the 1970s. Growth targets are just over twelve percent annually for the 1980s. The government's strategy is one of sustained high growth, which must also be balanced, relying to the maximum on domestic resources—and with an economy that is both diversified and maximally integrated. The development of a comprehensive machine tool sector, in which ninety-eight percent sufficiency is claimed, is central to this strategy.

Outside observers have questioned some of the regime's claims. Detailed analysis of growth rates has slightly deflated the official claims. Chung convincingly questions the extent to which light and heavy industry were really as well balanced up to 1970 as the regime claims.[42] The quality of many consumer goods is manifestly poor, and military demands must have placed heavy pressure against consumer goods production.[43] In addition (see below) Pyongyang does not give due acknowledgement to foreign aid.

One specific area in which the North seems to have had notable and little-noticed success is in energy. It has no oil and yet it has one of the highest per capita consumptions of energy in East Asia, estimated at 3072 kg. of coal equivalent in 1979, not far below the figure for Japan and well ahead of both Singapore and South Korea.[44] But what is most striking is that oil accounts for only a very small percentage of primary energy consumption— probably about ten percent. About three-quarters of its energy is produced from coal. The rest is from hydroelectric sources. Although energy usage may be quite inefficient, the DPRK's energy achievement is a remarkable one which, to my knowledge, has no parallel anywhere in the world: a highly industrialized economy which is minimally oil-dependent and minimally dependent on external energy sources, even though lacking any oil of its own.

If official Pyongyang claims are sometimes exaggerated and often very vague, Western and especially Seoul downgradings are usually also inaccurate. A well-informed Soviet source said in 1984 that industrial production "almost quadrupled" in the previous decade.[45] There are undoubtedly major structural problems. Transportation and infrastructure lag badly behind. There are about 4,380 kilometers of railway track, which carry almost all the country's goods. Very little seems to move by road. There has been a big drive to electrify the system and by the end of 1984, eighty-eight percent electrification was claimed, although outside estimates do not confirm this.

The other less tangible area involves the general level of education of the society and the ideology of economic management. The regime claims a very high level of education, with 1.2 million technicians. Outsiders generally consider that the North has a fairly broad stratum of middle-level technicians, but that technical training, like much of the industrial plant itself, is rather backward. The editor of *Ceres* wrote that "the present stage of agrarian revolution in the DPRK can fairly be likened to a well-disciplined regiment marking time,"[46] and something of the same can be said about industry and industrial management.

No one disputes the assertion that the North carries a heavy defense burden, but no one agrees on what it actually is. The official figures are that defense spending accounted for 14.1 percent of the 1986 budget and that the armed forces totalled "about 350-400,000" in 1980.[47] Western sources claim that the defense budget accounts for anything between 10.2 and twenty-five percent of GNP (or twenty-seven percent and upwards of public expenditure), and that the armed forces total up to 880,000 people.[48] No definitive reconciliation of these widely varying figures is possible. From visible observation, it is manifest that the armed forces in the North are extremely numerous. On the other hand, no one in the West or in Seoul has been able to explain how the DPRK economy has been able to function successfully with the crippling percentages attributed by U.S. and ROK sources to DPRK defense spending, which truly would constitute an "economic miracle."[49] In most armies, pay accounts for just over half of any defense budget. Since the Korean People's Army (KPA) plays a major role in both industry and agriculture, it is not clear that this part of military spending is detrimental to the working of the economy. The KPA also undoubtedly plays a major role in training troops in such things as driving trucks and medium-level technology. The high level of military preparedness must also have stimulated the arms industry, which, in addition to earning much foreign exchange (e.g., big sales to Iran), must also have had some spin-offs in the non-military sector. In brief, defense spending must be a net drain but it is not at all clear how big.

Finally, any assessment of juche must confront two major problem areas: the role of foreign aid and the size of the external debt. The DPRK is conspicuously silent, and indeed downright misleading, on both issues, which severely undermines its credibility and weakens the juche "model." Official figures on aid say that the DPRK received $550 million from all sources. Outside estimates range up as high as "probably $5 billion" by the early 1970s.[50] Western sources suggest, quite plausibly, that foreign aid accounted for nearly twenty-five percent of budget revenues prior to the Korean War, forty to fifty percent during the war and thirty-three percent immediately afterwards, falling rapidly in the late 1950s. In addition, the enormous quantity of free labor provided by the Chinese troops during the Korean War and in the years following up to 1958 was crucial in helping the DPRK to reconstruct very fast after the Korean War. All this can, of course, be considered an exceptional period.

Nevertheless, Soviet sources have recently given many details of very extensive Soviet aid continuing up to the present day. These Soviet accounts also indicate that Soviet loans were re-scheduled over very long periods up to thirty-five years.[51] According to the Soviets, "The projects built with Soviet assistance comprise the backbone of the DPRK national economy...and encompass practically all major branches of the economy." This is quite a different picture from the one presented, partly by omission, by Pyongyang. The official DPRK version of events is thus not of much use, since it fails either to confront the hard facts or, therefore, to spell out how well Korea has been able to use Soviet aid. It even fails to make explicit Korea's quite interesting and unique position as a participant in Comecon on relatively independent terms.⁵² Unsaid by both parties is the fact that Soviet aid on this level is hardly generalizable.

Pyongyang is, if anything, even less forthcoming about its external debt. In spite of Kim Il Sung's attempts to dismiss it as a "temporary phenomenon" and a simple trade deficit (in 1977),⁵³ it is something much more than this. First of all, it is now clear from Soviet accounts that the DPRK has been heavily in debt to the USSR for the past thirty-five years, and still is. It is probably similarly in debt to several East European countries and China. Secondly, from the early 1970s Pyongyang racked up a sizable debt with Japan and some West European states. Calculations about the size of this hard currency debt are bedeviled by Pyongyang's evasions and Seoul's bad-mouthing. In September 1984 the (London) *Economist* estimated the debt to non-communist countries at about 2.3 billion dollars.⁵⁴ The highest reliable estimates for overdue sums have been about $400 million.⁵⁵

What is a fair overall assessment of this debt, which has to be confronted frankly if one is to make any useful assessment of juche and of North Korea's chances of "re-linking" with the world capitalist economy? First of all, the debt is quite large compared with the DPRK's total hard currency trade. The debt service ratio over the years 1981-85 has been estimated at thirty to thirty percent of the DPRK's hard currency export earnings.⁵⁶ Secondly, it is not nearly so menacing if set against the size of the economy as a whole and resources, such as gold, which would allow it to raise hard currency quickly. But there is more to it than this, on both sides.

There should be absolutely no doubt that the DPRK mismanaged its debt very badly. It was the first communist state ever to default on its loans. It earned a deservedly atrocious reputation in world banking and trading circles. It was blackballed on the Baltic Exchange in London. And, perhaps most serious, it endangered its own ability to borrow money and import the advanced technology and plant it badly needs. On the other hand, although its cranky behavior deprived it of access to some advanced technology, the DPRK did not do so badly as its critics make out. There is no evidence that the growth rate slowed down as a result of the debt. It could therefore be argued that the state did its job; it protected the citizens of the DPRK against the fluctuations and pressures of the world economy. Pyongyang did not allow the IMF in to go through the books, force a devaluation, or a cut in social services (although this may now be in effect in disguised form because more of production is being geared for export to earn foreign currency). But overall, it is clear that Pyongyang mishandled the whole affair badly. Although bankers love lending money, it is hard to shake off the reputation of being a bad debtor.

In 1979 Kim Il Sung announced that "precedence" was to be given to the production of goods for export,⁵⁷ a formulation which was itself unprecedented and raises a question about the concept of self-reliance, in the sense of self-centered (*auto-centré*) development.

In September 1984 the Supreme People's Assembly, the North Korean parliament, enacted a joint venture law designed to attract foreign investment. DPRK spokespersons have said that they are looking for capital from Western Europe and Japan, and from Koreans living overseas. So far, apart from arrangements with pro-DPRK Koreans in Japan, the only such venture with a capitalist country known to be under way is the construction of a large modern hotel in Pyongyang with French investment. Talks are reportedly under way on a joint venture with a West German company to build a cement factory. The joint venture law allows for export of profits. It has also been hinted that foreign management would be able to pay wages fifty percent higher than normal rates to DPRK employees, and to exercise freedom in hiring and firing. Senior DPRK figures, including heir-apparent Kim Jong Il and ex-Premier Kang Song San, are known to have taken a keen interest in some of China's new experiments with foreign capital. But the DPRK has much less experience than China in coping with foreign technology and foreign personnel and work methods. It is very much an open question whether the DPRK will be able to handle this new phase with more aplomb than it handled the external debt issues in the 1970s.[58]

- Capitalism in the South

As with the North, there are two starkly contrasting view of the South's economic development. The South and its admirers describe Japan." Seoul's critics suggest the ROK economy is a "house built on sand" or even that the South's industrialization is "fictitious" (Fidel Castro).[59] Yet anyone who examines South Korea's development and its presence in the world economy cannot but recognize that extraordinary growth has taken place, especially in the industrial sector, in the past two decades.

Per capita GNP in mid-1986 was estimated at almost exactly two thousand dollars from eighty dollars in 1961. Average growth in GDP over the years 1965-73 was ten per cent. It reached 7.3 per cent in the decade 1973-1983, in spite of sharp fluctuations around 1980.[60] The structure of the economy changed markedly over the decades of the 1960s and 1970s, as can be seen from Table V, which gives the shifts in the contributions of the different sectors in 1960 and 1982.

Table V[61]

	GDP	Agriculture	Industry	[Manufacturing]	Services
1950	3,810	37	20	14	43
1982	68,420	16	39	28	45

As has the North, therefore, the South has shifted the balance between agriculture and industry radically, while producing a much bigger service sector. But both agriculture and industry have developed quite different profiles from those in the North.

Prior to the division, the South was the main agricultural area of Korea. Now, in spite of the fact that the South is proportionately slightly less urbanized than the North, it is not self-sufficient in food production. In addition, the so-called rate of self-sufficiency (which in this case is not self-sufficiency) has been declining. Between 1974 and 1983 cereal imports went up by almost two and a half times—from 2,679,000 metric tons to 6,354,000 metric tons.[62] Between 1960 and 1981, during two decades of intense industrialization, food imports rose from ten to twelve percent of total imports.

As has the North does, the South manipulates and conceals statistics to suit its case, particularly in agriculture. Under President Park, it was claimed that self-sufficiency in rice had been achieved by the late 1970s. After Park was assassinated in 1979, the Ministry of Agriculture announced that the level of self-sufficiency in rice in 1979 had reached only eighty-six percent. *The Asia 1986 Yearbook* states that net imported food accounted for 51.1 percent of consumption.

Critics of the ROK can point to the following weaknesses. The South, a rich agricultural area, is increasingly dependent on food (especially grain) imports. Food imports are increasing absolutely and as a percentage of total imports. Perhaps most important, the amount of arable land, currently about twenty-three percent, is shrinking rather fast. None of the remedies tried so far, e.g., miracle rice, has managed to stem the tide. Socially, too, the shift off the land has led to harsh conditions for sizable numbers in both the villages and the towns. Many rural communities have been damaged, and large numbers of those who have flocked into the cities live in bad, or very bad (slum) conditions. Many others, though, have seen their incomes and living standards rise. Likewise, supporters of the ROK's development can argue that increasing food imports are not necessarily bad. It all depends on the terms of trade.

In industry, the ROK can show very high growth rates—an average of 17.2 percent annually over the decade 1960-1970, and an average of 13.6 percent annually over the period 1970-1982, in spite of severe problems in the years 1979-1982. According to some estimates, the ROK was the most productive economy in the world over the decade from the mid-1960s to the mid-1970s. The incremental capital-output ratio (the amount of capital necessary to produce an additional unit of output) was 0.022, the lowest in the world.[63] This extraordinary boom has fairly been described as "export-led." In the early and mid-1970s exports grew at an annual rate of forty-five percent.

Over the period since Syngman Rhee was ousted in 1960, the ROK has moved impressively from a relatively small-scale, basically import-substituting economy, to one which can compete on the world market in most of the major branches of industry—steel, shipbuilding and cars, in particular. It has also moved into newer high-technology and electronics. In addition, it must be emphasized that the ROK has managed to create a fairly broad-based and comprehensive industrial base. It is heavily dependent on industrial imports, both raw materials and machine tools and technology. Its industrialization can fairly be termed import-dependent as well as export-dependent. Yet it has, unlike Taiwan, with which it is frequently compared, created the kind of industrial and financial base which can, in principle, ensure continued growth and solidity. It does not by any means produce all the manufactured goods it needs, but it has an industrial economy which is both sufficiently large (twice the size of Taiwan's) and sufficiently comprehensive for the domestic gaps not to be an inherent obstacle to growth. In this sense, it is unique among the newly industrializing countries of Asia.

The other striking feature of the ROK economy has been its ability to break into the market for giant international construction projects. Building on skills acquired during the Korean War and later on major construction projects in Vietnam, South Korean companies like Hyundai moved into the Middle East in a big way, thus incidentally earning valuable foreign exchange. In each of the years 1981 and 1982 the ROK earned more than $13 billion in new construction contracts overseas. In 1984 it won the bid to build a huge water project in Libya, worth $3.3 billion, and reportedly the largest single contract of its kind ever. But since 1984 earnings and new contracts for business in the Middle East have been in decline. As of mid-1986, however, ROK firms were reported as still having some $20 billion of construction contracts outstanding in the Middle East—though in some cases companies were expecting losses due to defaults and bad debts.[64]

The South is developing a fairly sophisticated service sector to accompany its industrial drive. Although the financial sector has been very carefully protected by the state from foreign pressure, it has so far been able, through a mixture of orthodox and unorthodox methods (including a wild "curb market" which has produced major scandals), to handle the country's rapid growth demands. Seoul is currently engaged on a cautious "liberalization" program.[65]

The South has a more extensive railway system than the North (6,168 kilometers of track), as well as a much more developed road system, which plays a much bigger role in the economy than do roads in the North. The South also has a very sophisticated international communications network, with a major airline, Korean Air (formerly Korean Airlines: KAL). Korean shipping has been carrying an increasing proportion of the country's trade.[66]

Like the North, the ROK has heavy military expenditures and a large army. The armed forces total 622,000 (supplemented by some forty thousand U.S. troops). Military spending is officially stated to have been $4.4 billion in 1985. *The Asia 1986 Yearbook* gives this as 6.7 percent of GNP or twenty-five per cent of total public expenditures.[67] Unfortunately, these statistics do not tally much better than those about the North, and it is very hard to assess the weight of the military on the economy, either in terms of subtraction of manpower (the ROK military is exclusively male) or of diversion of financial resources. Unlike the North, the military in the South does not play a major role in the civilian economy, although the pressures of the arms industry probably have much the same overall effect as in the North. The great military-industrial complex at Ch'angnyong, for example, has continually operated at large deficits. The spin-offs from high militarization and from the high-technology U.S. presence have been considerable. In addition, the high level of militarization also helped produce a (probably one-shot) bonanza during the Vietnam War, when the ROK benefited from large military-related sales to the U.S. forces and also earned sizable income from, in effect, renting a part of its armed forces to the United States for fighting in Indochina.[68]

In trying to assess the South's economic success, it is also necessary to consider its vulnerability and external dependence. One factor which cannot be underestimated is the huge amount of foreign aid which the ROK has received: some $13 billion between 1945 and the late 1970s (military and economic). This amounts to $600 per capita.[69] Over the period 1946-1978 the ROK received almost as much money, nearly $6 billion) in U.S. economic grants and loans as the whole of Africa ($6.89 billion). Most important is the very high level of U.S. military assistance. Over the period 1946-1975 the ROK received $8,871,800,000 in military assistance from the United States, compared with $2,562,000,000 for the whole of Latin America and $1,030,400,000 for the whole of Africa.[70] In addition, although hard to quantify in purely economic terms, between 1950 and 1975 South Korea had 32,479 trainees at U.S. military schools, more than the whole of the Middle East, North Africa and South Asia put together (23,526).[71]

This aid, both military and economic, was crucial to the ROK's survival. During the 1950s U.S. aid accounted for five-sixths of ROK imports. Bruce Cumings cites a U.S. report on the U.S. aid program to the ROK in the 1950s: "If we were to characterize the program simply, we would say that the Korean consumer has been subsidized by the International Cooperation Administration (ICA) and U.S. military expenditures in return for the maintenance of a large military establishment. The attitude one adopts toward this Korean military program very largely determines one's attitude toward the U.S. aid program in Korea."[72]

The second main feature of the ROK's external dependence is its foreign debt. This was estimated at about $47 billion as of mid-1986, the largest in Asia, and the fourth biggest in the world, after the Latin America "big three" (Brazil, Mexico, Argentina). The debt service ratio was estimated at 15.2 percent in 1984. Compared with the Latin American states, the ROK's debt is fairly high as a percentage of GNP, but relatively low as a proportion of exports. As of mid-1986, the debt situation was improving markedly. The ROK's reserves also topped the $8 billion mark for the first time in the middle of 1986 to reach $8.16 billion by the end of July.[73]

From 1979 to 1982, political uncertainty after the assassination of President Park came on top of major problems caused by the world recession. The severe crises of these years make any examination of trends which include this period very hard to evaluate. But it is important to note that over the period 1970-77 the debt service ratio fell quite markedly.[74] The country's debt is, of course, closely affected by its trade balance. Until the mid-1980s, the ROK ran a regular trade deficit. Although it often failed to meet its targets for reducing this up to 1985, it did (contrary to what many left-wing critics predicted) manage to reduce its deficits. And in the first half of 1986 there was, for the first time, a sizable surplus on trade ($1.07 billion to the end of July 1986). With this, the country can reduce both new borrowing and projected debt.

It is important to note that, due mainly to the very large amounts of U.S. grant aid in the 1950s and 1960s, the ROK contracted virtually no debt obligations in the early period of its industrialization, unlike most Third World countries. Also, along with the fact that direct foreign investment is fairly low, there is the absolutely key fact that the ROK state has exercised tight control over foreign borrowing. Although the debt is not of negligible size, the ROK's control over it is unusually strong. Lastly, it has to be pointed out that on a debt well over ten times as large, the ROK's debt service ratio is lower than that of the DPRK.

The South is vulnerable. Foreign trade was estimated to account for 84.4 percent of GNP by *The Asia 1985 Yearbook*. But it is also true, as Richard Luedde-Neurath has remarked, that even as Seoul has become more dependent on the world economy, it has become more independent within it. It is very heavily dependent on raw materials for its industries and on food imports for its population. The ROK is dependent on a few key markets for most of its exports, and it is therefore vulnerable to protectionism.

The South is also vulnerable because of its very close and unequal relationship with Japan. The complexities of this are the subject of much debate. Critics of the relationship can point to stark factors of "dependency," such as the "Yatsugi Plan" drawn up in 1970, envisaging a form of subordinate integration of the ROK economy into a new Japanese form of "Co-Prosperity Sphere."[75] It is certainly true that Japan has been running enormous trade surpluses with the ROK. In both 1982 and 1983 Japan's surplus with Korea exceeded the ROK's total trade deficit with the whole world. Japan has also dumped high polluting industries in Korea. The other side of the coin is that the ROK is gradually catching up and competing with Japan. Within the subordinate relationship, Korea has been able to upgrade its industrial structure, albeit at a high human and social cost.

In spite of what the ROK's critics have said, its industrialization is not fictitious. As 1986 showed, with a favorable conjuncture (low oil prices, high yen, low dollar, low international interest rates) the ROK can do extremely well, and even right some of its apparently chronic problems, such as the trade deficit. South Korea has an increasingly sophisticated financial sector. It even has sizable investments in industry in the United States. So far, its ability to overcome its vulnerabilities has been far more impressive than its much-criticized weaknesses.

Comparing the North and the South

No one has devised a foolproof system for comparing the real standard of living, including the quality of life, in socialist and capitalist societies. In the case of North and South Korea, there are many pitfalls in attempting a comparison. First is the problem of agreeing on what is actually important. Second is agreeing on a fair exchange rate for the DPRK won. Third is interpreting the self-serving and often downright false statistics put out by each state, both about itself and about the other (and, especially in the case of the DPRK, large statistical lacunae).

In 1978 the U.S. CIA published a comparison of North and South Korea whose main statistics have not, to my knowledge, been seriously challenged. Table VI shows the calculations of selected products.[76]

Table VI

Production of Selected Products

		1970		*1976*	
	Units	*North*	*South*	*North**	*South*
Electric power	billion kwh	16.5	9.2	21.8	23.1
Coal	mil. metric tons	27.5	12.4	39.5	16.4
Crude steel	mil. metric tons	2.2	0.5	2.75	2.7
Fertilizer	mil. metric tons (nutrient content)	0.3	0.6	0.6	0.8
Cement	mil. metric tons	4.0	5.8	5.0	11.9
Textiles (excl. yarn)	mil. sq. meters	418.0	329.0	450.0	936.0
Refined petroleum products	mil. metric tons	0	9.0	1.0	17.8
Fish catch	mil. metric tons	0.7	0.9	1.2	2.4
Machine tools	thousand units	10.0	7.5	24.0	8.4
Trucks	thousand units	4.0	5.5	10.0	19.5
Zinc	thous. metric tons	83.0	3.0	125.0	27.0
Lead	thous. metric tons	61.0	3.0	80.0	8.0
T.V. sets	million units	Negl.	0.1	Negl.	2.3

*Preliminary estimates.

This shows the South closing the gap between 1970 and 1976, but leaving the North still well ahead as of 1976—on average, roughly double per capita output of most basic items. Most sources in the West now tend to put the ROK ahead in real living standards, although it has to be said that it is never clear on what basis this claim rests. *The Asia Yearbook* gave average growth over the years 1978-1982 at 9.7 for the DPRK (the highest in Asia, except for Brunei), and only 3.4 percent for the ROK (admittedly poor years), and 4.5 and 4.74 per cent, respectively, for the years 1980-1984.[77] But if the CIA's figures are even roughly correct (and they hardly have an interest in biasing them in favor of the North) the ROK would have needed much higher growth than this to overtake the North by 1984-85. In addition, Western sources often credit the DPRK with higher gross capital formation than the ROK. *The Asia 1984 Yearbook* gave the DPRK thirty-eight percent in the years immediately preceding, with the lower but still very high figure of 26.2 percent of GNP for the South.[78]

It is generally accepted—except in Pyongyang—that per capita income in the South reached $2,000 in 1986. But no one agrees on the figure for the North. Kim Il Sung claimed per capita income in the North had reached $1,920 as of New Year 1980. This claim was not explained and was not widely believed. Most Western sources give per capita income in the North at about half that in the South.[79]

Apart from the basic items given in Table VI, what else can one reasonably include? First of all, food intake. In 1985, the World Bank gave the North a slightly higher figure: 130 per cent of the daily calorie requirement per capita, compared with 125 per cent for the South.[80] A second criterion is life expectancy. The World Bank gives the South figures of sixty-four years for males and seventy-one for females and the North sixty-three and sixty-seven respectively, a little higher than the *Asia Yearbook*.[81] But the North disputes these figures and claims average life expectancy of seventy-one and seventy-seven, respectively, for males and females.

The North claims to spend far more money on health and have a far higher ratio of doctors to population than the South.[82] But what actually happens with all this health care? It should produce a result, for example, longer life. If the Western figures are correct, it does not; equally, if the DPRK figures are true, it does.

Among other criteria one must include are male/female income and employment figures, urban/rural standards of living, and equity.

The DPRK states that it implements the principle of equal pay for equal work and that women have access to all posts. Certainly, the 1946 Law on Equality of the Sexes appears to lay down the legal basis for such an approach. But, leaving aside the special case of the armed forces, it is also apparent that most top jobs in the civilian economy are occupied by men. In particular, there are more men in top government jobs and in industry. On the other hand, wages play a much smaller role in total income than in any other socialist country (my own guesstimate is that they account for less than half real income), and this must be taken into account. Official statistics claim that women make up forty-eight percent of the total work force and 45.5 percent of the industrial work force (and this is believable), but there is no comprehensive breakdown by sector.[83]

The situation in the South is rather different. First of all, a much smaller percentage of women is employed for remuneration. According to official figures, about fifty-seven percent of women over the age of fourteen were classified as "economically active" in 1980, up from forty-eight percent in 1965.[84] Secondly, the ratio of wages to total income is quite different in the South from the North and social services in the South for those not employed are much less, or even non-existent. Average income for women working in the South in paid jobs was estimated at the end of the 1970s at 43.9 percent of average male earnings and, on the whole, for much longer hours.[85] In addition, although not strictly an economic factor as such, many women in the South are obliged to work in a sector which has been officially and probably in fact eliminated in the North, prostitution. This has been a major foreign exchange-earning sector for the ROK (under quasi-state control), taking in up to $1 1/2 billion annually, according to some estimates.[86]

Urban/rural standards of living are hard to assess in the North. The regime claims that differences have been eliminated. A Soviet source suggested in 1981 that urban living standards were still somewhat higher, as seems probable.[87] But there are other factors, not easily quantifiable. For example, there seems to be more housing space per person in rural than in urban areas in the DPRK, and basic foodstuffs may be more easily available. On the other hand, amenities and medical care are probably superior in the urban areas.

In the South, no one claims that rural living standards are the same as those in urban areas, but it is also difficult to evaluate how many people are living in dire straits in either rural or urban areas. In 1978 Rao calculated that, although average per capita consumption in rural areas had been growing at about four percent annually over the previous decade, "It is likely that per capita consumption is about twice as high in urban as in rural areas and...that there has not been much change in the relative position of urban and rural households in recent years."[88] About the same time, it has been calculated that more than eighty-five percent of Korean workers in urban areas were earning incomes below the government's recommended minimum living standards.

There is not space here to enter into any detailed discussion of the question of equity. Suffice it to say that from visual evidence, which is proably the best criterion, there is much less disparity of income and standard of living in the North than in the South. There is, however, a visible elite in the DPRK, smaller than in the ROK, made up of government officials engaged in some forms of conspicuous consumption, e.g., Mercedes cars. There is certainly less disparity between the incomes of men and women, and between urban and rural areas. There is also, overall, a better safety net in the North, and there are no visible extremes of poverty. Real living conditions in the most mountainous areas, in prisons and the armed forces are unknown.

The *Far Eastern Economic Review*'s 1985 survey of South Korea referred to "a dangerous trend towards social schisms and economic and political polarization" and an economic structure which was "perilously lopsided in its shape" (referring to the concentration of wealth among the chaebol, as well as "the sullen middle class" and "the genuine hatred with which people making a fortune are viewed." The North may have its problems; these are not among them.

It is more difficult to give an overall assessment of the quality of life. Both societies tolerate extreme forms of pollution. The South has accepted very high-polluting industries from Japan, with noxious results, and the capital, Seoul, now with nearly nine million inhabitants, suffers from atmospheric pollution on a serious scale. Pyongyang, the DPRK capital, does not, but Harrison Salisbury reported heavy pollution at Hamhung in 1972, with smog worse than Los Angeles.[89] Visitors to factories in both North and South have commented adversely on safety measures for workers.

The North has gone flat out for a system whereby virtually all adults of both sexes are pushed full-time into the work force. To do this, there has been considerable spending on education and on an extensive network of creches and kindergartens. My own impression, in 1977 and 1985, and that of most Western visitors has been that, if anything, the North has a labor shortage, although this is contradicted by a 1983 Soviet text.[90] However, even at the purely economic level, it is not at all clear that all resources are being well used. Energy is a case in point. The regime has done a tremendous job in minimizing reliance on oil, but there is also plenty of evidence for massive energy wastage. Everyone seems to work—but are they all making the best things possible? With gross capital formation apparently consistently very high, perhaps the standard of living ought to be higher, although, again, it is impossible to know how much is being diverted into the military sector. There is reportedly a whole city whose entire economy is devoted to the manufacture of hagiography about Kim Il Sung—a dreadful waste of human resources.[91] At the same time, there is a housing shortage.[92] Investment in education is high, but one may well question the amount of time given over to studying the works of Kim.[93] Heavy spending on external security can be justified, but expenditure on internal security must also be very high and can be questioned from both an economic and a non-economic standpoint. Basic economic questions such as employment, pensions, sick pay and the like seem to have been solved. There appears to be no inflation. In fact, the regime claims prices have been lowered, although the details and mechanisms behind this are not clear. Allocation of many goods is tightly controlled through a system of rationing (officially denied).[94] The variety and quality of consumer goods are poorer than in the South.

The South has gone all out for high growth and has achieved it. Above all, the South has created a fairly broad industrial structure which has over the past two decades shown itself able to compete in the world market, moving increasingly into the key sectors of heavy and advanced industry. The costs of this can be questioned. Luedde-Neurath, one of the fairest analysts of ROK growth, states flatly, "The social costs of the Korean model are not disputed here, nor in our view can they be justified."[95] Among the costs: very low wage levels for many workers, particularly women workers; very long working hours; poor or non-existent social services (sick pay, unemployment benefits, pensions); high inflation (at times); inadequate housing; poor safety precautions in industry; weak labor laws (often not implemented); high pollution; continuing unemployment and the marginalization of large sectors of the population; the devastation of rural communities; workers' need to emigrate to get jobs (North Korean workers apparently migrate on a seasonal basis to the Soviet Union). Most of the standard literature on the South's development concentrates on its successes, which are undeniable. Most of the South's critics tend to focus on its defects, which are also undeniable. Both sides of the equation must be taken into consideration.

Seoul claims it overtook the North in per capita GNP in 1969. The U.S. CIA claims this happened in 1976. It is undeniable that the South has moved into more advanced industrial sectors than the North, but whether it has a more advanced industrial structure is another matter. The South has a more advanced transportation system, both domestically and internationally. The South is more locked into the world market than the North, but it has also been incomparably more successful at penetrating the world market than the North. The North is less vulnerable to buffeting from external forces than the South, but also much less adaptable. The North is in a stronger position than the South in regard to its ability to feed its population with its own resources.[96]

The fairest measure for comparison is purchasing price parity (PPP), but unfortunately, to my knowledge, no detailed up-to-date comparison has been made of the North and the South on this basis. Taking $2,000 as a rough average figure for the South, what figure can one reasonably suggest for the North? Here it is a question of estimating on the basis of a combination of inadequate statistics and visual observation. An extrapolation from the World Bank figures puts the DPRK figure for per capita GNP in the $1,650 range for 1982. Parris H. Chang, citing his experiences during a visit to North Korea (and the USSR) in mid-1985, wrote in *Newsweek* (July 8, 1985) of "a standard of living comparable to Eastern Europe," where per capita income was well over $2,000 by 1980 even in the more backward states like Romania.

The South, according to almost all observers, including those who have been in both North and South fairly recently, is ahead of the North, and the evidence of these first-hand observers has to be respected. But it also has to be said that the South's superiority is not demonstrated by the available statistical data. The average standard of living seems to be higher in the South, but less evenly distributed among the different income groups, between women and men, and between town and country.

Conclusion: The Two "Models" and the Future

Both North and South tend to be over-optimistic and evasive about their own prospects, and each is hypercritical of the other. It has to be recognized that both have a history of confounding their critics. To some extent, they have both become models for other economies.

The North has shown that a fairly advanced form of relatively independent, self-reliant development, with sustained high growth, is possible for a medium-sized country, in the Third World, and within the "socialist camp." The conditions which made this possible are not clearly spelled out by Pyongyang, which greatly diminishes the credibility and applicability of the "model." Among the specific features which would need to be confronted are: the absence of neo-colonialism; no brain drain (at least to a metropolitan country); no external commitments; forcible de-linking from the world economy; the fact that Korea was the only such state with the "socialist camp" at a given period and that its economy was susceptible to Soviet-style industrialization. The DPRK regime presents itself and its president, Kim Il Sung, as the leaders of the whole of the Third World. Yet there is very little evidence of other Third World states really emulating North Korea. While it is necessary to puncture Pyongyang's ludicrous and often unpleasantly boastful picture of its influence, it is also important to register the fact that a leading and by no means uncritical authority on the DPRK can write in a book edited by an extremely conservative economist that, "It has contributed a credible concept, nay even an ideology, of autarkic Stalinism" and "*Chu ch'e*' [juche] is an enormously popular concept on the left-wing of the Third World."[97]

Perhaps the fairest way to sum up the DPRK's "model" status is to divide its influence into two parts. On the one hand, the DPRK itself, as a total entity, or even purely as an economy, is not a model for the rest of the Third World. But in certain specific fields, particularly in agriculture and irrigation, the DPRK's experience is valued by states like Tanzania and Zimbabwe. The evidence is that many DPRK aid teams in these fields have done a good job and that their help has been appreciated. The DPRK model may thus have some similarities with that of Taiwan, which could provide useful agricultural assistance to Nicaragua up until the break in relations in 1985, while no one would suggest that Managua was attracted by the Taipei model as a whole.

The South has shown that a fairly large Third World state can sustain high growth by constantly upgrading its industrial structure and breaking into world markets for more advanced industrial products. This achievement has given rise to admiration for "the (South) Korean model." The "Look East" policy of Malaysia, for example, explicitly states its interest in the ROK's experience. As with the

North, there are features of the South's experience which can be extracted for study, but there are also features which it is hard to envisage being repeated. First, there is the specific geopolitical situation of the ROK, which led to its receiving large amounts of U.S. aid, on unrepeatably favorable terms and, as pointed out above, at a stage in the country's development which has not been duplicated elsewhere (with the marginal exception of Taiwan). Second, there are the spin-offs from the Korean War, the U.S. military presence, and the Vietnam War. Third, there is the degree of political and social control, which in turn springs partly from the overall situation of confrontation with the North, as well as from the degree of U.S. backing available because of the strategic considerations involved.[98]

Paradoxically, perhaps the most important lesson that can be learned from the ROK's experience is one which is not often touted by the advocates of free enterprise, namely, the role of a strong state. The ROK state is a result of the merging of several authoritarian traditions: Confucianism, the Japanese colonial state, and the 20th century authoritarian U.S. client militarized regime. This combination is, in its own way, effective and the ROK has rightly been called "Korea, Inc."—which is more justifiable than "Japan, Inc." But whether this highly specific experience can be extrapolated is another matter. Malaysia's so far rather unsuccessful experience with its "Look East" tactic hardly strengthens the case for exporting a South Korean model.

Lastly, it has to be said that the brightest hope for Korea's future lies with a demilitarized and reunified country. There has not yet been, to my knowledge, any detailed study of the impact of demilitarization and/or North-South economic exchange on the peninsula. Certainly, in theory, the release of resources from military expenditure should greatly promote growth. But it must also be recognized that both the ROK and the DPRK, like Taiwan, have had sustained high growth with very high military spending, and this paradox has not been successfully analyzed.[99] There is also the unquantifiable stimulation of confrontation, which would be absent in a demilitarized and reunified country.

Reunification would, by itself, produce a tremendous stimulus to growth. First, it would bring about a very large unified domestic market of over sixty million inhabitants. Second, the striking and identifiable needs of this market could be filled immediately by resources available within the unified economy. Third, leaving aside the question of the political character of the reunification, the stimulus of reunification and the large domestic market thereby created would undoubtedly more than compensate for the competitive stimulus of confrontation.

My thanks to Roberta Foss, Gregory Henderson and Yeomin Yoon for very helpful critical comments on a first draft.

Notes

1. (U.S.) Central Intelligence Agency, National Foreign Assessment Center, *Korea: The Economic Race Between the North and the South,* (1978), p. 1.

2. Bruce Cumings, "The Origins and Development of the Northeast Asian Political Economy: Industrial Sectors, Product Cycles, and Political Consequences," *International Organization*, Vol. 38, no. 1 (Winter 1984), p. 3; this is an excellent text on the underlying issues.

3. Shiota Shobei, "A 'Ravaged' People: The Koreans in World War II," *The Japan Interpreter*, Vol. 7, no.1 (Tokyo: 1971), p. 45. 1 *koku* = 4.96 bushels.

4. Bruce Cumings, *The Origins of the Korean War: Liberation and the Emergence of Separate Regimes 1945-1947* (Princeton: Princeton University Press, 1981), is the outstanding source on this.

5. George M. McCune, *Korea Today* (Cambridge: Harvard University Press, 1950), p. 140. I have discussed the North's legacy and subsequent evolution in two texts which provide more sources and backing on contentious questions: "The North Korean Model: Gaps and Questions," *World Development*, Vol. 9, no. 9/10 (1981); and "The North Korean Enigma," *New Left Review*, no. 127 (May-June 1981)—also (in a slightly different version) in Gordon White, Robin Murray, and Christine White, eds., *Revolutionary Socialist Development in the Third World* (Brighton: Harvester, 1983; University of Kentucky Press, 1983).

6. Joseph Sang-hoon Chung, *The North Korean Economy: Structure and Development* (Stanford: Hoover Institution Press, 1974), p. 57, citing a Japanese source.

7. Cumings, *Origins of the Korean War*, ch. 11. I have listed the articles I found most useful on the North's economy in note 1 to "The North Korean Model," cited in note 5 above. I have done bibliographies on the DPRK in *Bulletin of Concerned Asian Scholars*, Vol. 11, no. 4 (1979) and Vol. 16, no. 4 (1984).

8. Robert A. Scalapino, and Chong-Sik Lee, *Communism in Korea* (Berkeley and London: University of California Press, 1972), Part I: The Movement, p. 416. The authors emphasize that these are North Korean figures which should be treated with caution.

9. "Why Try to Smear Achievements of Pyongyang Economic Seminar?" *Rodong Sinmun*, (Sept. 7, 1964), cited in Chung, p. 117. What seems to be a different translation of the same quotation is cited in Robert Owen Freedman, *Economic Warfare in the Communist Bloc* (New York: Praeger, 1970), p. 148 (from the *New York Times*, Sept. 11, 1964). *Rodong Sinmun* is the Communist Party daily. For detailed Soviet sources on aid, see V. Andreyev and V. Osipov, "USSR-DPRK: Mutually Beneficial Cooperation," *Far Eastern Affairs*, no. 4, (Moscow, 1983); and V. Andrianov and V. Melnikov, "Fruitful Cooperation Between the USSR and the DPRK," ibid., no. 2, (1984).

10. Cumings, *Origins of the Korean War* pp. 61, 562, where he calls this movement, involving about 370,000 Koreans, "probably the largest group of voluntary emigres to a socialist country on record."

11. This light industry included airplane and automobile assembly plants. [Harold R. Isaacs, *No Peace For Asia* (Cambridge: M.I.T. Press, 1967), p. 88.] The fascinating "Korean Labor Report" prepared by Stewart Meacham, labor adviser to the Commanding General USAFIK (U.S. Army Forces in Korea), submitted November 1947, points out that "in 1944 more than two-thirds of the establishments employing about four-sevenths of all workers in manufacturing industries were located south of the thirty-eighth Parallel." (p.3)

12. Much of what follows is based on W.D. Reeve, *The Republic of Korea: A Political and Economic Study* (London: Oxford University Press, 1963); cf. Cumings, *Origins of the Korean War*

13. Mark Gayn, *Japan Diary* (Rutland and Tokyo: Tuttle, 1981), chapter on Korea.

14. Reeve, *The Republic of Korea*; Irma Adelman and Sherman Robinson, *Income Distribution Policy in Developing Countries: A Case Study of Korea* (London: Oxford University Press, 1978), pp. 38-9.

15. Takashi Hatada, *A History of Korea* (Santa Barbara: ABC-Clio, 1969), p. 140.

16. Cumings, "The Northeast Asian Political Economy," p. 23.

17. L.L. Wade and Byong Sik Kim, *The Political Economy of Success: Public Policy and Economic Development in the Republic of Korea* (Seoul: Kyung Hee University Press, 1977), p. 16.

18. Hatada, op.cit., p. 140, and pp. 140-1 for what follows; cf. Reeve, op.cit., ch. 7. There was some improvement in the period 1949-1950.

19. Reeve, op.cit., p. 103 and pp. 103-4, for what follows. Joyce and Gabriel Kolko, *The Limits of Power: The World and United States Foreign Policy, 1945-1954* (New York: Harper and Row, 1972), pp. 614-6. Adelman and Robinson, op.cit., p. 39.

20. I owe this point to Cumings, "The Northeast Asian Political Economy," p. 23. Details of the land reform are available in BBC, *Summary of World Broadcasts*, Far East, no. 64 (July 11, 1950),

pp. 11-12; and in Kim Chum-kon, *The Korean War* (Seoul: Kwangmyong Publishing Co., 1973) pp. 384-7.

21. Leroy P. Jones, and Il Sakong, *Government, Business, and Entrepreneurship in Economic Development: The Korean Case* (Cambridge: Harvard University Press, 1980), especially Appendix B ("Chaebol Case Studies"). Spencer, Daniel L., "An External Military Presence, Technological Transfer, and Structural Change," *Kyklos*, Vol. 18, no. 3 (1965). Although it was the Korean War which gave the key impetus to the rise of the chaebol, it should be added that both in structure and in terms of founding personnel, these sprang from the Japanese mold.

22. Casualty figures are disputed. Some sources suggest as many as 2.5 million people died in the South. As Joyce and Gabriel Kolko point out, not all were killed in actual fighting (*Limits of Power*, p. 615). Cf. Wade and Kim, op.cit., p. 17.

23. There were also enormous losses in educational facilities (Reeve, pp. 88-9). It is worth emphasizing that, according to a U.S. military source, most of the damage was inflicted by the United States: "The devastation in the republic we were defending was wrought largely by us, not the (invader." Capt. Walter Karig, "Korea—Tougher to Crack than Okinawa," *Collier's*, (Sept. 23, 1950), p. 70.

24. Andrianov and Melnikov, op.cit., p. 43. (Unfortunately, no exchange rate is given for the won).

25. *Military Situation in the Far East*; Hearings Before the Committee on Armed Services and the Committee on Foreign Relations, U.S. Senate, 82nd Congress, 1st Session, p. 3075. Information below from Kolko and Kolko, op.cit., p. 615. John Gittings, "The War Before Vietnam," in Gavan McCormack and Mark Selden, eds., *Korea North and South: The Deepening Crisis* (New York: Monthly Review Press, 1978).

26. Dennis Lankford, *I Defy—The Story of Lieutenant Dennis Lankford* (London: Wingate, 1954), p. 156. Kolko and Kolko, op.cit., p. 785, state that thirty two thousand tons of napalm were dropped (almost all, presumably, on the North).

27. Kolko and Kolko op.cit., p. 615. Gittings, op.cit., pp. 68-9. Among neglected sources on the destruction are *We Accuse! Report of the Commission of the Women's International Democratic Federation in Korea, May 1951* (Berlin: WIDF, 1952); and International Association of Democratic Lawyers, *Reports on Investigations in Korea and China* (March-April 1952) (Brussels: IADL, 1952). I have discussed some of these neglected aspects of the war in "Anti-Communism and the Korean War," *The Socialist Register 1984* (London: Merlin Press, 1984).

28. V.V. Martynov, *Koreya*, (Moscow: Izdatel'stvo "Mysl'," 1970),p. 9. Cited in Robert Ante, "The Transformation of the Economic Geography of the DPRK," *Korea Focus*, Vol. 1 (1972), no. 3, p. 55.

29. Bruce Cumings, *The Two Koreas* (New York: Foreign Policy

Association, 1984), p. 65. Halliday, "The North Korean Model," op.cit.; Chung, op.cit.

30. For Chinese accounts, see Chi Lung, "A New Move for Peace," *Peking Review*, Vol. 1, no. 1 (March 4, 1958) and *Peking Review*, Vol. 1, no. 4 (March 25, 1958), p. 19.

31. Harrison Salisbury, *To Peking—And Beyond: A Report on the New Asia* (New York: Quadrangle, New York Times, 1973), pp. 200, 199. Rene Dumont, *The Hungry Future* (London: Deutsch, 1969) p. 137; and Joan Robinson, "Korean Miracle," *Monthly Review*, (Jan. 1965); both cited in Aidan Foster-Carter, "North Korea: Development and Self- Reliance: A Critical Appraisal," in McCormack and Selden, op.cit., p. 124.

32. Figures for 1946 and 1965 from Chung, op.cit., pp. 146-8. 1970 figure from G.V. Gryaznov, *Stroitel'stvo material'no-tekhnicheskoy bazi sotsializma v KNDR [The Construction of the Material-Technical Base of Socialism in the DPRK]* (Moscow: "Nauka," 1979). 1983 figures from M.E. Trigubenko, ed., *Koreyskaya Narodno-demokraticheskaya Respublika* (Moscow: "Nauka," 1985), p. 63 (percentage of aggregate social production). [I am grateful to Aidan Foster-Carter for bringing this source to my attention.] Figures below based partly on estimates in Jun Nishikawa, "El desarrollo economico de Corea del Norte," *Estudios de Asia y Africa* (Mexico), Vol. 12, no. 2 (1977). The World Bank's *World Development Report 1985* gives forty-nine percent of the labor force in agriculture (in 1981), thirty-three percent in industry and eighteen percent in services (p. 259). In my opinion, these figures are questionable, particularly since the same source gives the North exactly the same figure for urban population as a percentage of the total (sixty-two percent) as the South, yet only thirty-four percent of total population in agriculture in the South (1981). Trigubenko, ed., op.cit., citing official DPRK sources, gives 45.8 percent in agriculture (including forestry and fisheries) and 54.2 percent in industry and services combined for 1980 (p.58). The *Asia 1986 Yearbook* appears to have given up and has only "n.a." [not available] for this and several other entries for North Korea for which in previous years it provided specific figures (which often did not change over many years).

33. Kim Il Sung (to a visitor from Benin), *Pyongyang Times*, (Aug. 4, 1979); cf. n.a., *Our Party's Policy for the Building of an Independent National Economy* (Pyongyang: FLPH, 1975).

34. "The independent national economy we speak of has nothing to do with the (*sic*) 'autarky'," (*Our Party's Policy*, op.cit., p. 10).

35. Kim Il Sung, *Pyongyang Times*, (Aug. 4, 1979).

36. *Asia 1984 Yearbook*, p. 8, (*1986 Yearbook* has "n.a."). The *1984 Yearbook* gives food and agricultural products as accounting for thirty-one percent of merchandise exports. *World Development Report 1985* gives cereal imports falling by more than two-thirds between 1974 and 1983, but no net figure for food trade balance.

David Barkin, "Food Self-Sufficiency in North Korea," *Bulletin of Concerned Asian Scholars*, Vol. 18, no. 4 (1986) takes an optimistic view of the situation. The well-informed Australian scholar Adrian Buzo suggests, on the basis of the latest indications, that as of early 1987 "Pyongyang had actually made little progress in solving the serious problem of stagnating farm production" ("Agricultural malaise," *Far Eastern Economic Review*, May 7, 1987). Buzo suggests that the DPRK may be exporting as much as half its total rice crop to earn foreign exchange and notes that it is a substantial importer of wheat and flour.

37. Peter Hendry, "Waiting...and changing," *Ceres: FAO Review of Agriculture and Development*, Vol. 16, no. 4 (July-August 1983), p. 33.

38. *World Development Report 1984*, p. 265 (year unclear; apparently c. 1981). Cf. information below at note 80.

39. The DPRK officially claims "nationwide irrigation"; Hendry, op.cit., p. 33, says irrigation in 1983 "covers at least sixty percent of arable land"; he also points out that mechanized rice transplanters do not do a perfect job (p. 34).

40. I have tried to evaluate these more fully in "The North Korean Model" and "The North Korean Enigma", op.cit., with fuller references there; cf. Chung, op.cit. Hendry, op.cit., p. 34, notes the vagueness of DPRK accounts when it comes to the nitty gritty.

41. There is no adequate study of the role of taxation and revenue in the DPRK. Officially, all taxes were abolished in 1974. This claim may have some psychological value, but hardly anything else. There is no sign that the rate of accumulation slowed down with the abolition of taxes. The DPRK has refused to give figures for the domestic savings rate (the key category)—even rejecting the term in toto. The rate of extraction of the surplus has certainly been consistently very high. But systematic information is lacking on this, as on the redistribution of what is extracted. Cf. my "The North Korean Model," op.cit., p. 895.

42. Chung, op.cit., pp. 41, 73.

43. In an unusual admission, the pro-Pyongyang *People's Korea* cited Ms. Kim Sukchom, president of the Pyongyang Light Industry University, as saying: "Frankly speaking, our light industry is backward." *People's Korea* (Tokyo: Aug. 2, 1986).

44. *Asia and Pacific Annual Review 1980* (U.K.: Saffron Walden), p. 56, from World Bank figures. Cf. CIA, *Korea*, (1978), op.cit.; *World Development Report 1985* puts the figure for the North at 2,093 kg. of oil equivalent in 1983—nearly double the figure it gives for the South in the same year (1,168). There is a valuable survey of the oil situation in *North Korea Quarterly* (Hamburg), Vol. 6, no. 3/4 (1979), pp. 27ff. The Soviet Union was reported in 1986 to be engaged in joint offshore oil exploration with the DPRK off the Korean coast.

45. *New Times*, no. 33 (Moscow: August, 1984), p. 13.

46. Hendry, op.cit., p. 36. For an excellent survey of the industrial management system, see Kloth, Edward W., "The Korean Path to

Socialism: the Taean Industrial Management System," *Occasional Papers on Korea* (Seattle), no. 3 (1975). See also very useful up-to-date information in series of articles by Aidan Foster-Carter in *Far Eastern Economic Review*, (various issues from June 26 to August 14, 1986).

47. Figure given to Gavan McCormack, who kindly made it available to the author.

48. Economist Intelligence Unit, *China, North Korea*, no. 2, (1986), pp. 33,37; *North Korea Quarterly*, no. 36 (Spring 1984), p. 31.

49. At the end of the 1970s the United States upped its estimate of the DPRK armed forces from about half a million to over three-quarters of a million. The grounds on which this huge increase were founded were never explained. Just from a purely economic point of view, it should be said that such a huge increase in a country of this size would have to show up in economic indices (however vague these indices might be). Yet, no such indications have been detected. Interestingly, former President Jimmy Carter stated on April 2, 1985 that he had "never comprehended fully" the 1979 U.S. intelligence estimate suddenly upping the size of North Korea's armed forces (*International Herald Tribune*, April 4, 1985).

50. Salisbury, op.cit., p. 197. Figures below from Rinn-Sup Shinn, et al., *Area Handbook for North Korea* (Washington, D.C.: U.S. Government Printing Office, 1969), p. 389.

51. Andreyev and Osipov, op.cit., p.21. Quote below from same.

52. This is discussed in greater detail in my "The North Korean Model," op.cit., and references there.

53. Kim Il Sung interview, *Le Monde*, (June 26-7, 1977), p. 3. I discuss the debt question in "The North Korean Model."

54. *Economist*, (September 15, 1984); this figure may be too high.

55. *The Asia 1985 Yearbook*, p. 8, gives outstanding debt at $1.9 billion. *North Korean Quarterly* [henceforth NKQ] (Hamburg), nos. 37/38 (Summer/Fall 1984), pp. 32ff., carries useful material on the external debt.

56. *Far Eastern Economic Review*, (June 26, 1981).

57. New Year address, (Jan. 1, 1979).

58. Useful survey of the joint venture law and related questions in *NKQ* 37/38, pp. 15ff; cf. observations by Parris H. Chang, "North Korea's Wind of Change," *Newsweek*, (July 8, 1985), p. 4. The 1984 joint venture law was followed by two laws on taxes on such ventures and foreigners working in them (August 1985). Some clarification in a series on the issue in *People's Korea*, (April 5, 1986 and ff.) The hotel project with French interests was reported in trouble in mid-1986.

59. Fidel Castro, Opening Address to the Second Congress of the Association of Third World Economists (Havana, April 26, 1981), p. 16. North Korean material on the South is of noticeably worse quality than Seoul's publications about the North.

60. *Financial Times*, (April 8, 1986).

61. *World Development Report 1984*, p. 223; manufacturing in

brackets because it is part of industry. *Far Eastern Economic Review*, (July 18, 1985), p.47, says that as a percentage of GNP [close to GDP], agriculture had fallen to less than fifteen percent; mining and manufacturing accounting for twenty-nine per cent; social overheads and service industries accounting for fifty-six per cent.

62. *World Development Report 1985*.

63. Cumings, *The Two Koreas*, op.cit., p. 61. For interesting surveys of the fast-growing literature on the ROK's development, see Tony Michell, "Korean Economy in Transition," *Journal of Korean Studies* (Seattle: 1982-3), Vol. 4, and, for a more critical stance, Sung-il Choi, "South Korea Under Park Chung Hee: Development or Decay?," *Bulletin of Concerned Asian Scholars*, Vol. 15, no. 2 (1983). My own view is that there was development *with* decay. An excellent brief text which deals lucidly and fairly with many criticisms of ROK development is Richard Luedde-Neurath, "Export Orientation in South Korea: How Helpful is Dependency Thinking to its Analysis?" *IDS Bulletin* (U.K.), Vol. 12, no. 1 (Dec. 1980) [IDS: Institute of Development Studies, Sussex University]. Cf. Hagen Koo, "The Political Economy of Industrialization in South Korea and Taiwan," *Korea and World Affairs*, Vol. 10, no. 1 (Spring 1986); and Stephan Haggard and Chung-in Moon, "The South Korean State in the International Economy: Liberal, Dependent, or Mercantile?" in John Gerard Ruggie, ed., *The Antinomies of Interdependence: National Welfare and the International Division of Labor* (New York: Columbia University Press, 1983).

64. *FEER*, (August 26, 1986).

65. Ibid.

66. Luedde-Neurath, *IDS Bulletin*, p. 52.

67. *Asia 1986 Yearbook*: the ROK budget is, of course, a much smaller proportion of GNP than the DPRK's.

68. See Frank Baldwin, "America's Rented Troops: South Koreans in Vietnam," *Bulletin of Concerned Asian Scholars*, Vol. 7, no. 4 (1975); and Diane and Michael Jones, "Allies Called Koreans: A Report from Vietnam," ibid., Vol. 8, no.2 (1976)—collected together as an American Friends Service Committee pamphlet, *America's Rented Troops: South Koreans in Vietnam*, (Philadelphia: AFSC, 1976).

69. Anne O. Krueger, *The Developmental Role of the Foreign Sector and Aid* (Cambridge: Harvard University Press, 1979), ch. 1; Cumings, "The Northeast Asian Political Economy," p. 24.

70. North American Coalition on Latin America (NACLA), *Latin America and Empire Report*, Vol. 10, no. 1 (Jan. 1976), pp. 24-26.

71. NACLA, ibid, p. 28.

72. Cited in Cumings, "The Northeast Asian Political Economy," p. 26.

73. *International Herald Tribune*, (August 20 and 21, 1986).

74. Luedde-Neurath, op.cit., and for points immediately below.

75. On the Yatsugi Plan, see Jon Halliday and Gavan McCormack, *Japanese Imperialism Today* (Penguin, 1973; New York: Monthly

Review Press, 1973), ch. 5. For a more recent survey, see D. Moun, "Japan's Economic Penetration of South Korea," *Far Eastern Affairs*, no. 3, (1985). I am grateful to Aidan Foster-Carter for allowing me to see his draft paper, "Standing Up: The Two Korean States and the Dependency Debate—A Bipartisan Approach" (1985).

76. CIA, *Korea*, (1978), p. 11. Of earlier texts attempting to compare the economies of the North and South, Gerhard Breidenstein, "Economic Comparison of North and South Korea," *Journal of Contemporary Asia*, Vol. 5, no. 2, (1975), is still useful, especially methodologically. For an interesting attempt re China, see James E. Nickum and David C. Schak, "Living Standards and Economic Development in Shanghai and Taiwan," *China Quarterly*, no. 77 (March 1979). I am grateful to Nirmal Kumar Chandra for allowing me to consult his paper, "North and South Korea: A Study in Two Paradigms of Development," (1984).

77. *The Asia Yearbook, 1984* and *1986*.

78. *Asia 1984 Yearbook*, p. 6. Again the 1985 *Yearbook* gives up and has only "n.a." for the North (27.8 per cent for the South).

79. Kim's claim in his New Year address, 1980. According to Aidan Foster-Carter, the United Nations Development Program works on a figure of about $900 (*FEER*, August 14, 1986). A Soviet authority gave a figure of "about $800" to the author in 1985.

80. *World Development Report 1985*.

81. Ibid; the *WDR* gives exactly the same figures for North and South for both infant mortality (aged under one) and child death rates (aged one to four) for both years covered, 1960 and 1982 (p. 263). This is questionable.

82. *Asia 1984 Yearbook*, p. 6; cf. V. Andreyev and N. Beryozkin, "How the Democratic People's Republic of Korea Deals with Social Questions," *Far Eastern Affairs*, no. 1, (1981), p. 66. It should be said that the North's definition of "doctor" is not always clear. Nor is confidence in the DPRK's statistics strengthened by blanket claims for perfection, and even the elimination of all serious illnesses [Gavan McCormack, "North Korea: Kimilsungism —Path to Socialism?" *Bulletin of Concerned Asian Scholars*, Vol. 13, no. 4 (1981), p. 57 (claim by the chairperson of a collective farm)].

83. Kim Il Sung, "On the Revolutionization and Working-classization of Women," speech at the Fourth Congress of the Democratic Women's Union, October 7, 1971 (Pyongyang: FLPH 1974), p. 13; author's interview with officials of the Korean Democratic Women's Union, Pyongyang, July 29, 1977. Exactly the same figures given by Kim Il Sung in 1971 were being given as accurate in the mid-1980s: See Pak Il Bun, "Women at Work," *People's Korea*, March 23, 1985; cf. *People's Korea*, August 2, 1986. I have tried to sum up the available information on women in the North in "Women in North Korea," *Bulletin of Concerned Asian Scholars*, Vol. 17, no. 3 (1985).

84. Uhn Cho and Hagen Koo, "Economic Development and Women's Work in a Newly Industrializing Country: The Case of

Korea," *Development and Change*, Vol. 14, no. 4 (October 1983), p. 519. Although, according to the World Bank, the percentage of the total population aged 15-64 which was in the labor force in 1982 was higher in the South than in the North (sixty-two and fifty-six per cent, respectively); this seems most unlikely.

85. *Human Rights of Korean Women* (Tokyo: The Society to Defend the Human Rights of Korean Women, 1979), p. 14. The same source gave average working hours for all Korean workers as 58.1 per week as of the end of 1977.

86. Ibid, p. 25.

87. Andreyev and Beryozkin, op.cit., (note 76), p. 66. There is also a problem of definition since the DPRK will not define "urban" and "rural" and there is also quite a lot of industry sited in rural areas.

88. D.C. Rao, "Economic Growth and Equity in the Republic of Korea," *World Development*, Vol. 6, no. 3 (1978), p. 388. But Paul Ensor states that since 1975 urban incomes have been growing faster than rural ones (*Far Eastern Economic Review*, July 18, 1985, p. 69). Information below from unpublished ILO source. For illuminating discussion of government statistics in the early 1970s, see Chung Kyungmo, "The Second Liberation of South Korea and Democratization of Japan," *The Japan Interpreter*, Vol. 9, no. 2 (Tokyo: Summer-Autumn 1974).

89. Salisbury, op.cit., p. 200.

90. M. Glebova and V. Mikheyev, "Some Aspects of Economic Development of the Democratic People's Republic of Korea," *Far Eastern Affairs*, no. 1, (1983), p. 89.

91. I was told this by the late Genaro Carnero Checa, a Peruvian writer who visited the DPRK many times. He told me that when he asked how the DPRK managed to flood the world with its propaganda, he was taken to see this city.

92. *New Times*, (Moscow: 1984) no. 33, p.13.

93. McCormack, "Kimilsungism...?," op.cit. p. 57.

94. Confirmation of rationing is given by Andreyev and Beryozkin, *Far Eastern Affairs*, no. 1, (1981), p. 60. (It was denied to the author in 1977.)

95. Luedde-Neurath, op.cit., p. 50; cf. Choi, op.cit. Cf. Clive Hamilton, "Capitalist Industrialization in East Asia's Four Little Tigers," *Journal of Contemporary Asia*, Vol. 13, no. 1 (1983). Excellent analysis in Hagen Koo, "Center-Periphery Relations and Marginalization: Empirical Analysis of the Dependency Model of Inequality in Peripheral Nations," *Development and Change*, Vol. 12, no. 1 (Jan. 1981); and Hagen Koo and Doo-Seung Hong, "Class and Income Inequality in Korea," *American Sociological Review*, Vol. 45, no. 4 (Aug. 1980).

96. This emerges clearly even from statistics produced by the South. *Vantage Point* (Seoul) gave the North 5,215,000 M/T of *polished* grain production in 1983, compared with 7,134,000 for the South (October 1985).

97. Pong Lee, "The Korean People's Democratic Republic," in Peter Wiles, ed., *The New Communist Third World* (New York: St. Martin's Press, 1982), pp. 329, 308. Lee's use of "autarkic" seems to go further than what the DPRK claims for itself (see quote at note 34 above). From my own observation, I would question Lee's remark. In 1981 I attended the Conference of Third World Economists in Havana, Cuba, where Castro called ROK industrialization "fictitious" (see note 59). The chief DPRK delegate made a monist speech about his country's development, failing totally to engage with the problems of other Third World countries' development experiences. He was questioned on exactly this issue by three delegates (from Nepal, Togo and Nigeria) and failed entirely to confront the points they raised.

98. I have discussed some of these points at greater length in "Capitalism and Socialism in East Asia," *New Left Review*, no. 124 (1980).

99. McCormack, "Kimilsungism...?," op.cit., p. 54, makes the point that, while weapons must be a drain in the DPRK, personnel are not necessarily so, at least inasmuch as they contribute to the non-military economy (on incomes not known to be higher than those of civilians). For interesting observations and comparisons on this field, see Mary Kaldor, "The Military in Development," *World Development*, Vol. 4, no. 6 (1976).

Jon Halliday is a British economic historian who has written extensively on East Asia. He is the author of *A Political History of Japanese Capitalism* (1975) co-author (with Gavan McCormack) of *Japanese Imperialism Today* (1973). He has visited Korea twice and has written extensively on Korea, including chapters in several books and in such journals as *World Development*, *Bulletin of Concerned Asian Scholars* and *New Left Review*.

Chapter 4

The Military Situation on the Korean Peninsula

Stephen D. Goose

Introduction

The high level of tension between North and South Korea in recent years—due to the Rangoon bombing and the KAL incident among other things—has once again focused attention on the military situation on the Korean peninsula. Those tensions coupled with the deteriorating health of Kim Il Sung, who has vowed to unify the Koreas before his death, and the increasing economic disparity between the North and South have led many to conclude that the chances of war are greater now than at any time since 1953.

In early 1986 South Korean President Chun Doo-Hwan said, "Not only our government but also military specialists in foreign countries share the view that there is a great risk of war on the Korean peninsula during the next few years."[1] Indeed, Chun's words have been echoed widely. South Korea's defense minister has said that "the most precarious period for national security would be for this year through 1988."[2] General William Livsey, commander of U.S. forces in Korea, has said, "The optimum time for the North Koreans [to invade] is in the next three-to-four-year period."[3] Deputy Assistant Secretary of Defense James Kelly told Congress, "With the Asian Games scheduled this year and elections and the Olympics in 1988, Korea is entering perhaps its most dangerous era in thirty years."[4]

Both sides are preparing for major war at an increasing pace, producing and buying more and more weapons of ever-increasing deadliness, and stepping up the readiness of their forces. The Korean peninsula is already one of the world's most militarized areas. There are nearly one and one-half million military forces squaring off on the peninsula, with a combined total of almost forty-six hundred tanks and over twelve hundred combat aircraft. An estimated two million troops face each other along the Sino-Soviet border, but that border stretches over 4,600 miles, compared to the 155-mile long Demilitarized Zone (DMZ) separating North and South Korea. The European theater has more weaponry, as does the Middle East/Persian Gulf region, but it is not nearly so concentrated on a small land mass.[5]

North and South Korea have two of the most militarized societies in the world by any measurement, be it per capita military spending, military spending as percent of government spending and gross national product (GNP), or incorporation of the "civilian" population into the military structure.

Many people in the United States tend to forget that North and South Korea are still at war. A very unstable truce has been in effect since 1953. Both sides keep armed guard posts within the DMZ, and firefights break out with surprising regularity, some lasting hours. Over one thousand Koreans and ninety U.S. troops have been killed (and 131 U.S. personnel wounded) in battle since 1953.[6]

South Korea occupies a very special place in U.S. military strategy and structure. The level of involvement and integration of U.S. and foreign military forces is higher in Korea than anywhere except Europe. This is evident in the large number of U.S. combat troops in the Republic of Korea (ROK), the stationing of U.S. nuclear weapons there, the combined command structure, the extensive joint training and planning for war, the equipping of both ROK and U.S. forces in Korea with the latest U.S. weapons, the high degree of compatability and interoperability of U.S. and Korean weapons and equipment, the pre-positioning of war supplies on the peninsula, and many other factors.

It is common wisdom that there is no military "balance" between North and South Korea. Government officials from the United States and South Korea for years have talked about the need to redress the overwhelming military advantage of the North. One constantly hears about a massive, aggressive North Korean military buildup over the past fifteen years or so.

In testifying to the House Appropriations Committee in March 1986, Deputy Assistant Secretary of Defense Kelly said, "The ROK has been unable to match the massive North Korean military buildup which began in 1970 and continues to this day. The North Korean military now poses as great a threat to the ROK as at any time since the Korean War."[7] Testifying in support of the administration's FY 1985 military construction request for South Korea, Assistant Secretary of Defense Richard Armitage warned of the "growing threats posed by North Korea," stating that "North Korea continues the unrelenting buildup of its offensively postured military forces."[8]

Assistant Secretary of State Paul Wolfowitz has told the Senate Foreign Relations Committee that "for the past decade North Korea...has carried out a major force buildup which has seriously affected the military balance on the peninsula."[9] He pointed to the "extremely heavy military purchasing requirements forced on South Korea by the continuing North Korean buildup" as justification for U.S. military aid for the ROK.[10]

Officials are quick to recite certain statistics: that North Korea has forty percent more manpower, that North Korea spends over twenty percent of its GNP on the military compared to six percent for the South, that North Korea has more than a three-to-one advantage in tanks, artillery, and aircraft, and four-to-one in ships.[11] The implication is always that if not for the presence of U.S. troops and weapons, including nuclear weapons, Kim Il Sung would be marching south momentarily.

There are kernels of truth in most of the statistics cited, but they are usually overstated, almost always misleading, and often meaningless. It is essential to look beyond numbers at capabilities, missions and other non-quantifiable factors. Sometimes direct comparisons of any type, quantitative or qualitative, make little sense because the ROK and Democratic People's Republic of Korea (DPRK) have structured their forces differently and emphasized different types of weapons.

North Korea does enjoy a numerical advantage in nearly every category, but that advantage is frequently offset by other factors. First and foremost is the superior quality of South Korean weapons; they tend to be newer, more powerful, and more reliable. The qualitative edge of the ROK is probably the single most important aspect to consider when comparing the militaries of North and South Korea.

A second key advantage for the South is its superior training, experience, and leadership. While North Korea also rates high, most military analysts agree that these areas would be a big plus for the ROK in a major war.

A third factor of extreme importance in the South's favor in case of attack would be geography, terrain and defensive posture.

In the event of a long war, South Korea also has the advantage of a much larger population (43.3 million vs. 20.5 million)[12] and much more developed economy (a GNP of $90.1 billion vs. $23 billion).[13]

From time to time, U.S. and Korean officials will acknowledge that all is not gloom and doom on the peninsula. In 1982, for example, then-Assistant Secretary of State James Buckley stated, "We have in Northeast Asia a strong and economically vital South Korea that is able to deter its northern neighbor from military adventures."[14] The 1982 *Handbook of Korea*, produced by the ROK government, stated, "Today...the fully mature ROK armed forces are ever firmly resolved to defend the nation, single-handedly if necessary....The Republic's defensive power is fully capable of meeting North Korean tank assaults and aerial offensives."[15]

A congressional delegation that visited South Korea in August 1983 reported that Korean leaders predicted that by 1986 South Korea will reach military parity with North Korea.[16] Also in 1983, General Sennewald, then commander of U.S. Forces, Korea, told Congress that "...our forces, combined with those of the ROK, will acquit themselves well in any conflict with North Korea."[17] Mr. Armitage testified in 1984, "The ROK maintains a sizable armed force which, in conjunction with U.S. forces stationed on the Korean peninsula, provides a strong deterrent to possible North Korean aggression."[18] Admiral William Crowe, then commander-in-chief of the Pacific Command, told Congress, "There are encouraging signs on the Korean peninsula. South Korea's military posture is improving steadily."[19] He also stated, "If South Korea has advance warning of an impending North Korean attack, they would be capable of defending the DMZ with in-place forces and with follow-on augmentation of regular and reserve forces."[20]

More recently, General Livsey said in 1985 that, "Korean and U.S. forces are now able to defeat any renewed aggression from North Korea."[21] He also said, "I believe that, by the early 1990s, all comparisons between South and North Korea, including the military, will favor the ROK."[22] Secretary of Defense Caspar Weinberger, when asked during a March 1986 press briefing, "How do you overcome the imbalance between the North and the South?" replied, "Well, there are very great strengths in South Korea and in the American forces in South Korea. We have very capable weapons, very sophisticated weaponry....South Korea is making very large and necessary investments in very effective weaponry and very effective training."[23]

It is no wonder that the House Foreign Affairs Subcommittee on Asia and the Pacific lamented, "The Subcommittee remains seriously concerned about the differing judgments it has received from the Defense Department in recent years as to whether North Korea's military superiority was widening or not, what the trend in the respective military strengths of the North and South was likely to be in the years ahead, and the magnitude of the effort that would be required by the Republic of Korea to close the gap in a reasonable period of time."[24]

A careful and detached analysis of the military situation is essential because it is the specter of the threat from the North that President Chun uses to justify large and increasing military budgets and continued military domination of national politics. It is the threat that the United States uses to justify large and increasing military aid to the South and the presence of forty thousand U.S. troops.

This chapter will compare in detail North and South military spending, arms imports, military production capabilities, manpower, air forces, naval forces, and ground forces. It will then examine the U.S. military presence, the UN command structure, and the interaction of the U.S. and Korean militaries.

Military Spending

In comparing the military efforts of North and South Korea, perhaps the greatest anomaly is that in the period of alleged "unrestrained, unrelenting growth" by the North, the South has spent significantly more money on its military forces. This may be one of the best kept secrets in Washington.

Most analysts agree that North Korea began a significant military buildup in 1969-1970. Prior to that, the North had relied on a strategy of extensive infiltration, hoping to incite the southern population to revolt against the Park government. What does an examination of the data since 1970 show? According to the U.S. Arms Control and Disarmament Agency (ACDA), from 1970 to 1983 North Korea spent $24.4 billion on the military, compared to $30.5 billion for South Korea.[25] In other words, in the period of military growth by North Korea which so concerns the U.S. and South Korean governments, the South has outspent the North by twenty-five percent. South Korea passed the North in spending in 1975 and has outspent it every year since.

ACDA's figures show that North Korea's defense budget increased more than six-fold from 1970 to 1983 ($576 million to $3.6 billion), but South Korea's increased nearly ten-fold ($491 million to $4.7 billion). In fact, it is ROK military spending that has been growing in a "steady, unrelenting" fashion. North Korea invested heavily in the military in the first half of the 1970s, but since then spending has been erratic: in real terms (adjusted for inflation), it decreased in 1975, rose in 1976, decreased in 1977, 1978, and 1979, rose in 1980, decreased in 1981, rose in 1982, and decreased in 1983. The variations in spending in real terms from 1980 to 1983 have been very slight; the DPRK budget has essentially held steady.[26] North Korea actually spent more on the military in 1972 than in 1979 in real terms.[27]

The last two editions of the ACDA publication on military spending contain an unusual, and confusing, development. The 1983 report, which included data for the years 1971-1980, listed North Korean expenditures in 1980 at $1.3 billion.[28] However, the last two editions revised the 1980 figure to an estimated $3 billion, with increases to $3.5 billion in 1982 and $3.6 billion in 1983.[29] Strangely, these astronomical jumps are not specifically mentioned in other government sources, in the congressional testimony of Defense and State Department witnesses, or in authoritative non-governmental sources. The following chart compares recent estimates of North Korean military spending:

	ACDA (83)	ACDA (85)	IISS	SIPRI
1979	$1320	$1320	$1363	$1429
1980	$1300	$3000 est.	$1337	$1533
1981	—	$3240 est.	$1601	$1677
1982	—	$3500 est.	$1755	$1807
1983	—	$3600 est.	$1916	$1968
1984	—	—	$4086	$2129
1985	—	—	$4196	$2213 est.

Note: All figures are millions of dollars (not adjusted for inflation); ACDA—U.S. Arms Control and Disarmament Agency, *World Military Expenditures and Arms Transfers*; IISS—International Institute for Strategic Studies, *The Military Balance 1984-85 and 1985-86;* SIPRI—Stockholm International Peace Research Institute, *SIPRI Yearbook 1986.*

Even with its revised estimates of very high North Korean military spending, ACDA shows that South Korea outspent the North in 1983 by thirty-one percent ($4.7 billion vs. $3.6 billion).[30] The London-based IISS puts South Korean military spending in 1983 at more than two and one-quarter times that of the North ($4.4 billion vs. $1.9 billion).[31]

ACDA has not released figures for military spending after 1983, but other U.S. government documents have pegged the ROK military budget in 1984 at $4.5 billion,[32] and in 1985 at $4.8 billion.[33] No U.S. government figures are available for North Korea, but SIPRI estimates North Korean military spending at $2.1 billion in 1984 and $2.2 billion in 1985,[34] while the IISS records a big jump to $4.1 billion and $4.2 billion, respectively.[35]

•The GNP Smokescreen

When addressing the issue of the "threat" from the North, the first thing most U.S. government officials will state is that the North spends over twenty percent of its GNP on the military, while the South spends only six percent. It is rarely mentioned that the ROK's gross national product is well over four times that of the DPRK—$90.1 billion vs. $23 billion in 1983—and that, therefore, the South is spending more.[36]

The percent of GNP spent on the military is one of the most useless and meaningless measures for comparing military forces. A large percent of GNP spent on the military does indicate a highly militarized country that places a high priority on the military and carries a heavy military burden. But it indicates very little about the military capability of a nation. Obviously, the total amount spent is a much more relevant gauge. What counts is how much money is spent and how well it is spent.

For many years, U.S. government officials have repeatedly asserted that the DPRK spends twenty percent or more of its GNP on the military, with some citing figures as high as twenty-four to twenty-six percent.[37] Yet the ACDA publications reveal a different story. The North Korean percentage hovered around twenty percent in the early part of the 1970s, but averaged eleven percent in the five-year period 1975-1979, declining each year from 1976 to 1979, and hitting a low of 9.2 percent in 1979. ACDA's original estimate for 1980 of 8.2 percent was revised to 19.4 percent. The percent has fallen each year since then to 16.7 percent in 1983.[38]

As is the case with overall military spending, authoritative nongovernmental sources call into question the high figures cited by the U.S. government on North Korea's percentage of the GNP spent on the military. The IISS estimates the North Korean percentage in 1983 at 9.6, the South Korean at 5.7.[39] For 1984 it estimates 10.2 percent for the DPRK and 5.4 percent for the ROK.[40] SIPRI's latest estimates are 12.3 percent for North Korea in 1983 and 5.1 percent for South Korea in 1984.[41]

ACDA shows the South Korean percentage of GNP growing steadily from 3.8 percent in 1973 to 6.2 percent in 1981, then falling to 5.8 percent in 1983.[42] That compares to 6.6 percent for the United States, 5.8 percent for all developing nations, 3.9 percent for European NATO, and 3.5 percent for all of Asia.[43]

U.S. officials have recently started claiming that North Korea spends a larger percent of its GNP on the military than any other country in the world,[44] but other sources list at least ten that spend more, including U.S. allies Israel, Saudi Arabia and Oman.

There are other measurements of the military burden on a nation besides percent of GNP. Two of the most common are percentage of central government expenditures (CGE) spent on the military and per capita military spending. According to ACDA, during the past ten years (1974-1983) South Korea spent an average of twenty-nine percent of its CGE on the military compared to twenty-three percent for North Korea. The revised ACDA estimates show the DPRK at 29.7 percent in 1982 and the ROK at 27.9 percent in 1983.[45] The CIA estimates that South Korea will spend 31.2 percent of its central government budget on the military in 1986.[46]

Although South Korea's population is more than twice that of North Korea, it began to catch up to North Korea in yearly per capita military spending in the late 1970s. The IISS data shows the South exceeding the North for the first time in 1978, with the gap growing to $110 versus $100 in 1983.[47] ACDA's revised estimates show the Northern expenditure significantly larger ($179 vs. $109 in 1983).[48]

- Who's Fooling Whom?

It is obvious that while North Korea invested more in its military in the first half of the 1970s, the South has outspent it by an even greater margin in the latter half of that decade and in the 1980s. The important question then becomes why U.S. and Korean officials continue to speak of the growing threat from the North and the increasing gap in North/South military capabilities. There are several possible answers, none very pleasing to contemplate. Perhaps the North spends its money more wisely, getting "more bang for the buck." Perhaps the North's military industries are more efficient. Perhaps the South's procurement strategy of fewer but more modern (and expensive) weapons systems is incorrect. Perhaps the larger portion of the South's military budget spent on personnel and other non-hardware costs is not leading to better trained, more effective soldiers and a superior military establishment.

More likely, there is no increasing gap in North/South military capabilities. Talk of such a gap may be nothing more than a tactic used by U.S. officials to justify the continued extensive military involvement of the United States on the peninsula, the presence of forty thousand U.S. soldiers, and rising military aid requests for South Korea. The United States does not want to upset the status quo on the peninsula. It wants to make sure that its troops remain there as part of its forward deployment strategy. It wants to make sure that the friendly government in Seoul remains in power. A good way to insure that is to convince Congress and the U.S. public of the threat from the North.

Weapons Imports

Weapons imports have played an important role in the militarization of the Korean peninsula. Until the 1970s, when North and South Korea began to develop an indigenous military industry, both nations had to rely entirely on weapons from other countries—primarily the United States for the ROK and the Soviet Union for the DPRK.

Although it has a military industrial base superior to that of North Korea, South Korea imports far more weapons. ACDA estimates that South Korean arms imports from 1973 to 1983 were more than two and one-third times larger than those of the North ($3.8 billion vs. $1.6 billion) and nearly two and one-half times greater over the past five years ($2 billion vs. $840 million from 1979 to 1983).[49]

•Arming the South

South Korea's weapons have come almost exclusively from the United States. In spite of a worldwide trend toward diversification of arms suppliers, South Korea has continued to look to the United States for over ninety percent of its imported weapons.[50] More than twenty-five percent of the ROK's military budget is spent in the United States.[51]

Since 1950, U.S. military assistance agreements (cash sales, grants and loans for equipment, training and construction) with South Korea have totaled $10.7 billion. Nearly half ($5.3 billion) have been signed in the past ten years (1976-1985). U.S. weapons deliveries since 1950 totaled $9.1 billion, leaving $1.6 billion in the pipeline.[52]

South Korea's arms imports from the United States are going to remain at a high level. Since the 1979 reassessment of North Korean military strength, the United States has made an intensified effort to supply South Korea with the latest U.S. weaponry. Foreign military sales agreements totaling a record $1.1 billion were signed in FY 1982, the bulk coming from the sale of thirty-six F-16 fighter-bomber aircraft.[53] U.S. military sales and aid to South Korea in FY 1985 totaled $301 million. The administration estimates that FY 1986 sales and aid will more than double to $652 million and will continue to rise to $752 million in FY 1987.[54] Since FY 1985, the United

States has been extending military aid to South Korea on more favorable terms, by extending the repayment schedule from five-year grace and seven-year repayment to ten-year grace and twenty-year repayment.[55]

The ROK is expected to buy half its estimated $9 billion in weapons and military equipment from the United States during its Force Improvement Plan (FIP) II from 1982 to 1986.[56] The U.S. government has estimated that South Korean military purchases from the United States will exceed $8 billion from 1985 to 1989.[57] In addition to the F-16s, recent acquisitions from the United States include F-4 fighter aircraft, A-10 close support aircraft ("tank-busters"), OV-10 Bronco counter-insurgency aircraft, AH-1S Cobra attack helicopters with TOW anti-tank missiles, Stinger anti-aircraft missiles, Harpoon anti-ship missiles, Maverick air-to-surface missiles, and Sparrow air-to-air missiles.[58]

South Korea has requested E-2C Hawkeye airborne early warning aircraft. The E-2C is similar to the E-3A AWACS aircraft and is used by Japan and Israel, among others. U.S. officials have said South Korea is the most likely customer for the overland version of the Hawkeye, being developed by Grumman for service in 1988. In October 1984, tests of the overland version were conducted in South Korea.[59]

South Korea is considering purchasing the F-20 Tigershark from the Northrop Corporation. It would be the first major sale of the aircraft. The F-20s would replace F-5s in the ROK inventory and complement the more advanced F-16s. South Korea's interest may have waned after one of the three Tigersharks built thus far crashed on October 10, 1984, during a demonstration flight at Suwon Air Base, killing the U.S. test pilot.[60] South Korea has also expressed an interest in the McDonnell Douglas F/A-18.[61]

•The North Is On Its Own

In the 1950s, 1960s, and early 1970s, North Korea imported nearly all the arms in its arsenal from the Soviet Union. During the next decade, however, it imported few weapons and looked mainly to China for those. The People's Republic of China (PRC) accounted for twenty-seven percent of the weapons delivered to North Korea from 1979 to 1983, compared to twenty-five percent for the Soviet Union.[62]

The Soviet Union did not send any significant weapons to North Korea for more than ten years, until after Kim Il Sung's visit to Moscow in May 1984 (his first in twenty-three years).[63] Since then, the Soviet Union has delivered most, if not all, of an estimated forty to fifty advanced MiG-23 fighter aircraft, AA-7 Apex air-to-air missiles for the MiGs, SS-1 SCUD surface-to-surface missiles, SA-3 surface-to-air missiles, and early warning radars.[64]

North Korea seems to be returning to its policy of seeking support from both the USSR and China. The turn to the Soviet Union may be a reaction to China's improved ties to the United States and South Korea and certainly reflects North Korea's recognition that the USSR is better able than China to provide the type of modern weaponry needed to match ROK systems such as the F-16.

Politically, North Korea still appears to be closer to China than to the Soviet Union. Admiral Crowe has told Congress, "I suspect that Moscow considers North Korea at best an unreliable and ungrateful ally."[65] It is clear that neither the USSR nor the PRC wants a war on the Korean peninsula. It is unlikely either would be anxious to lend massive assistance to North Korea if it attacked the South. Admiral Crowe has commented, "Stability on the Korean peninsula is also of primary concern to the USSR and China, as each nation recognizes the enormous risks to its own national interests that would be involved."[66] He went so far as to tell the Senate, "I believe that both Moscow and Beijing have compelling reasons to avoid a new Korean war and, therefore, act as restraining influences."[67]

Domestic Military Production

South and North Korea have two of the most advanced indigenous military production capabilities in the Third World, matched or surpassed only by China, India, Israel, Brazil, South Africa, and Taiwan. Both nations are working toward self-sufficiency in building weapons and both are close to that goal. They can produce nearly the full range of ground, sea, and air equipment, with the major exceptions of modern jet military aircraft, sophisticated missiles, and high technology items, especially electronic equipment. Both have moved from the ability to maintain and repair weapons provided by other nations, to assembly in-country of weapons components provided by other nations, to producing entire weapons under license (co-production), in some instances, to the final step of researching, designing, and developing new weapons systems domestically.

South Korea's arms industry began in earnest in the early 1970s. It can now produce roughly seventy percent of its military needs domestically.[68] There are over fifty military contractors in the ROK.[69] Most of its weapons are copies or modifications of U.S. equipment, many of which are locally assembled or produced under license.

The ROK military industry is very adept at producing ground equipment. It makes almost everything from barbed wire to tanks, including rifles, communications gear, grenade launchers, howitzers, recoilless rifles, mortars, armored personnel carriers, anti-tank missiles, mines and more. It co-produces M-48A3 and -A5 tanks, M-109A2 self-propelled 155mm howitzers, M-79 grenade launchers, and Vulcan air defense systems.[70] Co-production of an indigenously designed tank, known as the XK-1 or the Republic of Korea Indigenous Tank (ROKIT), began in 1986. It weighs forty-five to fifty-two tons, is armed with a 105mm gun, and has a digital fire-control computer.[71]

As early as 1982, *Proceedings*, the journal of the U.S. Naval Institute, noted that "South Korea is fast becoming the naval shipyard of Asia....South Korea is, in terms of indigenous naval construction, one of the most advanced maritime nations in Asia."[72] It began building its own advanced naval vessels such as missile-armed fast attack craft and amphibious craft in 1977, frigates in 1980, submarines in 1983, and minehunters in 1985.[73]

The U.S. Navy has awarded overhaul contracts to South Korean firms.[74] In 1984, the U.S. Coast Guard for the first time selected a foreign firm for large boat design; Daewoo of South Korea will be providing the basic design for sixteen large patrol boats to be built in Seattle.[75]

South Korea's capability to build military aircraft lags behind that of ground and naval systems, but it has advanced from repair and overhaul, to assembly, to licensed production. The ROK started co-producing F-5E fighter aircraft (the most modern version of the F-5) in 1982 and licensed assembly of Hughes 500 Defender helicopters with TOW anti-tank missiles in 1978.[76] In 1985 the first repair facility for F-100 jet engines (used in F-15s and F-16s) was established in South Korea.[77]

North Korea's domestic military industry is equal or superior to the South's in ground equipment, but inferior in naval and air weapons systems. Like the ROK, the DPRK can and does produce the entire range of ground systems. Significantly, it produces substantially more ground weaponry than the ROK and probably benefits from economies of scale. Apparently all new armor being added to North Korean forces is domestically produced. Tanks now include a version of the Soviet T-62 model.[78] Some estimates put North Korean production of tracked vehicles at three hundred per year (one hundred tanks, one hundred APCs, one hundred self-propelled guns).[79] U.S. and Korean officials have charged that North Korea is producing and stockpiling "lethal chemical offensive weapons."[80] The ROK Defense Minister has said that five factories in the North produce fourteen tons of chemical agents annually and that 250 tons have been stored.[81] South Korea also reportedly produces some chemical agents.[82]

North Korea's naval production is not very impressive and aircraft force production is almost nonexistent. The DPRK began building patrol boats in the 1960s, then graduated to primitive frigates in the 1970s. Most significant is the production since 1975 of twelve Romeo class submarines. In the 1980s the North has been accelerating its production of missile fast attack craft and amphibious vessels.[83]

- Weapons Exports

Both South and North Korea have emerged as important weapons exporters in recent years. ACDA ranked the ROK and DPRK as the second and third largest arms exporters in the Third World for the period 1979-1983, with $2 billion and $1.8 billion in military exports respectively. Only China ranked higher.[84] Most other sources, however, rank Israel and Brazil as the top Third World exporters.

The major systems that the ROK exports are naval vessels, especially fast attack craft. In recent years South Korea has sold PSMM-5 type fast attack craft to Indonesia and the Philippines, as well as amphibious craft to Venezuela and Argentina, and patrol craft to Malaysia.[85]

Some estimates put DPRK exports in 1982 at $470 million.[86] North Korea has become a major supplier to Iran, including (according to some reports) F-6 fighter aircraft, 150 T-62 tanks, four hundred field artillery pieces, one thousand mortars, anti-aircraft artillery and missiles, and small arms.[87] Ironically, South Korea has also provided weaponry to Iran during the course of its war with Iraq.

North Korea and South Korea have criticized each other for increasing arms sales to foreign countries. In September 1984, North Korea blasted the South for exporting "$400 million" in arms in 1982, shortly after the ROK accused the North of extensive shipments to Iran and attempts to penetrate the African market.[88]

The United States, while joining the ROK in condemning North Korean shipments to Iran, has not objected to increasing South Korean weapons exports. In fact, in 1983 then-Commander of U.S. Forces, Korea, General Sennewald, noting that the ROK had an excess capacity in many of its military plants, said, "We should find ways to permit them to increase sales of military equipment to third countries."[89]

Force Comparisons

It has been demonstrated that South Korea spends more on its military than North Korea and has for many years. South Korea has a superior domestic military production capability and it imports more weapons. As we now turn to a comparison of the military forces of North and South Korea, it will be seen that the DPRK does indeed have very large, very capable armed forces. North Korea's military strength proportionate to its size and population is matched by few countries in the world. Israel and Taiwan may be the only other candidates for that distinction. The size and strength of North Korea's forces cannot be denied. Often passed over in the United States, however, are the advantages that South Korea possesses—advantages which make it highly unlikely that North Korea could successfully attack the South, or have sufficient confidence even to make the attempt. South Korean forces today, particularly if U.S. air and naval reinforcements are added in, are strong enough to deter and if necessary defeat a North Korean invasion force. As the International Institute for Strategic Studies put it in the 1985-86 edition of *The Military Balance*, "The opposing forces on the Korean peninsula are roughly equivalent. Neither is capable of a successful major offensive against the other without significant foreign assistance."[90]

Manpower

North Korea's regular armed forces now number 838,000, compared to 598,000 for South Korea—an advantage of 240,000 people, or forty percent.[91] The South's regular armed forces outnumbered the North's until 1978, but DPRK troops have expanded considerably since then while ROK troops number about the same.[92]

The North's numerical superiority is mostly in ground forces, where it has an advantage of 750,000 to 520,000. The North also has an advantage in air forces of 53,000 to 33,000. The North has 35,000 naval forces, while the South has 23,000 navy men and 22,000 marines.[93]

There is a strange inconsistency in U.S. government figures on North Korean troop levels and military spending. They show North Korea's manpower holding steady during the first half of the 1970s when DPRK military spending was rapidly rising, then show manpower greatly expanding in the late 1970s when DPRK military spending was falling. In fact, ACDA's data shows North Korean manpower rising by only seventy thousand during the six-year period from 1971 to 1977, then jumping by 112,000 from 1977 to 1978.[94]

In wartime, North Korea's advantage in regular armed forces may be offset by South Korea's edge in reserves and para-military forces. The South has a very large advantage in all services in well-trained, first-line reserve forces. The ROK's reserves are estimated between 1.24 and 1.5 million; the DPRK's between 270,000 and 540,000.[95]

The South's ground force reserves number 1.1 to 1.4 million, the North's 230,000 to 500,000. The South's naval and marine reserves number about 85,000, the North's forty thousand. The South has about 55,000 air force reserves; the North has none.[96]

Besides well-trained reserves, both nations have enormous numbers of para-military forces—people who have received some military training, but are not integrated into the regular military establishment. South Korea has about 7.4 million para-military forces: a 3.5 million Civilian Defense Corps, a 3.3 million Homeland Reserve Forces, and a 600,000 Student National Defense Corps.[97]

Estimates of North Korean para-military forces vary widely. Analysts agree that there is a 38,000-man security force, but numbers on the Workers, Farmers and Youth Red Guard vary from 1.76 million to 3.7 million.[98]

In a long war, South Korea's larger population (43.3 million vs. 20.5 million) would prove a big advantage. South Korea presently has 8.1 million males fit for military service compared to 2.9 million for the North. More over, the South has a total of 464,000 males reaching age for military service each year, compared to 260,000 for the North.[99]

With people as with weapons, it is not just raw numbers that count. It is generally accepted that South Korea's forces are better trained than their northern counterparts. ROK leadership and experience are other important pluses. North Korean forces have not fought in over three decades, while South Korean troops had extensive combat experience fighting alongside U.S. forces in Vietnam.

Air Forces

In any war between North and South Korea, the battle of the skies would clearly be won by the South. If U.S. air forces are added in, the devastation would likely be akin to what Israel did to Syria over the skies of Lebanon in the summer of 1982. There is absolutely no question of ROK/U.S. air superiority; the only question is to what degree that air power would offset North Korean advantages in ground forces.

Air power is the key area which demonstrates South Korean qualitative advantages overcoming North Korean numerical advantages. North Korea has about 780 combat aircraft compared to about 490 for the South, a significant margin of nearly sixty percent (though nowhere near the oft-claimed two-to-one advantage).[100] But the South's aircraft are more modern and incorporate higher technology. They have better range, greater speed, a higher ceiling, more firepower, superior maneuverability, better avionics and weapons delivery capabilities. In other words, they can fly faster, farther, and higher; they handle better; they can deliver more powerful weapons more accurately. South Korean pilots are far superior to North Korean. DPRK pilots are believed to be relatively unskilled, largely because of very limited flying time.

Lt.General Charles Donnelly, Jr., commander of the 5th Air Force and U.S. Forces, Japan, said in 1983, "The North Korean aircraft are fairly old and have limited range. We think we can negate them pretty quickly."[101] Colonel Thomas Olsen, commander of the 51st Tactical Fighter Wing at Osan echoed that view: "We expect to be operating initially in a semi-permissive environment, and soon after in a permissive environment" as far as North Korean fighters or air defenses are concerned.[102] So much for the threat from the air.

North Korea does have large numbers of combat aircraft, but they are very old and of low quality.[103] About three-quarters of their combat aircraft are 1950s vintage. Until the delivery of the MiG-23s during the past two years the latest fighters in their arsenal were 1960s-vintage MiG-21s.

Of the approximately 780 North Korean combat aircraft, 480 are ground attack aircraft and three hundred are interceptors. The ground attack planes are particularly antiquated. Nearly forty percent (290 aircraft) of the North's combat aircraft are MiG-15s and MiG-17s. MiG-15s were the first modern Soviet jet fighter, appearing in 1949 and used during the Korean war. MiG-17s came on the scene four years later. Both are subsonic, cannot be used at night or in bad weather, have very poor radar (essentially eyeball contact), high vulnerability (strong infrared signature) and low ammunition capacity. The North also has seventy Il-28 light bombers and twenty Su-7B Fitter A bombers, both of which were first introduced in the late 1950s.

Another two hundred of the North's combat aircraft are MiG-19s. Half are configured as fighters, half as interceptors. MiG-19s were introduced in 1955, and the Soviets stopped production later in the decade. Like the MiG-15s and -17s, they are very primitive aircraft by today's standards.

The MiG-21 Fishbeds, of which they have 160, are extremely limited. They have short range, crude avionics, poor navigation, very light armament, and serious engine problems. East Germany reportedly lost 48 MiG-21 and -23s in 1983 and approximately another dozen in the first four months of 1984.

The MiG-23s are much more advanced aircraft than anything else in the North Korean arsenal. First deployed with Soviet forces in the early 1970s, the MiG-23 is the aircraft of choice for most close Soviet allies. Its sophisticated radar, superior avionics, more powerful engine, and better armaments are a big leap forward for the DPRK air force. It is, however, far from the "top-of-the-line" for Soviet aircraft and not nearly as modern as the F-16. The delivery of forty to fifty MiG-23s to North Korea will not significantly affect ROK-U.S. air superiority.

In early February 1985 the U.S. Commerce Department revealed that a West German company had illegally shipped eighty-seven U.S.-made Hughes Model 300C, 500D, and 500E helicopters to North Korea using a circuitous route through Japan, the Netherlands, and other nations. While these were civilian versions, the Hughes helicopters can be powerful military machines. The DPRK will probably convert most of them to carry air-to-surface missiles, rockets, and machine guns. To compound the trouble, they are the same type of helicopter that South Korea produces under license for its own armed forces. They could improve the DPRK's ability to infiltrate into the South and launch a surprise attack; at the least, they will make detection in wartime difficult.[104]

The United States and South Korea have agreed to take steps to offset any advantage the North may have gained—primarily "tactical methods" of dealing with the expanded DPRK helicopter fleet such as improved identification measures and new helicopter countermeasures systems.[105]

South Korea signed a deal for thirty-six F-16 fighter/ground attack aircraft in 1981. The first aircraft was delivered in March 1986, with ten more scheduled for delivery by the end of the year.[106] The F-16 is widely regarded as the best airplane of its type in the world. Currently, the 250 F-5 aircraft are the mainstay of the ROK air force. They have both the original F-5A/Bs and the upgraded F-5E/Fs. The F-5 was the main U.S. export aircraft of the 1970s. It is far superior in all aspects to any plane in North Korea's inventory, except the MiG-23. F-5s can be used either as fighters or interceptors.

The ROK also has 70 F-4D/Es. The F-4 Phantom is still considered one of the world's best ground attack aircraft, better than the F-5s. It is fast, powerful, and versatile. It is being replaced in the USAF inventory with F-16s. South Korea is phasing out its seventy F-86F Korean War-vintage fighter-bombers.

In addition, the ROK has numerous "specialty" aircraft. It has six A-10 "tank busters." These are considered the best close air support aircraft in the world. South Korea also has twenty-four OV-10 and approximately thirty A-37 counterinsurgency aircraft. Additionally, the ROK has ten RF-5A reconnaissance aircraft, twenty S-2A anti-submarine aircraft, and fourteen Army O-2A observation planes.

South Korean air armaments are far superior to the North's. The DPRK's air-to-air missiles are mainly old AA-2 Atolls, although newer AA-7s were recently delivered from the USSR, while the ROK has Sidewinders, Sparrows and Mavericks.

In sum, South Korea's air force, though outnumbered, is much more capable than North Korea's. When U.S. air assets are added in, the advantage is overwhelming. According to the way in which a possible North-South war developed, U.S. air support could be important, particularly in stopping a North Korean ground offensive. There is no need, however, for U.S. air forces to be based in the ROK. Reinforcement could be made effectively from Japan and from aircraft carriers.

Naval Forces

It is difficult to compare the navies of North and South Korea because they are structured differently and each nation has emphasized different types of vessels. Both navies are built for coastal operations, but North Korea's navy is the more offensively-oriented.

As in air forces, the North has a quantitative advantage, but the South a qualitative advantage. North Korea has about a 3.3 to 1 edge in number of naval vessels (527-159).[107] That comparison, however, has no more relevance than the fact that the South has about thirty percent more tonnage (93,000 vs. 71,000). While the DPRK has built large numbers of large patrol craft and small fast attack craft, the ROK has concentrated on large surface ships. Thus, the South has twenty-one destroyers, frigates, and corvettes compared to two for the North. The North has nearly four hundred patrol and small fast attack craft compared to seventy-five for the South.

The South Korean navy is generally about a decade ahead of North Korea in terms of its modernity. They have a large technological edge in electronics and weaponry which is increasing. South Korean ships tend to be faster, less vulnerable, and have more powerful, accurate weapons.

North Korea has emphasized submarines and small surface ships, such as fast attack craft and small, high speed landing craft, for coastal operations and offensive actions. Over the years, North Korean vessels have frequently gone into South Korean waters for the purpose of harassment and espionage, and it can be anticipated that in wartime the subs and fast attack craft would be used mainly for coastal raids and mining operations. A major handicap for the North Korean navy is the forced geographic division into two fleets, one in the east based at Wonsan and one in the west based at Nampo. The division greatly limits flexibility, a naval imperative.

The largest ships in the North Korean fleet currently are the two frigates of the "Najin-class" built domestically in 1976 and 1979. These frigates, with 3.9-inch guns, have been described by experts as primitive and crude.[108]

The North's nineteen subs, which are old, but nonetheless capable, have received much attention in force comparisons. Fifteen are of the ex-Soviet Romeo class; seven were built in China and delivered in 1973-75, twelve were built in North Korea between 1975 and 1982.

These are stationed on the west coast. The other four are ex-Soviet Whiskey class, of 1940s and 50s-vintage, which were transferred from the USSR in 1960 and are based on the east coast. Adm. Sylvester Foley, Jr., then commander-in-chief of the Pacific Fleet, has stated in 1984 that he is confident that once North Korean subs put to sea, his fleet can sink them.[109]

Also of concern are the thirty missile-carrying fast attack craft (FAC). The twelve Osa-I (delivered from the USSR between 1968 and 1983) and eight Komar FAC carry Styx missiles with a twenty-three mile range. They would provide a powerful strike force against the South Korean coastal areas. Ten FAC (six Soju-class, four Sohung-class) built locally are copies of the Osa and Komar boats.

In addition to the missile FAC, North Korea has a large number of ships for coastal operations, including a total of 301 gun and torpedo FAC (155 and 146, respectively). The North Koreans also have thirty-two large patrol craft and thirty coastal patrol craft, some built by the USSR, some by China, some by North Korea. Most of these are 1950s and 1960s vintage, although two were commissioned in 1939. Twenty of the patrol craft are old enough to have wooden hulls.

The North has about 113 landing craft. While this is a very large number, only a few are large enough to carry tanks and other heavy equipment. The biggest are four Hantae class ships (LSMs) built domestically since 1980, each of which can carry three or four medium tanks. There are about one hundred 84-foot Nampo class vessels, each armed with four machine guns and capable of transporting nineteen troops.

In sum, the DPRK Navy is basically a coastal force with very limited intervention capability and a small-scale surprise attack capability.

South Korea has eleven ex-U.S. destroyers of World War II vintage which have been upgraded considerably. Seven ex-Gearing class carry anti-ship missiles and one Alouette III helicopter each; two have advanced Harpoons. All eleven have five-inch guns and anti-submarine weapons.

The ROK Navy has six frigates, each with five-inch guns and anti-submarine weapons. Four are ex-U.S, WWII age, and two are South Korean Harpoon missile-carrying Ulsan class, launched in 1980. *Proceedings* called the Ulsan-class "unusual and innovative...good weapons and sensors."[110] South Korea has also built four corvettes of the HDP 1000, or Ma San Ho-class (1400 ton displacement) in the past few years.

According to *Jane's Fighting Ships*, South Korea's first submarine, a 175-ton domestically built vessel, entered service in 1983. It is reported to be the first of a class of four or five.

South Korea has eleven missile fast attack craft, ten of which are locally built: eight PSMM 5 types with Standard and Harpoon missiles, two Wildcat class with Exocet missiles, and one ex-U.S. boat with Standard missiles. Also in the inventory are more than sixty-two fast attack craft armed with guns, two large patrol craft, some coastal patrol craft, and eight coastal minesweepers.

In addition, the ROK Navy has thirty-six amphibious vessels, eight of which can carry up to twenty tanks each (LSTs), eight more of a size comparable to the biggest North Korean amphibious ship (LSMs), and twenty smaller craft (LCUs).

The most likely scenario has North Korea hoping to make surprise landings along South Korea's coasts with the small landing craft, protected by the hundreds of fast patrol craft, to outflank the ROK. North Korean subs would then attack ROK supply lines to threaten ROK logistics and U.S. reinforce ments, as well as conducting extensive mining. The ROK would strike back with its destroyers, fast attack craft, and air forces. Shipping would be escorted by frigates, corvettes, and patrol craft. There would probably be a full-scale counter attack involving amphibious forces.

North Korea has a more potent offensive navy than South Korea, but it is doubtful that it has the size, firepower, or technology to defeat the defensive prowess of the South Korean navy. In a full-scale war, assistance to the ROK from the United States and Japan, especially in anti-submarine warfare and mine countermeasures, could prove important.

Ground Forces

Ground forces are the area of greatest concern to the ROK and the United States. Any war on the Korean peninsula is likely to be dominated by ground forces. The DPRK and ROK have the world's sixth and seventh largest armies, respectively, exceeded only by China, the Soviet Union, the United States, India and Vietnam.[111]

North Korea has a significant advantage in numbers of troops and equipment on the ground. The qualitative advantage of South Korea is not so pronounced as with air and naval forces. In fact, much of North Korea's artillery is more powerful and of longer range than the South's. North Korea's ground forces are highly mechanized and mobile. Moreover, more than seventy-five percent of North Korea's ground forces are within fifty miles of the DMZ and Seoul is only twenty-five miles from the DMZ.[112] The high priority the ROK and the United States have placed on the defense of Seoul means the South cannot fight a defensive strategy of trading territory while extracting attrition.

Yet it is interesting to note that as late as 1977 Secretary of Defense Harold Brown was saying, "The ground forces of South Korea are comparable in numbers and capability to those of the North and should be able to hold defensive positions north of Seoul."[113] At that time, the Carter Administration had determined that the military balance on the peninsula was such that the withdrawal of a large number of U.S. ground forces was justified.

Then in 1979 there was a major U.S. government re-evaluation of North Korean ground forces. Overnight, the United States boosted its estimates of North Korean army personnel by 160-260,000 (including 100,000 commandos), tanks by 650, APCs by 250, field guns by 500-1,000, and anti-aircraft weapons by 2,500-3,500.[114] Suddenly, the U.S. government refused even to contemplate the withdrawal of U.S. troops. The threat itself had not changed at all, only the perception of it.

Today, the North has roughly forty percent more army manpower (750,000 vs. 520,000), a 2.75 to 1 advantage in main battle tanks (3,275 vs. 1,200), seventy-five percent more APCs (1,240 vs. 700), and fifty-five percent more artillery (4,650 vs. 3,000).[115]

Clearly, the numerical advantage of the North is significant, but there are important offsetting factors. First, the North Korean quantitative edge still falls short of current Soviet operational doctrine for success of offensive versus defensive forces: three to one manpower, five to one tanks, six to one artillery.[116]

Second, the defensive posture of the South would be a tremendous advantage. The ROK would be fighting from extremely well-fortified defensive positions on their own territory. The North Korean tank advantage disappears quickly when one considers the terrain the tanks would have to traverse. There are only three north-south attack routes, all of which are heavily defended with extensive in-place fortifications and which would channel DPRK forces, making them vulnerable to a barrage from anti-tank weapons, artillery pieces, and aircraft.

Third, the South Korean forces do enjoy a qualitative edge. Most of their ground equipment is superior, in terms of late model tanks and APCs, self-propelled artillery, and advanced ground missiles (surface-to-surface, surface-to-air, anti-tank).

Fourth, the structure of forces offsets many of the North Korean numerical advantages usually cited. For example, the South has emphasized anti-armor forces while the North emphasizes armor. The South has more anti-tank guns and weapons which can be fired from the ground or the air; the South has better close air support forces.

Fifth, the South has an advantage in training, leadership, and experience. These are two of the best trained armies in the world, but the South has the advantage of three hundred thousand men who fought in the Vietnam War, including many present-day commanders.[117] North Koreans have had no combat experience since 1953.

Sixth, as pointed out above, the South has more reserves and paramilitary forces, more males fit for military service and more males reaching military age annually. Given these facts, and the South's general advantage in population and industrial capacity, any war that lasts a long time would eventually favor the South.

Several issues have drawn special attention in recent years. Foremost is North Korea's deployment further south, closer to the DMZ, of troops, tanks, artillery, and other weaponry. Chun Doo Hwan first revealed the movement in October 1984 and Korean and U.S. officials were quick to point out that it reduced the South's warning time of a possible attack and increased the chances of a successful surprise attack.[118]

At the 1985 U.S.-ROK Security Consultative Meeting, the two nations agreed to enhance early warning capabilities and to expand the exchange of intelligence, as "both preventive and counter-measures against North Korean provocations." Defense Minister Yoon also revealed that "a presumed North Korean mode of attack scenario has jointly been developed by the United States and the Republic of Korea."[119]

What is usually left unsaid is that the movements were not a sudden, threatening, new buildup by the North. They were gradual in nature, occuring over the course of three years starting in 1982.[120] U.S. officials have admitted the movements represented no increase in overall North Korean military strength, only the shifting of rear echelon forces into more forward positions to make more efficient use of their resources (whether for offensive or defensive missions).[121]

Adm. Crowe did not seem overly concerned when interviewed in *Armed Forces Journal International* in May 1985. "I think we probably have put more attention and emphasis on our communications and warning systems in Korea than we have any other single piece of real estate in the world. We have a very reasonable capability. In fact, more than that, we've got a good capability....We work in many ways to detect communications and warning, and I think we're in pretty good shape...These steps [DPRK movements south] may cut down warning time, but I don't think they have destroyed all of our effectiveness; it's certainly made us work a little harder to compensate in other ways."[122]

Another issue is North Korean tunnels. Three tunnels have been discovered in the past—in 1974, 1975, and 1978. The last two were dug at least fifty meters below the surface, and were approximately two meters high and two meters wide.[123]

There is little doubt the DPRK has continued to attempt to build tunnels. There are five hundred U.S. and Korean technical personnel assigned to search for them.[124] Apparently they have been able to detect signs of underground activity, but not able to isolate individual tunnels. How many tunnels have been and are being built, and how large, is open to question.

Some sources claim that ten to thirteen more tunnels have already been built and have been detected by the South, but not precisely located, and that another ten to thirty are now under construction. The possibility has been raised that each of the more than twenty North Korean divisions along the DMZ is digging at least one tunnel. The tunnels are said to be large enough to move at least two thousand and perhaps as many as thirteen hundred troops an hour through each, as well as small trucks and artillery pieces.[125]

From a military point of view, the tunnels are not terribly worrisome. If they were able to reach deep into South Korea undetected, they would be something of a cause for concern, but it takes about a year to auger one mile of granite. It would be many years before tunnels could reach rear areas, and over the course of those years they would in all likelihood be discovered and destroyed. Tunnels that only serve to bypass the DMZ are probably counter-productive; soldiers could move faster and with more equipment above ground. In wartime, previously undetected tunnels could be quickly and effectively destroyed by blocking exits.

A third issue that has attracted much attention is the existence of eighty to one hundred thousand North Korean commandos/rangers. Government officials are quick to claim that this is probably the largest commando force in the world, and that it poses grave dangers for the ROK.[126] It is expected that the commandos would be the vanguard of an invasion, using the tunnels, AN-2 transport aircraft, and small naval craft to infiltrate at night into South Korea to disrupt ROK forces from the rear by attacking military bases, communications sites, ground control facilities, and other targets. Seventy percent of the commando force is thought to be ground/paratroop soldiers.[127]

While the commando threat should not be taken lightly, it should also be realized that South Korean forces are already capable of dealing with that type of warfare. As stated above, it is doubtful the tunnels will be of much use. The DPRK has 250 AN-2s, each capable of carrying only fourteen commandos. The AN-2 is a slow, noisy, weaponless propeller bi-plane which is extremely vulnerable.[128] The difficulty would be in tracking it on radar designed for faster, higher flying jet aircraft. The South Korean navy is designed for coastal defense. The vast majority of the commando force would probably end up using the same invasion corridors as the main ground troops and therefore would likely be detected early and encounter stiff resistance.

A fourth issue is the degree to which the North has "hardened" its military facilities by putting them underground and protecting them with concrete shelters. Apparently, artillery is buried in caves and concrete; aircraft hangars and repair facilities are inside mountains big enough to handle fifty or more fighters; air defense missiles are in buried bunkers; air defense radars are stored underground and brought up by elevators; submarines and patrol boats are in "drive-through" granite and concrete harbors.[129]

U.S. officials say that at the present time, U.S./ROK forces have no non-nuclear ordnance that could destroy most of these structures and that it may be years before any is available. Still, senior U.S. military officers have discounted the value to Kim of the hardened facilities: subs, aircraft, field guns, missiles and radars cannot do anything underground.

With respect to the airplanes, Gen. Jerome O'Malley, the commander-in-chief of Pacific Air Forces, has said, "If they stay unflushed, they won't be of very much use. So they've got to flush, and we may be able to do some things to flush them. There are certain targets they have to defend, and if they flush—that's our goal—we'll take them out in the air." Gen. Donnelly, commander of the Fifth Air Force, echoed those words: "I can make [Kim] fly. He can't afford to keep his assets inside a mountain if we are attacking targets in his country."[130]

Hardening of facilities in this fashion seems inconsistent with the all-out offensive strategy U.S. and ROK officials attribute to the DPRK. In fact, as John Keegan, noted military analyst and author of the encyclopedic *World Armies*, has noted, North Korea's forces may be best suited to a long, defensive war fought on its own territory, not an attempt at a quick offensive victory.[131] The DPRK could best take advantage of the "militarization of the whole population" and the "fortification of the whole country" in a protracted war fought in the North.

U.S. Forces In Korea

The United States has maintained combat troops and support units in South Korea on a continuous basis since 1950. After the Korean War, the United States pledged itself to the defense of South Korea by signing the Mutual Defense Treaty in 1954. Three U.S. infantry divisions remained in the country to help rebuild the ROK army and to insure that North Korea did not cross the thirty-eighth parallel again. One U.S. division was withdrawn in 1954 and the number of U.S. troops stayed around sixty thousand until 1971 when the Nixon Administration withdrew another division.

Since then, there have usually been about forty thousand U.S. military personnel in South Korea, although the precise number fluctuates. Until the latter part of 1985 the highest number in recent years was recorded at the end of March 1980; between the end of December 1979 and March 1980 the force level rose from 39,306 to 42,822.[132] General Chun Doo Hwan, of course, seized power in December 1979. During the Reagan Administration the number has dipped lower than 38,000 but has been steadily rising since the end of 1984.

There are apparently more U.S. troops in South Korea now than at any time since the Nixon withdrawal. At the end of March 1986 the exact number was 45,158, including 32,312 Army, 11,469 Air Force, 408 Navy and 969 Marine personnel.[133] Army General Richard Sennewald, former commander of U.S. Forces in Korea, recently revealed that the United States has made "modest increases" in the number of ground troops in Korea since 1981 and will continue to do so through 1985, adding a total of 2,000-2,500 soldiers.[134]

South Korea is the only place in the world where U.S. forces are permanently kept at DEFCON 4 (Defense Readiness Condition Four), one level above normal.[135] The United States has a total of forty military installations in Korea.[136] The most important are the army base at Camp Casey and air force bases at Osan and Kunsan.

The majority of U.S. forces in Korea are members of the Eighth U.S. Army, the major element of which is the second Infantry Division.[137] (Of the sixteen U.S. army divisions, only the Second Division and the four in West Germany are stationed in foreign countries). Other army forces stationed in Korea include a surface-to-surface missile command, an air defense brigade, a signal brigade, and surveillance, logistics, and intelligence units.

The Second Infantry Division, along with thirteen ROK Army Divisions, forms the Combined ROK/U.S. Field Army (also known as the I Corps Group). It is mostly deployed between the DMZ and Seoul with the mission of defending Seoul. The Fourth U.S. Army Missile Command, with Lance surface-to-surface missiles, is headquartered in Chunchon, about eighty kilometers northeast of Seoul. The Thirty-eighth Air Defense Artillery Brigade is headquartered at Osan Air Base.

The main U.S. Air Force unit in Korea is the 314th Air Division, headquartered at Osan, which is subordinate to the 5th Air Force in Japan. The 314th Air Division controls two tactical wings. The Fifty-first Tactical Fighter Wing is based at Osan, with F-4E, OV-10 and OA-37B aircraft. U-2R reconnaissance planes normally operate out of Osan also. The Eighth Tactical Wing, with two squadrons of F-16s, is based at Kunsan. Taegu is home to the 497th Tactical Fighter Squadron with fourteen F-4E fighters. Suwon houses the twenty-fifth Tactical Fighter Squadron with twenty-four A-10s.

The United States has equipped its troops in Korea with large numbers of its most advanced, top-of-the-line weaponry.[138] Major ground equipment that the United States has in Korea includes 155 medium tanks (M-60s and M-55s), 105mm and 155mm artillery, 107mm and 88mm mortars, Vulcan air defense systems, I-Hawk and Redeye surface-to-air missiles, and TOW and Dragon anti-tank weapons. U.S. forces in Korea will eventually get the new M-1 main battle tank. As in Europe, the United States has large amounts of munitions pre-positioned in Korea, for use in wartime by both U.S. and Korean forces.

Major U.S. air assets located in Korea include forty-eight F-16 fighter-bombers, twenty-four F-4 fighter-bombers (some F-4G "Wild Weasels"), twenty-four A-10 attack aircraft ("tank-busters"), sixteen OV-10 counter insurgency/reconnaissance aircraft, AH-1S Cobra TOW attack helicopters, and UH-60 Blackhawk transport helicopters.

The United States is constantly upgrading its forces in Korea with the latest weapons in the U.S. arsenal. General Livsey said in late 1985 that the Eighth Army would receive some 135 new systems over the next few years.[139] F-16s, A-10s, AH-1Ss, and UH-60s have been added over the past several years. New ground equipment includes the M-198 155mm howitzer, M60A3 tanks with night vision sights, and multiple rocket launch systems.[140] The first two U.S. Air Force airfields to have operational Stinger anti-aircraft missile systems (replacing 20mm Vulcan cannons and .50 caliber machine guns) were Osan and Kunsan Air Bases; deployment was completed in June 1985.[141]

Other recent efforts include readiness improvements, upgrading of airfields, activation of a new military intelligence battalion, and improvements in intelligence collection platforms. The United States is also building up its war reserve stockpiles in Korea; Congress appropriated $125 million in the FY 1984 supplemental bill and $248 million in FY 1985 for that purpose.[142]

There has been an increase in construction activities as well. The FY 1985 U.S. military construction in Korea total of $220 million was the largest request ever for facilities improvement.[143] Livsey reported in 1985 that the Eighth Army was getting rid of old, temporary structures and replacing them with "modern, semi-permanent facilities."[144]

•The UN Command and the Combined Forces Command

Technically, all U.S. troops in South Korea and all ROK forces are still under the operational command of the United Nations Command in Korea. The commander of UN Forces is always the commander of U.S. Forces, Korea. Thus there exists the unique situation of all of a sovereign nation's armed forces being headed by a foreign commander.

The UN command was established by a UN Security Council Resolution on July 7, 1950. The Taejon Agreement of 1950 between the ROK government and the UN Command stipulated that the operational control of Korean forces would be in the hands of the UN Command. Eight of the sixteen nations which originally formed the UN Command (and which in July 1953 pledged to unite again to resist renewed aggression on the peninsula) remain accredited: Australia, Canada, France, New Zealand, the Philippines, Thailand, the United Kingdom and the United States. No longer accredited are Belgium, Colombia, Ethiopia, Greece, Luxembourg, the Netherlands, Turkey and South Africa.[145] However, only the United States maintains combat troops in South Korea. Some of the other nations have token forces on duty at the ceasefire center at Panmunjom.

The UN Command's mission is to enforce the armistice agreement and settle any questions of violations, but in a practical sense its main purpose is to serve as the only internationally recognized channel of communication with North Korea. Through the Military Armistice Commission at Panmunjom, it is supposed to propose initiatives to reduce tensions and achieve a final peaceful settlement. It would also serve for rapid introduction of foreign forces if major conflict erupted on the peninsula. As early as 1971 Morton Abramowitz remarked. "The UN presence [in Korea] is little more than a hollow shell," a legal figleaf to cover the continuing operation of the armistice agreement which has always been a U.S.-ROK arrangement with the DPRK.[146]

In recognition of the fact that the United States and South Korea are solely responsible for the defense of the ROK, and to permit greater involvement of the ROK in war planning, the Combined Forces Command (CFC) was formed in 1978. The CFC is the only combined U.S./Allied command outside of NATO. The CFC is the war-fighting headquarters.[147] The purpose of the CFC is to "integrate ROK and U.S. forces into a cohesive organization capable of fighting coalition warfare" and to achive an "integration of tactics and doctrine with an emphasis on interoperability and complementarity."[148]

The ranking officer of the CFC is the commander of U.S. Forces, Korea. The CFC headquarters is manned by equal numbers of U.S. and Korean personnel from each of the services. The CFC has over 650,000 military personnel under its operational control, including almost all ROK forces, plus U.S. Air Force, air defense, and logistics units.[149] As mentioned above, the U.S. Second Division is under a separate command, the Combined ROK/U.S. Field Army, which also controls thirteen Korean divisions. The ROK Capital Garrison Command is a separate unit under the direct operational control of the ROK president, and has the mission of the protection of Seoul.[150]

If there were any doubts previously, the establishment of CFC insures that a new Korean war cannot be fought without U.S. forces. U.S. troops would be involved from the first shot fired. Deputy Assistant Secretary of Defense James Kelly once again made this very clear when he told Congress early in 1986, "If deterrence were to fail, these U.S. forces would be engaged immediately alongside ROK forces...."[151]

• "Team Spirit"

The CFC conducts five major annual exercises, the largest of which is Team Spirit. Outside of the "Reforger" exercise in Europe, Team Spirit is the largest exercise in which U.S. forces participate each year. The purpose is to practice fighting a war with the North. Team Spirit 86, held in February, was the eleventh in the series. It involved over 200,000 U.S. and Korean military personnel, including sixty thousand U.S. troops deployed from the continental United States and other U.S. military bases in the Pacific and about twenty-five ships from the U.S. Seventh Fleet. Team Spirit 86 was the first to include a mass airdrop of over nine hundred U.S. and Korean paratroopers.[152] The last several Team Spirit exercises have been used partially as tests for the new light divisions: the Twenty-fifth Infantry Division in Hawaii, the Seventh Infantry Division in California, and the Ninth Infantry Division in Washington.[153] Generally, the exercise consists of mock amphibious assaults, aerial and naval bombardment, anti-submarine warfare, commando/special forces operations, and field maneuvers, as well as training for chemical and nuclear warfare.[154]

• Paying for the U.S. Presence

The best estimate of the cost of stationing U.S. troops in Korea is approximately $2 billion per year. The South Korean government—through one means or another—picks up about half the tab. General Wickham told Congress in early 1986, "They [Koreans] offset the presence of U.S. forces in their country to the tune of $1 billion a year, year in and year out."[155]

The U.S. and Korean governments estimate that in 1982 U.S. forces realized $970 million in savings or cost avoidance from Korean contributions such as rent-free real estate, construction of training and warfighting facilities, force structure augmentation, industrial and utility support, and tax abatements.[156]

The biggest part of the Korean contribution comes from real estate provided at no cost. The rental value of real estate used exclusively by U.S. forces is estimated at $535 million.[157]

The ROK has built over $500 million in military facilities for the United States since 1980, including a hardened tactical air control center; hardened army and navy command, control, communications, and intelligence centers; airfields and aircraft shelters; and munitions storage areas.[158]

Force structure augmentation, or personnel offsets, primarily involves fleshing out the manpower-short U.S. units by the KATUSA (Korean Augmentation To the U.S. Army). Inititated in 1950, KATUSA now provides 7,240 Korean soldiers to support the Eighth U.S. Army, with the ROK paying their salaries. Additionally, there is the Korean Service Corps (KSC), a paramilitary organization of 3,200 personnel created to support U.S. forces during the Korean War. Plans are to expand the KSC to 22,500 in the event of another war.[159]

Industrial support consists mainly of Korean industry providing maintenance for U.S. equipment, such as repairing M-113 tracked vehicles. U.S. military installations are charged forty-three percent less for electricity than ROK forces. U.S. military personnel can get gasoline at one-fourth the price charged local residents. Privately-owned vehicles of U.S. personnel are exempt from the Korean road tax. U.S. forces are exempt from the value-added and special excise taxes that the ROK military pays on contracts.[160]

The ROK also provides support by paying U.S. munitions-handling costs, and charging little for transporting, storing, and maintaining U.S. munitions. (On the other hand, South Korea is the only country for which the U.S. buys munitions.)

The $2 billion total is somewhat misleading as it includes only direct costs of stationing troops in Korea. It does not take into account equipment costs, costs for reinforcements, or a host of other items. It is not reflective of the overall cost of U.S. preparations for fighting in Korea or the U.S. military commitment to Korea. Total cost of U.S. forces for fighting in Asia has been put at $47 billion in FY 1985.[161] The biggest portion of that would be for fighting in Korea, plus a substantial amount for the defense of Japan and a lesser amount for the Philippines, Thailand, and other U.S. friends in the region.

- U.S. Nuclear Weapons

Outside of Western Europe, South Korea is the only foreign country where it is acknowledged that the United States has nuclear weapons stationed. In the mid-1970s it was generally accepted that the United States kept over six hundred nuclear weapons in South Korea.[162] Since then, however, the United States has withdrawn warheads for Honest John surface-to-surface missiles, Nike-Hercules surface-to-air missiles, and other systems.

It is very difficult to be certain about the number of nuclear weapons in South Korea, but one authoritative source has put the current stockpile at 151: sixty aircraft bombs, forty 8-inch artillery shells, thirty 155mm artillery shells, and twenty-one atomic demolition munitions (ADMs, or land mines).[163] Kunsan Air Base is the storage location for U.S. nuclear weapons.[164]

While some nuclear weapons have been withdrawn, others have probably been replaced with newer weapons—older single yield weapons replaced with new selectable yield weapons, giving greater flexibility. For example, there are probably some of the new B-61 tactical nuclear bombs for aircraft stationed in Korea. The B-61 has four yield options, from one hundred to five hundred kilotons. (The bomb dropped on Hiroshima was about twelve kilotons.) It can be delivered at lower altitudes than older bombs and is probably considered a more usable nuclear weapon.

The eight-inch artillery shells have yields from less than one kiloton to twelve kilotons. The 155mm artillery shells have a yield of .1 kiloton. There are two types of ADMs, one man-portable (about 163 pounds) with a yield from .01 kiloton to one kiloton, and a larger version with yields from one to fifteen kilotons.[165]

It is possible that the United States will deploy the new W-79 eight-inch artillery shell, commonly known as the neutron bomb, in South Korea. From 1981 to 1984 the United States built about 325 eight-inch neutron artillery shells.[166] In October 1984 Congress stopped further production of the originally planned three thousand neutron warheads for eight-inch and 155mm artillery because of the refusal of West European governments to accept them on their soil. The completed neutron weapons are now sitting in storage in the United States. Neutron bombs produce radiation as their primary lethal effect, rather than blast and heat. They are thought to be particularly effective against massive concentrations of tanks and armor. It has also been speculated that the United States might deploy ground-launched cruise missiles in Korea in the future.

U.S. nuclear weapons in Korea have no military utility, are unnecessary, and only serve counter-productive purposes. They have always been justified as the ultimate deterrent to a North Korean attack. Yet, in contrast to Europe, there is no nuclear threat from North Korea. There are no nuclear weapons in North Korea, thus no need for U.S. nuclear weapons as a deterrent against the use of nuclear weapons by the North.

There is also no need for U.S. nuclear weapons as a deterrent against a conventional attack by the North. As demonstrated above, there is essentially military equivalency on the peninsula. The conventional military strength of South Korea, and even more so of the combined ROK/U.S. forces, appears sufficient to deter an attack by the North. Even if North Korea acts irrationally and attacks, the ROK, with some assistance from the United States, is strong enough to defend itself with conventional weapons.

North Koreans may believe that the likelihood of the United States ever using its nuclear weapons against a non-nuclear nation again is very low. It is doubtful the U.S. public would support such a use and world opinion would certainly be strongly against it. The United States did not use nuclear weapons in 1950-1953 even though it suffered serious military reverses and had a monopoly on nuclear weapons at the time.

But the Reagan Administration has adopted a nuclear war fighting strategy which presumably includes plans to use nuclear weapons in Korea. That would likely result in the destruction, not the saving, of the nation. Besides the obliteration of property, the use of tactical nuclear weapons would kill and injure a great number of Koreans and U.S. troops and civilians resident in South Korea. Fallout would endanger all Koreans, Japanese, Chinese, and Soviets. The use of nuclear weapons might even create the kind of widespread chaos that could lead to a North Korean victory. There is also the danger— probably limited—of capture or unauthorized, premature firing of the nuclear weapons.

- The Withdrawal of U.S. Forces

Why are U.S. troops stationed in South Korea more than thirty years after the signing of the armistice agreement? U.S. and ROK officials are always quick to answer: to deter the North, and to assist in combat should deterrence fail.

Deterrence, however, is really a state of mind. What is the U.S. contribution to deterrence of the North? Is it the U.S. mutual defense treaty with South Korea, or is it the presence of U.S. troops in the ROK, or is it the combat capability of those troops, or is it the presence of U.S. nuclear weapons in the South? While only Kim Il Sung and other DPRK leaders can answer with certainty, it seems evident that the U.S. commitment to the defense of the ROK is the essence of the U.S. contribution to deterrence. The question then becomes how best to demonstrate that commitment from a political, military, and economic standpoint.

It has already been argued above that U.S. nuclear weapons are not necessary to deter the DPRK. Likewise, the combat capability of U.S. forces stationed in South Korea is probably not a key element in deterring the North. While U.S. forces stationed in Korea would add significant firepower, especially from the air, to the ROK's armed forces, it is not likely that they would make a crucial difference in the case of a North Korean attack. The Second Division in particular makes little military sense. As Army Brigadier General John Bahnsen wrote in November 1985, he supports a continued U.S. military presence in Korea, but "the wisdom of maintaining any U.S. infantry in a country so rich in manpower is purely political. And with forty million people in South Korea opposing twenty million in the North, even the political wisdom of supporting the current design of the Second Infantry Division is wearing thin....The Second Infantry Division...is a political solution without any basis in warfighting requirements."[167]

U.S. forces elsewhere in the region could have a serious impact on a war in Korea and, therefore, serve as a deterrent to the North. This is particularly true of the aircraft carriers, other ships, and planes of the Seventh Fleet in the western Pacific, as well as the Fifth Air Force and the Third Marine Division in Japan.

It is probably true that the physical presence of some U.S. forces in South Korea helps to deter the North from attacking. Their presence not only reinforces the strength of the U.S. commitment to the defense of the ROK, it also creates a "tripwire" effect, insuring U.S. involvement in conflict. However, it should be abundantly clear that a tripwire force need not number forty thousand. A very small number of men—a battalion or less—could serve the same function.

There is reason to question the wisdom of having tripwire forces at all. It may enhance deterrence, but at too high a price. It is not at all clear that the U.S. public would favor U.S. involvement in another Korean war, or any war on the Asian mainland. "Automaticity" of immediate and massive combat involvement may not be desirable. It might be wiser to adopt a posture that would allow U.S. policymakers time to reflect on the necessity of extensive U.S. involvement, to judge the attitude of the country, to see whether or not the ROK can hold its own with logistical and material support from the United States or with naval and air support and without the commitment of ground troops.

In sum, there is no overwhelming military rationale for keeping large numbers of U.S. troops on the Korean peninsula. They are there primarily for a political purpose—to demonstrate the depth of the U.S. commitment to South Korea. It would be much safer, and less costly, to demonstrate that commitment in a different fashion.

Outside of the Korean context, the United States has other reasons for wanting to keep forces in Korea. Korea provides an excellent training ground for U.S. forces, and exposes them to something as close to wartime conditions as possible. The U.S. presence facilitates U.S. intelligence collection throughout the region. South Korean bases are an important element of U.S. post-World War II forward deployment strategy, which involves stationing one-half million men at hundreds of bases in dozens of foreign countries all around the globe, in an attempt to enable the United States to fight effectively any place, any time. South Korea could be an important location from which to fight Soviet forces in the future. U.S. military planners see the U.S. troop presence in South Korea as essential to remaining a viable Pacific military power and containing the Soviet Union.

Many other reasons have been put forth for the continued presence of U.S. forces, including protection of U.S. economic interests in Korea and maintaining control over South Korean forces, perhaps to prevent them from acquiring nuclear weapons or from invading the North. Some have even suggested the U.S. military wants to keep high-level billets and promotion possibilities open.

No matter how many arguments are made in favor of maintaining troops, the essential truths which led the Carter Administration to advocate a troop withdrawal in 1977 still exist today. Large numbers of U.S. ground troops are not militarily necessary, given the basic equivalence of ROK and DPRK forces, and the withdrawal of U.S. troops is not likely to lead to increased aggression by the North. Professor Edward Olsen, national security affairs specialist and coordinator of Asian studies at the U.S. Naval Postgraduate School, wrote in the *Naval War College Review* in early 1985, "Clearly it is not popular today to suggest that Carter was right about the troop reduction idea, but I will say so in a modified way. The Carter Administration's ideas were valid as far as they went...." Olsen believes the major flaw in Carter's proposal was the expectation the ROK should shoulder more of the defense burden. Olsen argues Japan could and should play a larger role: "It is time that the Carter troop proposal be taken off the shelf....A workable formula between South Korean manpower and Japanese and U.S. subsidies for equipment and support would be both feasible and reasonable. Such actions should not be taken as a failure of the United States to shoulder its commitments to Northeast Asia. But rather, its purpose is to equitably share the security burden for the area and, further, to enable the United States to keep its commitments in the region without resorting to nuclear weapons."[168]

In fact, because of the extreme hostility of the DPRK to the presence of U.S. forces, a U.S. withdrawal would more likely result in reduced North-South tensions and improved relations. The risk of war would be slightly greater, but the chances for conclusion of a meaningful peace treaty would be enhanced immeasurably.

In all probability, a withdrawal would also lead to improved U.S. relations with the Korean people. For years the U.S. troop presence has served to bolster the power of a series of repressive military dictatorships in South Korea. A withdrawal, if carefully and skillfully executed, could increase the possibility of the establishment of a true democracy in South Korea. There is very real danger, however, that a withdrawal improperly executed could lead to greater repression by military leaders, increased militarization, and dominance by the military in South Korea.

If accompanied by an end to U.S. operational control over ROK forces, a withdrawal would probably be viewed as an expression of respect for the Korean people. South Korea would no longer face charges from other states of being a U.S. puppet. ROK national independence and integrity would no longer be compromised, in either the military or political realm. The military elements which have dominated U.S.-Korean relations would be de-emphasized.

If carried out, a U.S. withdrawal would have to be done slowly and gradually under the proper conditions. It should be part of a bargaining process with the North, taking advantage of the opportunity to lessen military tensions and force levels on both sides. U.S. and especially Korean public opinion would have to be taken into account. All citizens involved would have to be well informed of what was being done and why. A planned, gradual withdrawal with intermediate steps and stages, and a high level of education of the people, still makes a great deal of sense.

The place to start would be the removal of all U.S. nuclear weapons from the peninsula. Elements of the Second Infantry Division could then be systematically withdrawn over a period of years, followed by Air Force units. This would still leave behind the less controversial, but militarily important U.S. air defense, intelligence and support units. These are important, necessary and militarily-feasible steps toward the desirable goal of a militarily self-reliant South Korea and a Korean peninsula with no nuclear weapons or foreign troops.

Notes

Introduction

1. *Washington Times*, (March 19, 1986).
2. *Jane's Defense Weekly*, (March 9, 1985), p. 395.
3. *Atlanta Constitution*, (April 5, 1985).
4. Statement to House Appropriations Committee, (March 12, 1986), p. 7.
5. For numbers and types of weapons in all regions of the world, see the International Institute for Strategic Studies, *The Military Balance 1984-1985*, (London: 1984).
6. Sgt. First Class Michael Brown, "The DMZ Beat," *Soldiers*, (February 1986), p. 14.
7. Kelly to House Appropriations Committee, (March 12, 1986), p. 6.
8. House Appropriations Committee, Military Construction Appropriations for 1985, Pt. 6, p. 611.
9. Statement before the Senate Foreign Relations Committee, (March 22, 1984), reprinted in *Department of State Bulletin*, (May 1984), p. 54.
10. Ibid., p. 57.
11. See, for example, Adm. Hays' Statement to Senate Armed Services Committee (March 11, 1986), p. 12; Wolfowitz to Senate Foreign Relations Committee (March 21, 1985), p. 4; statements of Armitage and Wolfowitz cited above; the annual Congressional Presentation Documents; and the annual statements by the Commander of U.S. Forces, Korea, to congressional committees.
12. Central Intelligence Agency, *World Factbook 1986*, pp. 134-136, (July 1986 data).
13. Ibid., (1984 real GNP).
14. House Appropriations Committee, Foreign Assistance Appropriations FY 1983, Pt. 1, p. 152, (March 11, 1982).
15. *A Handbook of Korea*, Korean Overseas Information Service, (Seoul: Ministry of Culture and Information, 1982) 4th Edition, pp. 453-454.

16. *DMS Intelligence Report*, (September 19, 1983), p. 1.

17. Statement by General Robert Sennewald before the House Armed Services Committee, (March 8, 1983), p.1.

18. House Appropriations Committee, Military Construction Appropriations for 1985, Pt. 6, p. 612.

19. Senate Armed Services Committee, Department of Defense Appropriation for FY 1985, Pt. 2, p. 1195.

20. Ibid., p. 1253.

21. *Korea Herald*, (July 7, 1985).

22. *Army*, (October 1985), p. 134.

23. Department of Defense Briefing Transcript, (March 24, 1986), pp. 20-21.

24. House Foreign Affairs Committee, Foreign Assistance Legislation for FY1985, Pt. 5, p.xii.

Military Spending

25. U.S. Arms Control and Disarmament Agency, *World Military Expenditures and Arms Transfers 1985*, p. 69 for 1973-1983; three previous editions for 1970-1972.

26. U.S. Arms Control and Disarmament Agency, *World Military Expenditures and Arms Transfers 1985*, p. 69.

27. U.S. Arms Control and Disarmament Agency, *World Military Expenditures and Arms Transfers 1972-1982*, p. 33.

28. U.S. Arms Control and Disarmament Agency, *World Military Expenditures and Arms Transfers 1971-1980*, p. 55.

29. U.S. Arms Control and Disarmament Agency, *World Military Expenditures and Arms Transfers 1985*, p. 69 and *World Military Expenditures and Arms Transfers 1972-1982*, p. 33.

30. U.S. Arms Control and Disarmament Agency, *World Military Expenditures and Arms Transfers 1985*, p. 69.

31. International Institute for Strategic Studies, *The Military Balance 1985-1986*, p. 172.

32. Secretary Armitage to House Appropriations Committee, Military Construction Appropriations, Pt. 6, p. 612, on April 4, 1984 says that the ROK military spending "approximates $4.5 billion." Kelly to Senate Foreign Relations Committee (March 21, 1985) says $4.5 billion.

33. Kelly to House Appropriations Committee (March 12, 1986), p.7.

34. Stockholm International Peace Research Institute, *SIPRI Yearbook 1986*, p. 235.

35. International Institute for Strategic Studies, *The Military Balance 1985-1986*, p. 126.

36. CIA, *Factbook 1986*, pp. 135-136.

37. Admiral William Crowe, Senate Armed Services Committee, Department of Defense Authorization for FY 1985, Pt. 2, p. 1190 (26%); Adm. Hays to Senate Armed Services Committee (March 11, 1986), p. 12 (25%); Gen. Wickham, House Appropriations Com-

mittee, Department of Defense Appropriations for FY 1987, Pt. 1, p. 138 (24%).

38. U.S. Arms Control and Disarmament Agency, *World Military Expenditures and Arms Transfers 1985*, p. 69.

39. International Institute for Strategic Studies, *The Military Balance 1985-1986*, p. 172.

40. Ibid., pp. 126-127.

41. *SIPRI Yearbook 1986*, p. 244.

42. U.S. Arms Control and Disarmament Agency, *World Military Expenditures and Arms Transfers 1985*, p. 69.

43. Ibid., pp. 85 (U.S.), 47 (developing countries), and 48 (NATO and Asia).

44. For example, Adm. Crowe to Senate Armed Services Committee, Department of Defense Authorization for FY 1985, Pt. 2, p. 1190.

45. U.S. Arms Control and Disarmament Agency, *World Military Expenditures and Arms Transfers 1985*, p. 69.

46. CIA, *World Factbook 1986*, p. 137; Kelly to House Foreign Affairs Committee (March 12, 1986), p. 7, said military spending accounted for about one-third of the government's budget.

47. International Institute for Strategic Studies, *The Military Balance 1978-1979*, p. 89; *The Military Balance 1985-1986*, p. 172.

48. U.S. Arms Control and Disarmament Agency, *World Military Expenditures and Arms Transfers 1985*, p. 69.

Weapons Imports

49. U.S. Arms Control and Disarmament Agency, *World Military Expenditures and Arms Transfers 1985,* p. 111.

50. Ibid., p. 132 (95% for 1979-1983); see also annual SIPRI Yearbooks.

51. Kelly to Senate Foreign Relations Committee (March 21, 1985), p. 6; House Foreign Affairs Committee, Foreign Assistance Legislation for FY 1985, Pt. 5, p. 123.

52. Department of Defense, *Foreign Military Sales, Foreign Military Construction Sales and Military Assistance Facts as of September 30, 1985*, passim. Includes sales through FY 1985.

53. Ibid.

54. *Congressional Presentations Document, Security Assistance Programs for FY 1987*, pp. 66, 98, 101. Includes Foreign Military Sales (cash sales and loans), IMET (grant training), and private commercial sales.

55. *Department of State Bulletin*, (May 1984), p. 54; Wolfowitz to Senate Foreign Relations Committee (March 21, 1985), p. 4.

56. Kelly to House Appropriations Committee (March 12, 1986), p. 7; Wolfowitz to Senate Foreign Relations Committee (March 21, 1985), p. 4; Department of Defense, *Congressional Presentation Document, Security Assistance Programs FY 1986*, p. 93, cites $8 billion, half from the U.S.

57. See footnote 51.

58. See *SIPRI Yearbook 1986*, p. 386; annual International Institute for Strategic Studies, congressional testimony and many sources.

59. *Aerospace Daily*, (November 5, 1984), p. 18, and (May 17, 1984), p. 101.

60. Korea has been interested in the plane for years—see *Aviation Week and Space Technology*, (December 13, 1982), p. 21. Accounts of the crash can be found in *Aerospace Daily*, (October 11, 1984), p. 210; *Aviation Week*, (October 15, 1984), p.25; *Defense Week*, (October 15, 1984), p. 4; *Jane's Defense Weekly*, (October 27, 1984), p. 716; *Armed Forces Journal International*, (September 1984), p. 26.

61. *Aerospace Daily*, (May 17, 1984), p. 94.

62. U.S. Arms Control and Disarmament Agency, *World Military Expenditures and Arms Transfers 1985*, p. 132.

63. *Defense and Foreign Affairs Weekly*, (May 14/20, 1984), p. 1.

64. Adm. Hays to Senate Armed Services Committee (March 11, 1986), p. 12; Gen. Wickham in House Appropriations Committee, Department of Defense Appropriations for FY 1987, Pt. 1, p. 138; *Air Defense Artillery* Winter 1986, p. 26; many public sources on MiG-23s, including *Far Eastern Economic Review*, (November 7, 1985), p. 18; *Wall Street Journal*, (June 16, 1986); *Washington Post*, (August 14, 1985).

65. Senate Armed Services Committee, Department of Defense Authorization for Appropriations for FY 1985, Pt. 2, p. 1187 (February 1984).

66. Ibid., p. 1253.

67. Ibid., p. 1195.

Domestic Military Production

68. Larry Niksch, "South Korea," in *Fighting Armies*, ed. Richard Gabriel (Westport, CT: Greenwood Press, 1983), p. 134; *Armada International*, (August 1985), pp. 18-20.

69. *Armada International*, (August 1985), p. 18.

70. Numerous sources, including the *SIPRI Yearbook 1986*, pp. 416-417; Wolfowitz to Senate Foreign Relations Committee (March 21, 1985), p. 4; *Congressional Presentation Document, Security Assistance Programs FY 1986* (CPD), p. 93; *Armada International*, (August 1985), pp. 18-20; CPD FY 1985, pp. 76-77; *Jane's Defense Weekly*, (October 5, 1985), p. 737; *Jane's Armour and Artillery 1984-1985*, pp. 49-50; International Institute for Strategic Studies, *Military Balance 1984-1985*, pp.102-103; Larry Niksch, Congressional Research Service Issues Brief, "Korea: U.S. Troop Withdrawal and the Question of Northeast Asian Stability," (September 19, 1980), p.4.

71. *Asian Defense Journal*, (November 1984), p. 110; *Jane's Armour and Artillery 1984-1985*, p. 49; *Jane's Defense Weekly*, (January 28, 1984), p. 104 and (May 19, 1984), pp. 774-775; *International Defense Review*, #7 (1984), p. 859, and #10 (1984), p. 1547.

72. *Proceedings*, (March 1982), pp. 60-61.
73. See annual volumes of *Jane's Fighting Ships*; *Proceedings* (March 1986), p.66; *International Defense Review*, #6 (1985), p. 991.
74. *Defense and Foreign Affairs*, (January/February 1983), p. ii.
75. *Armed Forces Journal International* (AFJI), (July 1984), p. 31.
76. *SIPRI Yearbook 1984* p. 276.
77. *Armada International*, (August 1985), p. 22.
78. Statement by Gen. Robert Sennewald to House Armed Services Committee, (March 8, 1983), p. 4.
79. *Armed Forces Journal International*, (September 1984), p. 94.
80. Wickham in House Appropriations Committee, Department of Defense Appropriation for FY 1987, Pt. 1, p. 138; *Korean Newsletter* (Embassy of ROK), (June 1985), p. 3.
81. *International Defense Review*, #12 (1985), p. 1978.
82. *Armada International* (August 1985), p. 20, identifies manufacturer as National Plastic Co., Ltd., in Dongrae-ku.
83. See annual volumes of *Jane's Fighting Ships*.
84. U.S. Arms Control and Disarmament Agency, *World Military and Arms Transfers 1985*, passim.
85. *SIPRI Yearbook 1986*, pp. 373, 381, 389, 404.
86. *Defense and Foreign Affairs Weekly*, (April 2-8, 1984), p. 2.
87. Ibid.; *SIPRI Yearbook 1986*, p. 381.
88. *Jane's Defense Weekly*, (September 29, 1984), p. 525.
89. Sennewald to House Armed Services Committee, (March 8, 1983), p. 13.

Force Comparisons

90. International Institute for Strategic Studies. *Military Balance 1985-1986*, p. 118.

Manpower

91. International Institute for Strategic Studies *The Military Balance 1985-1986*, pp. 127-128. *Korea Herald*, (September 6, 1985) quoted Adm. Crowe, citing 880,000 for DPRK.
92. See annual *Military Balance* volumes or annual U.S. Arms Control and Disarmament Agency, *World Military Expenditures and Arms Transfers* volumes.
93. See footnote 91.
94. U.S. Arms Control and Disarmament Agency, *World Military Expenditures and Arms Transfers 1971-1980*, p. 55, and *World Military Expenditures and Arms Transfers 1972-1982*, p. 33.
95. Lower estimates are *CIA Factbook 1985*, pp. 127 and 129; higher estimates are International Institute for Strategic Studies, *The Military Balance 1985-1986*, pp. 127-128.
96. Ibid.
97. International Institute for Strategic Studies, op.cit., p. 128.
98. See footnote 95.
99. *CIA Factbook 1986*, pp. 135 and 137.

Air Forces

100. Figures are drawn primarily from International Institute for Strategic Studies *Military Balance 1984-1985* and CIA *World Factbook 1985*, updated with *Jane's All The World's Aircraft 1985-1986*, congressional testimony, and other sources.

101. *Aviation Week and Space Technology*, (February 7, 1983), p. 42.

102. Ibid.

103. See footnote 100.

104. Good details in *Washington Post* (July 14, 1985).

105. Joint News Conference (Weinberger and Yoon) (May 8, 1985), transcript, p. 3.

106. *Defense Week*, (February 24, 1986), p. 14; *Defense News*, (March 24, 1985), p. 19.

Naval Forces

107. Data is drawn primarily from *Jane's Fighting Ships 1985-1986*, pp. 312-322, and supplemented with International Institute for Strategic Studies, CIA, and congressional testimony.

108. Jean Labayle Couhat, *Combat Fleets of the World 1982-1983*, p. 385; *Proceedings*, March 1986, p. 66.

109. *Armed Forces Journal International*, (August 1984), p. 95.

110. *Proceedings*, March 1986, p. 66.

Ground Forces

111. See International Institute for Strategic Studies, *The Military Balance 1985-1986*.

112. Niksch, op.cit., p. 117.

113. Dr. Stefan Leader, "An Assessment of the Korean Military Situation," *Center for Defense Information Monograph*, (May 1977), p. 1.

114. Some of the important sources on the withdrawal and the reassessment include House Armed Services Committee "Report on the Impact of the Intelligence Reassessment on the Level of U.S. Troops for Korea," (September 7, 1979), pp. 4-5; Senate Armed Services Committee, Report of the Pacific Study Group, "Korea: U.S. Troop Withdrawal Program," (January 29, 1979), p. 8; House Armed Services Committee, "Review of the Policy Decision to Withdraw U.S. Ground Forces from Korea," (1978).

115. The basic data comes from International Institute for Stategic Studies, *The Military Balance 1985-1986*.

116. Donald Cotter and N.F. Wikner, "Korea: Force Imbalances and Remedies," *Strategic Review*, (Spring 1982), p. 67.

117. Niksch, op.cit., p. 128.

118. Quoted in *New York Times*, (October 2, 1984).

119. Joint News Conference (Weinberger and Yoon) (May 8, 1985), transcript, p. 2.

120. *Washington Times* (May 2, 1985), citing State Department officials.

121. *Far Eastern Economic Review*, (May 16, 1985), citing U.S. officials.

122. *Armed Forces Journal International*, (May 1985), p. 108.

123. A useful chart with details about the tunnels appeared in *Armed Forces Journal International*, (August 1984), p. 95.

124. *Asian Defense Journal*, (August 1984), p. 109, quoting Gen. Sennewald.

125. *Armed Forces Journal International*, (August 1984), pp. 95-96.

126. See, for example, Wolfowitz to Senate Foreign Relations Committee on March 22, 1984, reprinted in *Department of State Bulletin*, (May 1984), p. 57. Gen. Livsey put the number of commandos at eighty thousand in *Army*, (October 1985), p. 135. *Korea Herald*, (July 28, 1985) also cited a UN Command figure for commandos of eighty thousand.

127. *Armed Forces Journal International*, (September 1984), p. 103.

128. *Jane's All The World's Aircraft 1971-1972*, p. 427.

129. *Armed Forces Journal International*, (August 1984), pp. 94-97.

130. Ibid., p. 94.

131. John Keegan, *World Armies*, (New York: Facts on File, Inc., 1979), p. 410.

U.S. Forces in Korea

132. The source for number of U.S. troops in the ROK is the quarterly Department of Defense Fact Sheet, "U.S. Military Strengths Worldwide."

133. Department of Defense Fact Sheet, "U.S. Military Strengths Worldwide as of March 31, 1986,"(June 3, 1986).

134. *Asian Defense Journal*, (September 1984), p. 144; *Jane's Defense Weekly*, (July 28, 1984), p. 94.

135. William Arkin and Richard Fieldhouse, *Nuclear Battleships*, (Cambridge, Massachusetts: Ballinger Publishing Co., 1985), p. 120.

136. Department of Defense, *Defense 1985 Almanac*, (September 1985), p. 51.

137. There are numerous sources on types of U.S. forces in Korea. A good outline of the organizational details of U.S. forces in Korea was in *Jane's Defense Weekly*, (August 18, 1984), p. 228.

138. Each year the commander of U.S. Forces, Korea gives details on U.S. equipment in Korea in testimony to the House and Senate Armed Services Committees.

139. *Army*, (October 1985), p. 148.

140. Ibid.; *Armed Forces Journal International*, (May 1985), pp. 27-28.

141. *Jane's Defense Weekly* (May 8, 1985), p. 1056; *Defense Week*, (June 11, 1984), p. 12.

142. House Foreign Affairs Committee, Foreign Assistance Legislation FY 1985, Pt. 5, p. xiii.

143. House Appropriations Committee, *Military Construction Appropriations for 1985*, Pt. 6, pp. 576 and 625.

144. *Army*, (October 1985), p. 149.

The UN Command and the Combined Forces Command

145. Keegan, *World Armies*, pp. 345-346; *Pacific Defense Reporter*, Annual Reference Edition, p. 56.

146. *Pacific Defense Reporter*, Reference Edition, p. 56.

147. *Army*, (October 1985), p. 139.

148. Statement by Gen. Robert Sennewald before the House Armed Services Committee, (March 8, 1983), p. 7.

149. Ibid.

150. Niksch, op.cit., p. 129.

"Team Spirit"

151. Statement to House Appropriations Committee (March 12, 1986), p. 5.

152. *Armed Forces Journal International*, (June 1986), p. 24; *Asian Defense Journal*, (March 1986), p. 136; *Air Forces Times*, (April 14, 1986), p. 31.

153. *Soldiers*, (August 1985), pp. 13-17; *Armed Forces Journal International*, (May 1985), p. 27.

154. Department of Defense News Release (January 17, 1986) and previous years' releases on Team Spirit; *Armed Forces Journal International* (November 1985), p. 31; *Armed Forces Journal International* (May 1985), p. 27; *Navy Times* (January 23, 1984), p. 2; *Asian Defense Journal*, (August 1984), pp. 69-70.

155. House Appropriations Committee, *Department of Defense Appropriations for FY 1987*, Pt. 1, p. 138.

156. Brig. Gen. Robert Pointer, Jr., and Major Howard Nichols, "Host Nation Support the Korean Way," *Army Logistician*, (September/October 1984), p. 23.

157. Ibid., p. 24.

158. Ibid., House Appropriations Committee, *Military Construction Appropriations for FY 1987*, Pt. 5, p. 229.

159. Pointer and Nichols, op.cit., pp. 24-25.

160. Ibid., p. 24.

161. Earl Ravenal, *Defining Defense: The 1985 Military Budget*, (Cato Institute, 1984), p. 16.

U.S. Nuclear Weapons

162. "Korea and U.S. Policy in Asia," *Defense Monitor*, (January 1976), p. 5.

163. Arkin and Fieldhouse, op.cit., pp. 120 and 231.

164. Ibid., pp. 121 and 231; House Appropriations Committee, *Military Construction Appropriations for FY 1987*, Pt. 5, p. 216.

165. For details on nuclear weapons, see Cochran, Arkin, and Hoenig, *Nuclear Weapons Databook, Vol. 1: U.S. Nuclear Forces*

and Capabilities, (Cambridge, Massachusetts: Ballinger Publishing Co., 1984).

166. *Washington Post,* (January 17, 1986).

167. *Armed Forces Journal International,* (November 1985), pp. 82, 86, 88.

168. Edward A. Olsen, "Security in Northeast Asia," *Naval War College Review,* (January-February 1985), p. 19-21.

Stephen D. Goose is senior analyst with the Center for Defense Information, a private, non-government research organization in Washington, D.C. His primary areas of expertise are conventional arms transfers, power projection forces, and U.S. military involvement in the Third World. Goose holds a master's degree in International Relations from the Johns Hopkins School of Advanced International Studies, and has published articles in the *New York Times,* the *Chicago Tribune, Pacific Defense Reporter, South,* and *Korea Scope,* among others.

Chapter 5

The Politics of Korea

Gregory Henderson

Korea is one of the world's most continuous surviving nation-states. The Korean people have developed a highly literate culture and unusually homogeneous political life traceable for some fifteen hundred years. These developments have occurred within a strategic peninsula sharply defined in geographic and racial terms. Its division in 1945 between the communist and non-communist worlds greatly heightens the political significance of this background.

Korean politics, since the start of relevant records fifteen hundred years ago, is far more continuous than discontinuous. The Koreans are a people little affected since 500 A.D. by major migration or exile, a people often invaded but little ruled in an effective way by alien cultures. Exceptions were Mongol rule for a century following 1260 and Japanese rule for forty years following 1905.[1] The Mongol presence left traces which, so far as present institutions are concerned, are either very minor or exceedingly difficult to measure. Japan's legacy was far greater and more recent. Although different and regarded as alien, it was not unrelated to Korea's own traditions and sometimes continued, sometimes broke with Korea's political traditions.

Less changed than her economies or rapidly changing societies, Korea's ancient political culture thus transmits to both contemporary Koreas more powerful traditional influences than come to her from any other parts of her culture. This relative continuity, however, creates a problem: each Korea's retarded political development is in tension with each state's rapid, though differing, pace of economic, social and cultural change. In neither Korea can politics adequately express the changes that have occurred in other fields.

In traditional Korea the situation approached the reverse—excessive political discussion and dogma impeded development, rather than being impeded by development.

Traditional Political Characteristics

Korea's indigenous political traditions might be said to have the following general characteristics, which, with somewhat different degree, mark both North and South Korea today.

1. It had a relatively great and continuous centralism with conspicuously weak, discontinuous and uninfluential regional or local power.

2. Related to this centralism, there was a highly-developed central bureaucracy which is usually perceived as the key to both national and local power and has been the chief focus of aspiration and political contest for a millenium.

3. Approximately half a millenium of strong Confucian influence (ca. 1400-1900) constituted perhaps the major influence on the social system, on political and social behavior, and on ideals of government.

As an extremely political belief system, Confucianism greatly politicized Korean culture, making central bureaucracy an even more profound aspiration for a larger number of Koreans than ever before. It increased the desire for and helped develop the institutions of education whose lessons it directed toward good government and the central bureaucracy. It strengthened family and the royal court but side-stepped the development of institutions between village and court, eroding institutionalization generally. It emphasized ethics, including loyalty, rather than practical performance as the prime standard to which politics should adhere, i.e., an ideological orientation. It connected social status with government service. It honored seniority and, theoretically, age. It exalted men over women, civilians over soldiers and merchants and generalists over specialists.

4. The exact nature and influence of an indigenous social system dominant prior to Confucianism are unclear in political respects but it seems to have tended in the direction of a social caste system based on blood rather than education; to have emphasized strong personal leadership within a government of clans or councils; and to have laid less emphasis than Confucianism—perhaps no emphasis—on the subordination of women. Confucian values seem largely to have overlaid these previous social emphases.

5. Buddhism was a major influence and the country's dominant religion from 500 to 1400, but it seems to have had diminishing effects on the political culture. Buddhist influence on art and religion, on the other hand, stands out clearly.

6. The continual need to defend the small peninsula from its powerful neighbors casts a constant shadow over Korean politics. Military might and a lowering of Korea's profile through poverty, isolation and inconspicuousness did not do much after 1200 A.D. other than delay disasters which the cultivation of an image of weakness tended to invite. External threat forced politics chronically

into defensive postures. The sense of threat contributed to a heightened general sense of Korea as a community, but not necessarily a unified community. The need to balance defense needs with social stability in a civilian-oriented Confucian polity bred political controversy and breakaway factions, especially during the Yi dynasty, 1392-1910. Some factions then acted as ephemeral kinds of pre-modern political parties. These were created, as always in Korea's centralized ethos, largely from the top down. In them one sees a characteristic tendency of Korea's politics to be disputatious without being strongly institutionalized, an apparently odd dichotomy in political science. By and large, with somewhat different degrees, these characteristics mark both North and South Korea today.

Japan's Colonial Political Legacy

The Japanese colonial period reinforced the country's high degree of bureaucratic centralism while altering the role of elites, Korean access to government, and the conduct of government. Aging leaders were pensioned off. All elites were separated from political power, the upper bureaucracy being largely pre-empted by the Japanese. With the economy considerably expanded, the Confucian style of generalism gave way to specialization which was rather rapidly introduced. A greatly expanded education system facilitated the process in which, as elsewhere, Japanese were greatly favored over Koreans. Despite this favoritism, a new Korean modern, specialized elite of businessmen, lawyers, bankers and bureaucrats was in process of formation, especially in colonial Korea's last decade, 1935-1945.

Military values were emphasized, the Japanese military forming an elite to which, until 1941-45, few Koreans were admitted. Security became a preoccupation in policy which, especially after 1930, was increasingly linked to anti-communism. All governors-general were former top-ranking military officers. Politics was discouraged, removed from top priorities or aspirations, and finally, in the last decade, forbidden to Koreans altogether. Ordinary Koreans were supposed to be economically productive drones leaving politics and policies to their (Japanese, often military) betters. From 1920 on—but only for a small minority who paid over five yen a year in taxes—voting was permitted for largely advisory township and city and, later, provincial councils. Political parties were not allowed in campaigns.

The grudging politics of militarist Japanese Chosen, new to modern Korea, proved more a model for the grudgingly-permitted politics of Korea's militarist 1970s and 1980s than any other political system had been. The Japanese model, however, was institutionally slightly more advanced in terms of local administration than those of the 1986 Koreas.[2]

Meanwhile, in exile or emigration or through the printed word, Koreans came in touch with U.S. democracy, Soviet communism and the Chinese right and left. The Yi government, its rulers and its elites, had been swept by the Japanese into history's dustbin. Untried foreign ideologies developed their adherents and their claims. In 1945, few could predict which way Korea's politics would go after thirty-five years of suppression under an unloved alien leadership.

Initial Postwar Politics

Underneath Japan's repression, Korea's ancient style of competition for self-rule among ambitious rivals for central power had not died; repression and education stimulated it and it only awaited freedom for its renewed expression. Upon liberation, this political competition was honed by the new ideologies influencing Koreans from Soviet, U.S., Chinese and Japanese sources. The politics of August and early September 1945—the first month of liberation—thus proved explosive throughout the peninsula. Japan's repression suddenly dissipated. Thousands demonstrated. Myriads of social and political groups, parties, unions, committees and federations were started in succeeding days and weeks. The instinct behind them was ancient, but lacking institutionalization, they combined and usually died.

Local people's committees, unions and peasant organizations, with "peace preservation corps" to replace Japanese police, were formed all over the peninsula. These local committees included moderates but they soon leaned left in both North and South following the liberation of thousands of Korean political prisoners from Japanese jails on August 16th. These committees were the starting point of postwar political activity.[3] They sent representatives to Seoul to found, on September 6, a "Korean People's Republic" under a leftist liberal activist named Lyuh Woon Hyung. The formation was hasty, but enthusiasm for a new leftist-nationalist beginning abounded. Against this setting the incoming conquerers soon cast their shadows.

Soviet troops began battle with the Japanese on August 10, 1945, near northeast Korea's Soviet border and entered the three main cities of the north on August 21-24. The Soviets generally did not try governing directly. With them they brought some thirty thousand Koreans who had been in exile in the USSR. To a great extent these Koreans effectively diluted the Soviet presence. Though the Soviets at first lacked a uniform policy, they soon recognized the people's committees they found and placed them in local charge. On October 14 in Pyongyang, the Soviets introduced Kim Il Sung, a prominent Korean guerrilla leader in the 1930-1941 struggle in Manchuria against Japan. Partly through Kim, the Soviets influenced central government composition. Until central power was reconstituted, they exerted little direct influence on local committees, which effectively purged Korean collaborators with Japan and began property re-distribution north of the thirty-eighth parallel.

In the South, U.S. troops under Gen. John R. Hodge arrived on September 8, nearly a month after the Soviets. They had few Korean-Americans to bring; even those who were available, never properly organized, were rarely brought. The rule of U.S. forces was direct and undiluted. They refused to recognize the Korean People's Republic or meet with its representatives. As rapidly as they were able, they countered and abolished the local committees. Thereafter, they worked through Japanese-trained Korean policemen and officers, those in the South augmented by those fleeing the North. Generally, collaborators were used, rarely purged. They threw Korean alumni of the Japanese police and armed forces against the disorders resulting from their repression of the left. These disorders and the attempts to crush them initiated the "security issue" which has been prominent in South Korean politics. This contrast in the treatment of the Japanese collaborators is basic to the politics of the two Koreas, a part of their mutual hostility and of the legitimation of communist rule.

Political Development in North Korea

While the United States found few believing democrats in the South, the Soviets found numerous communists locally and also imported them to North Korea. Among them were native communists who had been underground during the Japanese occupation, those working with Mao in Yenan, those who had been in exile in the Soviet Union, and those born and raised in the USSR. These variegated communists founded—or refounded—a Korean Communist Party and joined the People's Committees, nudging moderates aside. Kim Il Sung now performed the difficult job of amalgamating these potentially contentious groups. Kim became head of the northern branch of the Korean Communist Party on December 17, 1945, and in February 1946, as Hodge undermined the People's Republic in the South, Kim became chairman of the North Korean Interim People's Committee, the first separate Northern regime.[4] A year later, after single-slate, open-ballot "elections," a convention of People's Committees created a Supreme People's Assembly, and elected a Presidium and a Supreme Court. A North Korean Workers Party was formed from the merger of Kim's Korean Communist Party and the Yenan group's old Korean Independence League. A further merger of the North Korean Workers Party in June 1949 with the old South Korean Labor Party created the supreme Korean Workers Party, bringing the political bases of rival communist leaders firmly under Kim Il Sung and creating today's monolithic party system.[5]

Meanwhile, on August 25, 1948, elections were held for the new Supreme People's Assembly, then as now a rubber-stamp body. The Assembly ratified a new constitution and proclaimed the establishment of the Democratic People's Republic of Korea (the DPRK) on September 8, 1948. Kim Il Sung was named premier on September 10. The DPRK was recognized on October 12 by the Soviet Union and became formally independent when Soviet troops withdrew by December 26, 1948, though Soviet-Korean vice ministers and numerous Soviet advisory personnel maintained extensive influence for a further five years.

In three years, 1945-48, Kim Il Sung achieved what Stalin took seventeen years to accomplish. He became leader of both party and state. Meanwhile, by mid-1947, some 1.8 million North Koreans, about seventeen percent of the population, had fled to South Korea, including in their number the bulk of the political opposition. Approximately another 1.2 million fled during the Korean War.[6] These refugees sapped strength from the North but took with them their dissent. This movement helped Kim's control. He used his command of party and administration to eliminate, in 1953-55, the rival native communists under Pak Hon Yong whom he unjustly blamed for Korean War reverses. In 1955-56 Kim was criticized by the Soviet and Yenan factions for excessive concentration on heavy industry and—in the wake of Khrushchev's February 1956 denunciation of Stalin's personality cult—for building an excessive Kim cult. From 1956 until 1958 Kim, in retaliation, eliminated critical partisans of both the Soviet and the Yenan factions. He then sealed his independence in the doctrine of *juche* (self-sufficiency) founded to justify distance from all tainting foreign, even when socialist, influences.[7] All barriers to the forming of a political orthodoxy and a dictatorship with a personality cult had been removed.

Since the end of 1958 or 1959 Kim has completely dominated North Korean government and politics with a personality as well as a salvation cult of unbounded political and virtually religious power. Despite ominous occasional references to "anti-party elements," no leader, no faction has emerged in rivalry. Distance, secrecy, and penalties against foreign ties make Pyongyang's politics opaque and unknowable to an extent unique among major societies. Names and formal functions of institutions are known but the political transactions occurring within and among them remain almost traceless.

Opinion in the North is not completely monolithic. The visitor finds traces of different views which must reflect debate within the government, especially regarding degrees of openness to the foreign world, policy toward South Korea and, no doubt, economic and social priorities. Some North Koreans acknowledge that what they claim is a misreading of juche impedes normal communication between North Koreans and foreigners. Such an impediment certainly exists—even with other communist peoples. Students who pore over the lists of committee memberships also decipher traces of debate, probably disagreement. One presumes that the large armed forces (according to some estimates nearly 800,000) constitute a security-conscious, inward-turning group.

There is a lack, so far, of concrete evidence that differences have ever solidified into anything like a discernible group or faction—though such may well have occurred within military circles. Enormous social, indoctrination, and surveillance pressures undoubtedly work against group advocacy politics and force advocacy and whatever exists of politics into obscure, small personal networks which so far have evaded outward scrutiny. Compared to the North in these respects the South is mild. But it is noteworthy that the same tendencies have always existed and continue to exist there, only politics is far less obscure, far more public and more scrutinized—most of the time—in Seoul than in Pyongyang.

The Kim system, though initiated in part even before the Korean War, was strengthened by the extreme trauma of U.S. bombing which destroyed ninety-nine percent of all above-ground structures in two and a half years. More bombs were unleashed per acre than on Europe in World War II. North Koreans apparently admired Kim's composure under bombardment and reversal, and his determined planning; his initiatives in invading the South were concealed from most of his citizens. He became his despairing nation's sole hope. He has since become the world's senior living national leader, the sole source of the North's government, law, and salvation cult.

Today less than a third of North Koreans remember the 1950s as adults. His early days of contention or aggression passed or forgotten, an enshrined aging leader (b. 1912) has apparently passed daily controls to his son, Kim Jong Il, in a transition carefully planned since 1974. This transition started with a shift in the center of power when Kim Jong Il was entrusted with the operation of the Party, being known, from 1974-80, as the "party center." It was revealed that Jong Il fought "anti-party elements" in the latter half of the 1970s.[8] He replaced most party secretaries, created his own cadres and lately has taken over most of his father's local visits and "on-the-spot-guidance."

Many new North Korean leaders seem to be the political progeny of the old, but their outlook seems different. Isolation has been great but has somewhat lessened through years of relations with one hundred nations and gradually increasing visits to and contacts from a far more open China and many concerned Japanese. In its isolation, as in much social behavior, the North seems far more than the South like Yi-dynasty Korea, not wihout reason called "the Hermit Kingdom." Trade, though miniscule beside South Korea's, also raises consciousness of the outside world. The old guard of guerrilla fighters around Kim Il Sung and the leaders of the Korean War have given way to a new generation of bureaucrats more traveled and experienced than their predecessors. The outlook is for a gradually more open policy.

During the transition to a new leader, the old fabric is wearing thin and loosening a little. This can be glimpsed in the marked turnover in the elite membership of party and state institutions and in the launching of political campaigns, such as the Red Flag and the Three Revolution Workteam movements, Maoist-style drives for solidarity, patriotism and increased production. These are sure signs that the change of leaders, however smooth on the surface, is not being achieved without opposition.[9]

Perhaps both the pressure of younger bureaucrats on Kim Jong Il for more openness and the fruitlessness of past confrontational tactics account for recent, a little more open, communication as in the September 1984 law to facilitate joint ventures with foreigners; the delivery of relief goods to Seoul flood victims during the same period; and 1985's increased North-South meetings and family reunions, which unfortunately dried up in 1986. In addition there have been visits from many foreign groups, including even the first tourists, and continuing efforts to establish bilateral relations with the North's old bête noire, the United States.

Under its obscurity and Maoist-Kimist modern tunic, politics in North Korea seems to retain many traditional Korean characteristics. Since early 1946 it has featured extraordinarily centralized leadership. It has been weak in encouraging or institutionalizing grass-roots organization; like South Korea, it implants its institutions from above. It is highly influenced by security and defense priorities. More than South Korea, but reminiscent of the Yi dynasty, it is highly ideology-oriented.

Politics in the South

Conservative U.S. military direction plus considerable collaborator leadership from the time of Japanese rule determined government in the South, so that it became a kind of rightist counterbalance to Kim's dictatorship. It was based on a network of rightist police and youth groups who monopolized arms. These helped frustrate even a U.S. State Department-supported middle-of-the-road political coalition in 1946. Nor could such a coalition exist under the Soviet occupation in the North.

Thus, foreign occupations polarized the peninsula. The Korean People's Republic having been abolished in the South, no native, peninsula-wide political framework on which unification could be constructed could be identified in the 1946 and 1947 U.S.-Soviet Joint Commission meetings. Washington, seeing danger of entrapment and no further useful role for itself, decided to pull out its troops and control from Korea. This left no significant alternative to supporting the right under Syngman Rhee, the aging U.S.-educated leader whom Gen. Hodge had introduced in October 1945. Rhee himself had won popular respect and legitimacy as a nationalist. The rightists on whom he had to rely to rule, however, had little, if any, such status and were thus largely dependent on the police for their support. In the South of this time lay probably as great a tendency to create politics and institutions from the top down as marked the 1946-48 North. Grass roots were eliminated rather than nurtured.

In this writer's judgment, Washington had not actually sought the division of Korea, but it maintained insufficient control over the U.S. forces command. The occupation command, for its part, was so focussed on security questions that it failed to correct the consequences of an earlier mistaken decision, namely, to accept Japanese surrenders separately from the Soviets at separate points south of the thirty-eighth parallel. The Soviet Union thus achieved what many observers, including this one, believe it always wanted: a buffer zone in Korea.

Confrontation continued to mark the South's politics. The withdrawals of both occupation commands—of Soviet troops by the end of 1948 and of U.S. troops by the end of June 1949—left two Korean governments whose structures had been forming since 1946. They reflected the hostile occupations, and were hence designed to defy each other. The Korean War greatly exacerbated the bitterest and most intractable of confrontations, each Korea acting with especial cruelty toward the other, branding and eliminating as collaborators all who sought mutual cooperation.

The politics growing within such a milieu could not be happy. The politics of Rhee and his regime were authoritarian, but did not develop the systematic controls introduced after his fall by the more organizationally disciplined military regimes. Incipient signs of defiance by the National Assembly were squelched in arrests, trials and intimidations in 1949-51. From 1951 on, a powerful government party, oddly entitled "Liberal," was created by command of the government. Constitutional restraints on Rhee's autocracy were more or less forcibly broken. The press, long quite vibrant under Rhee, was increasingly controlled in the late 1950s. Local government remained unimplemented and autocracy was enlarged. In an increasingly urban Korea, however, democracy stirred. To combat authoritarianism, opposition forces increasingly coalesced. The years 1956-60 were the highwater mark of a two-party system in which the opposition carried ever-larger parts of urban Korea, electing the vice president in 1956. Nevertheless, politics in the South vibrated within a narrower frame than before—between differences in the degree of democracy, of rightist autocracy and in the use of force; ideological differences between right and left all but disappeared. The political spectrum came to be painted in different yet still vivid tints of right.

An increasingly educated, urbanized and democratically aspirant population chafed under restrictions which were sufficient to anger people but not systematic enough to cow them. Bold student demonstrations, with wide public sympathy, succeeded, after unjust presidential elections, in overthrowing the aged President Rhee in late April 1960. The party called Liberal promptly disappeared almost without trace. Police power was overthrown, never completely to recover. There was a peaceful transition to a fairly elected democratic government under Prime Minister Chang Myong, with a bicameral assembly.[10]

Almost unseen, the military was taking the place of the police as the prime instrument of security. It had by 1960 become the best-financed and trained South Korean institution, buttressed by the closest ties to the United States. Its anti-communism was virulent and institutionalized. On seizing power in a May 1961 coup under Maj. Gen. Park Chung Hee, it promptly created the Korean CIA (since January 1, 1981, renamed the National Security Planning Agency), built up systematic surveillance, and implemented a stern and extreme anti-communism. Banning politics and suspending civil rights, the Park regime proved lastingly suspicious of civilian politics in general and of competitive parliamentary democracy in particular. Nor did it favor judicial independence or niceties of legal process. Its predilections, besides defense, lay in forced-march, centrally-planned economic and export expansion to build up the essential power of the nation. To do this, the military quickly and effectively co-opted civilian technical and bureaucratic expertise, a process lightly ideologized under Park's formulation "administrative democracy". This proved a brand of central bureaucratic specialist rule uncurbed by parliamentary or judicial power, unspokenly modeled on Japan's last decade (1936-45) of rule in Korea. As under Japan, Park's Koreans were supposed to be hard-working, economically productive drones, leaving politics uncomplainingly to their (now Korean but still military) betters who could be counted on to purge it of "dangerous," demagogic elements.

Politics controlled largely by crisis under Rhee became, under Park, politics more systematically marshalled. A new party blithely called "Democratic Republican," founded in 1962, ran, elected, and re-elected President Park in 1963, 1967, and 1971, also controlling the assembly. In 1971 Park narrowly defeated Kim Dae Jung, losing to him in urban areas by 44.9 percent to Kim's 51.4 percent.[11] The government's assembly control also eroded. Feeling threatened, Park initiated a bloodless coup against his own 1963 constitutional system, declaring a quite unjustified state of emergency on December 6, 1971, and martial law on October 17, 1972.[12] Under emergency powers, he lacerated the constitution with some seventy-two amendments, cutting whatever slight muscle the legislature and judiciary had had. He also instituted indirect elections by an electoral college, which he headed, and which then dutifully elected him by a vote of 2,357 of 2,359 delegates to an expanded six-year term on December 23, 1972. Government control of a weakened assembly was assured by the presidential appointment of one-third of its members. Draconian Emergency Measures suppressed student movements, demonstrations, or any criticism; eight persons then being unjustly held were executed for disobedience. Park called this the Yushin ("Revitalization") System.

Until 1975, Park's authoritarianism at least produced sensational economic and export growth, greatly strengthening South Korea internally and externally. After that time, however, inflation grew and a huge debt accumulated, which was perceived especially negatively as being related to adverse trade balances with Japan. Political pressures built and the stifled political system could no longer contain them. 1978-79 saw mounting demonstrations against Park's pre-emption of a fourth term and the government's maintenance of assembly control with a minority of votes.[13] Further riots in Pusan and Masan, following the expulsion of their favorite son, Kim Young Sam, from the Assembly, convinced the Korean CIA Director, Gen. Kim Jae Kyu, that only President Park's death could change an unpopular but ingrained system. He therefore assassinated Park and his security chief on October 26, 1979, in order to end the crisis. This action dramatically ended eighteen years' rule and with it many elements of the Yushin system and South Korea's deepest immersion in authoritarian rule.

Transition to Chun

Amid high hopes for democracy and much public discussion, a cautious civilian bureaucrat, Choi Kyu Ha, Park's last prime minister, became acting president. On December 5, 1979, Choi unpopularly utilized the Yushin electoral college to become president. A week later, Major General Chun Doo Hwan, head of the army's Defense Security Command, a Park devotee and investigator of the Park assassination, staged a palace coup in defiance of the U.S. Joint Commander, General Wickham. He arrested the Korean chief of staff and martial law commander and other generals on charges of involvement in Park's murder and of corruption. Those arrested and, subsequently, most other generals senior to Chun were then retired. Behind a facade of civilian government, the military was restored as the chief operative repository of political power in South Korea, with Chun as its *éminence grise*. Nevertheless, early 1980 found citizens around Korea participating in democracy—discussing a new constitution, political parties and elections. Kim Dae Jung, failing to find a basis for joining Kim Young Sam's opposition party, made plans to form his own. Then, on May 17, falsely implicating Kim in the leadership of the Kwangju disturbances, Chun's forces arrested him; other leaders followed him to jail the next day.

On May 18, 1980, peaceful demonstrations took place in Kwangju in Kim Dae Jung's home province to protest martial law and the end of open political process. To quell these demonstrations, General Chun sent in Special Forces paratroopers, trained for brutal combat behind North Korean lines and not under the control of the U.S.-ROK Combined Command. Their extreme, unexplained savagery caused hundreds or thousands of deaths and mutilations to unarmed students. Traumatized by shock and rage, the Kwangju citizenry rose and drove the paratroopers out, seizing arms in the process. After nine days of turmoil, Gen. Wickham as joint commander acceded to Chun's urgent request to release regular Korean forces in his command. These forces, with comparatively less brutality, quelled still-defiant students and returned a traumatized and resentful Kwangju to government control. Hopes for political change were again violently crushed.

Kim Dae Jung and twenty three co-defendants were tried and convicted by courts-martial of "insurrection" on charges described by the U.S. State Department as "far-fetched." Kim's unjust death sentence, though cravenly upheld by the supreme court, was ultimately commuted by Chun amid international outcry and Kim was allowed in 1981 to go to Washington, purportedly for medical treatment. The Martial Law Command under Gen. Chun became the de facto government and dismissed eight thousand government employees, two hundred ministers and directors, and eight hundred press personnel, many through mergers and the closing of one hundred and seventy two publications. Politics was once again proscribed.

Politics in the Chun Era

On August 16, 1980, shadow President Choi resigned. Promptly on August 22, General Chun, rapidly self-promoted from major-general, retired and on August 29 was elected president by 2,524 votes out of 2,525 cast by the servile National Conference on Unification. On September 29, the text of a draft Constitution amending the Yushin Constitution but retaining indirect presidential election was rushed to print and, on October 23, approved in a national referendum by 91.6 percent of those voting. From late 1980 to early 1981, under continuing martial law, an appointed "Legislative Council for National Security" began a rapid-fire legislative sprint through some one hundred executive-provided, highly authoritarian laws, sometimes at a clip of twenty a per day. This legislation in essence continued Park's "administrative democracy" and substantially circumscribed the effects of a new, somewhat improved constitution announced on September 19, 1980, and ritualistically approved by plebiscite under martial law on October 11. The Council's laws "shall remain valid and may not be litigated or disputed for reasons of this constitution or other reasons"; thus they still enchain democratic process.

The Chun government, like its predecessor in 1961-63, now forged ahead to create a new political order. All old political parties were abolished in 1980. In their place, without a thought for local roots, the new government rapidly mapped, then created, a new multi-party system. The government party was to be united. The opposition was to be dismembered, separate parties being created for each brand of (non-communist) ideology and each rubric, however slight, of previous political history and factionalism.

From late November through December 1980 there abruptly appeared eighteen political parties, a creation unparalleled in the world's political history. These ranged from the new government's Democratic Justice Party (DNP), the large New Korea Democratic Party (NKDP), the older opposition Korean Democratic Party (now a sliver of three), the Park-related Korean National Party (KNP) a Social Democratic Party, to the Korea Farmer's Party and a party of Buddhist affiliation. In the end, only six survived—the first five above plus the sliver defectors' Democratic People's Party. Only the DNP, NKDP and KNP are of any present institutional importance.

Claiming that "sources worry over political confusion," the president proclaimed that all parties must have local chapters in at least one-fourth of seventy-seven electoral districts before being inaugurated. Amalgamation movements immediately arose and, one after another, these parties have disappeared or have been amalgamated, leaving the above six, only three of substantial importance.[14]

From December 1984 on, Korean people showed a disdain for the government's divisive tactics by strongly backing a new, independent opposition party, the New Korea Democratic Party (NKDP) formed by politicians newly released, by popular demand and quiet U.S. pressure, from political restraints. Two months after formation, and shortly after Kim Dae Jung's well-publicized return to Seoul from the United States, the NKDP miraculously captured twenty-nine percent of the popular vote in the February 12, 1985, assembly elections. It won sixty-seven out of two hundred seventy-five representative seats, a number subsequently boosted to one hundred and two through absorption of almost all the Democratic Korea Party into the NKDP. The government party, with only thirty-five percent of the vote, kept its legislative majority of 151 by means of the distorted proportional representation system, but nearly two-thirds of the popular vote was in opposition; a resounding trend toward a two-party system had been made. Moreover, interest in and even media attention to politics greatly rebounded throughout 1985. Politics was no longer exiled to bottom listings, even in government media.

Emboldened by these successes, the opposition spearheaded a popular nationwide drive in the last months of 1985 and throughout 1986 for a signature campaign for a constitutional revision to permit direct presidential elections in 1987-88. At first this was repressed, but the government was reluctantly forced to concede constitutional revisions of some sort before the February 1988 end of Chun's term. On April 30, 1986, President Chun called for the formation of a constitutional revision committee in the National Assembly which would study all options; it took months to form and had not, as of late September 1986, shown signs of achieving a compromise draft. The government party remained, as of September 1986, opposed to direct elections, for which the opposition is still unitedly pushing. The government introduced in late August 1986 a draft amendment for a parliamentary system responsible to a cabinet, something which the main opposition thus far opposes. Whether compromise around this system will emerge and a free electoral process become established remains in doubt in September 1986.

The political outcome also remains in doubt. The political prospects through 1987 and very possibly beyond augur passion and instability. A few doubts have begun to be expressed in the world press as to whether the summer Olympics should take place in South Korea as scheduled. If instability escalates, so will these doubts. Greater democracy, or a return to repression through the Chun government or through another coup, remain alternatives for the 1987-88 period; a popular groundwave against military hegemony and the old over-centralism with its accompanying authoritarianism seems gradually to be swelling.

Through 1983, Chun succeeded in some self-legitimation; but the illegitimacy of coming to power through coups and over hundreds of corpses at Kwangju still shadows his government. Yet Chun cannot clean the slate without placing on trial officers whose exposure would destabilize the military and erode its support. So demonstrations continue. Indeed, from October 1984 through 1985 and the first half of 1986, they rose to over three hundred a year involving upwards of one hundred thousand students. There is some evidence that some demonstrations are fabricated to create popular revulsion against violence, but students, in part, do display increasing violence and anti-U.S. sentiment. The students also stand apart from the present opposition parties which have not quieted all doubts regarding the new programs they would implement or the unity and stability they would achieve.

Legislative Restraints on Politics

North Korea does not rule by law and only in small part by police or jail. It rules through exceedingly concerted and consistent propaganda and socialization programs in an isolated polity. Since 1958 this control system has worked without any opposition appearing on the surface. Pyongyang needs no legal restraints on politics; they inhere in its massively disciplined social system in which little complaint and no redress is possible.

Seoul's government is not yet one of law. Yet restraints on politics are deeply embedded both in social conditioning and in law legislated under the Chun regime. On the whole, the new (1980) constitution, though far less liberal than the 1948 constitution, is less offending than the repressive 1972 Yushin Constitution. A relatively brief document, it adheres far more closely to the 1962 Park Constitution.[15] Only in the provisions applying to presidential power has the Yushin Constitution substantially survived. The president continues to be elected indirectly and not, as in the 1948 constitution, by the National Assembly or, as later, by the public, but by a controllable "presidential electoral college" of 5,278 members. The presidential term is now increased to seven years though it is sternly limited to one term with no constitutional amendment possible to enable the present president to extend his term. National Assembly powers to lift emergency presidential rule are somewhat increased over the 1972 constitution but prolonged presidential emergency rule continues to be quite possible, the 1980 constitution lying between the 1962 and 1972 constitutions in restraining it. The president continues to enjoy his 1972-initiated right to dissolve the National Assembly.

Appointive members of the National Assembly, introduced by the Yushin Constitution, are abolished in the 1980 amendments. On balance, however, the assembly retains only a vestige of its 1948 power though it is still more significant than Pyongyang's Supreme People's Assembly. Except for open criticism of the president's person, exchanges within the assembly are relatively free; the media, however, are restrained from reporting much more than sanitized summaries. The courts seem slightly more independent than in 1972 but it remains impossible for a "political" defendant to receive a fair trial in South Korean courts in accordance with fair standards of civil procedure as the 1980-81 trials of Kim Dae Jung and his colleagues demonstrated. Kim was given the death sentence for instigating, through a person he had never met, demonstrations taking place following his arrest in a place where he was not present.[16] Threat of such trials—the impossibility of mounting any effective defense—obviously restrains free politics. In North Korea legal independence or the right to redress a political grievance through trial does not exist. In South Korea, one can still hope.

The chief restraints on South Korea's political life are not within the constitution itself but in the laws of the eighty-one-member Legislative Council on National Security appointed by President Chun, which, in effect, supplemented the constitution. Of these, the most obviously repressive, the Political Renovation Law, deprived 587 politicians of their right to participate in politics until after the end of President Chun's seven-year term. Between February 1984 and February 1985, all 587 were removed from these restraints, although the chief leader Kim Dae Jung remains barred from political activity because of his sentence. The Renovation Law, which imposed penalties for normal political activities during a time when they were legal, clearly violated the *nulla poena sine lege* ("no penalty without law") Article 12 of the constitution. Lack of any separation of powers or constitutional review prevented, as it always has, judicial action on this illegality.

The Chun government also has a Political Party Act, amended from one in effect since 1962. Under it, parties must have promoters, a preparatory committee and detailed registration, which must be updated with the Central Election Management Committee. This committee, a government body, has the power to cancel registrations, hence parties, for improper registration, for failure to obtain a seat or poll two percent of the votes, or failure to provide complete financial or membership information.[17] Seat allocation in the law also favors majorities. Assemblymen are elected from ninety-one districts in which the top two vote-getters are seated. The chance that at least one of these will be a government candidate is great, whereas if each representative were elected separately, two opposition candidates would be elected from many urban districts. The party getting the largest number of seats is additionally awarded sixty-one or more of an additional ninety-two seats at large. By this manipulation, the government party, while elected with only thirty-five percent of the votes cast, controls the Assembly with 151 of 275 seats. A thirty-five percent vote hence turns into fifty-five percent control.

New and more extreme is the Political Funds Act of December 31, 1980, quite possibly the most picayune regulator of political funds on the books of any nation.[18] Too complex to detail here, it has the effect of fiscally distancing parties from their main natural supporters. As a result, the government tends to become the chief financial support of all—even opposition—parties. The law, which may well in practice be circumvented, reflects the Korean government's view of politics as a closely-run state enterprise subject to sedulous scrutiny and control.

The National Assembly Act, promulgated January 29, 1981, specifies four-year terms for all members. Assembly sessions are not to exceed ninety days. Special sessions, called by the president, are not to exceed thirty days, and "shall deal only with matters submitted by the government" and last only so long as the president requests. The power of the chairman to limit debate or discipline members is considerable, the act strongly implying that maintenance of assembly order occupies a higher priority than does freedom to legislate.

Conduct of elections is controlled by a Presidential Election Law with unique minuteness. Candidates cannot "barnstorm" and must campaign "only through posters and mass media" and only twice in each medium.[19] Campaign funds are, in essence, provided for each candidate by the government. Political parties may not put up candidates for the presidential electoral college. Those wishing such representation must get signatures of two to three hundred voters in an electoral district.[20]

Press and media are very closely controlled by the Basic Press Law of December 20, 1980, empowering the state to confiscate the contents of periodicals or broadcasting programs "when there are sufficient reasons." All media must be registered, as was the case under Japan, and the Ministry of Culture and Information may cancel registered publications "when their contents deviate from their original purpose or endanger national security or public order." Additional control comes from the amalgamation of all private news broadcasting into the state-run Korean Broadcasting System and of all news agencies into the official Yonhap Agency, whose importance is increased by the fact that Seoul newspapers are enjoined from having regional news organizations.

There is no formal censorship. The National Security Planning Agency (formerlly KCIA) distributes "guidance" to the media. This agency has considerably weakened since 1980 and by 1985 some of its guidance was ignored by the press. But there remains a high level of awareness and concern about how far one may go. The 1980 purge of several hundred leading press personnel greatly reduced the spirit of press independence. An amazing uniformity is the result, especially as it relates to the scope and proportion of attention given to politics (small), economics (large), and sports (greatly inflated). Uniformity is also seen in the coverage of such touchy foreign subjects as the activities of Solidarity in Poland, the Aquino assassination, or the overthrow of Marcos, all of which were, at first, barely mentioned.

Nevertheless, a degree of freedom was present until the fall of 1985 as government confidence expanded. Some circumvention of these controls seemed tacitly permitted. Student demonstrations, once not reported at all, received gradually expanding press attention until 1986 when the press shifted its attention to their unpopular violence. In 1985, there was a little criticism of government (though never of the president), more in magazines and newspapers than on the air.

Even here, however, a degree of manipulation was present; such criticism was often directed at officials the government sought to replace. Occasionally in 1985 articles were allowed to report in a less consistently defamatory tone the nature of North Korean conditions and policies. 1986 has, however, seen perceptible backsliding in press freedom, and control of the media remains very much in place.

Many other laws repress political activity. The National Security Law forbids activity in any way supporting or appearing to favor anything connected with communism or North Korea. Its provisions are subject to broad, almost uncurbed, interpretation. A 1980 Act Concerning Assembly and Demonstration forbids any "demonstration that violates or is feared to violate pertinent control laws and regulations on maintenance of public peace and order" or "that is feared to conspicuously cause (sic) social unrest." Notification of any demonstration must be made to the police forty-eight hours before it takes place; this law is continuously violated. In addition, much labor legislation was passed by the Legislative Council controlling, to the point of rendering impossible, a free labor movement. This legislation included the Labor Standard Law, the Labor Union Law, the Labor Dispute Settlement Law, the Labor Committee Law, and, later, the new Labor-Employer Council Law of January 1, 1982. Prohibited in these inter alia was the work of Christian missionaries for the welfare of industrial workers. [21]

The legislation of particularly the first five years of the Chun regime makes the following clear:

1. Democratic opposition politics in South Korea has been made almost impossible by law. Only the greatest national determination works through pressure and some circumvention to make opposition partly possible. This determination is concentrated in the NKDP, in student movements, and in some union and church activities. In essence, Korean politics is administered hierarchically and fairly uniformly by the Seoul bureaucracy. The same is true of all else in Korea—law, the judiciary, industry, the economy, labor unions, the press, agricultural cooperatives and industrial research.[22] As during the colonial administration, today's South Korean bureaucrats are wary of politics, more wary, perhaps, than were their Yi dynasty predecessors.

2. Unlike Yushin rule, this legislative control has not been placed in the constitution directly or in one or two draconian edicts; it has been distributed through a multiplicity of legislation, a thicket wearying to penetrate, which therefore presents a poor target for attack, especially simplified media attack. The republic's laws seek not only the control but the confusion of its critics.

3. The government claims that present politics are a cautious beginning of what will become full democratization. It says that the constitution has been improved and the situation better accepted. 1984-85 presented some evidence for this in gradual liberalization of media coverage, in the return of banned students and professors to campuses, in the lifting of the curfew, and in the barring of security forces

from campuses from March 1984 until the fall of 1985. Economic growth and prosperity, moreover, gave large population segments a stake in stability and a penchant for down playing the persistent restraints on open politics.

4. On the other hand, the politics which does take place is, in effect, a caricature of the democratic process. The controlled media, in their distorted depiction of repressive controls as democracy or the path thereto, have probably added to the problems Koreans have in achieving a freer system. In a country of ancient and powerful central bureaucratic rule whose bureaucracy has now achieved substantial success in economic development, it remains far from clear whether politics stands much chance of bringing central government under the control of a freely elected assembly with strong local roots. Contests between bureaucrats and parliaments are endemic to democracy, but Korea's political experience and beliefs plus the dominant interpretation of its economic development tend to weight this contest in Korea toward the bureaucracy.

Indoctrination

Control of present policies is accompanied in the South as well as, far more ubiquitously, in North Korea, by indoctrination to create a united and loyalist future. Since President Park founded the *Saemaul* (New Village) Movement in 1971, six programs have continued or emerged, most during the Chun years.

1. The Saemaul Movement (Home Ministry). Saemaul itself remains by far the most widespread and important rural movement. In President Park's last years, a proto-ideological movement gradually incorporating indoctrination and known as the *Saemaum* (New Mind) Movement developed under the President's daughter. Saemaum had interesting analogies to juche in North Korea, both in its stress on self-help and its use with a government rural development program so vast that it went far toward replacing traditional local government. Saemaum featured pep sessions in twenty- to thirty-household *pansanghwe* meetings stressing work, local initiative, local cooperation and togetherness in discussing and solving problems. Accompanying this was an explicit or implied loyalty to local and national leadership—a kind of developmental national Confucianism. These sessions provided the government with added grass roots penetration; local meeting agendas were often prepared in the Home Ministry.[23] Such penetration was also aided by the changes in local leadership brought by the movement. These substituted more malleable, new, army-trained leadership for that of established local families. The result has incipient totalitarian overtones.

President Chun, while dropping the somewhat ridiculed term saemaum, expanded the indoctrination aspects of the movement and placed them under his brother. Under this new leadership all South Korean organizations set up selection procedures for the training in rotation of their personnel. The movement includes schools (thus far, above primary grades), factories, government offices from ministers down to sweepers, village chiefs, businesses, and churches. In the vast headquarters in Suwon and many local centers, thirty-six thousand people were trained in 1982, some forty thousand in 1983, still more in 1984 and 1985. Beneath this superstructure, all larger companies have "spiritual training" programs which report to Saemaul headquarters. In these programs national songs, anti-communism, "consciousness reformation," developmental tales of village obstacles overcome, diligence, and loyalty to leaders and nation mix and are cultivated. Invitations to participate are not intended to be refused. No provision for protest and dissent is programmed for intrusion in any session. An atmosphere of consensus, togetherness and conformity is nurtured, much as in similar party, Kimism and juche sessions in North Korea. In effect, the very political atmosphere that the government seeks to establish throughout the nation is inculcated.[24]

2. The Unification Study Institute (Unification Ministry). The Ministry of Unification maintains a Unification Study Institute which works with the Anti-Communist League which, under the leadership of retired generals, provides anti-communist training in Changch'ung-dang, Seoul, for those whom the institute and the league select.

3. *Minjong-dang* Consciousness-Reforming Programs (Democratic Justice Party). The government party, perceiving the utility of indoctrination for partisan ends, established a Party *Usik Kaehyon Ponbu* (Consciousness-Reforming Headquarters) headed by a former leading Unification Ministry official with an intimate knowledge of North Korean techniques of participation. The program trains mostly party members (of whom some one hundred seventy thousand are claimed) by rotation at such centers as Togyu-san where it sponsors solidarity conferences.

4. *Ch'ongsin Munhwa Yon'gu-won* (Research Institute on Spiritual Culture, Ministry of Education). This institute, supervised by the Education Ministry, trains bureaucrats, professors and high-ranking army officers in prolonged joint sessions in a center outside Seoul where highly nationalistic and propagandistic reviews of Korean culture and history instill a "healthy national consciousness."

5. The *Hwarang* Program (Ministry of Education). This Education Ministry program honoring the "knights" (Hwarang) of Silla (an elite military leadership of the 500-700 A.D. era) "invites" (summons) thousands of young students who generally constitute the upper ten percent of classes up to high school to a grandiose, traditional-style center in Kyongju, the old Silla Kingdom capital where, for considerable stretches of summer and winter vacation, fidelity to and pride in the nation and its military leadership are inculcated.

6. Armed Forces Spiritual Programs. In addition to heavy anti-communist and South Korea loyalty indoctrination from boot camp on, every military unit has its own Saemaul training program of discussion and action. Korea's universal male draft for about three years brings almost all Korean men into prolonged contact with these

programs.

7. Education Board Programs. Each provincial board of education trains young students through the high school level in solidarity, pride and consensus through camping trips, exercise, and training in history and culture. It is a kind of "strength through joy" effort in which promotions reward special merit.

8. Others. The above do not include the instruction on morals and patriotism woven into all school curriculum levels, including increasingly intense consensual interpretation of national history.

Summary

The people of both Koreas are among the world's most highly mobilized and nationalistic populations. Ideological conformity has been intensively inculcated for more than thirty years in the North. For nearly fifteen years it has been inculcated in the South, though so far less intensively and in less isolation than in the North, where dissent is hardly possible. Dissent continues in the South, but increasing indoctrination attempts to cast it in a deviant, dangerous, and "un-Korean" light. Nevertheless, an increasingly vibrant opposition struggles to achieve unity against these obstacles. South Korea's previous party traditions, dogged student disaffection, and great openness to other countries will limit the extent to which the South Korean indoctrination system is likely ever to smother dissent as has seemingly occurred in the North. What has begun to happen, however, is the creation within South Korea of what Disraeli called in the 19th century "the two nations"-not the rich and the poor as in England, but the conformists and the dissenters. Both camps are large, compromise between them seems to be ebbing, and further unrest seems likely.

Despite long political traditions, both Korean regimes seek to depoliticize—or, at the minimum, to consensualize—their societies, reducing debate and opposition to superficial effects. That the South has not fully succeeded in this does not prevent it from trying. The North uses contact by leadership and administration more than the South to achieve expansion of popular support for the government. Each uses the government party. In both societies, public debate is inhibited or prevented on such important but sensitive issues as military factionalism, military influence on politics and policies, human rights, the political influence and organization of labor unions, and faults of top leadership. The South adds to these its problems of pollution and the hazards of industrial or military nuclear materials. The North so far lacks these problems but removes genuine public debate from virtually all controversial subjects including trade and foreign relations, which are constantly debated in the South.

Overall Conclusions

The central emphasis of the middle 1940s on political development has, in the past twenty-five years of monolithic Kim Il Sung control in the North and military control in the South, shifted to a priority on economic and social development in the two Koreas. Politics needs to catch up in both countries but the directions and pace are uncertain, more so in the North than in the relatively open South.

Though Pyongyang is quite isolated, foreign influences on it slowly increase while the prestige and effectiveness of Kim Il Sung's monolithic control ebb. However carefully he plans, Kim Jong Il can never fully succeed his father. The opening of the North, already beginning, is likely to proceed further at an unpredictable but probably slow pace. Political forces desiring participation are more likely to take the form of factions around Kim Jong Il rather than distinct political institutions. Sudden, unexpected change is conceivable, especially if Kim Jong Il is unable to maintain his position. Large scale military action seems unlikely.

South Korea will continue to have divided political aspirations which are hard either to contain or to reconcile. Conservatives stress bureaucratic controls and primarily economic objectives while viewing political change with cautious suspicion. On the other hand, students, workers, and many urban middle class groups favor political development and participation and decreased military hegemony over politics, policies and relations with North Korea. The two groups may be fairly evenly divided in relative political strength. Both have their aggressive, activist, to some extent strong-arm salients, which sometimes clash. The outlook is for continued tension. A workable compromise which permits the country to carry off the 1987-88 presidential election immediately before the summer 1988 Olympic Games continues (as of September 1986) to be a critical question, not eased by the antiquated and politically controversial position of the United States as tactical commander of most combat South Korean forces, which reinforces Washington's own political inclinations toward supporting the military, repressive side of the Korean political equation and stimulates anti-U.S. sentiments among student activists.

Up to the fall of 1986, some spirit of compromise has been shown by both government and opposition leaders. Nevertheless, even the issue of direct vs. indirect elections still under debate in September 1986, approaches the intractable; mutual concessions about parliamentary government still involve electoral reform, compromise, and issues of overall governmental stability. The outlook is cloudy and unlikely to be calm. The politics of the Korean peninsula will attract mounting attention during the next years as each Korea seeks ways to move past a quarter century of political repression.

Notes

1. Though Japan's formal annexation dates from 1910, Japanese governmental and political institutions dominated the peninsula from 1905. The dating of Mongol rule also involves elaboration at either end, which is, for present purposes, of little relevance.
2. Gregory Henderson, *Korea: The Politics of the Vortex*, (Cambridge: Harvard University Press, 1968), pp. 102-103. Plans to implement local administration in 1987 were underway in September 1986. Plans so far (*Korea Herald*, July 4, 1986) call only for local elected councils which would enact ordinances and inspect local governments but would neither elect nor be able to propose non-confidence votes in them. An elaborate Local Autonomy Act, passed at the end of 1949 and amended in 1969, 1972, 1973, and November 25, 1980, is on the books with the stipulation that it come into effect when promulgated: (*Current Laws of the Republic of Korea*, Fourth Edition, (Seoul: Korean Legal Center, 1983), Part I, pp. 117-145.) "Chosen" is the Japanese pronunciation of the most ancient name for Korea, a term Japan revived.
3. Bruce Cumings, *The Origins of the Korean War*, (Princeton: Princeton University Press, 1981), Chapter 3, pp. 68-100.
4. Cumings, ibid, pp. 403-405.
5. Gregory Henderson, "Korea," in G. Henderson, R.N. Lebow and J.G. Stoessinger, *Divided Nations in a Divided World*, (New York: David McKay and Co., 1974), pp. 70-72.
6. A portion of the 1.8 million were returnees to South Korea from Manchuria. A small number, possibly a few thousand, fled from South to North, and Cumings, op.cit., p. 562, notes 370,000 Koreans, mostly of southern origin, who went from Japan to North Korea in the first post-liberation years.
7. Vreeland, Shinn, Just and Moeller, *Area Handbook for North Korea*, (Washington, D.C.: 1976), pp. 34-35. Other well-known sources for North Korean politics are Robert A. Scalapino and Chong-sik Lee, *Communism in Korea*, (Berkeley: Univ. of California Press, 1972), and, for early years, Dae-sook Suh, *The Korean Communist Movement 1918-1948*, (Princeton, Princeton University Press, 1967).

8. Dai-sook Suh, "Changes in North Korean Politics and the Unification Policy" in *Korea and World Affairs*, 9, No. 4, 1985, pp. 693-694.

9. Ibid, pp. 684-706.

10. The widely cited view that Korea has never known a peaceful governmental transition is a false myth perpetuated to buttress military rule. The transition from Prime Minister Huh Chong to Chang Myon, summer 1960, was eminently legal and peaceful. The fact that Mr. Huh's regime was "interim" is of minor relevance. It controlled police and army and could have used them to influence the political result had Mr. Huh or his regime in any way so intended.

11. For full treatment of this election see Sung Il Choi and Chae Jin Lee, "Environment, Policy and Electoral Participation: A Comparison of Urban and Rural Areas," in Chong Lim Kim, *Political Participation in Korea*, (Santa Barbara, California: Clio Books, 1980), pp. 165-180.

12. For a summary of events in the 1970s, see Young Whan Kihl, *Politics and Policies in Divided Korea: Regimes in Contrast*, (Boulder and London: Westview Press, 1984), pp. 55-65.

13. For a summary of these events, see Gisbert H. Flanz and Hakjong Andrew Yoo, "Republic of Korea," in A.P. Blaustein and G.H. Flanz, *Constitutions of Countries of the World*, (Dobbs Ferry, NY: Oceana Publications, Inc., 1975).

14. *Korea Herald*, Seoul, December 4 and 10, 1980.

15. Kim Dae Jung, conversation, September 24, 1986. For analysis, see Flanz and Yoo, op. cit., pp. 1-6.

16. A member of the Legal Department of the Department of State was dispatched to observe Mr. Kim's trial; the embassy indicated that the records would be made public. They never were. In calling the charges against Mr. Kim "far-fetched," it is apparent that the State Department's opinion of the legal process involved was no higher than it has been in previous trial observations.

17. Political Party Act, *Current Laws*, op. cit., Vol. 1, Pt. 1, pp. 45-59.

18. Idem, pp. 37-44 for Political Funds Act. Some resemblance between the South Korean and the West German systems for funding political parties should, in fairness, be noted.

19. *Korea Times*, Dec. 13, 1980, preparing the public for these provisions. For labor laws, see *Current Laws*, idem., Part II, pp. 101-185.

20. The electoral college is an unusually striking illustration of centralized politics, preventing, as it seeks to do, the emergence of interest groups.

21. Young Whan Kihl, op. cit., p. 89, citing Nakagawa Nobuo, "Problems Confronting the Struggle for Democratization in Korea,"*Gekkan Shakaito* (Today's Socialist Party), (Tokyo: August 1981).

22. In fact, the increasing infiltration of the central bureaucracy into all these segments of Korean life is an important part of Korean

political process during the last quarter-century. See remarks on this process for agricultural cooperatives in U.S. Agency for International Development, "Korean Agricultural Services: The Invisible Hand in the Iron Glove: Market and Non-Market Forces in Korean Rural Development," (Washington: March 1984), Appendix D and passim.

23. USAID report, idem, D-8-12; also James R. Schiffman, "Militant Patriotism Draws Young and Old to a Korean Movement," *Asian Wall Street Journal*, Oct. 8, 1984. There is a considerable Saemaul literature, much laced with propaganda.

24. Despite their public and, in most cases, their mass nature, these indoctrination programs have been handled in a semi-secret manner, certainly as a totality, undoubtedly because of the questions they would raise regarding South Korea's democratic pronouncements. For this reason, sources outside of the Saemaul Movement are few; I have had to rely on Korean political scientists within Korea for information on programs (2)-(7).

Gregory Henderson is a research associate with the Center for East Asian Studies at Harvard University and has recently served as guest professor at universities in Bochum and Berlin, Germany. His service in Korea has been extensive, first as political officer with the U.S. Embassy in Seoul during the pivotal years 1948 to 1950; then, after serving in Washington as Korea desk officer, again at the U.S. Embassy in Seoul from 1958 to 1963. Henderson, who holds an M.B.A. from Harvard University, has published numerous books, monographs, and articles on Korean politics, the primary work being *Korea: The Politics of the Vortex*.

Chapter 6

The Major Powers and the Korean Triangle

Ilpyong J. Kim

It is the thesis of this paper that the success or failure of the North-South dialogues and negotiations for reunification of Korea will largely depend on the ways in which the four major powers formulate and implement their policies toward Korea. To the extent that they create a climate in which the two Koreas can conduct dialogue and negotiations, the possibility of peaceful reunification increases and stability can be maintained. However, if a major power dominates the policies of either Seoul or Pyongyang, tensions increase and there is greater likelihood of North-South conflict.

Since the success or failure of inter-Korean relations largely depends on the effective influence, conduct of policy and articulation of interests among the four powers, it is necessary to analyze and understand the positions of the powers and their policies toward Korean unification.

Background

In the 1970s there was a dramatic shift in the relations of the four major powers with the Korean peninsula. Where there had been a bipolar confrontation, there emerged a multipolar constellation. Significant changes occurred in the foreign policies of the four major powers—China, the Soviet Union, Japan and the United States. North Korea had been allied closely with the Eastern bloc headed by the Soviet Union, while South Korea was in alliance with the Western bloc led by the United States. For a time the Korean peninsula was a major focus of East-West conflict. The Korean War of 1950-53 was undoubtedly a textbook illustration of the cold war exploding regionally into armed conflict between elements, but not the totality, of the blocs. In the event, it was the Chinese, not the Soviets, who fought on the side of North Korea, while U.S. troops that fought on the side of South Korea were deployed under the flag of the United Nations. The conflict contributed for almost two decades to the frozen relations between the United States and the People's Republic of China and remains unresolved today.

The rapprochement between the United States and the PRC and the detente between the United States and the Soviet Union in the 1970s created a new international climate in which North and South Korea made serious efforts to open communications, conduct dialogues and negotiate reunification issues. In addition, as the result of the Sino-Soviet dispute in the 1960s, the North Korean leadership assumed an independent and self-reliant posture toward her allies. The South Korean leadership had begun to have doubts about the U.S. commitment as the result of U.S. rapprochement and detente with the PRC and the Soviet Union. The emergence of a multipolar constellation based on a balance of power and the shifts in U.S. foreign policy paved the way for the two Koreas to explore their shared sense of nationhood.

East-West detente helped bring about the North-South Korean dialogues beginning in 1972; changes in East-West relations as well as the deep mistrust and antagonism between the two parties helped to cut the dialogue short. The breakdown of dialogue in 1973 lasted until 1983, and during that period relations between the two Koreas reverted to cold war conditions. Tensions and armed skirmishes persisted along the 150-mile demilitarized zone that divides the peninsula. Although efforts were made by both sides to reopen the inter-Korean dialogues following the assassination of Park Chung Hee in October 1979 the real negotiations and agreements for Red Cross talks and exchange of separated family members and of performing artists did not materialize until 1984-85.

A significant change in attitudes came about in January 1984 when North Korea proposed a tripartite conference with the participation of the United States, North and South Korea. This was a departure from its earlier stance of refusing to meet with anyone from South Korea. The North also advocated changing the armistice agreement to a peace treaty, a position it has held for some time. No action was taken on these proposals, but in the autumn of the same year, North Korea offered to send 14,300 tons of rice, 550,000 yards of cloth and one hundred thousand tons of cement to aid flood victims in the South. The South accepted this offer and the goods were sent by ships and trucks in September and October.

There was some speculation about why the South Korean leaders accepted this aid. It was thought, for example, that the South needed to achieve a favorable image befitting its role as host of the Asian Athletic Games in 1986 and the Olympic Games in 1988. South Korea needs a favorable climate for the games if China and the Soviet Union, the friends of North Korea, are to participate.

Another component in the North-South thaw and changed international climate is the frequent exchange of visits and expression of views by the top leaders of the United States, China and Japan, as well as the active diplomacy of the two Koreas with their respective friends and allies in the early 1980s. Chinese leaders, including Deng Xiaoping, the architect of the open door policy, and his close associates, visited Pyongyang to participate in various ceremonial functions. Among these were the Sixth Congress of the Korean Workers' Party (KWP) in October 1980 and the celebration of North Korean leader Kim Il Sung's 70th birthday in the Spring of 1982. During their visit to North Korea, Deng and his protege Hu Yaobang, General Secretary of the Chinese Communist Party (CCP), were reported to have endorsed the succession of Kim Jong Il, the eldest son of Kim Il Sung and his heir apparent, to the leadership of the KWP.

While this active diplomacy was occurring in the Northern Triangle (North Korea, China, USSR) in the early 1980s, there were also stepped-up exchanges in the Southern Triangle (South Korea, Japan and the United States). The South Korean president, Chun Doo Hwan, went to Washington in February 1981 as one of the first heads of state to do so following President Reagan's inauguration. In return, Reagan visited Seoul in November 1983 as a part of his travel to East Asia.

Japanese Prime Minister Yasuhiro Nakasone visited Seoul after his inauguration in 1983. This was a dramatic change in Japanese posture toward South Korea. Previously, all prime ministers of postwar Japan had paid their first foreign visits to the United States. To reciprocate this important gesture, President Chun went to Japan in September 1984, the first Korean president to do so. He met with Japanese Emperor Hirohito and accepted an expression of "regret" for Japanese actions in Korea during the colonial period (1910-1945).

In March 1984 Prime Minister Nakasone visited China. During meetings with Chinese leaders in Beijing he discussed the possibility of reducing tensions and maintaining stability on the Korean peninsula. In the process he offered his services as an intermediary between China and South Korea. This was something of a new approach on the part of at least one member of the Southern Triangle toward the Northern Triangle.

Yaobang paid an official visit to Pyongyang following Kim Il Sung's trip to China in September 1982. The Chinese official held a series of consultations with North Korean leaders and delivered a number of speeches. In June 1983, Kim Jong Il, Kim Il Sung's heir apparent, went to China. He was followed in August by North Korean Premier Kang Sung San. Kim Il Sung made an unofficial visit to Beijing in November 1984.

From May 16 to July 1, 1984, Kim made an extended trip to Moscow and Eastern Europe, meeting with then General Secretary Konstantin Chernenko and Politburo members, including Mikhail Gorbachev, in the Kremlin. Kim's previous visit had been in 1961.

Relations between the Soviet Union and North Korea have improved considerably since Kim's 1984 trip.

While active and close relations between China and North Korea were fostered through these exchange visits by the top leaders, Soviet First Deputy Minister of Foreign Affairs, M.S. Kapitsa, came to Pyongyang in November 1984 to negotiate the boundary lines between the Soviet Union and North Korea at the Tumen River. The Japanese news agency Kyodo speculated on the possibility of a visit by Kim Jong Il to Moscow sometime in August or September of 1985 to obtain Soviet endorsement of his succession to his father, but the visit had not taken place by the end of 1985.

The frequent exchange of visits by the heads of states and other officials in both the Northern and Southern Triangle seemed to indicate that the interests of the four major powers relating to Korea had begun to converge in some respects.

The Northern Triangle: China, North Korea and the Soviet Union

North Korea's relations with China and the Soviet Union may best be understood in terms of certain stages and periods of development. When Korea was divided in 1945 after World War II, the northern part was occupied by the Soviet Union and initially ruled by a Soviet military government. The southern part, below the thirty-eighth parallel, was occupied by the United States and ruled by a U.S. military government until 1948. In that year two separate governments were established—the Republic of Korea (ROK) in the south and the Democratic People's Republic of Korea (DPRK) in the north. Both the North and South depended heavily on the economic and military support of their respective allies. In this early period North Korea's closest ally was the Soviet Union, which played the major role in shaping the North Korean political system.

A new factor in the Northern Triangle was the founding of the People's Republic of China (PRC) in 1949. The PRC established diplomatic relations with both the Soviet Union and the DPRK. In June 1950 the Korean War broke out and all of the southern part, except the Pusan perimeter, was overrun by the North Korean army. U.S. intervention in the war restored to South Korea most of the territory which had been occupied by North Korea. The United States crossed the thirty-eighth parallel, attempting to liberate the northern part and unify the peninsula under U.S. influence. This brought Chinese intervention to sustain North Korea as a buffer state for the security of China. Sino-North Korean relations after the Korean War have been characterized as the relationship of "lips to the teeth" and as solidarity sealed in blood. At this point North Korea was more dependent on China than on the USSR for her security, and established closer relations with her.

Until 1956 Pyongyang maintained close and active relations with both Moscow and Beijing. During this period China and the Soviet Union provided massive economic and military assistance to North Korea for postwar rehabilitation and defense build-up. However, in

1956-1961, as the result of the Sino-Soviet conflict, the close and friendly relations North Korea had maintained with both China and the Soviet Union were beginning to show strains. At the Fourth Congress of the KWP in Pyongyang in 1961 North Korea adopted a policy of neutrality in the Sino-Soviet dispute.

This dispute became an open struggle in 1962-64 and the Soviet Union withdrew its economic and technical aid from both China and North Korea. It was inevitable that Pyongyang would change its posture toward the Soviet Union and shift its neutral position to one of close alignment with the PRC. During this period the Chinese head of state, Liu Xiaoqi, visited North Korea and placed China's full support behind the Pyongyang government. The North Korean head of state, Choe Yong Kun, paid a return visit to China and Sino-North Korean relations were further consolidated. It was also during this period that China provided Pyongyang with eight hundred million *yuan* in aid.

The close relations between China and North Korea did not last long, as Sino-Soviet competition over influence in Pyongyang mounted and the Soviet Union's efforts to woo North Korea to its side began to bear fruit. China and North Korea did not agree on a strategy to counter U.S. escalation in Vietnam. North Korea proposed joint Sino-Soviet action to aid the North Vietnamese, but the Chinese rejected the idea. This factor contributed to the growing tension between Beijing and Pyongyang. Also, during the Cultural Revolution in China in 1965-69 the Red Guards attacked North Korean leader Kim Il Sung as a "fat revisionist" and the "Khrushchev of Korea." Despite this, and although Kim Il Sung had reiterated his policy of independence in October 1966, the end of the Cultural Revolution declared at the Ninth Congress of the Chinese Communist Party in 1969 helped to improve relations between China and North Korea. On October 1, 1969, the North Korean head of state, Choe Yong Kun, rushed to attend the twenteith anniversary ceremony of the founding of the PRC and in April 1970 Chinese Premier Zhou Enlai paid a state visit to North Korea. It was Zhou's second visit to Pyongyang; his first was in February 1958.

Meanwhile, in 1968 North Korea's posture toward the Soviet Union began to change as the result of the Soviet Army's suppression of Czechoslovakian resistance and the enunciation of the Brezhnev Doctrine under which the Soviet Union claimed the right to invade its fraternal countries in order to salvage their socialist systems. Moreover, the Sino-Soviet armed clash over Qingdo (Damansky) Island in the Ussuri River (near North Korea) in the spring of 1969 brought about a real possibility of military threat to North Korea. The tension over border issues between China and the Soviet Union persisted and created great anxiety and insecurity in the minds of the North Korean leadership. This in turn produced unpredictable North Korean behavior and attitudes toward the United States, Japan and South Korea in the late 1960s and early 1970s.

U.S. policy toward the PRC changed dramatically in the 1970s, from containment to rapprochement. This created a new set of pressures on the leaders in Pyongyang and Seoul, who were pushed toward some understanding with one another in order to accommodate to the external changes. The improvement of U.S. policy toward China as well as detente with the Soviet Union opened the way for North Korea to adopt an equidistant policy toward China and the Soviet Union. This policy was based on the North Korean goals of achieving *chajusong* (independence) in politics and of implementing *juche* (self-reliance) in economics as well as non-alignment in diplomatic relations.

To sustain this policy in the 1970s North Korea rapidly improved relations with the developing countries of the Third World and within the developed countries of the "Second Tier" in the West. North Korea attempted to open a line of communication with the United States by sending signals in the form of letters and appeals to the U.S. government in Washington. Also, in 1973 North Korea attained the status of permanent observer at the United Nations after it became a member of some specialized U.N. agencies such as the World Health Organization (WHO), United Nations Educational, Scientific and Cultural Organization (UNESCO), and Universal Postal Organization (UPO). More than one hundred countries provide diplomatic recognition to North Korea and maintain diplomatic relations with Pyongyang. Sixty of these countries also recognize South Korea.

One of the most important developments in the first half of the 1980s was a change in the relationships of China, the Soviet Union and North Korea. After a series of negotiations, China and the Soviet Union finally agreed to improve relations and in December 1984, signed an agreement on four items of economic and technological cooperation. This represented a giant step toward a thaw in Moscow-Beijing relations, which had been strained for some twenty years. Kim Il Sung's visit to the Soviet Union in May 1984, his first official visit in twenty-three years, helped to improve Soviet-North Korean relations. What emerges from these events and exchanges is a strengthening of interdependent relations, though not necessarily an alliance system, among Moscow, Beijing and Pyongyang. It is, therefore, worthwhile to evaluate the perceptions and policies of the Soviet Union and China toward the Korean question in the context of North Korean proposals for reunification.

The Soviet perception of the Korean problem and its policy toward reunification have been well reflected in the pages of Soviet newspapers such as *Pravda, Izvestia,* and *Red Star* as well as other journals that speak for the views and policies of the government. The statements of the late Soviet Premier Konstantin Chernenko during Kim Il Sung's visit to Moscow in 1984 clearly articulated the Soviet viewpoint. The Soviet leader said that Korea is considered the most dangerous place bordering Soviet territory, one where conflict could easily break out. This makes Korea a source of insecurity and uncertainty in the Soviet Union's international relations. Chernenko said the USSR perceives the Asian continent as the eastern front line of the United States where it confronts the socialist states of the East. For the Soviet Union, the Korean peninsula has thus become a strategic area for defending its own territory and maintaining its security in the face of the threat posed by the Western military bloc.

The obstacles to a solution of the complex Korean problem are, the Soviets believe, the continued presence and actual increase in the strength of U.S. troops in the South and the participation of Japanese military forces, as well as South Korean forces, in the annual exercises of combat coordination among the United States, South Korea and Japan. The emerging military alliance in the Southern Triangle, the Soviet leader asserted, would inevitably perpetuate military tensions rather than promote peace on the Korean peninsula. As long as a threat is posed by the U.S.-South Korea-Japan military bloc, the Soviet Union and North Korea are committed to uphold the Treaty of Friendship, Cooperation and Mutual Assistance signed in July 1961. (It should be noted that Kim Il Sung earlier announced a willingness to abrogate this treaty if the United States signed a peace treaty with North Korea to replace the armistice agreement that ended the Korean War.)

An important related element in Soviet policy has been the proposal for withdrawal of U.S. troops as the first step toward a peaceful resolution of the division. In the Soviet view, the U.S. troop presence perpetuates the division and is the greatest obstacle to a peaceful resolution. In addition, the Soviet Union has supported North Korean positions on issues such as replacing the armistice agreement with a peace treaty, the adoption of a non-aggression declaration, the mutual reduction of forces in the North and South, and the establishment of a nuclear-free zone in the Korean peninsula. To achieve these goals, the Soviet leaders believe, North and South Korea should stabilize the situation in Korea and hold discussions to create conditions favorable for negotiations. The stated Soviet policy over the past four decades has not changed despite the strains in Soviet-North Korean relations in the 1960s and early 1970s.

The most important event in Soviet-North Korean relations in 1984 was the visit of Soviet Deputy Foreign Minister Kapitsa to North Korea in November. The Japanese news agency Kyodo reported on November 30 that during Kapitsa's visit the Soviet Union and North Korea reached agreement on a border settlement and on the expansion of bilateral trade, communication and railroad facilities by opening the Tumen River area. This area is in the northeast where the borders of China, North Korea and the Soviet Union meet, and has often been an area of dispute. Kapitsa conferred with Kim Il Sung on November 20 and met Kim Jong Il on November 23 in Pyongyang. The content of their discussions has not been disclosed to date. However, some Japanese sources speculated in December 1984 that Kapitsa's visit to Pyongyang strengthened Soviet-North Korean ties and cited Pyongyang's permission for Soviet fighter planes to fly over North Korean airspace and use North Korean air force bases. In return, the Soviet Union agreed to provide MiG 23 fighter planes and economic assistance, and to recognize the succession of Kim Jong Il.

The Japanese newspaper *Sankei Shimbun* reported in August 1985 that the Soviet Union had dispatched ten of the promised forty MIG 23s to North Korea. This build-up of the North Korean Air Force was an attempt to counterbalance the U.S. sale of F86 fighter planes to South Korea. The Soviet Union rebuilt the port of Najin in 1978 and began to reinforce its Pacific fleet in the 1980s to counter the U.S.-Japan-South Korean naval and air forces in the Pacific region. On August 15, 1985, the Soviet Union dispatched a high-level delegation headed by First Deputy Premier Alieff to Pyongyang on the occasion of the fortieth anniversary of Korea's liberation from Japanese colonial rule. Included in this delegation were Vice-Chairman of the Presidium of the Supreme Soviet Voliyakof, First Deputy Minister of Defense Petrof and several other Soviet leaders.

In the areas of economic cooperation and assistance, the Soviet Union has helped in the construction of sixty major plants, while, according to Moscow broadcasting, eight more factories were under construction with Soviet assistance in March 1984. The Soviet Union was proud of helping North Korea produce sixty-three percent of its electric power, forty-two percent of its steel, and fifty percent of its petroleum supplies. In recent years, thirty-five percent of North Korea's total trade has been with the Soviet Union.

To follow up the series of agreements concluded between the Soviet Union and North Korea on June 19, 1984, after Kim Il Sung's visit to Moscow, North Korea dispatched Foreign Minister Kim Young Nam in April, Deputy President Park Sung Chul in May and then Premier Kang Sung San in December 1985. The Soviet News Agency reported on December 16, 1985, that Soviet Premier Rizkof and Premier Kang signed a number of economic and technological pacts, including an agreement for Soviet aid in the construction of a nuclear power plant. According to a Japanese source, the North Korean premier also agreed to support the Soviet proposal for Asian collective security, reversing the North Korean position on security issues.

While there were these frequent DPRK-USSR visits between the Chernenko-Kim summit meeting in May 1984 and Kapitsa's visit to Pyongyang in November of that year, the Soviet Union also moved to improve its relations with China. In December 1984, First Deputy Prime Minister Ivan V. Arkhipov visited Beijing, the most senior Soviet official to do so in fifteen years. He reached agreement with Chinese officials on four areas of economic and technological cooperation: a long-term trade pact (1986-90), an economic cooperation accord, a science and technological cooperation pact and an agreement to establish a joint commission for these exchanges. The impact of these changes on North Korea has been so great that the Pyongyang government was also persuaded to adopt an open door policy, not only to the Soviet Union and China but also to the United

States and Japan.

In September 1984, as part of its open door policy, North Korea proclaimed a joint venture and foreign investment law in order to elicit Japanese and Western investments. A Japanese company is currently constructing a department store while a French firm is building a tourist hotel in Pyongyang. A Canadian engineeering firm has signed a $250,000 agreement with North Korea to explore a deposit of gold at the Woonsan mines. In order to expand its business with Japan, North Korea invited Japanese business leaders, including President Kawakasu of Nankai Electric Railway Company in September and Chairman Soejima of the East Asia Trade Research Committee in November of 1985. All Nippon Air Line's Councilor Okazaki was also invited to Pyongyang in January 1986 to explore the possibility of expanded airline services linking Tokyo, Pyongyang and Beijing. Despite Japan's favorable response to these initiatives, the United States has been slow in responding to North Korea's open door policy, perhaps due to pressure from South Korea.

China's primary interest in Korea has traditionally been to keep the Korean peninsula within the Chinese sphere of influence. The Sino-Japanese War of 1894-95 was fought over the question of hegemony in Korea. The Chinese entered the Korean War in 1950 to deny the United States occupation of North Korea. Domination of the Korean peninsula by a hostile country would, in China's view, pose a great threat to its own security. North Korea is needed, therefore, as a buffer state. China's perceptions of Korean problems and its policies toward reunification issues have been greatly influenced by her security considerations. One must understand Chinese policies toward Korea in the context of Sino-American, Sino-Soviet, and Sino-Japanese relations, all of which have an impact on Korean affairs.

During my visit to China in the summer of 1984, I heard from a Chinese government official, a specialist on Korean affairs, that the best solution now to the problems of Korea is to begin the proposed tripartite talks among the United States, North and South Korea. When the North Korean government called for the tripartite conference, the spokesman of the Chinese Ministry of Foreign Affairs endorsed the proposal the next day. "China takes the position of supporting without reservation the convening of the three-way conference," the *People's Daily* stressed on January 12, 1984. All the press reports and editorials in China emphatically supported the North Korean call for the tripartite conference and urged the United States to respond positively.

Such talks would seek to reduce tensions, replace the armistice agreement with the peace treaty and pave the way for the Democratic Confederal Republic of Koryo (DCRK). This, it was said, would allow the two political systems to coexist in a condition of peace and stability in the Korean peninsula. "Is there any better solution to the Korean problem than this?" the Chinese official asked.

This official seemed to rule out reunification in the near future, but sought to maintain a balance between North and South by eliminating such sources of conflict as U.S. troops, nuclear weapons and continued escalation of troop levels. According to him, China is interested in serving as an intermediary between North Korea and the United States, fostering direct discussions between them. China argues that North Korea has made a series of proposals for discussions and has opened its door to the United States. It is the United States that has been recalcitrant and has sustained the conflict situation in Korea, putting the interests of the U.S. government ahead of the interests of the Korean people.

After Kim Il Sung's prolonged trip to the Soviet Union and Eastern Europe in the Spring of 1984, Pyongyang's policy of self-reliance shifted to an open door policy that is somewhat comparable to that promoted by Deng Xiaoping since 1979. Following a reassessment of international and domestic situations, the North Korean leader seems to have concluded that an open door policy would address economic problems at home and would contribute to the reduction of tensions in the Korean peninsula.

The approach of the Northern Triangle to the Korea problem has involved tension reduction between North and South Korea through communication, dialogue and negotiations. The eventual establishment of the Democratic Confederal Republic of Koryo would ensure peace and stability on the peninsula, all of which would contribute to the ultimate goal of reunification of the two Koreas. The changes in North Korean attitudes, reflected in such actions as providing relief materials and responding to the South's call for an economic conference and Red Cross talks, should be analyzed and understood against the background of changes taking place in the Northern Triangle. In mounting a peace offensive the Northern Triangle has apparently attempted to undermine the emerging military cooperation in the South between the United States, South Korea and Japan.

The Southern Triangle: The United States, South Korea and Japan

Briefly stated, this is the story of the growth of military and security relations in the Southern Triangle. The triangular relationship of the United States, Japan and South Korea developed as a political alliance in the 1950s and 1960s. Following the Korean War of 1950-53 the United States signed a security treaty with South Korea. This was followed by a massive build-up of the ROK army and the introduction of nuclear weapons to the Korean theater. After fourteen years of strain, relations between South Korea and Japan were normalized in 1965. The renewal of the U.S.-Japan Security Treaty in the 1960s and South Korean participation in the Vietnam War on the southern side further strengthened the military alliance in the Southern Triangle. The present state of these security relations affects North-South Korean relations, as it will the future policy direction of the four major powers toward the Korean peninsula. Some observers in Japan and China are concerned that the development of such a military alliance will prolong the North-South conflict and perpetuate the division of Korea.

For the past three decades the United States has played an important role in creating and maintaining the strategic triangle in the South. The United States has been the security shield for Japan and South Korea, as well as their major trading partner. South Korea has depended heavily on the United States for security protection and on Japan for economic assistance and trade partnership.

As explained below, the inauguration of the Reagan Administration in January 1981 brought new strength to the military alliances between the United States and the other two states in the Southern Triangle. Relations between South Korea and Japan have also improved in the 1980s.

The alliances of the Southern Triangle developed in the context of the cold war and the Korean War, as these new allies sought to counter what they perceived to be the expanding influence of China and the Soviet Union. The U.S. security commitment to South Korea since 1945 should also be understood in this context, as should U.S.-Japanese defense cooperation.

At the height of the cold war era, in the 1950s and 1960s, the United States provided not only a security shield but also military hardware to South Korea and Japan. U.S. troops have remained in South Korea since the end of the Korean War; their presence helps to keep the peninsula divided. The nature of the U.S. security commitment to South Korea is indicated in Article 3 of the 1954 U.S.-ROK Mutual Defense Treaty:

> Each party recognizes that an armed attack in the Pacific area on either of the parties in territories now under their respective administrative control, or hereafter recognized by one of the parties as lawfully brought underthe administrative control of the other, would be dangerous to its own peace and safety and declares that it would act to meet the common danger in accordance with its constitutional processes.

During the three decades of the U.S.-ROK military alliance the U.S. government has provided some nine to ten billion dollars in security assistance to create, train and equip the six-hundred-thousand-man ROK military with advanced F16 planes, modern tanks and missiles. A large number of ROK military leaders received their training in the United States and have worked closely with U.S. military advisers. The ROK is Washington's most reliable ally in its policy of containing Soviet expansion in East Asia. Moreover, the combat experience, joint operations and transfer of U.S. military technology to South Korea during its participation in the Vietnam War in the late 1960s further strengthened the capability of the ROK Army.

In 1977 the Carter Administration announced that U.S. troops would be withdrawn from Korea. This decision was based on the assumption that the large amounts of U.S. aid had made the ROK military strong enough to defend itself. The United States provided

$1.5 billion in a military modernization program during 1971-77. In 1974-75, the United States sent $219 million worth of military hardware to South Korea, and in 1975-76, $509.5 million worth of military equipment, missiles, and advanced planes in the foreign military credit (FMC) sales. In 1978, the U.S. Congress appropriated $1.2 billion for South Korea as part of a military assistance program that included eight hundred million in military equipment transfer. The United States also sold F-4E Phantom jets to the ROK in 1979 and approved the sale of 60 F-16 fighters in FMC sales in the 1980s. All in all, the ROK army strength was greatly expanded in the 1980s and South Korea caught up with or surpassed North Korean military capabilities by 1985.

There was debate about Carter's proposed troop withdrawal in the U.S. Congress and among the public. The questions were whether the North Korean Army was superior to that of the South, whether South Korea could defend itself, and whether the role of Japan and U.S.-Japanese defense cooperation would be damaged in the event of war in the Korean peninsula. Reassessment of North Korean military strength and capability by U.S. intelligence agencies was one factor that led to the cancellation of the U.S. troop withdrawal policy in 1979. In 1981 the Reagan Administration announced that U.S. troops in Korea would stay there indefinitely, thereby committing the United States to a direct role on the Korean peninsula.

During his visit to South Korea in November 1983, President Reagan reaffirmed Washington's continuing strong commitment to the security of South Korea. He stated that the security of the South Korean Republic is "pivotal" to the peace and security of Northeast Asia and, in turn, vital to the security of the United States. He emphasized that the United States would continue to maintain its forces in Korea and strengthen their combat capabilities.

The Reagan Administration has sent an additional two thousand troops to South Korea and stepped up its military assistance program. From Washington's perspective, the security and stability of South Korea have top priority. Reducing tensions or taking steps toward dialogue and negotiation with North Korea are apparently at the bottom of the list of Washington's Korea policy objectives. The logic of Washington seems to ask why there should be reunification of the two Koreas so long as the division serves the security interests of the United States.

Korean-Japanese relations have been stormy and turbulent at best since Korea was liberated from Japanese colonial rule after World War II. With the division of Korea and the creation of the ROK and DPRK, Japan fostered an "equidistant policy" between the two states and was able to play one side off against the other. This policy suited Japan's postwar interests until 1965 when the normalization treaty between Japan and South Korea tilted Japan toward South Korea.

Under the terms of this treaty the two nations established diplomatic and consular relations, settled property claims and fishing disputes, and regularized the status of Koreans in Japan. They also reached agreement on economic cooperation in the form of Japanese government credits, commercial loans, and equity investment in Korea. The Japanese government agreed to provide three hundred million dollars in grants, two hundred million in soft loans, and three hundred million million in private commercial credits. The transfusion of Japanese money into the ailing South Korean economy produced the "Miracle on the Han" in the 1960s and 1970s.

However, South Korea's relations with Japan in the 1970s were more complex than the terms of the treaty would indicate. In 1973, Kim Dae Jung, the prominent opposition leader of South Korea, was kidnapped from a hotel in Tokyo by South Korean intelligence agents. There was the attempted assassination of President Park Chung Hee, allegedly by a Korean resident of Japan, in which Madame Park was killed. South Korea violated civil liberties and human rights in the name of the Yushin constitutional system. All these events had an impact on the relations between Japan and South Korea.

At the same time any strain between Seoul and Tokyo was somewhat alleviated by the end of the war in Vietnam, the announcement of the intended U.S. troop withdrawal from South Korea, the signing of the Sino-Japanese peace treaty and the normalization of relations between the United States and China in 1972. Japan was under great pressure from the United States to share the security burden in Northeast Asia when the United States began to retreat from battle stations in Asia after the Vietnam War.

The assassination of President Park by his own security chief, Kim Jae Kyu, in October 1979 changed the posture and policy of Japan toward Korea. The Japanese were willing to open channels of communication. Prime Minister Nakasone's visit to Seoul was followed by President Chun Doo Hwan's trip to Tokyo, the first of its kind by a South Korean leader in the post-World War II period. Under Chun's guidance, new military leaders emerged, heralding a new era in military cooperation and alliance in the Southern Triangle. A former chief of the security command in Seoul and a major general in the ROK Army, Chun Doo Hwan pursued pro-U.S. and pro-Japanese policies after he was inaugurated president in 1981. The inaugurations of President Reagan in 1981 and Prime Minister Nakasone in 1982 provided for further strengthening of the military alliance in the Southern Triangle.

In the 1980s ROK-Japanese relations have improved considerably from a "love/hate relationship" to a more cooperative and cordial relationship, at least on the official level. During Chun's visit to Tokyo, Nakasone reaffirmed through the Chun-Nakasone Joint Communique that peace and stability on the Korean peninsula are essential to the peace and security of East Asia, including Japan. Tokyo pledged support to Seoul's proposal for national reconciliation and democratic unification and to its efforts for dialogue. Nakasone also reaffirmed that South Korea's defense efforts combined with North-South dialogue would make a significant contribution to the maintenance of peace and stability on the Korean peninsula. Japan provided four billion dollars in credit to South Korea in 1983 in order to rejuvenate the ailing economy and to shift the balance of payments in favor of Japan.

According to some Japanese analysts, the key to the solution of the Korean problem is for Japan to establish a balanced and equidistant policy toward the two Koreas and to take North Korea into consideration as it formulates its policy. Japanese intellectuals and the opposition parties, including the Japan Socialist, Democratic Socialist, and Komeito parties, argue that the Nakasone government should pursue expansion of cultural, economic and trade exchanges with North Korea as a balance to its relations with the South. Such a policy, they contend, would foster peace and security on the Korean peninsula.

On the other hand, some U.S. scholars have suggested that Japan reciprocate for the U.S. security shield and trade partnership by increasing its security commitment and providing more aid to South Korea. In this view Japan should actively participate in the military alliance system of the Southern Triangle

Though Japan is increasing somewhat its contacts with North Korea, its basic policy seems to remain one of commitment to a divided Korean peninsula.

Conclusion

When Premier Zhao Zhiyang of China came to Washington in January 1984, he transmitted to the Reagan Administration North Korea's proposal for a tripartite conference of the United States, North Korea and South Korea. Reagan's response was to propose a four-way conference of China, the United States, North Korea and South Korea, since China was also a signatory to the armistice agreement at the end of the Korean War. When Reagan visited China in April that year, he held discussions with Chinese leaders on ways to resolve the Korea question in the context of maintaining peace and stability in East Asia. Washington perceives Beijing as having more influence in Pyongyang and better relations with North Korean leaders than the Soviet Union. The U.S. ambassador to China suggested during Reagan's visit that China should host a tripartite conference in Beijing, thereby finessing Soviet partipation.

The Soviet Union is not enthusiastic about the convening of a tripartite conference. Exclusion from such a conference might reduce Moscow's influence on future developments in the Korean peninsula. Though the Soviet Union was opposed to the tripartite proposal, Rumania, Yugoslavia and East Germany (GDR) supported the idea. Soviet leaders told Kim Il Sung in May 1984 that they would welcome any talks on the Korea question without any interference from external powers. The Soviet Union has consistently supported North Korea's position that the Korean problem, including reunification issues, should be resolved by the Koreans themselves without foreign interference.

Meanwhile, Prime Minister Nakasone of Japan visited China in March, a month earlier than Reagan, and discussed Korea with the Chinese leaders. Nakasone asked China to increase its contacts, trade, and economic relations with South Korea, while the Chinese leaders expected Japan to respond by expanding its economic relations and cultural exchanges with North Korea.

China had already made a series of contacts with South Korea. In May 1983 Xen Du, director of the Civil Aeronautics Administration of China (CAAC), successfully concluded an agreement with South Korean authorities to return a plane hijacked that month. China has allowed South Korean sports teams to participate in international competition in China and has dispatched Chinese officials to take part in the organizational meetings for the Asian games and the Olympic games to be held in Seoul in 1986 and 1988 respectively. In 1981-82 the Chinese government lifted its ban on scholarly contact with South Korea. China's trade with South Korea through third parties increased to $970 million in 1984 from a meager twenty million dollars in 1979. According to an analyst and a Korean specialist at the Institute of International Studies of the Foreign Ministry in Beijing, China has been playing an active role in promoting better relations with China and South Korea, thereby contributing to the process of maintaining peace and stability in East Asia. However, the specialist contends, the United States has done nothing to establish contacts with North Korea.

If the United States persists in closing the door to North Korea, the Chinese official warned, and continues to maintain a recalcitrant attitude toward the Pyongyang government, despite Pyongyang's willingess to talk, there will be grave consequences for any U.S.-Chinese efforts to reduce tensions and promote peace and stability in Korea. If the United States continues its hostile policy toward North Korea, the Chinese official asserted, there will be an increase of tension between the North and South and possibly no Olympic Games in Seoul in 1988. If the United States is seriously interested in peace and stability in Korea and East Asia, China expects the United States to take the initiative and contact North Korea, increase cultural and sports exchanges and promote better relations.

From the Chinese perspective, the Northern Triangle has already made great efforts to reduce tensions, maintain stability, and promote peace in Korea. These efforts have been enhanced by Sino-Soviet rapprochement, Kim Il Sung's visit to Moscow and Eastern Europe in May 1984, and the improvement in Sino-North Korean relations after Kim's visit to Beijing in November 1984. However, the Southern Triangle has not made any serious effort to reduce tensions and resolve the conflict situation in Korea. Rather it has transformed itself into a strategic triangle and a military alliance. Without changes in this military alliance system there will be no peace, the Chinese official believes, in Korea or Northeast Asia.

To sum up, the Korean people in North and South do not want another war or a permanent division of their country. They aspire to peaceful reunification without negative interference by foreign powers. There has been hopeful movement among the outside powers: China has expanded its cultural and economic contacts with South Korea, Japan has expanded similar contacts with North Korea, the Soviet Union has expressed its support of North-South negotiations. North Korea has asked the United States to join in tripartite talks with the two Koreas. But U.S. policy toward North Korea has not budged. That is where the next move must come, if peace and stability are to come at last to the Korean peninsula.

Ilpyong J. Kim is a professor of Political Science at the University of Connecticut, specializing in international politics in East Asia. Holding a Ph.D. from Columbia University, Kim has written and edited five books and published numerous articles in professional and academic journals. He is chair of the Columbia University Seminar on Korea and is past president of the New England Association for Asian Studies. He recently taught a course at Columbia University entitled, "The Politics of North and South Korea in International Perspective."

Chapter 7

Korea Today, Korea Tomorrow
— *A Korean Perspective* —

Kyungmo Chung

The Biblical story of Exodus depicts the rapture of emancipation experienced by the Israelites but goes on to tell of their subsequent suffering for forty years in the wilderness. For Koreans, August 1945 was a similar time: first the rapture, then the suffering, which came afterward and has lasted as long. Continuing the religious metaphor, we may say that the Koreans gave thanks to the Lord for humbling the Japanese, their hated colonial masters, and joyously sang praise of Him and of the U.S. troops who, working as His visible hand, defeated the emperor and his legions. That joy was fleeting. To the utter astonishment of Koreans, the same hands they naively thought were working the divine will had drawn an arbitrary line across the country at the thirty-eighth parallel and cut in two a nation established thirteen centuries earlier.

The division made the peninsula a tragic arena where Koreans were induced to hate one another. Millions were killed and wounded. Millions more became refugees in the fratricidal conflict of the Korean War (1950-53). General Matthew Ridgway, who replaced General Douglas MacArthur as commander of UN forces in Korea in 1951, termed it a tragedy unprecedented in human history. The threat of still another war hangs over our heads and Koreans in two hostile camps suffer repression because of this unending crisis.

Koreans now find that the Japanese, who left the country in humiliation forty years ago, are back to exploit us again as part of their sphere of economic domination. The only difference is that the whips are cracked this time not by the Japanese themselves, but by

Korean surrogates. We Koreans now find ourselves in the wilderness, threatened by vipers and hunger. Desperately we seek a promised land where there is no exploitation or hatred among brothers and sisters, and where freedom and justice flow like rivers.

My task is to offer some thoughts on how we Koreans might find and tread the path to unification. I must first comment on how we got into the present predicament. I warn the reader that I shall not present a step-by-step process for unification within the framework of international power politics. I am neither a political scientist nor a detached observer. Nor will I propose any policy changes to decision-makers in Washington. I fear that is futile. These remarks are addressed to people who can empathize with the agony of others. I do not deny that there is anger in my heart. To be for the unification of Korea seems to require that I be against many things. Hard truths will have to be stated. I shall avoid abstractions that deflect attention from the human situation or muffle the cry for salvation. I want to describe the ethos of the Korean people because I believe that the Korean ethos will determine the direction of Korean history regardless of how foreign powers meddle in our homeland.

I

Oda Yasuma was an obscure minor official in the Japanese colonial government in Seoul when Japan surrendered on August 15, 1945. On September 6, two days before Lt. Gen. John R. Hodge and his 24th Corps arrived at Inchon, an advance party of thirty-one military personnel headed by Brig. Gen. Charles Harris flew from Okinawa and landed at Kimpo Airport in Seoul. As the plane approached Kimpo, I think Harris must have recalled Oda's name. A missionary friend who had spent some years in Korea had recommended that the general find Oda, who worked for the Japanese Y.M.C.A. and was "trustworthy and fluent in English."

Gen. Harris, on his way to the plush Chosun Hotel in downtown Seoul, where the Japanese governor general Abe Nobuyuki had arranged for the party to stay, asked the Japanese official riding with him where he might find Oda. The inquiry must have astounded the Japanese. He was none other than Oda Yasuma himself.[1]

The cameraderie between the U.S. general and Oda, who was soon promoted to be one of Abe's key aides, was probably instantaneous. Oda became a prime informant for the U.S. Military Government (USMG) which replaced the Japanese governor general. He helped the U.S. officials secure interpreters, arranged interviews with Japanese dignitaries, and wrote memoranda on the situation in Korea after August 15.

About 350 memoranda were prepared in English by Japanese officials such as Oda and presented to the Americans during September and October 1945, which proved to be a crucial period for Korea's future.[2] The Japanese did not prepare these documents to promote U.S. goodwill toward Koreans. In fact, an effort to discredit Koreans had already been started by the Japanese well before U.S. forces reached the peninsula. Japanese tactics were effective. By the time the U.S. officials arrived in Korea, they had a strong propensity to distrust Koreans and rely exclusively on Japanese for information. According to Japanese sources,[3] the first radio contact between Japanese authorities in Seoul and the twenty-fourth Corps in Okinawa was made on August 31. The material is silent on what was reported to Okinawa about Korean activities. Did the Japanese leave no record for fear that some day Koreans might see it? U.S. records show that the Japanese launched a fierce smear campaign that characterized Koreans as a lawless mob bent on obstruction of whatever the U.S. forces might do in Korea. A flood of messages poured out of Seoul to Okinawa. In Bruce Cumings' words, "The Occupation command on Okinawa hearkened more to the Japanese definition of the mise en scene in Korea than to whatever passed for established American policy on Korea,"[4] such as the Cairo Declaration, which promised Korea would be treated as a nation to be set free in due course.

How else could the U.S. command have reacted? On September 1, General Kozuki Yoshio, commander of the Japanese forces in Korea, radioed from Seoul, "There are communists and independence agitators among Koreans who are plotting to take advantage of the situation to disturb peace and order here." In other messages on that day and the next two, Kozuki warned of possible sabotage of the U.S. landing in Korea by "red" labor unions and told of "Korean mob violence against the police, theft of munitions, and strikes." He expressed his eager desire to meet the U.S. forces as soon as possible so he could be extricated from his "difficult position."[5]

These Japanese messages from Seoul must have had a decisive influence on Hodge. On September 4, when his twenty-fourth Corps was about to embark, Hodge instructed his officers that Korea "is an enemy of the United States," and therefore "subject to the provisions and terms of surrender." Needless to say, altruism was not part of the reason why U.S. forces came to Korea. The cold war had already begun, and the prime U.S. objective in Korea was to form a bulwark against communism; liberating Koreans was only an incidental consideration.

U.S. forces considered the journey to Inchon as dangerous as the European D-Day landing on Omaha Beach. A leaflet dropped in Korea on September 10 in Gen. Douglas MacArthur's name warned that any Korean who harmed either Japanese or American personnel would be punished by death. The Normandy landing was undertaken to save France and destroy the Nazis, but the landing at Inchon seemed to be to save the Japanese and destroy Korea.

To many Koreans this was reminiscent of the time earlier in this century when President Theodore Roosevelt extended a helping hand to Japan in its contest with Russia over hegemony in Korea. A host of "patriotic" Japanese were then engaged in winning the hearts of U.S. citizens to their cause.

Okakura Tenshin was one of those Japanese. Even today he is regarded as a towering intellectual and a leading philosopher of the Meiji period (1868-1912). He wrote several books in polished English, including *The Ideals of the East*, and *The Story of Tea*. The Japanese versions are still regarded as classics in Japan. However, the work that made the author's reputation is *The Awakening of Japan*, published in 1904.[6] Okakura's argument centered on the claim that Japan's rule over Korea was manifest destiny, a historical imperative. Mobilizing his extensive knowledge of pseudo-history, Okakura confidently declared that Korea was "originally a Japanese province" because "Empress Zhingo of third century Japan led an invasion to the peninsula and established Japanese sovereignty over the country." Okakura even claimed that the mythological Japanese god Susanoo-no-mikoto was the father of the Korean ancestral deity, Tan'gun.[7]

Okakura concluded that "Japan is compelled to regard our ancient domain of Korea as lying within our lines of legitimate national defense...because Korea lies like a dagger pointed toward the heart of Japan," and that "starvation awaits the ever-increasing population of Japan if it be deprived of its legitimate outlet in the sparsely cultivated area of Korea" and the lands beyond.[8]

Okakura made these claims in the same book in which he wrote: "The very nature of our civilization prohibits aggression against foreign nations."[9] He added that it was utterly inconceivable that "Japan should be animated by the same spirit of aggrandizement of European nations that has often led them into war."[10]

The Japanese disinformation campaign at the turn of the century proved a great success. The notion that Koreans were cowards and the Japanese full of martial virtues was deeply instilled in the minds of the U.S. decision-makers. In January 1905 President Theodore Roosevelt wrote to Secretary of State John Hay that "we cannot possibly interfere for Korea against Japan," adding also that "Koreans could not strike one blow in their own defense."[11] Six months later, Roosevelt had his secretary of war, William Howard Taft, conclude the infamous Taft-Katsura Agreement. In a memorandum, kept secret until 1924, Washington recognized Korea as a Japanese protectorate and Tokyo recognized U.S. sovereignty in the Philippines. The Taft-Katsura Agreement is not a bit of bygone history; it is directly relevant to the contemporary situation in the Philippines as well as in Korea.

However, let us return to General Harris and his thirty men in Seoul, courteously guided by Oda Yasuma and other Japanese, on that day in September 1945.

The advance party's mission was to secure billets, hospitals, and warehouses for the main units to follow. The Japanese offered facilities in center city and at a meeting informed the U.S. party that all the pertinent documents for government administration had already been prepared and would be submitted the following morning. Given the short, simple agenda, the meeting should have ended quickly, but it did not. It was 3:30 a.m. when it finally adjourned.[12]

Rather than a meeting, it actually was a party staged by senior Japanese military and government officials. It turned into "a glorious drunken brawl with Japanese, which lasted for several days."[13] Any Korean who approached the U.S. personnel was "summarily shown the door with a minimum of courtesy."[14]

The highlight of this affair came the following morning. At ten o'clock Endo Ryusaburo, chief administrator of Political Affairs, received the U.S. dignitaries, including Gen. Harris and Col. Reamer Argo. Gen. Harris explained his intention to the Japanese: the structure and the personnel of the colonial administration would be kept intact to rule the southern half of Korea. Surprised and elated, Endo asked what would be his and the governor-general's function. Harris explicitly stated that the Japanese would be allowed a free hand, and the U.S. commander would confine himself to "the role of control and supervision" of a joint U.S.-Japanese administration.[15]

Harris declined Endo's request to put the statement in writing, and events thereafter prevented implementation of the Harris-Endo agreement. But imagine Endo's exhilaration at the prospect of retaining Korea as an "original province" of the Japanese empire. Barely three months earlier, in May 1945, Japan had informed the Soviet Union that it wanted to terminate the war and requested Moscow's good offices. As a concession for assistance, Japan promised to cede the Kurile Islands and southern Sakhalin to the Soviet Union. However, the concession was conditional on her right to retain Korea.[16] Of course, Japan was unable to retain Korea, since the Potsdam Declaration stipulated that the Japanese sovereignty would be limited to the four main islands of the archipelago. But it should be noted that in the Japanese mind, Korea was and still is more a part of greater Japan than the Kurile Islands and southern Sakhalin.

The Harris-Endo encounter in the very first hours of the U.S. arrival in Korea testifies to their shared disdain for Koreans. It also foreshadowed the present situation where South Korea plays its role within the framework of formal and informal political and economic understandings between Japan and the United States. It might be said that South Korea's destiny was set.

II

The attempted implementation of the Harris-Endo agreement was met by violent Korean opposition, which caused the *New York Times* to ask editorially, "Are we to be 'soft' with the colonial riffraff of Japan and hard with the people we have come to set free?"[17] Soon thereafter, the Japanese officials were ordered by the U.S. Military Government to leave Korea.

The process by which pro-Japanese collaborators became the core of the power structure in 1945-48 and subsequently moved en masse into Syngman Rhee's government deserves a brief explanation. These postwar events are part of every Korean's historical legacy and they shape today's attitude of the ruler and the ruled, constantly challenging the legitimacy not only of the regime but also of the state itself.

In October 1946, a large-scale revolt swept through Taegu and neighboring counties. Rebels stormed Taegu police stations and hacked policemen to shreds. The Korean police responded with a brutal ferocity that exceeded even that of the Japanese.

One of the leaders of the revolt was the son of Prof. Yi Yun Jai of Yonhi College (predecessor of Yonsei University in Seoul), a well-known scholar who was murdered in prison during World War II. Prof. Yi's "crime" had been a secret compilation of a dictionary of the Korean language, which had been outlawed by the Japanese. He was taken by the police to Hamhung, a city in northern Korea, for interrogation. In the winter of 1943 he died of torture inflicted by a Korean working for the Japanese police. After Japan's defeat in 1945, the torturer came south and was promoted by the Americans to be chief of the Central Taegu Police Station. When Yi's son learned of this, he organized a mob to get the man who killed his father.

Later, after young Yi's arrest, many Koreans defended him, citing his "justifiable grievances." But the pro-Japanese bureaucrats were already in firm control of the prosecution and judiciary. Also, to the U.S. Military Government a rebel was a rebel. The young man was summarily sent to the gallows.

There were many other reasons for the Taegu revolt—inflation, unemployment, and a rice shortage. But the biggest single factor was resentment against the former collaborators employed by the USMG. About half of the twenty-thousand-man colonial police force had been Koreans. Trained in the art of torture, they had suppressed the Korean nationalist movement for Japan. Ordinary Koreans hated them more than they hated the Japanese.

Mark Gayn, a *Chicago Sun* correspondent, visited Korea in October 1946. He reported a meeting with Col. William Maglin, Chief of the Police Division, USMG. Col. Maglin said, "Many people question the wisdom of keeping men trained by the Japanese. But many men are born policemen. We felt that if they did a good job for the Japanese, they would do a good job for us. It would be unfair to drive men trained by the Japanese out of the force."[18]

According to the same correspondent, the U.S. military had set up in Korea "a government by [pro-Japanese] collaborators representing a conspiracy of insufferable corruption," and "a police state so savage in its suppression of man's elementary liberties that it was difficult to find a parallel for it."[19] When the Republic of Korea was established in 1948, this state apparatus went to Syngman Rhee.

Noh Dok Sul was probably one of the most infamous people who served the Japanese police. Decorated many times during his twenty-seven years with the Japanese police, Noh attained the prestigious post of chief of the Sonkyori Police Station in Pyongyang, although his formal education had ended at the second grade. After Japan's defeat, Noh went to work for the USMG. As soon as he was installed as chief, Investigation Section, Metropolitan Police, Seoul, Noh began arresting "pinkos," just as he had ferreted out "futei senjin" (Japanese police jargon for disloyal Koreans). Torture was standard practice against any Korean with a critical mind. During the severe winter of 1947, Noh killed a prisoner in his torture chamber and dumped the body into the Han River.

For this crime and his conduct during the Japanese period, Noh was arrested in January 1949 by the Special Commission for the Investigation of Collaborators. This was a congressional agency given independent power by the constitution to investigate notorious collaborators. Punishments included the death penalty. Noh's arrest triggered a violent confrontation between Syngman Rhee and the commission. Rhee demanded Noh's immediate release. The commission refused. Rhee said state security required trained men like Noh, regardless of their past conduct. The commission responded that punishment of those like Noh was an absolute necessity if the new republic was to enjoy popular support and inspire patriotism. But Rhee won. In June 1949 the commission was crushed by the police. Rhee later imprisoned not the collaborators but the commission members, all elected parliamentarians, on framed charges of working for North Korea.

For the assassination of his political foes, center-left Lyuh Woon Hyung and nationalist Kim Ku, Rhee mobilized police thugs like Noh Dok Sul or men like Kim Ji Wung, a dope peddler and an agent for the Japanese Kwangtung Army.

Lyuh Woon Hyung tried to bring moderate leftist and rightist elements into a coalition to form a unified government. Kim Ku was opposed to the separate elections sponsored by the United Nations and traveled to the North in search of a last chance to prevent the permanent division of Korea. If a coalition movement by Lyuh or Kim Ku had succeeded in developing a unified Korea, Syngman Rhee and his ally Kim Song Su feared they would have no place in it.

The two murder cases of Lyuh Woon Hyung and Kim Ku were shrouded in thick mystery during Rhee's time. Many additional murders were committed by such state institutes as Tukmudai (Special Investigative Corps) and Honchong (General Headquarters of the Military Police). Today, nearly two-score years after the incidents, few Koreans would doubt that the ultimate culprit was Syngman Rhee himself.[20]

The wealthy landed gentry, represented by Kim Song Su, whom Mark Gayn called a political Jekyll and Hyde, were also involved. During the colonial period the Japanese, for efficient political control and economic exploitation, had carefully nurtured a thin layer of Korean landlords. This landed class was indispensable to colonial rule. Over the years these Koreans developed a Machiavellian ability to ingratiate themselves with those in power. Within a month after the arrival of U.S. forces, Kim Song Su had himself appointed chairman of the advisory group to the USMG. This was an acrobatic feat of the highest skill since, until the day of Japan's defeat, Kim had served the Japanese as a member of the Central Advisory Council of the Governor-General. The pro-Japanese element led by Kim Song Su found expedient allies in the police and the army, both of which were composed of former collaborators. They worked together to rid the country of nationalists such as Lyuh Woon Hyung and Kim Ku.

By the late 1940s South Koreans felt that "liberation" from the Japanese had brought not freedom but a complete reversal of the moral order. True to the word of the fifth chapter of Isaiah, the new Korean rulers, supported by the United States this time, called evil good, and good evil; turned darkness into light and light into darkness; made sweetness bitter and bitterness sweet. Koreans gradually sensed a *haan*. The word means a kind of hard knot formed from accumulated frustration and resentment due to grievous wrongs done to a person. The knot demands *puri*, the psychological resolution of catharsis. Otherwise, the person explodes like a volcano.

Syngman Rhee's government was incapable of redressing popular grievances. Yet he pushed through one illegal constitutional amendment after another in order to perpetuate his corrupt power. The abuse of his presidential power reached its zenith when he ran for a fourth term at the age of eighty-five in 1960 and rigged the election to a degree unprecedented in Korea. The accumulated *haan* developed into the April 1960 Student Revolution that toppled Rhee's regime and led to a new government.

For the first time since the inception of the Republic of Korea, there was a ray of hope. There might be possible a democratic state in which the people were truly sovereign. The students shouted, "Go north, come south, meet at Panmunjom." They questioned established authority: "Whose land is this anyway? Who can stop us from traveling back and forth between the north and south?" It was a period of dramatic catharsis of *haan*. But it was short lived. Park Chung Hee seized power at gunpoint in 1961 and ruled brutally.

III

For nearly forty years, the government of South Korea has told the people that it is the only lawful government on the peninsula, and that this legitimacy was bestowed by the United Nations. The legal basis for this claim is General Assembly Resolution 195 (III) of December 1948 adopted by the UN body convened in Paris. This document was drafted by James Plimsoll of the Australian delegation, which was headed by Dr. H.V. Evatt who was also serving as president of the assembly at the time. The inescapable impression is that the resolution's wording is deliberately vague and misleading. It seems to be a compromise between Plimsoll and John Foster Dulles, head of the U.S. delegation. Dulles wanted to present "the government of the Republic of Korea" not as a body with limited jurisdiction but as a "national government" fulfilling the promise of the Cairo commitment, provided in General Assembly Resolution 112 (II), adopted on November 14, 1947.

Judging from U.S. policy at the time and the cold war, Dulles obviously wanted the world to believe the following four points: (1) the UNTCOK (United Nations Temporary Commission on Korea) fully consulted with all political elements in Korea, and they had endorsed the separate elections held on May 10, 1948; (2) UNTCOK was able to observe the elections and judged that they were free, unhampered either by the U.S. military or the indigenous police and armed forces commanded by the USMG; (3) since the elections were a valid expression of the free will of the people and were held in an area that had nearly two-thirds of the entire Korean population, the Republic of Korea that resulted from these elections should be recognized as the sole legitimate polity with jurisdiction over all of the peninsula; (4) the other "government" in northern Korea, the Democratic People's Republic of Korea, was presented in a resolution submitted by Czechoslovakia and supported by other communist countries and is, therefore, illegal.

There were many discrepancies between the U.S. contentions and the facts known to the Interim Commission. First, even such prominent political figures in the rightist camp as Kim Ku and Kim Kyu Sik informed Krishna Menon, the Indian chairman of UNTCOK, that they were absolutely opposed to a separate election sponsored by the United Nations. Kim Ku stated publicly that a separate southern government would be a form of permanent trusteeship administered by a single power, the United States, and therefore even worse than the five-year trusteeship by four powers, which he had staunchly opposed. Both Kim Ku and Kim Kyu Sik boycotted the UN-sponsored election.

Second, of twenty-four South Korean rightists of various shadings whom UNTCOK consulted, only nine indicated a willingness to cooperate with a separate election. The rest either opposed it or expressed no opinion (opposed eleven, no opinion four) The temporary commission was unable to contact any leftist leaders since most were "outlawed, imprisoned, dead, exiled or tortured into silence."[21]

Third, observation of the elections by UNTCOK was a physical impossibility. UNTCOK never had a staff of more than thirty non-Korean members. UNTCOK could not "observe" an area of forty thousand square miles with a population of twenty million.

Fourth, the principle of separate elections was first adopted on February 26, 1948, by the Interim Commission of the General Assembly after intensive U.S. lobbying. The Interim Commission instructed UNTCOK in Seoul to proceed with separate elections that would lead to the establishment of "a national government."

Surprisingly, Australia and Canada, the two staunchest allies of the United States, rebuffed the UN instructions. The concept of a "national government" in the southern half of the Korean peninsula was a semantic contradiction. This was not the form of Korean government promised by the Cairo Declaration. Furthermore, the commission lacked the manpower to verify such elections. The Canadian representative, Dr. George Patterson, during a meeting held in Seoul on March 11, declared the assembly instruction both "unwise and unconstitutional." The Australian representative, Mr. S. H. Jackson, opposed the elections on the additional grounds that "the elections would surely be boycotted by all parties in Korea except the extreme right group" and this was "a vital development which might have altered the views of the Interim Committee had it appeared earlier."[22]

Finally, after heated debates within UNTCOK, the issue was put to a vote. Of the eight members of the commission, France and Syria abstained. Of the remaining six, China (Taiwan), the Philippines and El Salvador were expected to support any U.S. position. Canada and Australia were clearly opposed. Therefore, the final outcome depended on how the chairman, Krishna Menon, voted.

Menon had pointed out the semantic contradictions in the concept of a national government of South Korea, saying that "a separate government, which may be established in South Korea, cannot be a national government, as defined in the resolution of the General Assembly."[23] On January 15, 1948, on leaving for Korea, Menon told the Interim Commission of his unequivocal opposition to separate elections: "Separate elections in the South would only deepen the present schism between the two Koreas and may result in the tragedy of permanent division."[24]

On arrival in southern Korea, he also made the following remarks in a radio speech on January 21: "Korea is an inseparably homogeneous nation speaking the same language and sharing the same heritage. If there ever was a unified nation in the oldest days of human history, it was Korea."[25] Menon also confided to Kim Ku in a meeting on January 22: "What was made by God as one entity should not be separated by men....The division line must be eliminated. Without unification, there will be no independence."[26]

However, in a move that must have flabbergasted everyone, Menon endorsed holding a separate election. The Republic of Korea was created by a four to two vote, due to this strange about-face by Menon. The drama that caused Menon's change of heart was known to many Koreans, but not to the rest of the world.

Menon later wrote in his memoirs,[27] "This [his tour of duty in Seoul] was perhaps the only occasion in my service when I allowed my heart to prevail over my head." The woman who touched his heart was the beauteous Mo Yun Suk (Marion Moh), a well-known poet who was "dearest of all the friendly Koreans" to Menon who "spent many a hallowed hour (with her), talking not of politics...but of such elemental things as the sun and moon and stars, love and grief and joy." She wrote about her friendship with Menon: "The creation of the Republic of Korea was intimately related to my friendship with Krishna. Had there been no such friendship, there would have been no separate elections and no chance for Dr. Syngman Rhee to become president of the republic."[28] Her condescension to Rhee is understandable, especially if the "friendship" with the UNTCOK chairman was less a spontaneous romance than an arranged affair agreed to by Mo at Rhee's behest.

During the elections some 323 people were killed and ten thousand arrested.[29] The paramilitary Homeland Protection Corps (Hyangbo-dan) created by the USMG, was used to control the elections. At the same time, a "pacification campaign" was in full swing on Cheju Island where a violent revolt had broken out in protest against the separate elections. The campaign, launched by combined U.S. and South Korean forces under the command of Brig. Gen. William L. Roberts, lasted until 1955. By that time the island's population of three hundred thousand had shrunk by one-third.

With these developments in mind, let us return to the General Assembly Resolution 195 (III). The resolution says nothing about the protests and violence accompanying the elections. Without the frills and legal jargon, the document has three main points: (1) that a government was created in southern Korea through elections held in that area; (2) that the elections were observed by the UNTCOK and judged to be free; and (3) that therefore this government having the control and jurisdiction over the southern half of the peninsula should be declared lawful. The last paragraph's comment, "This is the only such government in Korea," is both redundant and misleading. UNTCOK's claims that the elections were the "valid expression of free will," and that it had made satisfactory observations, were unsupportable. This was the "legitimacy" the United Nations bestowed on the South Korean government, and was later persuaded to defend in a war that killed and maimed millions.

The United States was founded on the principle that legitimacy is derived from the people, never from an external source. This is enunciated in the Virginia Bill of Rights and endorsed by the Declaration of Independence. How different it was with the Republic of Korea. When John Foster Dulles, a U.S. citizen, ardently bestowed legitimacy on the Republic of Korea, invoking the authority of the United Nations, did he not know that the whole exercise was a contrivance and not based on the true will of the people?

An increasing number of South Koreans have come to realize that the UN flag that flutters in the skies of their country is legally fraudulent and morally indefensible. The least the world community can do is to demand that the U.S. government lower the UN flag to show that the regime in Seoul is not "the only legal government." This will be a meaningful first step in helping Koreans achieve their national reunification.

IV

Gen. Park Chung Hee ruled the Republic of Korea—from his military coup d'etat in May 1961 until his ignominious death in October 1979—for eighteen years, half the new state's existence. Understanding Park's background and mentality will assist comprehension of Korea today.

When the news of Park's coup d'etat reached Tokyo, a number of Japanese undoubtedly knew him. They were ex-military officers of the Kwantung Army and men like Kishi Nobusuke, who ruled Japan's puppet state of Manchukuo (Manchuria) during the height of Japanese militarism in the the 1930s. They would have been able to recognize from photographs that Park Chung Hee was Lt. Takagi Masao who graduated from Manchukuo Military Academy in 1940 and completed his training in the elite Japanese Military Academy in 1942. Some of them might have remembered Cadet Park's graduation pledge to the puppet Emperor Fu Yi: "I am determined to dedicate my life, which will fall like a cherry blossom, for this sacred war to establish the Greater East Asia Co-prosperity Sphere."[30]

While in the Military Academy in Tokyo, Park tried so arduously to hide his Korean traits that Gen. Nagumo Chuichi, the superintendent of the Academy, told the assembled cadets, "Cadet Takagi may be Korean by birth. But in his loyalty to the Emperor, he is more Japanese than an ordinary Japanese." Park thus earned the nickname from his classmates of "tokuto Nipponjin" (super-Japanese).[31]

Takagi Masao was Park's Japanese name at the Tokyo military academy, but he used the name Okamoto Minoru while serving in Manchuria. This suggests he was involved in intelligence activities against Korean guerrillas operating in the region. The Japanese used Korean turncoats to suppress Korean armed resistance.

In 1961, the Japanese reacted swiftly to the takeover by Park Chung Hee. His coup took place on May 16. Prime Minister Ikeda Hayato flew to Washington on June 19 and conferred with President John F. Kennedy on June 21. One major item on the agenda was Korea. Ikeda had the following to say to Kennedy: "Ever since the prehistoric time of Okuninushino-mikoto (brother to the mythological deity Susanoo-no-mikoto), Korea has been intimately related to Japan, and its geographical proximity holds vital importance to our security. Should red flags ever be raised on the southern tip of the peninsula, the peace and security of Japan would be in jeopardy. Japan is compelled to pay strict attention to the emerging military regime which is avowedly anti-communist. The new regime may not necessarily be democratic. Yet Japan will have to negotiate with this regime for diplomatic normalization. We cannot afford to wait until a more democratic government turns up."[32]

The United States was initially reluctant to accept Gen. Park as the new ruler. The Pentagon knew that Park was once sentenced to life in prison for involvement in the 1948 Yosu insurgency. Organized by leftist elements in the South Korean Army, this was a revolt against the U.S.-backed military expedition sent to suppress the popular uprising on Cheju Island. Park later won his freedom by divulging the names of the insurgents, including his own elder brother, Park Sang Hee, who was executed by a firing squad.[33] Washington thus had reason to suspect Park's loyalty.

Presumably, Prime Minister Ikeda's argument was too compelling for Kennedy to resist, however. Park consolidated his position and visited Washington at Kennedy's invitation in November. U.S. support of Park's place at the pinnacle of power was influenced largely by the crucial intervention of Premier Ikeda.

The Japanese never forgot this. In February 1962 former Prime Minister Yoshida Shigeru, on his return from a trip to the United States, said, "Japan will have to establish roots in the Korean soil in the same way that former Governor General Ito Hirobumi did."[34] Yoshida made this confident statement on the strength of encouragement by President Kennedy. According to Yoshida, Kennedy said, "Since the United States is short on experience with Korea, we hope Japan will help us out."[35]

Takasugi Shin'ichi headed the Japanese delegation to the seventh Korean-Japanese Conference which led to the Basic Treaty between the two countries, concluded under strong U.S. pressure, in June 1965. In January 1965 Takasugi called a press conference at the Foreign Ministry and said, "Japanese rule over Korea was a good thing for Koreans. Certainly, we outlawed their language and imposed Japanese-style names. But these actions stemmed only from our good intentions. We wanted to give them the status of true Japanese. Unfortunately, the war frustrated our efforts, but Korea today would be a more civilized country if Japan had ruled it another twenty years."[36]

Japanese support to Park Chung Hee was direct and overt. For example, in Park's three successful presidental campaigns, twice against the former president Yun Bo Son (1963, 1967) and once against Kim Dae Jung (1971), money from Tokyo poured into Park's coffers. Ono Banboku, an elder Japanese politician and vice-president of the ruling Liberal Democratic Party (LDP), attended Park's inauguration ceremony. Ono expressed his satisfaction at Park's election by saying at the airport in Tokyo, "President Park and I are like son and father."

The comment made Park a laughing-stock in South Korea, but it seemed reasonable to Ono. Even before the formal signing of the 1965 normalization treaty, which provided eight hundred million dollars in Japanese aid, a substantial portion of the money had already been transferred to Park. This money was probably crucial in Park's electoral victory in 1963. Who could blame Ono for his paternalistic condescension to the South Korean president?

The third election in 1971 was particularly crucial to the Japanese. Park pushed through a constitutional amendment in 1969 to make a third term "legal." The election was a prelude to the 1972 *Yushin* (revitalizing) reforms designed to make Park president for life. Tokyo made an all-out effort to assure his victory.

Support was provided in the form of rice and cars for the Seoul subway system. In 1969 and 1970, Tokyo shipped to Korea a total of 650,000 tons of rice on extremely lenient long-term credit terms, which provided that repayment be made in installments over twenty years, after a ten-year grace period. To Park's regime this was a bonanza. Since the interest rate was set at five percent per annum, the government earned billions of *won* by depositing the money from sale of the rice in commercial banks in Korea that paid at least twenty percent interest.

The three hundred subway cars delivered by Japanese firms were another windfall to Park's campaign. Takasugi Shin'ichi was the head of the Overseas Economic Cooperation Fund, a government agency, when he conferred with Park in Seoul in 1970. Actual delivery was made in 1973 and later. But a consortium of four conglomerates (Mitsubishi Shoji, Mitsui Bussan, Marubeni, and Nissho-Iwai) paid millions of dollars to Park's political machine in time to finance his election campaign. The payments were possible because the price was padded to about twice the actual commercial value.

After the election, South Korean newspapers reported that the total amount of money spent by Park's party exceeded thirty billion won or about $100 million. In the U.S. context, this would be equivalent to a presidential candidate's spending six or seven hundred million dollars. More serious to Koreans than these preposterous expenditures was the fact that his election funds were provided predominantly by Japanese.

In October 1979 *haan* exploded again in the fierce anti-Park revolt in the Pusan-Masan area. With unrest about to spread to Seoul, Kim Jai Kyu, Park's closest confidant and the chief of the South Korean CIA, chose the only way he saw to avoid imminent disaster. He shot his boss on the night of October 26. The finger that pulled the trigger was Kim's, but the force that compelled the shooting was the frustration of the people of South Korea.

For a second time, *haan* found an outlet, but again, the resolution was temporary. Gen. Chun Doo Hwan, after killing thousands in Kwangju in May 1980, emerged as strongman with the blessing of Tokyo and Washington. Chun was the first foreign leader invited to Washington to meet the new president, Ronald Reagan. In September 1984 Chun became the first South Korean president to visit Tokyo as a state guest. His objective was to gain some legitimacy with a pat on the back from the Japanese emperor. The emperor's remarks may have been welcome to Chun, but they rubbed Korean nationalism the wrong way.

V

South Korea is usually viewed as a great success story. Those who disagree have little credibility. South Korea today certainly looks different from twenty years ago. The giant steel mills, shipyards, petrochemical complexes, towering modern buildings, and superhighways that have altered the Korean landscape are impressive. But the success does not touch the lives of all Koreans.

The rapid growth of the South Korean economy started in the 1960s with the economic "assistance" of Japan and the United

States. Soon after diplomatic relations between Seoul and Tokyo were normalized in 1965 and economic cooperation was set in motion, Yatsugi Kazuo, a prominent Japanese conservative, predicted at the annual conference of the Japan-ROK Cooperation Commission (Nikkan Kyoryoku Iinkai) held in Seoul in April 1970 that South Korea would eventually be integrated into Japan's Kansai (Osaka-Kyoto) economic zone. Yatsugi's prediction has been proven accurate.

In the ten-year period following diplomatic normalization (1965-75), South Korea's imports from Japan accounted for forty percent of total imports, while exports to Japan were about twenty-five percent of the total. In 1976 South Korea's gross national product was approximately twenty billion dollars; trade volume with Japan was five billion dollars (exports $1.8 billion, imports $3.2 billion). Thus, approximately one fourth of South Korea's GNP was generated through trade with Japan. Japan's influence touches every facet of South Korean society, and inevitably spreads to political and military fields as well.

Mr. Yun Bo Sun, former president of the republic, said the following to the court that tried him for signing a "Declaration of Independence" in 1976: "The economic domination of Japan over Korea is now spreading into the field of politics and military. Thus, the realization of our national unification is seriously threatened by the Park regime which, in connivance with her ultra-nationalistic element, seeks a closer military alliance with Japan."[37]

Japan benefits enormously from these relationships at the expense of South Korea. Japan's trade volume with South Korea might seem to be insignificant. Annual exports to South Korea are approximately 4.4 percent of total Japanese exports, while imports account for about half that figure. These ratios remain fairly constant year after year. However, they do not reflect the real significance of Korean trade for Japan's economy. In 1976, for instance, Japan's trade surplus with South Korea was $977 million while its total foreign trade surplus was $2.4 billion; more than forty percent of the surplus was from trade with South Korea. In 1975, Japan had a trade deficit of $2.2 billion. However, it had $937 million surplus in trade with South Korea.[38] Japan's trade with South Korea is indispensable to its own prosperity.

These figures are not for one or two exceptional years. For the sixteen-year period from 1966 to 1982, the accumulated total of Japan's foreign trade surplus was $27.4 billion. In the same period, Japan accrued a surplus from South Korea of $23.9 billion. Thus, the trade with South Korea was so lucrative to Japan that it accounted for 87.4 percent of the total surplus.[39]

One more statistical example might shed some light on this relationship. In 1978, the trade deficit for South Korea vis-a-vis Japan topped three billion dollars. In terms of GNP, the scale of the U.S. economy at the time was about 70 times larger than South Korea's. Proportionally calculated, three billion for South Korea would be equivalent to more than two hundred billion dollars for the United States. But in 1977, when concern in the United States over the deluge of Japanese merchandise was already acute, the U.S. trade deficit with Japan was a mere eight billion dollars.

Impressed by the outward appearance of progress and modernization, foreigners often fail to see the costs of this modernization to the Korean people. Needless to say, not all Koreans are exploited. Exploitation by outsiders has created a stratum of the indigenous population with a high stake in the system.

Nevertheless, in his book *How Will Unification Be Achieved?* the Presbyterian activist The Rev. Moon Ik Hwan says that 0.3 percent of the total population (approximately one hundred thousand individuals) control forty-five percent of South Korea's wealth and that thirty major corporations, controlled largely by these individuals, account for seventy-three percent of South Korea's GNP.[40]

The "T.K. Letter from Seoul" in the February 1985 issue of *Sekai*, a monthly journal published in Tokyo, says that fifty-nine percent of urban workers (total number 4,380,000) earn less than a hundred thousand won ($110) per month for a fifty-eight-hour week and that the women textile worker's daily wage is between two thousand ($2.00) and twenty-five hundred won ($2.49). By keeping wages low and prohibiting effective union organizing for better working conditions, the Korean government can offer the world's businesses a profitable, "stable" climate in which to invest.

VI

The Korean situation once again recalls the Exodus. The children of Israel, unable to bear the suffering in the wilderness, wanted to return to Egypt and their former servitude. As slaves, they could at least slake their thirst from the Nile and lose their hunger with the crumbs Egyptians contemptuously threw them. They grumbled against Moses and Aaron, "Would to God we had died by the hand of the Lord in the land of Egypt, when we sat by the flesh pots and when we did eat bread to the full." (Exodus Ch. 16, verse 3)

South Korean society is divided today between those who advocate a return to "the land of Egypt," and those who insist on continuing the arduous journey to the promised land. Those looking backward are supported by foreign powers that have a stake in the status quo. Particularly for Japan, a unified and independent Korea would be an awesome rival. In addition, the Japanese may still consider the Korean Peninsula a "dagger pointed toward the heart of Japan."

Many Japanese have spoken of the desirability of keeping Korea divided. The late Ushiba Nobuhiko, formerly Japanese ambassador to the United States, declared, "The Korea most desirable to Japan is a Korea permanently divided."[41] Compare this statement with that of Gen. Oyama Iwao, Japanese Army Chief of Staff, in 1904: "Korea is our (Japan's) bed; I cannot bear the thought that someone else might sleep in it."[42] Japanese attitudes about Korea have not changed in eighty years.

I may seem obsessed with Japan. I do not deny it, but I feel that Japan poses the biggest obstacle to the unification of Korea. Let it be recalled that I promised to describe the Korean ethos. This seems to be the place to dwell on it. South Korea is armed to the teeth, deploying six hundred thousand soldiers against their blood kin, while Japan, firmly positioned in our front yard, is dictating to us what to do and not do, as a thinly disguised colonial master.

In August 1985 *The Japan Times* ran an article entitled "Japan's Arrogance is Showing" by a columnist named Arjuna. The article quotes "a prominant Japanese businessman" as saying, during "the next century Japan will use Australia as a mining concession, the United States as a grain silo and Europe as a boutique." An Australian, a European or an U.S. citizen may just grimace a moment and forget it as a bad joke. Will a Korean be able to do likewise when he hears remarks like the following: "Stability of the Far East requires the establishment of the *United States of Japan*, which will include Taiwan and South Korea." The man who made this statement in 1958 is Ono Banboku, who claimed his political "paternity rights" to President Park Chung Hee.[43]

Will such a Japan sit idly by and watch benevolently as Koreans attempt to determine their own fate and achieve unification?

The primary responsibility for the division of Korea should be borne by the United States. But even the United States must be aware that it cannot maintain troops there forever to enforce the split. Washington must at least consider a policy by which the occupation troops in South Korea can be withdrawn before the situation becomes untenable. The position of U.S. troops in South Korea will become increasingly precarious. As time passes, unification will appear the only feasible option for the United States, unless it really wants to try to continue a military garrison in South Korea indefinitely, an effort doomed to eventual failure.

Would a unified Korea, neutral and non-aligned, pose a military threat to the United States? Washington knows it would not. And increasingly Washington can expect accusations from the Koreans that the presence of the U.S. troops in Korea is not for protecting Koreans from anything, but to align them and use their country in the event of a possible war with the Soviet Union.

The 1972 July 4 Declaration, endorsed by both Seoul and Pyongyang, and also approved by Washington, stipulates that Korean unification be achieved independently without external interference. Washington tacitly acknowledged that withdrawal of U.S. troops was a prerequisite to unification.

But Korean unification frightens Japan. Japan reacted strongly when President Jimmy Carter attempted to implement his campaign pledge of 1976 to withdraw U.S. troops from South Korea. A systematic campaign waged by the Japanese government to prevent Carter from carrying out that promise is indicated in the partial list of government officials who attacked the policy in the Japanese and U.S. news media in November 1976:

- Kosaka Zentaro, Foreign Minister, interview in "Newsweek," Nov. 1.
- Togo Fumihiko, Ambassador to Washington, speech in Minneapolis, reported in *The Japan Times*, November 10.
- Nishiyama Akira, Ambassador to Seoul, interview in the *Yomiuri Shimbun*, November 9.
- Maruyama Ko, Deputy Minister of the Self Defense Agency, speech at the Japan Press Club, reported in *Asahi Shimbun*, November 9.
- Kubo Takuya, Maruyama's predecessor, essay in the *Asahi Shimbun*, November 11.

This chorus of opposition asserted that troop withdrawal would create a dangerous vacuum vis-a-vis Japan's security. Foreign Minister Kosaka Zentaro claimed U.S. troops were necessary to restrain North Koreans, whom he called mentally immature. The Japanese ambassador to Seoul, Nishiyama Akira, said South Koreans were incapable of practicing democracy in the same manner as Japanese and, therefore, the human rights problem in South Korea should not be a reason for troop withdrawal. To Nishiyama, Park was the best president South Koreans could possibly hope to have.

If this overt campaign was of such intensity, there must have been enormous covert pressure from Tokyo. President Carter reneged on his election pledge. The announced reason for canceling withdrawal plans was that a reassessment of North Korean military capabilities had shown them higher than previously estimated. This sudden Pentagon discovery seems a flimsy pretext. Many Koreans believe that the real cause was Japanese pressure, especially that of such persons as Ushiba Nobuhiko, who advocated a permanently divided Korea. He was the co-chairman of the influential Japan-American Advisory Council and perfectly positioned to influence Washington, particularly about Korea.

VII

Given such obstacles, on what basis do I believe that a joyous reconciliation is possible? The history of East Asia since the middle of the nineteenth century might be summarized as a process of destruction under the impact of the West and subsequent resurrection into individual nation states. Until the nineteenth Century, East Asia was a world unto itself, with China at its hub. East Asia civilization was not unlike medieval Europe centered on Rome from which popes prevailed over secular rulers.

The East Asian world began to crumble when a few British gunboats attacked Kwantung in 1840 and forced once-mighty China to kneel ignominiously before the West. The Opium War (1840-42) set off a chain reaction throughout East Asia. French troops landed at Cam Ranh Bay and occupied Saigon in 1858. The destruction of traditional Vietnam had begun.

Japan was also destabilized by the West. Commodore Matthew C. Perry's squadron sailed into Uraga Bay in 1853 to demand commercial relations. The traditional Japan and Tokugawa Shogunate in power for 250 years began to crumble. But Japan was luckier than her neighbors. The French were preoccupied with the colonization of Vietnam and with the conquest of Mexico as well. The British were tied down by the Taiping Rebellion in China, the Crimean War in Russia, and the Sepoy Mutiny in India. They lacked the military force for an attack on Japan. The U.S. Civil War precluded U.S. colonization of Japan under the Manifest Destiny doctrine. Thus Japan, starting with the Meiji Restoration in 1868, became the first member of the East Asian community to transform herself into a unified, independent modern nation-state.

Luckily for Japan, the time span between the "death" of the old order and the birth of the new was only fifteen years. This timing was fortuitous for Japan but it led to hubris, and Japan became a ruthless aggressor against her Asian neighbors, often blazing the trail for Europe. Sun Yat Sen had good reason to condemn Japan as "a falcon and a hound in the service of the Westerners."

The Chinese had been humiliated by foreign interventions, but in 1912 Sun Yat Sen proclaimed a Chinese republic. It was, however, soon ripped by civil wars which were interrupted only by the shaky coalition of the Kuomintang and the Chinese Communists to defeat the Japanese invaders of China at the end of World War Two. Civil wars began again when the Japanese were defeated and it was not until 1949 that Mao Tse Tung consolidated the new nation state. Until that time, the Chinese people had endured division and disunity for 109 years.

The Vietnamese struggled for 117 years, becoming a unified nation state in 1975. As historians have noted, Asian communism has been a powerful nationalizing force, although not the only one.

Korea is the only member of the East Asian world that has not formed a postwar unified nation state. After France (1866) and the United States (1871) failed to open Korea, a Japanese gunship, Unyomaru, attacked Kanghwa Island in 1875. Traditional Korea was doomed. Thus 110 years have passed but Korea's resurrection has not yet occurred.

Will Korea remain in historical limbo forever? Certainly not. Koreans are convinced that there will be a day of rebirth into a unified nation state. A unified Korean nation state is a historical imperative. No foreign power can stop it. Any nation that tries will meet the determined resistance of the Korean people.

A shared sense of nationalism will impel the two Koreas toward each other. Reconciliation will be encouraged by common claim and antipathy toward Japan, which has, in the eyes of many, never abandoned its designs on the peninsula, its "original province." Koreans on both sides of the thirty-eighth parallel will feel increasingly that not a single life, North Korean or South Korean, should be sacrificed for the interests of the great powers. No part of the peninsula should again be a battleground where other nations pursue their strategic or economic objectives.[44]

Some people seem to believe that anti-communism is a hereditary trait of South Koreans. When Secretary of State Cyrus Vance attended Park Chung Hee's funeral in 1979, he praised South Koreans for their enthusiastic anti-communism and urged them to persist. But Vance invoked a false god. Certainly anti-communism is the raison d'etre of the South Korean state, but anti-communism is not an inborn characteristic of South Koreans.

The question then is whether Korea must await the driving force of Asian communism to achieve its aspiration of becoming again a united nation. China, Vietnam and Korea all fought against imperialism, which subjugated them to colonial humiliation. They have heard Marxism and Leninism preach the evils of imperialism. But they have seen that Asian communism is not a carbon copy of Soviet communism and that their historic experience is different from the conditions that produced Marxism or Leninism. They never denied the value of nation states nor believed in the withering of the state as Marx and Lenin did. If they had been convinced that a market economy would modernize their societies, they might well have embraced it wholeheartedly. Such an attitude has surfaced in the People's Republic of China. If U.S. citizens had realized the truth of Asian pragmatism they might not have felt compelled to fight the Chinese, Vietnamese, and North Koreans, squandering millions of human lives and exhausting their own economic resources.

Time is running out for the United States in South Korea. Many South Koreans are abandoning a pro-U.S. sentiment which was rooted in what they thought was a shared antipathy to Japanese colonialism. This is rapidly turning to vehement anti-Americanism. As nationalistic sentiment grows stronger, intensified by repression by the pro-Japanese dictators propped up by the United States, Koreans see U.S. policy as a born-again Taft-Katsura Agreement.

In South Korea the democratic movement by Christian groups and increasingly intense protests by university students are creating a radical nationalism. This consciousness, combined with democratic activism, will negate the perennial curse of extremist anti-communism which has been the most malevolent restriction on our freedom and intellectual growth.

At the outset I said I would not lay out a step-by-step process for unification. It is partly because I do not believe that the future of Korea can be fathomed by extrapolating a simple straight line from the quantifiable present factors, such as GNP. Korean history will proceed forward along a discontinuous line of an unpredictable nature.

What will a unified Korea be like? In his "Declaration of Conscience," contemporary South Korean poet Kim Chi Ha said he is unable to visualize the landscape of our Canaan. He said he would merely strive to help the Korean people find the path to it. A blueprint for the future of Korea must be drawn collectively by the people as a whole.

The interest of the four mightiest nations in the world—the United States, China, the Soviet Union, and Japan—meet at the armistice line. These powers account for forty percent of the world population, and their combined military expenditures are close to seventy percent of the global total. The Korean peninsula is not the only place where the United States has rattled its nuclear weapons against a foe not similarly armed.[45] But in "Defense Report 1983," Defense Secretary Weinberger "assured" South Koreans that, in order to occupy Soviets elsewhere, the United States would automatically launch a nuclear attack against North Korea in the event of Soviet military intervention in the Middle East. We also recall, with a shudder, what Gen. Edward Meyer, U.S. Army chief of staff, boasted in Seoul in February 1983. He said, "The use of nuclear weapons is simpler here than in Europe where consultations have to be made with fifteen different sovereign nations." If tension over Korea explodes into a major conflict, it is not only Korea that will be devastated. But if the deadly rivalry between the two Koreas can be solved by peaceful means, and the universal brotherhood envisioned by Isaiah can be realized on the Korean peninsula, all of humanity will be saved from an enormous threat.

Ham Sok Hon, revered Korean Quaker champion of democracy and unification, contends that the fate of all humanity depends on the Korean people just as the destiny of the Israelites rested on the shoulders of the lowly shepherd boy David. However this conviction strikes the reader, did not St. Paul say, "Faith is the substance of things hoped for, the evidence of things not seen"?

Notes

1. Morita, Yoshio, *Termination of the War in Korea*, [Chosen Shusenno Kiroku], (Tokyo: Gannando, 1964).
2. Cumings, Bruce, *The Origins of the Korean War*, (Princeton: Princeton University Press, 1981), Chapter 5.
3. Morita, op cit, p. 268.
4. Cumings, op cit, p. 127.
5. Ibid., Ch. 4, p. 127.
6. Okakura, Tenshin (Kakuzo), *The Awakening of Japan*, (New York: The Century Co., 1904).
7. Ibid., p. 204.
8. Ibid., p. 208.
9. Ibid., p. 202.
10. Ibid., p. 201.
11. *The Treaty of Amity and Commerce between the United States of America and Corea*, concluded in May 1882, states in its Article I, "If other powers deal unjustly with either Government, the other will exert their good offices, on being informed of the case, to bring about an amicable arrangement, thus showing their friendly feelings."
12. Morita, op. cit., p. 272.
13. Richard D. Robinson's unpublished manuscript, *Betrayal of a Nation*, kept in Harvard-Yenching Library, Harvard University.
14. Ibid., p. 15.
15. Morita, op cit, p. 273.
16. Haruki Wada, "The Soviet Policy Toward Japan," (Tokyo: Tokyo University, Institute of Social Studies, 1974).
17. *New York Times*, (Sept. 11, 1945), quoted in Cumings, op. cit., p. 494, (Footnote 19 to Chapter 5).
18. Mark Gayn, *Japan Diary*, (Charles E. Tuttle Co., Oct. 24, 1946).
19. Ibid., (November 6, 1946).
20. For further details, see "Terrorist Kim Ji-wung; A Man with One Thousand Different Faces," *Wolgan (Monthly) Chosun* (February 1983), published in Seoul.
21. Gavan McCormack, *Cold War Hot War*, (Sydney: Hale and Iremonger, 1983).

22. Ibid., p. 43.
23. McCormack, op.cit., p. 42.
24. Sun Sung Cho, *Korea in World Politics*, [Hankuk Pundansa], (Seoul: Hyongsong-sa, 1982), p. 159.
25. Nam Hon Song, ed., *Post-Liberation Korea, 1945-1975*, [Haibang Samshimnyon-sa], (Seoul: Songmun-gak, 1976).
26. Kon Ho Song, ed., *Kim Ku*, (Seoul: Hangil-sa, 1980).
27. K.P.S. Menon, *Many Worlds, An Autobiography*, (London: Oxford University Press, 1965).
28. Monthly magazine, *Shindong'a*, (March 1983).
29. McCormack, op.cit., p. 44.
30. Il Myon Kim, *Japanese and Koreans* [Nihonjin to Chosen-jin], (Tokyo: San'ichi Shobo, 1967).
31. Ibid., p. 12.
32. Kazuto Ishimura, and others, *Sengo Nihon Gaikoshi* [The Diplomatic History of Post-war Japan], (Tokyo: Sanseido, 1984), p. 329.
33. The source of this story is Adm. Yi Yong-wun (now residing in Los Angeles) who was chief of staff of the Korean navy during the Korean war. It is commonly believed that President Park's brother, Park Sang Hee was killed by the police during the Taegu Uprising in 1949. This writer, however, is inclined to put more trust in Adm. Yi's version since his elder brother, the late Gen. Yi Yong Mun from whom the admiral learned the story, was the judge who presided over the military tribunal that tried Park Chung Hee in 1948.
34. Udai Fujishima, ed., *Reflections on Japanese-Korean Relations* [Nikkan Mondai O Kangaeru], (Tokyo: Taihei Shobo, 1965).
35. *Jiyu Sekai* [The Free World], (April 1964), (Tokyo: Jiyu Sha).
36. Goro Terao, *Introduction to Korean Problems*, [Chosen Mondai Nyumon], (Tokyo: Shinnihon Shuppansha, 1965).
37. Former President Yun was indicted in 1976 by the Park regime for having signed an anti-Park manifesto announced on March 1 of that year.
38. "White Paper on International Trade," Japanese Ministry of International Trade and Industry (MITI), (1977).
39. In Ho Yu, "What is Wrong with Korean-Japanese Economic Cooperation?" [Hanil Kyongje Hyomnyok ui Pansung] in *The Theory of Unification and Liberation,* (Seoul: Hyongsong-sa, 1984).
40. Ik Huan Moon, *How Will Unification Be Achieved?* [Tongirun Otoke Kanmunghanga], (Seoul: Hakminsa, 1984).
41. *Tong'a Ilbo*, (December 16, 1984).
42. Quoted in a speech by Nakatsuka Akira, history professor at Nara Women's College, "Modern Japan and Korea," (November 17, 1984).
43. Udai Fujishima, op.cit., p. 210.
44. See "The Qualitative Changes in the Situation Around the Korean Peninsula and Our Task", by Prof. Lee, Yong Hee, *Korea Scope* (March 1984), a quarterly magazine published by the Inter-

national Christian Network for Democracy in Korea, P.O. Box 904, New York NY 10027.

45. Gerson, Joseph, ed. and the New England Regional Office of the American Friends Service Committee, *The Deadly Connection: Nuclear War and U.S. Intervention*, (Philadelphia: New Society Publishers, 1986); see especially Part V, "Third World Nuclear Triggers."

Kyungmo Chung is a Korean national and formerly a technical consultant to the South Korean government. Chung has has been a resident of Japan since 1970. He is a graduate of Emory University, and has written extensively in Japanese, English and Korean. His publications concern Korean and Japanese politics and history. He currently publishes *Siarehim*, a journal that covers issues about Korea.

Chapter 8

A FUTURE FOR KOREA
An AFSC Perspective

The preceding chapters have presented a range of viewpoints and analyses about events on the Korean peninsula and the current realities of a divided country. This final chapter provides an AFSC perspective and offers a number of suggestions that seem to speak to the current situation and give promise of opening the way to a brighter future for Korea.

The AFSC perspective reflects the Committee's Quaker roots. Because of their particular perception of the divine-human relationship, for three centuries Quakers have regarded all persons as children of God, not to be debased or destroyed for any reason under any circumstances. For them, nonviolence has been more than a tactic; it has been a way of life. They have insisted that means determine ends, and that if conflicts are to be resolved without sowing the seeds of new conflict, they must be resolved by peaceful means.

This is the philosophy, tested by the Committee's direct experience in Korea itself and around the world, that governs our approach to the tensions that plague this divided nation caught at a focal point of Great Power conflict. In Korea, we seek paths for North-South reconciliation that will lead toward reunification, shaped by the Korean people themselves on both sides of the DMZ. In our view, such an approach is not visionary; it is an attainable goal whose achievement should command the efforts of all men and women of good will.

It will not be easy. The division of Korea by the United States and the Soviet Union in 1945 at the end of World War II has in the years since been widened by war and the conflict of ideologies, and what was traditionally a single state and a single people has been split into two separate states deeply suspicious and hostile toward each other. A particularly poignant aspect of the division that goes beyond geography and politics is the reality that ten million Koreans are separated from family members on opposite sides of the thirty-eighth parallel. Despite the passage of more than forty years, the tragedy of split families remains a powerful reminder of the human consequences of the division. But it also provides a dynamic for reconciliation and reunification; in spite of all that has happened, the American Friends Service Committee has found that people in both the North and the South continue to keep alive their hopes for a better future. Indeed, we have found this hope for family reunion and national reconciliation one of the two most powerful emotions a visitor encounters in Korea today. The other is the people's profound fear of war.

This fear is exacerbated by Korea's geographic location, which makes it a locus of cold war tensions. The United States maintains nuclear weapons and forty thousand troops in the South, while both China and the Soviet Union are in a position quickly to introduce major military forces across the borders they share with North Korea. Miscalculation or escalation of a minor incident could lead to a military confrontation and renewed war between North and South. These realities are deeply troubling to a people who have known first hand the suffering that war and occupation bring.

Eloquent pleas for reunification have been made by many Koreans. In the words of Ham Sok Hon, the venerable Quaker leader in Seoul:

> The thirty-eighth parallel is an absurdity from every angle, contrary to reason, something inconceivable. There is every reason that it ought to be eliminated, and it should in fact be easy to do so, once one's mind is set on it. The thirty-eighth parallel is not a line to be resolved by the sword, but one to be settled by reason, principle of right, the heavenly way, and human character. What is required is a will to life, with the realization of what life is and what the path to life is. This is a line that can be lifted in no time.
>
> No army, however large or powerful, on either side of the line can possibly keep a nation asunder, a nation which says "We are one...." (*Queen of Suffering*, p.162)

Given such longing, made more urgent by the fear of war, what are some of the positive factors that might give substance to hope, and what are some of the obstacles that must be overcome?

One important positive factor in working toward reconciliation is to be found in the commonalities among all Koreans. They share a Confucian heritage, the values of which remain a powerful influence today. The primacy of the family and the importance of education, keystones of this Confucian legacy, are evident not only within the boundaries of the Korean peninsula, but also in Korean communities overseas. Additional factors are a common language and culture which have enabled Koreans to resist being assimilated into the culture of occupying powers over the centuries. Even during the thirty-five year period of Japanese colonization, Koreans maintained a strong sense of national tradition and identity despite extreme pressures to deny their Korean heritage, language, names and religion.

Some observers argue that this strong sense of Korean identity will be the most important factor in achieving Korean independence and reunification. They believe that this identity, rather than imposed ideologies, will enable Koreans to recreate wholeness on the peninsula. There is a mystical element in this, an expression of faith. It leads some who yearn for reunification to resist defining concrete strategies or steps. Reunification, they say, will happen because it must. If there are no contrary external interferences, the Korean people will make it happen and will determine the form it will take. This belief in the inevitability of reunification is a positive and important factor in Korea's ability to reunite peacefully, although it is unlikely to provide sufficient impetus in itself. Specific steps are also needed.

A series of positive steps was taken by government and Red Cross representatives of North and South Korea in 1984 and 1985 as they engaged in talks and sponsored family visits across the DMZ. However, neither the people of the North nor of the South have had a determining voice, or have even participated in these negotiations. Certainly any efforts to negotiate, even at the governmental level, are a welcome move away from unremitting tension and periodic hostilities between the two governments. At the same time, most of the sixty million people on the two sides of the DMZ have been so isolated from each other, and so kept in the dark by their governments, that they are now incapable of informed discussion. In order for negotiations to be meaningful and enduring and for a solution to represent the will of the people, ways must be found for popular participation in the process.

Such participation of the Korean people will be the primary factor in determining the future of Korea. At the same time, Korea does not exist in a vacuum. Outside powers have had and continue to have significant impact on events there. Over the centuries, Korea has borne the brunt of the aggressive policies of its neighbors, especially Japan. The division of Korea by the United States and the Soviet Union after World War II has had profound effects on several generations of Koreans.

For a combination of reasons, China's current policies have helped in a modest way to reduce tensions between North and South. China has been serving as a mediator between North Korea and the United States and has entered into discussions with South Korea about direct trade and economic cooperation. This welcome development may continue, since China believes that peace in Asia is essential for the success of its current priority on domestic development. The Soviet Union has also placed revitalization of its economy second only to its own security. Like China, the Soviet Union would greatly benefit from peace in Asia. Yet, while the Soviet Union has supported the North's proposal of tripartite talks among North Korea, South Korea and the United States, it has also recently provided modern military planes and equipment to the North, an act that can only further heighten military tensions.

As Moscow and Beijing seek to address their own internal economic problems, they are also attempting to end the rift that has divided them. In addition, leaders in both Moscow and Beijing have held high-level discussions with U.S. policy makers about Korea, discussions which presumably are aimed at tension reduction on the peninsula.

In many ways, Korea's most difficult major power relations are with Japan. North and South Korea share the thirty-five-year history of Japanese occupation and colonization and the negative legacy of that period. People on both sides of the thirty-eighth parallel celebrate August 15 as the day of liberation from Japanese rule, and both the South and the North responded quickly and negatively to Japan's textbook revisions of a few years ago which minimized Japan's actions in Korea and elsewhere in Asia prior to and during World War II. It would be ironic and unfortunate if the perception of Japan as the common enemy were one of the forces helping to draw North and South Korea together. Chung Kyungmo's chapter, above, indicates the depth of his feelings toward Japan. These feelings are not atypical among Koreans and are of great concern to many sensitive Japanese who deplore their country's record in Korea.

On balance, Japan's ruling party prefers the present division to a united Korea which might be an economic and political threat to Japan. At the same time, many Japanese recognize that current tensions in Korea and the uneasy status quo could develop into a war between North and South that would threaten Japanese investments in the South and possibly spread to the Japanese islands. While maintaining its relations with South Korea, Japan has made a number of overtures toward agreements with the North. Among these are a fisheries agreement, agreement on direct charter flight service between Tokyo and Pyongyang, visas for visiting North Korean gymnasts and others, and travel by Japanese to North Korea. It is not clear that Japan's relations with both the North and the South are intended to encourage the interest of eventual reconciliation between the two Koreas. Rather, they may represent efforts to recognize both, while continuing to support division.

A desirable step for Tokyo toward tension reduction in all of Northeast Asia would be to reinforce its commitment to remaining a peaceful nation. That would mean standing up to pressures from Washington to increase its military budget and abrogate its constitutional commitment against war.

One South Korean has observed that one of the greatest obstacles to reconciliation and reunification in Korea is the export to Korea of the U.S. security doctrine, which places primacy on the military and on military solutions to political problems. There is little question that modification of military and political attitudes toward Korea in Washington would reduce the threat of war. U.S. policy has been frozen in a cold war attitude toward Korea since 1945. However, recent indications are that some changes may be underway. Washington has shown some flexibility and willingness to hold top level discussions about Korea with leaders in both Moscow and Beijing and for the first time granted visas (for a three-day stay) in 1985 to three North Korean scholars to attend an academic meeting in Washington. This is a welcome beginning, but much more is needed to support constructive negotiations and open communications with North Korea.

If the United States government is to be encouraged to find a more flexible policy toward Korea, and especially an openness to relating to North Korea, there will need to be greater popular understanding of the people and issues involved. Information about the North as well as the South must be widely available in the United States. Knowledge about both sides may begin to create awareness that each side in the Korean division has had substantial success in building a viable society. The more people know about Korea, the more they will see that each side is neither as bad as its detractors would have us believe, nor as good as its government's own information bureaus and official statistics would indicate. The expansion of U.S. visits to North Korea would not only let Americans see for themselves but would also help North Koreans be exposed to a diversity of views. This process would assist a loosening of tension on both sides.

We turn now to some concrete suggestions based on AFSC discussions with North and South Koreans, with other religious organizations, with representatives of the U.S. State Department, with diplomatic officials at the United Nations, and in conferences with Korean residents in North America. From these varied sources, we conclude that progress toward reconciliation and reunification requires the following steps.

1. Easing North-South Tensions: South and North Korea should agree to continue and to sustain the momentum of talks begun in 1984-1985. Both sides should seek immediately to encourage open discussion about the issues and popular participation in the reconciliation process and both should continue and expand family visits and exchanges across the DMZ with private time allowed for reunited family members.

As an immediate measure to prevent outbreak of hostilities and to address the fears of war in North and South Korea, both sides should cease mutual vilification and inflammatory propaganda, and should agree on a mutual non-aggression pact and immediately reduce the number of troops on either side of the DMZ. These measures would be steps toward eventual elimination of all military personnel at the DMZ and toward a unified Korea, which would also eliminate the need for the mutual non-aggression pact.

China, the Soviet Union, Japan and the United States should be supportive of North-South negotiations but at the same time agree to a policy of non-interference in Korea. For instance, they could encourage direct negotiations between North and South on sending a joint Korean team to the 1988 Olympic Games, scheduled to be held in Seoul.

2. Shifts in U.S. Policy Toward Korea

Nuclear Weapons: The United States, as the only party with nuclear weapons on the Korean peninsula, should take initiative to establish Korea as a nuclear-free zone, and as a first step should immediately remove all U.S. nuclear weapons from South Korea. This action, in addition to the positive factor that both North and South Korea are signatories to the nuclear non-proliferation treaty, would give impetus to discussion involving the major powers and the two Koreas on the larger nuclear-free issues.

Military Involvement: As a first step toward complete military disengagement in Korea, the United States should immediately cease military exercises in and around the Korean peninsula and undertake withdrawal of U.S. troops from South Korea. U.S. troops are in Korea because of perceived U.S. security interests, not for the defense of South Korea or in the interests of the Korean people. Removal of the U.S. troops from the peninsula would prevent their being drawn instantly into any new conflict. U.S. troop removal would also remove U.S. complicity in the human tragedies associated with any troop presence, including prostitution, subservience of Korean nationals, and corruption of minor and higher officials.

The high concentration of armed personnel and weapons is clearly dangerous to people on both sides of the DMZ. The deep fear of war in both North and South Korea has been mentioned above. People in the United States hear almost exclusively of the fear in South Korea, but we need also to be aware of the fear in the North, a fear that is exacerbated by the presence of U.S. forces, nuclear weapons, and the annual Team Spirit military exercises.

North Korea: In order to adopt a more open attitude toward North Korea, the United States should take these five steps:

　　a. Allow more North Koreans visas for visits to the United States and eliminate restrictions on travel by North Koreans in this country.

　　b. Release U.S. diplomats to have normal contact with North Korean diplomats throughout the world. Such contacts are valuable not only for their own sake but also because they offer opportunities for direct appraisal of North Korean personnel and policies and the chance to build personal relationships which may prove useful in unforeseen circumstances.

　　c. Use the good offices of China to find ways to open communications with the North.

　　d. Allow North Korean diplomats at the United Nations in New York expanded freedom of movement; they are now kept within a twenty-five-mile radius of New York City.

　　e. Be open to tripartite talks involving North and South Korea and the United States, with or without other parties present, as and if these seem appropriate.

South Korea: The United States should cease its direct support of South Korea's military government. While maintaining official recognition, the U.S. should also establish relations with those out of power, including religious leaders, opposition party figures, students and workers. To the extent that similar contacts are possible in the North, they too should be developed.

The United States should contribute to the easing of tensions by reviewing and changing those provisions of the 1954 Mutual Defense Treaty with South Korea that are provocative toward the North.

3. Positive Actions by China, the Soviet Union and Japan

China: China should continue its efforts to mediate differences, especially between North Korea and the United States.

China should continue its trade and economic discussions with South Korea, moving to improve exchange between the two countries.

China should make clear that it would not send troops to support North Korea in a conflict with South Korea, especially when and as U.S. troops are withdrawn from the South.

Soviet Union: The Soviet Union should cease its supply of sophisticated weapons and aircraft to North Korea, and make clear that it, too, would not send troops to North Korea's defense in case of a conflict with the South, especially when and as U.S. troops are withdrawn.

The Soviet Union and China should engage Japan in discussions aimed at tension reduction in Northeast Asia.

Japan: Japan should continue its contacts with both North and South Korea and the granting of visas to visitors from both the North and the South.

Japan should develop policies that will serve not only Japan's interests but also the cause of reversing Japan's negative legacy in Korea. A beginning could be made with more equitable and just policies toward Japan's Korean residents.

Japan should reaffirm its constitutional commitment to remaining a peaceful nation. To do so, Japan will have to stand up to U.S. pressures to increase its military budget and expand its military role.

Japan should abandon its de facto support for a divided Korea and the status quo. It should explore ways in which it might, through contacts in both the North and the South, contribute to reconciliation on the peninsula.

Japan should participate in discussions with the other great powers toward tension reduction in Northeast Asia.

4. *Human Contact With Both North and South Korea:*
Academicians, media personnel, Korean-Americans, ecumenical and other delegations should travel to both North and South Korea and report publicly on their experiences and observations, in the interest of providing accurate information and of demystifying the two Koreas.

5. *Shifts in U.S. Policy Toward Japanese Rearmament:*
The U.S. should review and reverse the 1960 Mutual Defense Treaty with Japan and eliminate U.S. pressure on Japan toward expansion of its military budget and strengthening the offensive capability of the Japanese military. Peace and security of Japan itself, and of Asia generally, have been well served for forty years by a disarmed Japan. To recreate it as a military power will only revive old fears and increase

insecurity throughout the Asian region, and especially in Korea, which has suffered grievously from Japanese militarism in the past.

To put these recommendations forward is not to suggest they are easy to accomplish. Entrenched hostilities, military tensions, an emphasis on military security, and a U.S. policy supporting the status quo are powerful factors in inhibiting positive change. Weighing against these negative factors are the visions of the Korean people and numerous pragmatic considerations.

Economically, a popularly reunited Korea would provide a large combined domestic market, many of whose needs could be fulfilled with its own resources. Reunification would ultimately allow an escape from foreign economic domination on the peninsula, and Korea could take advantage of trade with China and other major powers, according to its own priorities.

Given Korea's crucial location in Northeast Asia, creative changes in Korea could contribute to peace rather than tension in that region. Historically, peaceful reunification of Korea and its establishment as a nuclear-free zone would be of great significance. Korea is strategically located near three of the four great powers with which its present fate is entwined. It was occupied by Japan earlier in this century and by the two major powers after World War II. It has experienced the benefits and the liabilities of both capitalism and socialism. If Korea can transcend the current political division and establish a political and economic system specifically designed to meet its own diverse needs, the process could be a model for other Third World countries that are struggling to develop independent domestic systems appropriate to their histories and cultures.

Surely a unified, nuclear-free Korean peninsula relieved of interference from any outside power would offer greater security in East Asia and in the international community than does the present concentration of weapons and taut-nerved military personnel along a narrow strip of fortified land.

We close this study with the hope and belief that all who have been concerned with events on the Korean peninsula in the past four decades may find guidance in the reflection of Ham Sok Hon:

> It is time for the world to become one. This is the time for all who have been fighting and murdering each other, divided as they are by nation, by land, by race, by belief, by ideology, to put an end to all contradiction, all waste, and all misunderstanding. Failing that, the best efforts will be a brake on history, the highest level of morality a deadweight to sink history, the greatest talent will prove a deadly poison. Total mobilization thus becomes all the more urgent to bring humankind together. Nothing short of a new interpretation of world history can bring it about. Only the realization that we are brothers and sisters of a common ancestor will bring an end to fighting. *(Queen of Suffering*, p. 4)

About the Editors

John A. Sullivan served the American Friends Service Committee as Associate Executive Secretary for Information and Interpretation from 1969 until his retirement in 1982. Sullivan has traveled extensively, including trips to North and South Vietnam, the Middle East, and as leader of AFSC delegations to East and West Berlin and to China. The latter trip in 1972 resulted in an AFSC booklet, "Experiment Without Precedent," for which Sullivan was the technical editor. Prior to his work with the AFSC, Sullivan worked as a newpaper and broadcast journalist. He is a graduate of Harvard College.

Roberta Foss has been Co-director of Asia Programs for the American Friends Service Committee since 1975. Based in Philadelphia, Foss travels to Korea and Japan frequently, and has traveled extensively elsewhere in Asia. From 1971 to 1975, she served first as associate and then as director of the Service Committee's Quaker International Affairs Program in East Asia, located in Tokyo. Foss has a master's degree in East Asian Studies from the University of Michigan.